P9-DCU-834

# For Better,
# For Worse

*Susan Squire*

# For Better, For Worse

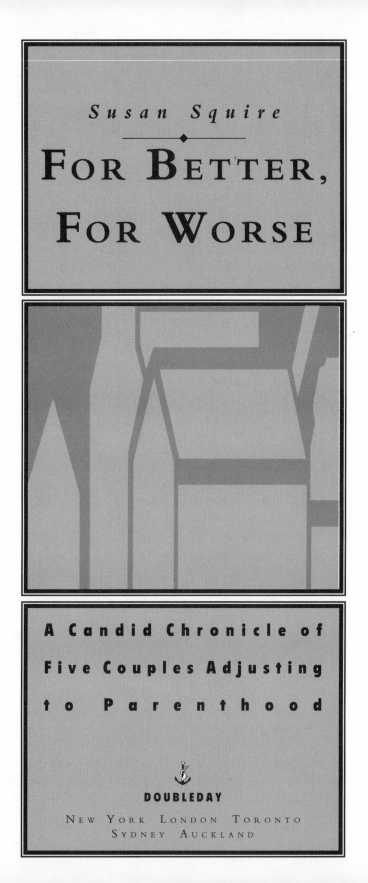

**A Candid Chronicle of Five Couples Adjusting to Parenthood**

DOUBLEDAY

New York London Toronto
Sydney Auckland

PUBLISHED BY DOUBLEDAY
a division of Bantam Doubleday Dell Publishing Group, Inc.
666 Fifth Avenue, New York, New York 10103

DOUBLEDAY and the portrayal of an anchor with a dolphin are
trademarks of Doubleday, a division of Bantam Doubleday Dell
Publishing Group, Inc.

Design by Glen M. Edelsten

Library of Congress Cataloging-in-Publication Data

Squire, Susan.
    For better, for worse : a candid chronicle of five couples
adjusting to parenthood / Susan Squire.
        p.    cm.
        1. Parenthood—United States—Case studies.    2. Marriage
—United States—Case Studies.        I. Title.
    HQ755.8.S7    1993
    306.874—dc20                                                  92-30562
                                                                         CIP
ISBN 0-385-41475-7
Copyright © 1993 by Susan Squire
All Rights Reserved
Printed in the United States of America
April 1993

10   9   8   7   6   5   4   3   2

*For David, and for Emily*

# Preface

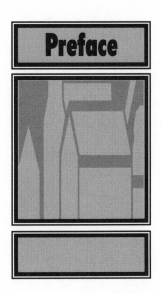

Y MOTHER AND FATHER BECAME PARENTS DURING THE SILENT 1950s. There were no sonograms, no amniocentesis, no Lamaze training, no husbands in the delivery room, and no warning of the marital transformation in store for them. "You had no sense of what you were getting into," my mother told me. But getting into it was a given. Young couples had children as soon after the wedding as their budgets permitted. They assumed that on the other side of pregnancy was the ineluctable state of family contentment enshrined on *The Adventures of Ozzie & Harriet* and *Father Knows Best*. If your life did not turn out to be quite that blissful (and of course it never did), you weren't supposed to say so. As I gathered from my mother, you hid your disappointment under the back seat of the station wagon and wondered what was wrong with you.

Fortunately, silence is out of fashion. Along with other aspects of private life that once were secret, the marital struggles that accompany the gestation and birth of a child have entered the public confessional. Particularly in the past fifteen years, the transition to parenthood, as the experts call it, has been analyzed feverishly at universities across the country, where researchers have devised indexes of "marital distress" to measure its impact. At the University of California at Berkeley, for instance, psychologists Philip A. Cowan and Carolyn Pape Cowan recently completed a ten-year study of San Francisco–area couples who had a first child. Contrary to one of the rosier myths of my parents' generation, the Cowans discovered that babies do not bring troubled couples closer together. In fact, according to the researchers, "the transition to parenthood seems to increase the stress in parents' lives, amplify the differences between the spouses, and thereby increase their level of marital dissatisfaction."

No kidding. Before I was aware of such studies, my personal experience led me to similar conclusions.

I already knew something about marriage. My first, to a man with whom I had little in common other than a determination to maintain civility at all costs, ended after a decade, with the same politeness with which it began. My second, to a man I consider my psychic twin, which can be good and can be bad, is now in its sixth year.

As for children . . . I was fourteen when I told my father I didn't want any. "That means you can't love," he said, with characteristic bluntness. His comment disturbed me. Somehow, even then, I was wary of motherhood and the complicated mix of devotion and worry and grief and hope it represented. The problem, I realized years later, wasn't that I could not love; I was simply afraid to.

When we met, my first husband had custody of two sons, aged eight and eleven, from a prior marriage, and they were enough for both of us. A few weeks after our wedding, he had a vasectomy. The doctor who performed the procedure questioned me closely beforehand. I was only twenty-five, he said; was I *certain* I did not want my own children? I assured him that I was. My stepchildren lived with us from the beginning, and though I believe I loved them, my role was a benign, uninvested one—half older sister, half friend. Was that the same as being a mother? I doubted it.

During my first marriage, while I was involved in my career as an editor and writer, a few of my colleagues started families; my younger sister had a son and then a daughter. I made my living interviewing people and could not resist grilling the most casual acquaintances about their interior lives, yet I had no interest in the new ordeals of my colleagues or my sister. The concept of parenthood seemed . . . I don't know . . . deadening.

David, the man who would become my second husband, was funny and smart and tender and quirky. I had no desire to contain or calibrate my feelings for him, even if I could. "Will you have babies with me?" he asked one night, early in our courtship. The question was unexpected, and so, at least to me, was my instantaneous response. "Yes," I said. My resistance to motherhood suddenly seemed antiquated and irrational.

Two months after David and I were married, I became pregnant, at the age of thirty-seven. I was terrified.

As a journalist, I know how to research and report information. As a human being, I believe in knowledge—not necessarily because it confers power, but because it helps to allay anxiety. So throughout pregnancy and afterward, I applied my professional skills to my personal predicament. I read *Dr. Spock's Baby and Child Care* and the work of my own era's gurus, Penelope Leach and T. Berry Brazelton. I read guides to nutrition, holistic birthing manuals, brisk introductions to breastfeeding, and the *What to Expect* series on pregnancy and the first postpartum year. When my daughter was born, I moved on to first-person accounts of fatherhood and motherhood (Bob Greene's disingenuously buoyant *Good Morning, Merry Sunshine,* Phyllis Chesler's solipsistic *With Child,* Jane Lazarre's candid, intense *The Mother Knot)* and the theories of Selma Fraiberg, Jean Piaget, and Bruno Bettelheim.

I learned quite a bit from these sources, but something important was missing. The guidebooks, though useful in terms of practical advice, were too generic. The personal narratives, while absorbing, seemed more intent on fostering the authors' chosen self-image than on offering a clear-eyed view of the transition itself, and I found myself doubting their applicability. The theories were provocative but lacked emotional texture.

In my case, the missing pieces were supplied only by experience.

So *this* is what it's about, I thought the first time David and I saw the fetus on a sonogram screen, just before Labor Day in 1988. My excitement was accompanied by a creeping ambivalence—feelings that thereafter would always go in tandem.

So *this* is what it's about, I thought one Sunday night in late January 1989, upsetting a friend's dinner party when I realized that my stomachache was not a reaction to pasta puttanesca. The pain, according to the second hand on David's watch, was coming in waves, rhythmic waves. It was labor, and we were both scared witless. There was no getting out of it—no turning back.

So *this* is what it's about, I thought at home a half-hour later. Labor was not proceeding in the manner that the books and the Lamaze teacher had suggested it would. Instead of distinguishable stages, steady increments of agony, I was dilating precipitously. I could no longer walk—but the mortgage was due the next day, and I had a frightening sense that I would never return home to pay it. *"What are you doing?"* David said incredulously, watching me crawl on hands and knees to the desk for my checkbook while he foraged anxiously through the drawers, hoping to come upon a stray Valium. Funny, how people respond differently to crisis . . . I would have laughed, but I could no longer do that, either. The typed sheet of Lamaze breathing exercises I had prepared weeks earlier was folded in David's shirt pocket, but we were both too overwhelmed by the magnitude of my contractions even to glance at it. We barely made it to the hospital. Our daughter, Emily, was born within an hour of our arrival.

For the next three days, life was perfect. David and I were enthralled with Emily and each other; I loved it when he called friends and family from my hospital bedside to announce proudly, "My girls are resting." The room was filled with flowers and attentive visitors, and a nurse came to fetch the baby whenever I wanted to sleep. I was a bit worried that my milk would never come in, but I was sure the worst was over. Pregnancy, labor, delivery—what else was there?

Then I went home.

So *this* is what it's about, I thought frantically a few days later, as I struggled to position Emily at my breast. I could not stop crying. I had assumed a certain level of competence in my adult life but now appeared to be a failure at the very first maternal challenge: nursing. I had milk, all right, but getting my newborn to suckle was another matter. "She's going to starve," I wailed. David was puzzled by my hysteria. "Why don't I buy some formula?" he suggested. I glared at him through my tears. He had never seemed so irrelevant, and I had never felt so alone.

So *this* is what it's about, I thought resentfully as I paced the apartment in the middle of the night, trying to calm three-week-old Emily, who had been screaming for centuries. David was sleeping. He had to go to work in the morning. Lucky him.

So *this* is what it's about, I thought furiously the fifth or hundredth time David forgot to pack any wipes in the diaper bag. "Do I have to think of *everything*?" I shrieked. (Was my transformation into this harridan going to be permanent?) David looked at me as if he didn't know me, and didn't want to. "You used to be so much fun," he complained, "and now you're always so beleaguered and frazzled . . ."

"What do you expect on two hours' sleep?" I snarled.

But then there was Emily, who could not yet wave or laugh or even shed tears, and still she filled us with joy that transcended the edginess, the confusion, and the panic of those early months. So *this* is what it's about: David and I had our arms wrapped around each other as we stared reverently at our daughter asleep in her crib, knowing that only the specific combination of our two sets of genes could have produced her. I could have had a child with another man, but it wouldn't have been *this* child . . . It was an epiphany, of sorts, which we still summon up whenever we feel like killing each other.

Thus what had been so aridly labeled "the transition to parenthood" was revealed to me. Deadening? No. I had gotten it wrong. It was like inhabiting a different planet, rich and dense, reminding me of the underground postal system Thomas Pynchon described in The Crying of Lot 49—a "separate, silent, unexpected world" that coexisted alongside the other, childless one but was hidden from the uninitiated.

You are oblivious to this world until you stumble into it, and once you do, your perception of all that has preceded it is changed irrevocably. The world I had stumbled into encompassed every conceivable emotion, all at once and in heightened form, shifting so rapidly that I couldn't stand back and take its measure. But it forced me to take my own. It exposed me to myself in a way that nothing had before.

I wanted to describe this world—in a sense, to reexperience it—as other couples entered it. I wanted to document their daily lives and thoughts from the surreal early weeks of pregnancy through the first postpartum year. I wouldn't interpret or analyze or offer advice, for that had already been done. My intention was to chart, in narrative form, this state of marriage in extremis and make it comprehensible to others, and in the process to myself.

Finding people to cooperate wasn't easy; the search took several months. Four couples, all expecting a first child, surfaced through a network of obstetricians who agreed to broach my project to their patients early in the first trimester. The fifth came more serendipitously: my father had a friend whose daughter had a friend who happened to be newly pregnant for the second time.

These five couples, selected from a group of potential subjects, represent a variety of religious, educational, cultural, and professional backgrounds. Their ages range from the mid-twenties to the mid-forties. Since I was interested in exploring what happens to relatively average people leading more or less average lives, I avoided the extreme ends of the economic spectrum. They had to live in the eastern part of the country, as I do, for the kind of intensive on-the-scene reporting I envisioned could not be managed otherwise, but I chose people from urban, suburban, and rural environments.

Beyond these objective reasons, there was something about each of these couples and their marriages that intrigued me.

Sam and Juliet met two decades ago at an Ivy League university—he was her professor—and have been together ever since. They retain an abiding delight in each other's company and a respect for each other's judgment that seem rare in a union of that duration. He is a prominent activist lawyer; she has never figured out what to do with her life and often feels frustrated by her lack of accomplishment. I wondered if motherhood would ease—or exacerbate—her frustration. Additionally, my long-standing interest in medical issues was piqued by their situation. While Juliet's mother was pregnant with her, she had taken diethylstilbestrol (DES), a female hormone prescribed in the 1940s and 1950s to prevent miscarriage, and its ironic legacy was a misshapen uterus that could lead to complications in Juliet's own pregnancy.

Sarah and Michael's marriage is fraught with tension and missed signals. They argue—or rather, Sarah argues and Michael retreats—over everything, starting with the dinner menu and escalating into conflicts over sex and the discipline of their three-year-old son. Michael holds a middle-management position in the food industry but fantasizes about becoming Mr. Mom. Sarah had a thriving career in fashion retailing, but when her son was born she gave it up, to what seems to be everyone's detriment. She now sells clothes part-time in a local boutique and complains of feeling imprisoned by motherhood. Their marriage, already rocky, was likely to become more so with the addition of a second child.

Tom and Erin attended the same high school. Tom runs a gas station he bought from his father, and Erin strives to move beyond her position as a secretary in a law firm. Both come from large, intact Catholic families and entered into married life with the illusion that it would be easy. Their union has already foundered and survived one separation. I was impressed with the steps they took to strengthen it. And their predicament at the beginning of pregnancy resonated with that of many other marriages I had observed: a man so preoccupied with his business that he is unwittingly blind to his wife's needs; a woman who fears that parenthood will permanently derail her personal and professional goals.

Maria is the office manager for a medical practice in a Manhattan hospital, and Joe is a mail carrier for the U.S. Postal Service. Both are Hispanic, with dreams of making a better life for their children than they had. I was attracted to Maria's fearlessness, to Joe's boyish energy, and to the courage and integrity they both projected. Joe comes from a tradition in which the man is the head of the household, a view he wholeheartedly endorses. Maria's perspective is more complex. She sees herself as independent, as an equal partner to Joe, but she also agrees with him that a woman's most important job is to raise her children. In an earlier era, their dreams might have seemed possible: four kids, a decent house in a safe neighborhood, and a mother at home. But they live in a tiny one-bedroom apartment in a big city, and without Maria's income they could not afford even that. Sadly, their dilemma is an all too common one these days for hard-working urban Americans who aspire to more than one child. I wanted to see how, or if, they would resolve it.

I connected immediately with Rob's sense of irony and self-mocking humor, with Alex's determination to establish herself as the equal of any man, and with their shared lack of pretension. Both have sales careers, in different industries; she makes considerably more money than he does. At times they seem like siblings, heckling and one-upping each other, and at times like newlyweds, playful and affectionate. But they also fight bitterly. Theirs is the kind of ongoing power struggle I had seldom seen in so overt a form. Moreover, Alex travels about two weeks out of each month on business. I was anxious about being away from my daughter for more than a few hours during her infancy; how would Alex take to leaving her child for several days at a time—a schedule she planned to resume two months after delivery?

In order to write about these strangers, I would be asking them to expose themselves and their marriages to me for a period of roughly two years. *I* would never agree to such intrusive inquiry. Why did they? "Ego—I love to talk about myself," said Sam, the much-quoted attorney. "It sounds like free marriage therapy," said Michael, the uncommunicative husband. "It would be like making a movie of how we were then, that we can always replay," said unflinching Maria. "I hope to learn something about myself," said ever-rational Alex. "It would be something for us to do together—something to share," said Erin, who once left her husband because they shared so little.

Because of the intimate nature of the material, I agreed at the outset to change the names of the couples and some of their associates. I also used pseudonyms for their doctors. Although all the doctors were willing to go on the record, I felt that since my interest was to filter medical interactions through the couples' eyes without regard for their doctors' point of view, it was only fair and appropriate to conceal their identities. No other biographical details have been altered except for one man's profession. He would otherwise be recognizable within his field.

We talked, my subjects and I, at length and on tape, at least once a week—several times a day when there was a crisis. I frequently interviewed husbands and wives separately so they would not feel compelled to shade the truth when they were around each other. Most often we spoke face-to-face, in their cars or offices or homes, in restaurants and in playgrounds, on trains and in shopping malls, at the beach and in beauty parlors, in the waiting and examining rooms of their obstetricians, on labor floors and maternity wards, at picnics and baby showers and birthday parties and christenings. I was there for most of the events described; when I was not, I reconstructed them to reflect both the husband's and the wife's perspective. All thoughts attributed to them were told to me firsthand; I have used italics to relate those that were expressed in particularly idiomatic language.

I assume my involvement had some effect on the course of events. Thoughts and emotions that might have been suppressed and conflicts that might have been glossed over or denied by one spouse or the other were examined in detail, which may have enhanced the couples' awareness of their problems. Beyond that, it is impossible to know how, or if, things might have turned out differently without me and my questions. I resisted the impulse to act as a go-between and remained as impartial as I could, letting the participants' stories unfold without comment or judgment.

There was, of course, no way to predict what would happen to any of these couples. There were times of trouble so acute that divorce loomed, and times of synchronicity so profound that living happily ever after seemed assured. There were many surprises, and no small amount of suspense. In the end, parenthood reconfigured their lives and their marriages—sometimes for better, sometimes for worse.

As for me, what began as a way to understand my own experience from a comfortable distance, and to indulge my voyeuristic curiosity about how other people managed it, soon became far more. I observed, I prodded, I recorded . . . but as my ten subjects revealed themselves to me, I developed a heartfelt affection for them and a deep admiration for their honesty, their resilience, and their perseverance in facing the hard truths—and making the resolute compromises—essential to any enduring marriage in these stressful times.

I hope that this chronicle of their lives will help capture for you, as it has for me, this most difficult, and most extraordinary, period of transition.

# For Better,
# For Worse

**1989**

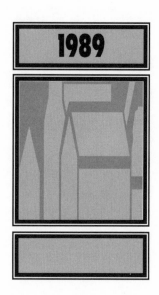

**OCTOBER 1989**

 HAF VERRY GOOD NEWS VOR YOU," SAYS DR. VOSS IN HER THICK German accent. Immediately, Juliet Nathan feels sad. Her husband, Sam Mayer, a celebrated activist lawyer, is en route to Los Angeles at this moment to give a speech. Juliet won't be able to see his face when she tells him she is pregnant, and he has wanted to hear those words for so long.

The nurse in the office suggests that Juliet wait until Sam returns tomorrow night. "Put on a pretty dress," she proposes, "and tell him over a candlelit dinner." Juliet is amused at this Total Woman scenario, which she could never pull off. She's no good at keeping secrets from Sam, certainly not this particular one.

At forty-three, Sam is nine years older than Juliet; he was ready to start a family long before she was. He's the one who kept careful records of her menstrual cycles and presented her with ovulation-predictor tests at the appropriate times. He's the one who grew morose when a uterine scan confirmed that Juliet, whose mother took diethylstilbestrol (DES) to prevent miscarriage while pregnant with her, has the misshapen uterus typical of women exposed to DES in the womb. But Juliet did not share Sam's pessimism. She has always had an uncanny sense of her physical self. This sense told her that she would be able to carry a child to term regardless of the medical realities.

Last spring, after nearly two years of attempted conception, Dr. Voss, a specialist in infertility medicine, proposed a laparoscopy. But Juliet, still convinced she could get pregnant without aggressive measures, decided to put it off until the fall. Secretly, she had felt relief each time she got her period. Juliet believed in some metaphysical way that she was in control: she would get pregnant when she was ready to get pregnant.

Late last week, just before her period was due, Juliet told Sam her body felt *different,* unlike its usual premenstrual self. When her period was three days late (which rarely happened, according to Sam's notes), he urged her to have a pregnancy test. Yesterday, the fourth day, she bled, though just a little. Sam hid his disappointment when Juliet showed him the doleful evidence on a Tampax, a gesture typical of the earthy nature of their relationship. But this morning, with Sam already airborne, there was no more blood. Juliet had to know what was going on.

Sam calls when he arrives at his hotel in L.A., around 4 P.M. West Coast time. Juliet says, "I'm pregnant."

"No!" Sam can't believe it. "My God . . ." He chokes up.

He composes himself and calls his best friend in Santa Barbara, already a father himself, to tell him the news. Then he tunes the TV to the World Series. He putters about his hotel room, feeling *strong, joyful, purposeful.* He thinks about the speech he will give tonight on a controversial civil rights case and how it is destined to be one of his best, because he is finally going to be a father. But when a news bulletin interrupts the ballgame to announce a major earthquake near San Francisco, Sam's elation turns to horror. He watches the Oakland–Bay Bridge collapse during the rush-hour commute; he sees a car crushed on screen. He thinks, *Juliet's is no longer the only news of the day that matters.* His speech that night is definitely not one of his best, but he assumes that no one notices. The audience, half the expected turn-out of four hundred, is as stunned and distracted by the catastrophe as he is.

Back in the hotel, Sam tries to focus on the earthquake reports, but his thoughts keep returning to the personal drama that has culminated in Juliet's pregnancy. The two of them met in 1973 at an Ivy League university, when she was a freshman and he a professor of law and political theory, a bachelor again after a brief marriage. Sam noticed Juliet instantly, though she was among a group of 150 students who were to be divided into sections for a class on conscientious dissent. There was something arresting about her, an intensity in her blue-gray eyes, a sensuous sway to her hips . . . Sam collected her registration card personally so he would know her name. He wanted to ensure that she would be assigned to his section.

Wary of plunging into an affair with one of his students, especially a freshman, he concealed his attraction to Juliet under a facade of indif-ference. All the while he was electrified, and sometimes intimidated, by what he still thinks of as her *life force*—her unflagging awareness of everything going on around her, *like an animal in the wild.* She chal-lenged him in class and out of it, at one point calling him a "stuck-up, uncontrollable egotist," and made him question himself in a way no woman ever had. But he knew by the attention she paid to his every flaw that she must be equally captivated. (Though physically attracted to Sam, Juliet was at first unimpressed with his intellect—until she read his comments on an early term paper she wrote and found them brilliant. Besides, he gave her an A.) Before the school year ended, they were lovers.

By the mid-1970s, Sam had an enviable tenured position at the university, but he no longer was satisfied by academic life, which had come to seem too cloistered and elitist. Instead of doing something about his situation, he moped. Juliet could tolerate only so much of this. After several months, she told him that their relationship would have to end if he continued to wallow in his gloomy inertia.

Sam took her threat seriously and resigned his faculty position. To-gether, though as yet unmarried, they moved to Manhattan, where he became a founding partner of a small, maverick law firm and quickly gained national recognition for his legal expertise—and for his talent for convincing members of the Hollywood-Washington power axis to donate money and services to his liberal political causes. He became the journalist's and TV reporter's dream interview subject, always will-ing to supply the kind of vivid quote that can punch a story.

As the 1980s dawned, Sam knew he had most of what mattered—a good marriage, an invigorating career, financial stability. But he felt a visceral need to sire a child and began to wonder what it would be like to be denied the experience of parenthood. His desire for offspring was tinged with melancholy, a sense that something important was passing him by. He discussed his feelings with Juliet, albeit in an off-hand way; she doesn't respond well to pressure. By 1986 she had at least decided to stop thinking of marriage as unromantic, *the end of life.* Marriage, they agreed, was something to get out of the way so they could have children. Whatever their bohemian predilections, they thought it silly and pretentious to saddle a child with the not-so-minor social stigma of being born out of wedlock.

On the last day of 1986, Sam and Juliet were married at City Hall, with their mothers in attendance. (Sam's father, who managed a small savings bank, died of heart disease twenty years ago; Juliet's parents are divorced, and her father, a professor of French literature, lives much of the year in Europe.) Almost a year later, in the fall of 1987, they were walking in the woods near their modest summer home on an island off the New England coast. They were struck with a sudden impulse to make love. Juliet said she didn't have her diaphragm; they looked at each other and shrugged. Sam found a spot under a tree and cleared away the leaves. Afterward, they realized a decision had been made. They stopped using birth control.

When Juliet wasn't pregnant by the following fall, she had a uterine scan. Sam was despondent as he stared at the image; Juliet's uterus was barely visible, shaped like a T instead of a pear. He thought to himself, *Forget it. No uterus, no kids.* Dr. Voss was cheery about their prospects

—there are plenty of procedures to try, she said—and sent Sam for a sperm test. The results showed an abnormal amount of misshapen sperm, which to Sam seemed at first a kind of poetic justice: his crippled sperm and Juliet's crippled uterus, equal contributors to infertility. But a second sperm test showed no abnormalities. Sam felt a rush of macho vanity: *Better her than me.*

Winter, spring, summer: 1989 was halfway over and Juliet was still not pregnant. That summer Sam noticed what seemed like hundreds of programs on TV about infertility. He learned that each in vitro procedure cost about $10,000, as did a privately arranged adoption, and he started wondering how much a child would be worth to him.

As Labor Day approached, he brooded. His focus on his own celebrity now seemed ludicrously devoid of meaning. He considered the idea of leaving Juliet if she couldn't bear children, but quickly rejected it. The prospect of life without her was even more dismal than life without a child. As summer turned to fall, Sam began to contemplate adoption.

There had been a few bright days just before his trip, when Juliet's period was late. Then she bled; Sam had chided himself for being hopeful. And now . . .

Sam arrives at the Los Angeles airport the next morning filled with the trepidation he always feels when he's about to board a plane. In general, he doesn't like relinquishing control—he wants *his* hands on the throttle—and ten years ago he was involved in a near-crash that permanently calcified his fear of flying. He has tried Valium, liquor, and beta blockers (prescription medication for high blood pressure that is thought to relieve anxiety), but nothing helps. He spends the trip staring out the window as if to ward off disaster, frozen with terror, thinking, *This is my last second on earth.* On the ground he's not superstitious, but in the air he looks for talismans. On this particular flight, the talisman is Juliet's pregnancy.

Suddenly he doesn't mind flying, because he doesn't mind dying. He will be leaving something behind.

ODAY IS THE COENS' EIGHTH ANNIVERSARY. MICHAEL FEELS RE-
lief: they've made it through the seventh year.

He and Sarah once laughed when people talked about
the seven-year itch, assuming that it would never apply to
them, but now he thinks there may be some validity in the hackneyed
term. Though he has never ceased desiring his wife, her interest in sex
has declined steadily since the birth of their son, Ben. Now in the
twentieth week of her second pregnancy, she has so little enthusiasm
that Michael often gets the sense, when they do make love, that she's
offering him some kind of charitable contribution. The passion she
showed him early in their relationship seems to resurface now only in
hotels, which he finds puzzling.

A few months into this seventh year of marriage, Michael began to
feel crushed by the weight of his domestic responsibilities and tugged
by a very short leash, held at one end by Sarah and at the other by
three-year-old Ben.

Michael's job as the purchasing manager for a New England–based
restaurant chain doesn't require him to travel farther than Boston. This
suits him perfectly; unlike Sarah, Michael becomes anxious in unfamiliar circumstances, away from his daily routine. He gets up with Ben at
seven, makes breakfast and brown-bag lunches for the family, feeds the
dog and cat, and arrives at work, after a ten-minute drive, by 8:30. He
leaves the office promptly at five, cooks dinner, bathes Ben, puts him
to bed, and helps Sarah fold laundry while watching TV. Still, every
few weeks he yearns to linger over a beer after work instead of rushing
home. It would be nice occasionally to walk in and find a fully cooked
meal. After all, Michael considers his job to be more important than
Sarah's—he's in management, and she works part-time selling fashion-
ably funky women's clothes in a local boutique. But that discrepancy
has always been irrelevant to their division of labor.

Sarah says he's passive, but Michael doesn't think she realizes that he serves an indispensable function in a household in which two of the three members are live wires. Somebody has to put up with Ben's tantrums and Sarah's testy moods. (Michael, only half-jokingly, has diagnosed her condition as CMS, for constant menstrual syndrome.) So he is the one who nurtures and soothes, while Sarah organizes his life and propels it forward.

From the beginning, Sarah took charge. Soon after she and Michael became lovers, back in 1978, she noticed that his body shook and he didn't eat or sleep. She asked him what drug he was on. "Crystal Methedrine," he said. "I have no intention of getting involved with a speed freak," she told him flatly. He had been looking for a reason to stop the drug habit that had ruled his life ever since he was prescribed diet pills as an overweight adolescent, and now he had found one. Without speed, Michael is by nature lethargic. He could see that Sarah was precisely the kind of woman he needed. She would keep him moving.

Michael proposed marriage to her shortly after making love, on their second date; his impulsiveness was driven by drugs. Sarah laughed at him. "You don't even *know* me," she said. It never occurred to Michael to ask her again; soon they were living together in what seemed to him a congenial arrangement that required no formalizing. But after two years of playing house, Sarah presented him with a choice: *Marry me or lose me.* The small wedding, financed by Michael, took place in the back yard of the house where they still live. Sarah wore an antique lace dress and pinned a lavender rose from her garden on the lapel of Michael's pin-striped suit; then the Protestant bride was joined to the Jewish groom by a justice of the peace. Sarah's mother gave her new son-in-law a wedding present: a copy of the New Testament, bearing the inscription *I'd like you to know about Sarah's background.*

When Sarah was pregnant with Ben, she converted to Judaism; she was drawn to the religion's emphasis on family unity. Her mother declared her demented. Soon after, with Michael's blessing, Sarah donated the inscribed copy of the New Testament to a yard sale.

ARAH'S AMNIO RESULTS ARE IN: NO EVIDENCE OF GENETIC DE-fects, and the gender is female. *Thank God,* Sarah thinks. She read in one of her pregnancy books that if the man takes a hot shower right before sex, the woman is more likely to conceive a boy, so for three months she wouldn't allow Michael to shower at night. Knowing that she's carrying a girl, hopefully with Michael's pliant personality instead of her own intractable one, is the only thing that makes this pregnancy tolerable.

Sarah couldn't take another Ben, who at three is bright and sensitive but too much like herself—willful and controlling. He rebels against her attempts to dominate him as she rebelled against her own mother, and when his behavior is at its worst, she feels she has no choice but to spank him. Her mother did it to her, and though Sarah resented it at the time, she now thinks it was useful: it taught her who was boss. Michael was raised in a more permissive household and believes in the gentler "time out" approach to punishment. When Sarah spanks Ben, Michael leaves the room.

Sarah agreed to have a second child primarily to please her husband, who has often said that he would like ten more. Two is her limit. She could ask Michael to have a vasectomy, but that doesn't seem fair; if anything happened to her—death, divorce, who knows?—she thinks he would want more children with someone else. So Sarah will have her tubes tied as soon as she delivers. There is, she thinks, nothing on earth that could change her mind.

During her first pregnancy, Sarah would come home and collapse on the couch in the living room. Michael was her obliging butler, serving nourishing dinners on a tray and plying her with herb tea. But now, with a fractious toddler underfoot, there's no opportunity to collapse. Sarah is tired all the time.

Sex is the last thing she wants.

In the beginning, she couldn't get enough of Michael's lovemaking.

She encountered him for the first time in 1975, in the bed of her cousin, Eileen, who was then Michael's girlfriend. It was midday; Michael was sleeping off a cocaine-propelled motorcycle ride from Miami to Cape Cod. Sarah studied the face of this darkly bearded stranger as he roused himself enough to mumble, in answer to her question, that Eileen was out back in the sauna. Sarah found Michael's brooding looks exotic; her boyfriends had always been blond, blue-eyed, clean-shaven Yankees. That afternoon, as Eileen and Sarah sweated together in the sauna, Eileen told her that the man in her bed was *a Jew from Palm Beach, of all things,* and that all he seemed to own was a motorcycle, a knapsack, a pair of jeans, and a few T-shirts.

Michael and Eileen's relationship was long over in 1978, when Sarah met him again on the Cape at a mutual friend's Thanksgiving dinner table. Sarah had never forgotten him, but Michael had no memory of this self-assured woman, whose warmth and audacity immediately sparked him. Sarah would have jumped into bed with him as soon as the turkey carcass was off the table, but decided, uncharacteristically, to heed her mother's advice: *A man will always want you more if you hold out.* She held out—until the next night.

Sarah considers Michael an adroit lover, tender and potent, with impeccable timing and the patience to bring her to orgasm no matter how long it takes. She relishes the tickle of his beard against her face; she admires the way their bodies fit when they dance. Michael is a superb dancer, and in his arms Sarah moves effortlessly, gracefully. She still feels a strong chemistry between them. But after seven years of marriage and three of motherhood, sex itself seems not worth the effort. Their only opportunity is at night, after Ben is asleep, but by then Sarah is a *zombie.* Mornings are her favorite time, but Ben is up at seven, and weekend afternoons are out because he no longer naps. In a hotel room, alone with Michael, free to make love whenever they please, Sarah is ardent. But at home . . .

Michael is so devoted a husband and father that she feels she can't continually deny him sexual pleasure. And so, much of the time, she *accommodates* him. She teases Michael by saying that she'll hire somebody to service him, but doesn't worry that he'll turn elsewhere. She knows family life is too important to him. Sometimes he tells that Jewish joke to their friends: *How do you get a girl to stop having sex? Marry her.* This doesn't embarrass Sarah, since she has made no secret of her disinterest. She suspects other women feel the same way she does but won't admit it. Only her manicurist and friend Betsy openly shares her attitude.

Sarah learned this recently, when she happened to whisper over the manicure table as Betsy worked on her nails, "My husband is a good lover, but I wish I didn't have to do it when I don't want to." To Sarah's delighted surprise, Betsy said, "I know what you mean. It's the same thing with my husband. I lie there like this"—she rolled her eyes —"and I'm thinking, Just let me know when you're done."

*Yes, exactly!* Sarah was thrilled to discover a kindred spirit. "When you meet someone who's the same," she confided to Betsy, "it's like, 'Thank God, I'm not a weirdo.' "

Sarah has the self-confidence of someone who is not burdened by introspection. Ambivalence is alien to her. If she likes you, you know it. And if she doesn't, you know that too. She prides herself on being the first to announce that the emperor has no clothes and to hell with the consequences.

Take breastfeeding, for example, a practice currently in vogue that reminds her of the hypocrisy about sex: you're supposed to do it and love it, and if you don't you're supposed to keep quiet about it. All the pregnancy books said it was important to breastfeed, and she remembers how the nursing staff at the hospital where Ben was born acted personally offended if Sarah breathed the word "formula." She nursed her son for the first few months because everyone, with the exception of Michael, pressured her to do so, but all she got out of it were sore, bruised nipples and such severe back problems that she had to see a chiropractor. She couldn't wait to go back to work because it meant she could wean Ben.

When Sarah was pregnant the first time, she was naive enough to believe the books, which made her think she would enter a permanent state of serenity the moment she gave birth. The baby would float into her arms and she would instantly feel fulfilled. Instead she felt anxious, depressed, and uncertain. She concluded that books about pregnancy did nothing to prepare a woman for the reality of what happens to her body, her mind, and her sense of control. Sarah now views with extreme skepticism those women who gush about the joys of child-bearing.

Sarah's voice is musical, sweet and sunny, belying her contentious temperament. When she is feeling overwhelmed by the constraints of small-town domesticity, which is frequent these days, she lashes out. Michael is a convenient target. Beyond making a snide comment or two, he won't engage her; he simply withdraws. Sometimes he leaves the house and drives around in his company-leased Chevy Caprice, returning after twenty minutes, muttering that he couldn't think of anywhere to go.

Sarah resists revealing emotions that she considers signs of vulnerability. If she feels like crying, she yells instead. This belligerence is a defense developed during childhood to hide what she really felt; her mother, she believed, was always looking for a way to exploit her. Sarah's self-protective strategy resulted in an ulcer at the age of twelve.

She grew up middle class in a town not far from Plymouth, where her ancestors arrived from the Old World on the *Mayflower*'s second voyage. When she was young, her father, then a Boston Harbor pilot with a drinking problem, was gone for weeks at a time, leaving her mother unhappily at home with three small children. Whenever he returned, the household would erupt with her parents' harsh fights. Sarah concluded that she wanted no part of marriage, which seemed synonymous with conflict, or of motherhood, which looked like unrelieved drudgery. (Her parents have since divorced.) She once asked her mother why she and her father argued so much; in a rare attempt to reassure her, her mother implied that fighting enhanced their sex life. This equation of strife with conjugal passion still makes Sarah uncomfortable. She wonders how much it has influenced her own lack of zeal for sex within marriage.

Sarah's grades were never high enough to please her demanding, extraordinarily strict mother, who lost no opportunity to call Sarah's attention to her younger sister's superior academic performance. As a teenager, Sarah was constantly sneaking out, running away, or getting into nasty fights with her mother, which sometimes escalated until they pulled out clumps of each other's hair. Her mother's brief second marriage (she now lives in the South with her third husband) was to a man twenty years her junior, a gas station attendant whom Sarah had once dated. At seventeen, Sarah left home for good. She now attributes her honesty and independent spirit to her mother's influence, but that's all she thanks her for.

Sarah changed her mind about marriage once she met Michael. He was the kind of man, she thought, who would make a good husband. He seemed (once off drugs) to be a grownup, as opposed to her father. She still considers herself fortunate to have found someone like Michael, though she doesn't believe it was blind luck. Sarah knew exactly what she was looking for: a stable, loving, highly domesticated man who works from nine to five and comes straight home. Over the years, however, she has found herself wishing he were more ambitious and less predictable.

Having children was Michael's idea. Sarah, fearful of recreating her mother's life, agreed on the condition that Michael would assume at least half the responsibility for child-rearing. "No problem," Michael said. Unlike some men, who agree to anything in the abstract and renege when personally inconvenienced, Michael has never failed her. He has far more tolerance for parenthood than she does. He cheerfully spends entire weekend days with Ben, whereas Sarah's nerves are frayed after two hours alone with her son.

Sarah is unfailingly loyal and generous to those who are close to her, and though she may sometimes use Michael as a punching bag in private, she protects him fiercely when it comes to the outside world. And for all her complaining about motherhood, she instinctively puts Ben's needs ahead of her own. Still, she always feels she is stuck behind the slowest driver or in the longest supermarket line. Whatever she has, wherever she is, there must be something better somewhere else.

**SATURDAY, OCTOBER 28**
**An island off the New**
**England coast**

 AM AND JULIET ARRIVE ON THE ISLAND FRIDAY NIGHT AND STAY IN a hotel, because their old wreck of a farmhouse, with its pretty lawn and ocean view, has been fumigated and closed up for three weeks. Juliet is six weeks pregnant.

On this Indian summer morning, she wakes in the hotel bed to a feeling of wetness between her legs. When she pulls the covers down, she sees blood. She wakes Sam; sadly, he looks at the sheets. Without discussion they get their things together, check out of the hotel, and drive to their house. Sam opens all the windows to release the fumes while Juliet goes upstairs to the bathroom. When she sees what comes out of her, she screams. Sam races upstairs to find her staring into the toilet at the large blood clots floating there. He looks in and thinks, *There is the baby we made; it's all over.* He fishes the evidence out with his hands and examines it, and then mutters *Fuck it.* He flings it back in and flushes it down.

Juliet sits on the couch in the living room with her feet up, sobbing. She calls Dr. Voss, who tells her that she has probably had a miscarriage and advises her to leave the island, where there is no hospital, in case she hemorrhages. Then Juliet calls her sister, a nurse in the Midwest, who also advises her to leave. "I hope it won't take so long to get pregnant again," Juliet tells her sister in a quivering voice.

She hangs up the phone and sits quietly. Slowly she feels her hysteria transforming into a strange, enveloping calm. She doesn't want to change her position on the couch, let alone leave the island. She wants to recover from her misfortune in her own way. She begins to feel cleaned out, rejuvenated. She has miscarried, and there is nothing she can do about it. She and Sam might as well relax and enjoy the island, now free of summer tourists.

Sam can see that Juliet is comfortable. Her life doesn't appear to be in danger. The sky is clear; there will be no fog to prevent them from flying off the island if they have to. He trusts her intuition. If she thinks they should stay, they will.

They take a three-mile walk, arms around each other's waists, and marvel at the unusually warm weather, the soft breeze from the south, the richly colored leaves. They feel completely in love. It seems like a honeymoon, a respite between the seriousness of pregnancy and the depression of going home and facing not being pregnant.

The next morning, Juliet is no longer bleeding. They assume the fetus has been flushed out of her system. They enjoy another walk, and that night they begin the journey back to Manhattan. In the car, Juliet suddenly announces that she feels queasy, bloated—pregnant. Sam thinks there might still be a chance but doesn't say so, not wanting to get anyone's hopes up.

On Monday Juliet lies on an examining table in Dr. Voss's office. Sam holds her hand as the doctor moves the sonogram monitor over her uterus. At first Sam and Juliet don't believe what they see: their child, snuggled in its sac, its heartbeat visible on the screen. They think they want to see exactly this so fervently that they have imagined it into being. They listen to Dr. Voss chatting away about how she bled all through her own pregnancy and how it is particularly common during the first trimester.

Sam's relief turns to annoyance. Why didn't the doctor tell them that on Saturday, instead of rattling them with the thought of a life-threatening hemorrhage?

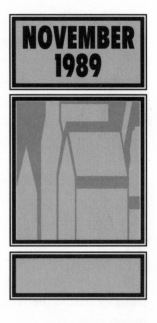

**FRIDAY, NOVEMBER 10**
**Cape Cod**

EFORE NOON ON HER DAY OFF, SARAH STANDS IN LINE AT THE supermarket checkout with a cartful of groceries, including a plump roasting chicken. She'll be the cook tonight, for a change. She wants to shake Michael out of his culinary rut, which has of late resulted in endless versions of Cajun-spiced fish.

Sarah loads the groceries into the trunk of her blue Mazda van, careful not to chip the fresh polish on her nails. Her light brown hair has recently been highlighted and cut in short layers, with wispy bangs. She wears denim leggings, a tunic top, sculpted gold hoop earrings, and glasses with round tortoise-shell frames. She consciously avoids the saccharine, strangely virginal effect that she thinks most maternity clothes impart.

She drives to the local synagogue to fetch Ben from preschool. He is slender and sandy-haired, with delicate features; a toy police badge is pinned to his red sweatshirt. As Sarah settles him in his car seat, he shows her the drawing he made of a Thanksgiving turkey, and she

praises his work. After a brief stop at the mall to reward Ben with a
He-Man sword, she heads home along the narrow country roads in
this relatively unspoiled part of the Cape, where simple wood fences
divide unassuming gray-shingled houses.

The Coens' 1,700-square-foot home is set away from the road on a
long, narrow lot that stretches for half an acre in back. Brie, their
golden Labrador, bounces into the driveway when she hears the car;
Alexis, their six-pod Siamese cat, doesn't move from her perch in the
sun. (Sarah named the cat for the Joan Collins character on *Dynasty.*)
Sarah drags the groceries into the large kitchen, which also serves as
the dining room. Sliding glass doors provide access to a square wooden
deck, where there is room for a barbecue grill and the sandbox Michael built for Ben.

While Ben lunges around with his new sword and a long-haired
plumber repairs the washing machine in the basement, Sarah fills her
roasting chicken with Pepperidge Farm stuffing and smears apricot jam
on top. She debates the wisdom of crowning the squash with brown
sugar and butter; Michael is on a diet again. She decides to wait on the
squash until he gets home. She can cook it quickly in the microwave.

Sarah is of average height and weight, with high, small breasts that
enable her to go braless. She accepts her body as it is and has never
cared much about food. She's astonished by the way some people,
including Michael, are constantly thinking about the next meal and
what they can and can't eat. Without speed or cocaine to cut his
appetite, Michael struggles with his weight, carrying ten or fifteen
extra pounds, dieting it off, putting it back on.

Michael lumbers through the kitchen door at precisely 5:10. He
wears his office uniform of chinos and a plaid button-down sport shirt
(he never bothers with a jacket and tie; his day is spent at his desk, his
ear attached to the phone). He has a gentle way about him that Sarah
describes as teddy-bearish. Underneath the gentleness is a droll, often
cutting sense of humor.

Ben has been waiting impatiently for Michael's arrival, asking Sarah
every five minutes, "When is Daddy coming home?" Now he runs to
his father. Michael lifts his son high in the air and puts him down with

a vigorous hug. He turns to the pile of mail on the dining table and flips through the latest issue of the Wine Enthusiast catalogue. Then he moves over to Sarah, who is rinsing dishes at the sink. He gives her a peck on the cheek and peers into the oven. He sees she has invaded his domain.

"You put the chicken in upside down," he tells her. "And you should have put the squash in. It takes an hour to cook, and it doesn't taste as good in the microwave."

Sarah doesn't explain that her concern for his diet caused the squash delay. She is hurt by his criticism, but instead of saying so, she retaliates. "You take over," she says irritably, hands on her hips. "Obviously I don't know how to cook."

"You didn't happen to watch what the plumber did, did you?" Michael is studying the bill the repairman left.

"All I know is he did whatever it was real quick."

"Was he here as long as an hour? That's what he charged us for, and you signed for it." Michael's tone is accusing.

"Remember when my mother first met you, she called you a sarcastic son of a bitch?"

"She asked me a stupid question and I gave her a sarcastic answer," Michael says with pride. "I like to get to her."

"I don't like her either, but you *are* a sarcastic son of a bitch."

"I want to feed Ben," Michael says, ignoring her crack. "I haven't seen him all day."

By 8:30, Michael has washed the dinner dishes, deboned the remnants of Sarah's perfectly cooked chicken, mixed the meat with mayonnaise and curry powder for tomorrow's lunch, and put Ben to bed. He joins Sarah in the small living room to watch *The Bill Cosby Show,* taped from the night before. It is an episode in which Cosby dreams that men get pregnant. In one scene, a wife places her hand suggestively on her pregnant husband's shoulder; the husband shrugs her off testily. Michael nudges Sarah and grins. "Sound familiar?" he says.

Early the next morning, Michael is back in the kitchen, combining ingredients for banana bread in the Cuisinart. He doesn't want to waste some rotting bananas, and besides, it's a cold morning and the furnace is broken. The oven heat, he reasons, will help to warm the house. Ben sits on the floor of the living room in pajamas, watching cartoons, while Sarah is still upstairs in the master bedroom suite.

A staircase leads from the living room to the suite, which was built at Sarah's insistence onto what was originally a one-story, two-bedroom, one-bathroom house. She designed the addition, which runs the length of the house. The large bathroom, with its fuschia walls and ivory tiles, has a glassed-in shower and a cavernous Jacuzzi tub surrounded by plants and woven baskets from Sarah's extensive collection. On one side of the staircase is a study, where Michael works on his computer, and on the other a sleeping/living area. (The king-size bed is new; Michael slept in the downstairs guest room during Sarah's third trimester with Ben, because their queen-size bed, she said, wasn't big enough for both of them.) Against the French windows, open to the vicissitudes of Cape Cod weather—the fresh sea breezes and the chowder-thick fog—is an arrangement of white wicker furniture enlivened by patchwork quilt throws.

Sarah goes downstairs in a terrycloth robe and enters the kitchen, where Michael is surveying the contents of the cupboards. When he sees her, he says, "You didn't follow the shopping list. There's five hundred jars of grape jelly, but no diet bread."

"Sorry," Sarah snaps. "You can do the marketing next time."

She grabs a mug of coffee and heads back upstairs to dress for work. Michael yells after her. He is about to make her a chicken salad sandwich for lunch and wants to know what bread to use.

"I don't want a sandwich," Sarah tells him, with a so-there inflection. "I'm going out to lunch today."

She leaves at 9:30. A half-hour later, Michael straps Ben into his stroller for the short walk to the beach. A dead dog, hit by a car, lies in the middle of the road near their house; Michael turns the stroller around so Ben's view is blocked. After the dog is removed by its tearful owner, Michael continues on his path, musing, as he often does, about how much easier it is to be a woman than a man. Sarah can decide to work a few days a week as a salesgirl, but Michael can't take some meaningless job as a waiter or bartender and stay home the rest of the time, which he would prefer. Sarah could resume her full-time career and make as much as Michael does now. (He supplements his $45,000 annual salary by dipping regularly into a family trust fund set up by his entrepreneurial grandfather; his share is currently valued at around half a million dollars.) But since she doesn't want to, she doesn't have to. Yet she thinks *he* has the easier life, beginning with the fact that his gender renders him incapable of bearing children.

When Michael is on his way out the door during the week and Sarah is trying to get Ben dressed for day care and Ben is resisting her, she often says resentfully to Michael, "Lucky you, you get to go to work." *As if,* Michael thinks, *sitting on the phone all day negotiating with meat and liquor salesmen is some kind of vacation.*

In a sense, he never wants to leave the house and Sarah always does. This strikes him as strange—and sad.

**WEDNESDAY,
NOVEMBER 15
Southern Maryland**

 OR MORE THAN A YEAR, ERIN WRIGHT AND HER HUSBAND, TOM, have been trying to conceive. Recently, her sister Joanie called to announce her pregnancy; Erin felt such envy that she doubted her congratulations sounded convincing. Joanie is thirty-seven, nine years older than Erin, and has been married just a year, compared to the Wrights' seven. *It's not fair,* Erin thinks, riddled with guilt over her selfish attitude.

Erin has several friends with infertility problems. She never believed she would be one of them, but now she wonders. Tom seems unconcerned, shrugging off each month's news of Erin's period with a quick "Don't worry, we'll get there." But Tom never seems to worry about anything other than that *goddamn gas station.* His father had owned the place since 1951. Tom started working there when he was fourteen, pumping gas and learning how to fix cars. Soon his father had enough confidence in Tom's managerial and technical skills to leave his son in charge when he had to be away. After school and on weekends, when his peers were at the beach or on the baseball diamond, Tom was working. As soon as he graduated from high school, he was there full-time.

Two months ago Tom, now thirty, bought the station outright from his father, who was ready to retire from what had become a twenty-four-hour-a-day, seven-day-a-week business. Tom got a $70,000 bank loan for working capital and financed the rest through a pay-back arrangement with his father. As the sole proprietor, with the financial burdens resting squarely on his shoulders, he has been far too preoccupied to focus on Erin's menstrual cycles.

Ironically, it has always been Erin who resisted starting a family. For some time after their wedding, in April 1982, she felt no maternal instinct whatsoever. Later, her mounting doubts about the marriage, which culminated in a six-month separation in 1987, prevented her from considering children. *I probably wouldn't have had a problem getting pregnant then, when I least wanted it,* she thinks. *Life is always like that.*

Tom and Erin went to the same high school in a Maryland suburb just north of Washington, D.C. Though he graduated three years ahead of her, they'd met a few times when their social circles overlapped at parties. But it wasn't until the summer before Erin's senior year that they connected. Erin, then a member of the cheerleading squad, a straight A student, and editor of the class yearbook, had a summer job as a night hostess at the restaurant next door to the gas station. When she got off work she would join the gang in the adjoining parking lot. Tom was always there, along with ten or fifteen other kids. They would all drink beer, smoke marijuana, throw Frisbees, sit on car roofs and talk. One night (Erin still remembers the exact date: July 1, 1979), Tom and Erin found themselves in a conversation that lasted for four hours and led to love.

Erin was attracted to Tom's self-confidence, his well-thought-out goals (he would take over the station when his father retired, he would make it *the best*), his certainty that college was not for him. She had never encountered anyone her age with such definite ideas about what he wanted from life. And he had this *sweetness*. He listened to her intently; he made her feel important.

Tom knew from that first conversation that Erin was special—unlike the other girls he had gone out with. She had a sense of humor he found irresistible: *Something off the wall would always come rolling out of her mouth.* He found her cheerful, friendly, warm, open—to life, to people, to him. In her company, he felt free.

Erin had been ambivalent about college. She was surrounded by people who built successful careers without benefit of an advanced degree—her father, her older sisters (both she and Tom are the youngest of several siblings), and now Tom. Early in her senior year, she decided that she wouldn't bother with further education. She would finish high school, get a job, marry Tom, have babies (eventually), and live happily ever after.

Soon after Erin's graduation, she and Tom became engaged. Tom bought a small condominium in northern Maryland in preparation for their marriage. Erin went to secretarial school, which placed her in a Washington law firm. Tom was increasingly consumed by his responsibilities at the station, but Erin didn't notice. She was too busy herself being a young working woman about town, trading office gossip over lunch with high school friends.

Tom and Erin married when she was twenty and he twenty-two, and for the first few years they coasted; their early, absorbing conversations got lost somewhere along the way. They didn't argue, because they didn't talk about anything more substantive than where to eat on Friday night. Erin shopped for Tom's clothes, choosing dark, neutral shades because she assumed that was what he liked. He never told her he preferred bright colors; he didn't want to hurt her feelings. The erosion was so gradual that neither of them perceived it, though in the fifth year of marriage it finally dawned on Erin that they hadn't had sex in months.

By then she had stopped regarding work as a social event and become aware of her own ambition. She deeply regretted her lack of a college education. She watched people come into the law firm who were no more intelligent or capable than she was, but by virtue of their degrees they were hired as paralegals or financial analysts. Meanwhile, she was *just a secretary,* which she associated with demeaning stereotypes she'd seen on TV—women who sit around filing their nails, chatting aimlessly.

She felt that the adult life she had so blithely entered had no future; in her mind's eye she saw a sign that read *No trespassing beyond this point.* She felt she had lost herself. Where was the effervescent cheerleader who couldn't wait to start the day? She bought a book on depression and identified with the symptoms. Occasionally Tom would wonder where her sparkle had gone. When he asked if anything was wrong, she would say no, and he would drop it. She couldn't tell him, as she grew more entrenched in the white-collar world, that it was . . . well, *embarrassing to be married to a guy with grease under his fingernails,* someone who had been around a gas station so long he spoke with a twang and dropped his *g*'s. She couldn't tell him she held him responsible for the loss of her future.

During that year, Erin took a month's vacation in England and Ireland with her oldest sister, Molly. When she returned, in April 1987, she announced to Tom that she wanted a separation. He was stunned. Erin had only the vaguest of explanations; "Something isn't right," she said. Tom helped her move into an apartment and hoped for a reconciliation. Erin started to see a therapist. When she asked Tom to join her for a few sessions, he went willingly. He learned there that Erin had blamed him for her malaise but was slowly realizing that the problem lay within herself. He made it clear, in front of the therapist, that he would do whatever he could to help Erin get the college degree that was her immediate goal. She sensed for the first time his steadfastness, his *selflessness.* When he spoke about the grinding pressure of management and the pride he took in his ability to handle it, Erin saw that she had unfairly denigrated him. He was no grease monkey; he was an *executive.*

That fall they resumed living together. Erin began to take courses toward a B.A. in business administration. Tom urged her to stop playing Superwife (she had always believed, despite Tom's protests, that housework was a woman's job) and allow him to assume some of the chores. They agreed that he would clean and she would cook. Erin has always been tough on herself, seizing on the smallest mistakes as proof of her unworthiness; Tom helped to bolster her self-esteem. He urged her to become more assertive at work, where she subsequently won a hard-fought battle with her company to have her duties split between secretarial and paralegal, with an increase in salary and responsibility. Tom involved her more actively in his life, seeking her counsel on important business decisions, and Erin made an effort to stop saying "nothing" when something was wrong and Tom asked about it. By the following summer, 1988, the relationship had greatly improved. They decided it was time to start a family.

Erin now feels secure enough about her marriage to be ready for motherhood. But her body, it seems, is not.

**DECEMBER 1989**

**FRIDAY, DECEMBER 1**
**Cape Cod**

 AST NIGHT SARAH HAD ANOTHER EROTIC DREAM ABOUT WINSTON. He was her boyfriend for five years, when she was in her early twenties.

This time Sarah dreamed they were in the cabin of his sailboat, having intercourse on a table that converted into a double bed. Before the act was completed, Sarah woke up—an expression, she thinks, of the unresolved sense she has always had about their relationship.

Sarah believes that the dream occurs in pregnancy (this was the third time) because she has often wondered what it would be like to have a child with Winston, though she considered him too irresponsible to be a suitable husband. (He still spends all of his time sailing in the Caribbean, picking up odd jobs when he needs cash.) And he wasn't great in bed. He was too quick, and too indifferent—but that was what made Sarah lust after him. He could take sex or leave it. Michael is by far the better lover, but he wants it too much. Sarah guesses there's something odd about her attitude, but doesn't care to analyze it.

Today, a headhunter she knows from her corporate days calls about a $90,000-a-year job in retailing. She tells him that she's having a baby in four months. "Try me in a year," she says. Sarah believes in keeping the doors open, though she explains to the headhunter she won't consider any job that isn't within easy commuting distance of her home. Still, one day she may take the guy up on one of his offers. It would certainly shock Michael.

Once Sarah was ambitious. After attending junior college in Florida, which to her was a two-year waste of time forced on her by her mother, she enrolled in Lord & Taylor's buyer's training program, knowing a New York retailing background would look good on her résumé. She learned how to dress and where to get her hair cut and how to make the right connections; she was sharp, canny, and driven. Through a vendor she met on Seventh Avenue, Sarah was hired as a buyer for a then-hip store in Harvard Square and relocated to Cambridge. She parlayed that position into a more powerful one, running a division of a nationally known catalogue company based in New Hampshire. She traveled to Europe and New York two weeks out of every month and made $40,000 a year, a sizable salary then for a woman who had gone only to junior college.

When she settled in with Michael, her drive began to dissipate. Sarah now believes she wanted an excuse to wind down her career and Michael provided one, just as she was his excuse for giving up drugs. She was tired of the traveling, the pressure, the strain of trying to mold her rebellious self into something she was not: a corporate player.

She resigned her executive position in New Hampshire and accepted an offer to manage a small women's clothing boutique ten minutes away from the home she shared with Michael on the Cape. (This was entirely her choice; Michael, not yet her husband, had offered to quit his job as a short-order cook and find something closer to New Hampshire so she could stay with the catalogue company.) She worked at the boutique until the day before Ben was born. Four months later she returned on a part-time basis, necessitating a demotion from manager to salesperson. Though she had some guilt about leaving her infant son with a sitter, staying home full-time made her feel like a *nonperson*, which was even worse. Now, with a second child on the way, she is unsure whether she'll go back to work at all. But she dreads being home and dependent on Michael for spending money. Sarah is a dedicated shopper, with a habit of running up large bills on credit cards.

Though Michael savors a great meal in a fine restaurant and a couple of ski weekends each winter, his material needs are few. He can see himself as a sailor on a small boat or an artist living in a rustic shack. He hopes the baby growing in Sarah's womb is born healthy, without complications; he prays that his mother, who was diagnosed with lung cancer in August, will survive long enough to see her first and only granddaughter. At this point, that's all he asks of life.

But Sarah requires shopping expeditions to New York, vacations in Europe, an occasional extravagant gift of jewelry, new appliances, a new bed, and now a larger house. Michael tries to give her these things, because when Sarah is happy, he is too.

**WEDNESDAY,
DECEMBER 6
Manhattan**

 ULIET LEANS OVER THE OLD WOODEN TABLE IN THE SQUARE, SKYLIT kitchen of her downtown Manhattan loft, nibbling on a piece of whole-grain toast. Mounted in a neat horizontal line against one wall of the room are ten brightly painted papier-mâché animal masks that she and Sam acquired in a marketplace in

Delhi. A collection of shells from Baja and the Caribbean are scattered on a table in a corner of the beamed living room, where a wood-burning stove provides heat in winter and books are stacked haphazardly in floor-to-ceiling shelves. The furniture is worn, reflecting Sam and Juliet's mutual dislike of shopping and their indifference to matters of style.

Juliet is in her twelfth week of pregnancy. Timid around strangers, she dreads the prospect of Lamaze classes and, later, the idea of making play dates for her child. She worries she'll be subsumed by motherhood in lieu of other distractions, for she has always been professionally unmoored. Sam makes enough money for them to live comfortably, so there is no pressure on Juliet to contribute financially. She works sporadically as a free-lance writer and researcher and has completed two unpublished novels, but her aversion to self-promotion, her tendency to wait for projects to materialize instead of making them happen, and her self-described laziness are obvious handicaps for a free-lancer. Several years ago she thought about going to law school, took the LSAT's, received a perfect score, applied to and was accepted at Columbia, and then decided not to enroll for reasons that are still unclear to her. She has never seriously considered an office job; she is naturally resistant to authority and would, she thinks, make a poor employee.

With people she knows well, Juliet offers bold opinions and provocative insights. But she is awkward at chitchat, and in social situations where she feels she has to prove herself, she is deeply uncomfortable and often defensive. She can also, at times, seem haughty and dismissive, putting people off. She envies many of Sam's qualities, particularly his self-confidence, social ease, and public stature. Yet her envy doesn't rankle him, nor does her low level of productivity. Sam depends on her to keep his ego in check, which she does by twitting him mercilessly whenever he preens with self-importance. He spent their early days together absorbing with good humor her assaults on what she deemed his cultural vapidity (she was annoyed, for example, that he confused Laurence Olivier with Michael Redgrave in the film version of *Uncle Vanya*). Juliet is a voracious reader, with a keen grasp of subjects ranging from psychoanalysis to politics, while Sam's interests are more narrow. He esteems her intellect and relies on her presence of mind—that *life force* which allows nothing to escape her attention—to compensate for his own general obliviousness. His deference keeps the power quotient of the relationship in balance, although to the outside world it appears to be tipped in his favor.

Juliet at thirty-five looks much as she did in college. She still wears her thick, cinnamon-colored hair straight and parted on the side, though now it stops at her shoulders instead of at her waist, and she continues to favor the natural approach to grooming—she doesn't use makeup or shave her legs or underarms. She wears glasses and dresses comfortably, in cotton slacks or funky dresses, and generally without accessories; but if the weather or her mood calls for it, she might throw on an embroidered ethnic cap or a richly colored scarf, adding an idiosyncratic flair.

She has become fixated on horror stories about labor and delivery. The most appalling one she's heard so far was recently recounted by the TV actor Ted Danson on *The Barbara Walters Show:* Danson's wife suffered a stroke during delivery and was physically incapacitated for a year afterward. Juliet has heart arrythmia and wonders if the stress of labor might lead her to a similar fate. But in the end, she figures, *practically every old fool who's ever lived has managed to have a baby, and labor can't be that bad or no one would ever have a second child.* She'd like to get through it without drugs, but if she's in pain, she'll ask for a painkiller; it's that simple.

The one thing that would upset her is being unable to breastfeed. Whenever she holds a baby on her lap, she has the instinct to nurse it. It seems so easy and so right, one of nature's more brilliant designs: the baby sucks, the milk flows, the uterus contracts. But recently Juliet saw a videotape about breastfeeding that didn't make it look easy at all. There were sequences of a mother pushing her breast at a baby and the baby crying and failing to latch on, problems she had never imagined. Sam is already jealous because he can't be the one to nurse their baby, but he plans to taste the milk. Some men, he has learned through talking to friends, find the idea repellent, but not Sam.

For weeks Juliet has felt physically insulated, as if every part of her is padded against the outside world. Her ears and nose are persistently congested and she has gained ten pounds. The strange calm that settled upon her in the first weeks of pregnancy remains, protecting her from anxiety. Even when she and Sam met with Dr. Bernstein, the specialist in high-risk obstetrics whom Dr. Voss recommended, to discuss the wisdom of going ahead with their planned trip to Egypt and Italy in two weeks, Juliet did not feel nervous. Everyone has warned them not to travel, since she is already in danger of premature labor and possible miscarriage. But Bernstein told them what they wanted to hear: he doesn't anticipate any problems until after the fifth month, when the baby will be large enough to put pressure on her cervix. "If you want to go," he said, "now is the time." They're going.

Juliet and Sam are eager to make love. They haven't been able to since late September because she is still bleeding. Bernstein explained that the prostaglandins in seminal fluid can make the uterus contract, as can orgasm; since the bleeding indicates that her uterus is already irritable, Juliet should avoid any activity known to exacerbate this condition. The doctor said forty-eight hours would have to pass with no sign of spotting before sex would be safe. So Juliet waits, watching the clock.

**TUESDAY, DECEMBER 12**
**Manhattan**

ARIA REYES, FIFTEEN WEEKS PREGNANT, TAKES HER LUNCH hour today at a coffee shop one block from the hospital where she works, making $26,000 a year as the office manager for a group of radiation oncologists. She orders a chicken salad sandwich on white bread, feeling guilty. Her husband, Joe, begs her to eat whole grains for the baby's sake, but Maria dislikes *brown food.*

Maria has known Joe since she was fourteen, when she lived with her older brother, Carlos. Joe would come over on Saturday nights to play cards with Carlos, usually as Maria was on her way out. She didn't pay much attention to him then—he was a twenty-three-year-old married man, and Maria was involved in her own teenage world.

At eighteen she got engaged to a boy her age, but she broke it off after six months because he seemed so immature. At twenty-one she ran into Joe at a Latin dance club. She hadn't seen him for five years, and didn't know he'd had a daughter and gotten a divorce. They were engaged a year later. This time Maria had no doubts: Joe was a *man,* responsible and strong, yet had an irrepressible sense of fun. He could always make her laugh.

Maria is only twenty-five, but she's an old soul. She grew up in a housing project under the Williamsburg Bridge on Manhattan's Lower East Side. She is the youngest of seven children, none of whom, despite the environment, turned out to be drug addicts or criminals—a fact that Maria believes is a testament to her parents' strict, old-fashioned notions of child-rearing.

Life in the projects toughened Maria. She learned to act as if nothing bothered her and no one could defeat her. She learned not to be afraid. As an adolescent, on her way to modeling school early one Saturday morning, she chased a man through a deserted subway station because he'd stolen her treasured black felt cowboy hat off her head. She didn't get it back, but she wasn't going to let herself be victimized without a fight.

Maria's mother, who worked as a chambermaid and a seamstress while her children were at school, sewed all the clothes the family wore (which were never fashionable enough for Maria's taste). Her father worked hard and took pride in his ability to care for his brood. When Maria was ten, he lost his job as a cook when the owners moved the restaurant out of state. Unemployed and depressed, he started drinking, a pattern that continued off and on for several years. Maria was his favorite child and the only one still living at home. She would return from school to find her father stinking of rum, waiting for her to comfort him. He'd slur, "Oh, Maria, I love you" and fall on the bed, begging her, "Help me." Her mother would hand her a cold rag to press to his forehead, and she would murmur reassuringly to her father as he wept, never revealing the terror she felt: *My big daddy, crumpled up like a baby . . .*

She was seventeen when her father spent several months on a psychiatric ward. Maria met with his social worker at the hospital; it was the first time she openly acknowledged her pain. She allowed herself to cry, and once she started, she feared she would never stop. Shortly after her father was discharged, he and her mother moved to Puerto Rico. Since then he has been fine.

Maria spent the years after high school graduation moving from one sibling's house to another, paying her share of food and rent. (Even though she was self-supporting, working as a cashier at a convenience store, her parents forbade her to live alone.) One brother didn't approve of her receiving phone calls in his home, and when Maria wouldn't comply with this rule, he changed the locks on her. She moved in with her sister, but her sister's husband objected to her hours —she worked the four-to-midnight shift and afterward went out dancing with her friends. Finally she rented a room from a cousin who left her alone.

Now Maria and Joe, who were married in July 1988, live in a quiet middle-class neighborhood in Queens. The brick apartment complex is only a half-hour's drive from the Lower East Side where she grew up, but to Maria it is a universe away.

Maria is a fatalist: she thinks that if things don't go the way you want them to, they weren't meant to happen, and it's better to change your course than to rue your misfortune. But so far everything has gone according to her plan, which was to get pregnant a year after her marriage to Joe.

Her obstetrician discussed amniocentesis with her, but she and Joe feel that even if she were ten years older and at statistical risk for genetic problems, they would do nothing to change the course of creating a life. Both are nonpracticing Catholics. Maria has never been to confession or received communion, and Joe believes he can talk to God more intimately at home than in a church, but they adhere to the concept of God's will: *You take what God gives, and you deal with it.*

Joe is grateful that God gave him Maria. He has been drawn to her since she was a teenager. When he was playing cards with her brother and she was on her way out someplace, he'd think to himself, noting her lush mouth, vibrant dark eyes, and full-breasted young body, *What a pretty girl.* He loves her spunk, her way of taking everything in stride, even the skinny legs he teases her about.

In Joe's first marriage, there was always a *cold zone*. His ex-wife was engrossed in her career working with computers, often traveling out of town. Joe felt, *if you're not here, then I'm not here either,* so he was always out playing ball, while his in-laws, who lived across the street, took care of his daughter, Cheryl, now twelve. Joe and his ex-wife didn't get along, though he refused to argue—he grew up with too much of that. Joe's mother and stepfather, who have been married for twenty-eight years, fought relentlessly, and Joe didn't want to expose Cheryl to such acrimony. She was five at the time of the divorce and now lives with her mother, stepfather, and two half-brothers. Joe is glad the marriage ended but regrets the effect of its dissolution on Cheryl, who has had trouble adjusting to the reconfiguration of her family—she grapples with feeling displaced by her baby half-brothers—and to enrollment in a new, nearly all-white school outside New York City. Joe sees her regularly, provides for her financially as needed (the child-support agreement with his ex-wife is informal), and involves himself actively in her upbringing—maybe, he thinks, too actively. His ex-wife often calls on him to discipline Cheryl, and though he doesn't like being forced into the role of the bad guy, his daughter needs someone to set limits. His ex-wife seems unwilling or unable to do so, and he already sees in Cheryl the beginnings of a wild, spoiled adolescent.

Joe makes about $31,000 annually as a mail carrier for the U.S. Postal Service, working from 6 A.M. to 2:30 P.M. Both he and Maria are diligent, devoted employees, but his job is less demanding than hers. Her responsibilities include billing patients for medical services rendered; sometimes her office is so busy she can't get the billing done during the day and has to complete the work at home. This disturbs Joe, but he knows she's just doing what she needs to do. Maria doesn't put her career before him as his first wife did.

Joe and Maria both have outgoing natures, and her stoical self-possession nicely balances his tendency to melodrama. They enjoy the same things—sporting events, Lotto, barbecues in the park with family and friends, raucous games of Parcheesi or Scrabble, weekend getaways to the Poconos. *Even when we're in different rooms,* Joe thinks, *it feels like we're together.*

He is rapturous about her pregnancy, hounding Maria to drink prune juice for her constipation, anxiously awaiting the moment when the baby first kicks inside her stomach, anticipating the thrill of delivery. If he can afford it, he wants four kids with Maria. He yearns for the kind of tight-knit, stable, two-parent family that was denied him as a child. Joe's mother has five children by four different men. Joe, who was born in Puerto Rico, was her second. When Joe was three his natural father abandoned the family without a penny of support, and his mother moved him and his older half-brother to New York. The only feeling Joe has for his father is contempt for his negligence.

Joe wants and needs to be relied upon. It feeds his self-respect and preserves his perception that he has nothing in common with his father. He is pleased that his mother and brothers turn to him for succor and advice; he thinks of himself as their *guardian angel*. But he believes in helping anyone who needs help (he has on occasion taken it upon himself to chase thieves and redirect traffic around highway accidents). The Good Samaritan is his defining role.

Joe considers himself a self-made man on every level. He should be fearful, he thinks, because his mother was—she kept him in the house to protect him from the dangers she imagined were lurking beyond her door, and didn't allow him to play outside with his friends until he was close to adolescence—but instead he confronts the world with unwavering self-assurance. He should be an easy target for bullies—he got picked on in grade school for his puny size and mortifying lack of athletic prowess—but by junior high he had conditioned himself rigorously enough to make the track team and had learned to use his fists.

Joe is often singled out at work for his initiative, and his bosses recently approached him about becoming a supervisor. But he is hesitant. He is gratified by the public relations aspect of being a mail carrier; he likes being on the street, meeting people, hustling to get them what they want. As a supervisor he would lose this contact with customers, and though he likes to be in control, he doesn't want to police his colleagues.

He has three buddies at work whose wives are pregnant. The men confide in each other, calling the women "Momma" and trading medical notes. When Maria was spotting a few weeks ago and Joe feared a miscarriage, he told the guys about it; they advised him not to worry. Joe has been entranced by the changes in Maria's body, particularly her swelling breasts, but at first he feared that lovemaking might hurt the baby. His coworkers again reassured him to the contrary.

He keeps waiting for Maria to turn into a "moody bitch," as one of his colleagues refers to his own pregnant wife. But so far Maria has been her usual unflappable self. In fact, she's always asking *him* why she's not depressed yet.

**SATURDAY,
DECEMBER 16
Southern Maryland**

L AST MONTH TOM NOTICED A DISCREPANCY BETWEEN THE AMOUNT of super gasoline being pumped and the amount measured in the underground tank. The gap kept increasing, indicating either a leak or a shortfall in the delivery of the product. By early December, he grew alarmed. The oil company of which he is a franchisee ran a test and concluded that the tank was leaking. Then the Environmental Protection Agency did its own inspection, and informed Tom that he cannot pump super gasoline until the leak is repaired.

Now it's ten days before Christmas, the busiest time of the year, with super gas normally accounting for 40 percent of his sales. Tom is frantic with worry. It barely penetrated his consciousness when Erin told him yesterday that once again she got her period. She asked about seeing an infertility specialist, which registered briefly—"I think that's jumping the gun," Tom managed to say—before he sank back into his own gloom. She mentioned something about an ovulation test kit, to which Tom nodded absently, thinking, *I've owned this business for less than three months and I may not make it past January.*

Erin cannot get through to him. He hasn't even noticed she has lost twenty pounds on the Slim-Fast diet she began in September in anticipation of getting pregnant. *The joke's on me,* she thinks, unable to experience any joy at her new svelteness. She has never been petite— she is five foot seven and has always been self-conscious about her large breasts—but her weight was not a problem until recently. Over the past three years she has become sedentary, with the combined demands of her job and her academic courses taking up the time she used to devote to aerobics. She was horrified to discover she had put on thirty-five pounds since high school.

Erin contemplates her husband. He seems both nervous and immobilized, hunched over the kitchen table, cracking his knuckles and staring off into space. She recognizes the gravity of his situation but cannot identify with it. Here they are, within touching distance, but it feels to her as if they are sealed off in separate chambers. *Merry Christmas,* she thinks bitterly.

**SUNDAY, DECEMBER 17**
**Westchester, New York**

I N THE TINY KITCHEN OF HIS TWO-BEDROOM CONDOMINIUM, ROB Weiner arranges a brunch platter of whitefish, lox, and bagels, then sets the platter on the dining table. In the bathroom, his wife is throwing up. She emerges and sinks into a chair, averting her eyes from the food.

Rob has been married to Alex della Croce for eight years. They are the same age, thirty-four, and height, five-nine, but Alex, now twelve weeks pregnant, appears taller. She is willowy; Rob is stocky.

Alex is a handsome woman, with strong features and a wide mouth that curves in a slightly crooked smile. Her lush dark hair falls in waves to her shoulders, and her fingers are long and slender, ending in well-tended nails. Rob's hair pains him because it's thinning; he spends close to a thousand dollars a year on Rogaine. He won't wear his wedding band because he thinks it will draw attention to his fingers, which he considers to be short and stubby, and to his nails, which are gnawed. With typical self-deprecation, he is quick to note the physical incongruities between him and Alex, so everyone knows *he* knows how lucky—and how completely undeserving—he is to have married someone like her.

Alex makes upward of $75,000 annually as the technical service representative for a chemical fiber company, which over the ten years of her employment has rewarded her frequently with raises, promotions, and increased autonomy. She relishes her work. Rob earns about $53,000 selling medical equipment, has changed jobs every two years, and denigrates every one of them because he cannot accept the notion of being a salesman. It conjures up to him a disturbing image: a guy in a plaid suit standing in front of a used-car lot, rubbing his hands together when he spots a little old lady coming down the street with a few bucks in her pocket.

Alex has an ability to charm and disarm everyone she meets; she is quick to size up a situation and discreetly manipulate it to get what she wants. Rob lacks her social cunning and tends to withdraw behind books or alienate people with his caustic, self-protective wit. Yet he can be a gifted raconteur, drawing on his knowledge of literature, music, politics, and sports. While Rob goes about daily life with a casual attitude, often running late or putting off tasks he views as inconsequential, Alex is ruthlessly efficient and detail-oriented. Though regimented, she is not grim; she has a ribald, tomboyish sense of humor, a full-throated laugh, and a lively curiosity.

Alex is a pragmatist who glories in her mastery of *male subjects* (she graduated from college with honors, majoring in engineering and chemistry) and prides herself on being one of very few women who have achieved prominence in a highly technical, male-dominated field. Instead of feeling her emotions, she articulates them, quite clinically; Rob acts his out.

Alex, the youngest of five siblings and the only one born in America, is the daughter of northern Italian immigrants who insisted that dinner-table conversation be conducted in Italian as a way of keeping the language alive. Her father, now deceased, was a bricklayer whose work was so artful and precise that people thought the fireplaces and chimneys he built had to be fake, they were so symmetrical. From him Alex inherited meticulousness and stubbornness. Her social wiles come from her mother.

Rob is a first-generation son of Russian Jewish immigrants. Unlike Alex, he does not exalt his background. His mother is a gentle, compliant woman who never makes direct demands but excels at subtly inducing guilt. Rob thinks of her as the martyr type, who will sit in a completely dark house until someone offers to change the light bulbs. His father, who operated a one-man, marginally successful stock brokerage, died of pancreatic cancer in October, just before Alex learned she was pregnant. He was an erudite and deeply cultured man, but in the working-class neighborhood where Rob was raised, the other kids never said, "Lucky Rob, his dad really knows Mozart." They said, "Lucky Steve, his dad can really throw a ball." Rob wishes, guiltily, that his father had been more of *a regular guy,* more *American.*

Despite their religious and cultural differences, Rob and Alex share a sense of the absurd and maintain similarly ironic perspectives on life. As Rob describes it, they can look at someone and decide independently that he or she is an asshole, for roughly the same reasons. They prefer each other's company, and rarely socialize with peers unless there's a business reason. Most of their leisure time is spent at home, where they indulge in pillow fights, cartoon fests, and friendly verbal sparring. Rob calls Alex "my princess" when he's not calling her "my mule," a reference to her unyielding nature; to Alex, Rob is "the slug." Aside from periodic screaming matches, usually instigated by Alex over some failing of Rob's and ascribed by Rob to Alex's misguided perfectionism, they seem to get along admirably.

They met during their junior year at college in upstate New York. Alex was then unenthusiastically engaged to a man named Jeffrey, who went to a different school.

"Harvard," Rob prompts her, wryly. "Tall, handsome *goy,* lots of hair, family estate in Greenwich . . . it made perfect sense that you threw him over for me."

"You were supposed to be just a good time," Alex reminds him, "but I realized something was wrong if I was having *that* good a time."

Alex broke up with Jeffrey; she and Rob soon became inseparable. A year after graduating, Alex moved in with him, sundering her relationship with her parents. Until that point they had demonstrated unwavering trust in her judgment and had rarely interfered with her decisions. Throughout adolescence she received straight A's; when it was time for college, she suggested that she take care of her own tuition (she won a partial scholarship) and spending money. Her parents, she said, could pay for room and board. Alex thought it was only fair that she contribute to her education, but more important, she didn't want to be *owned*. Her affair with Rob marked her parents' first significant intrusion into her life, and Alex would not tolerate it. She felt she had earned the right to live as she pleased.

The della Croces were warm, loving parents, but certain subjects were not discussed—especially sex, which was supposed to happen only within marriage. Alex learned about birth control by writing an eighth-grade term paper on the subject (she still remembers her most startling finding: in the Middle Ages, women devised their own version of condoms by inserting peapods into their vaginas) and had been careful not to shatter her parents' illusion of her virginity, which she lost long before Rob appeared in her life. For her parents, it was bad enough that their prized and accomplished daughter planned to live with a man outside of wedlock. But more painful was their belief that Alex had given herself to someone with no serious intentions. Rob, they said, would never marry a Catholic girl, and Alex would be hurt.

For two years Alex didn't see or speak to her parents, although she missed them strongly. It was Alex's mother, ever the diplomat, who finally brokered a reconciliation. Six months later, Alex's father was diagnosed with cancer. His illness accelerated Rob and Alex's marriage plans, but he died two weeks before the wedding. Rob's parents made their displeasure with his choice of a non-Jewish wife abundantly clear but didn't go through with their threat to boycott the nondenominational ceremony.

"Religion," says Alex now, sipping the chocolate milk she believes helps to minimize nausea, "is only an issue again because of the baby."

"Catholicism," says Rob, hoping to keep this ominous subject on a theoretical plane, "is such a horrible thing. Look at the antiabortion forces, and the people who say Mark Twain is obscene. All these people are in the church." He leans back in his chair and waits to be contradicted.

"I'm not arguing on behalf of Catholicism," Alex says. "I'm arguing on behalf of nothing."

"There's no such thing as nothing." Rob's tone is exasperated.

"I became nothing, by default."

"You're kidding yourself. If you were nothing by default, you wouldn't have a Christmas tree." Rob waves his hand in the direction of the lavishly ornamented tree that appears in their apartment each holiday season—without his mother's knowledge.

"I think it smells pretty," Alex says. "It has nothing to do with religion."

"Yes it does. Our kid will see Christmas trees and Easter bunnies and he'll think, 'Hey, Christianity looks like the way to go.' But I want him to know both sides of his heritage."

"I agree."

"Alex . . ." Rob expels an exaggerated sigh. "You don't understand. For you, heritage isn't about Catholicism, it's about being Italian. Jews never had a country of origin; our heritage is the religion. So to say we're not going to teach the kid about Judaism, it's like saying we're not going to teach him about being Italian."

"I'm not saying that."

"Good. If he's a boy, we'll have a briss."

"Then we'll have a baptism too. All or nothing."

"Okay." Rob picks up the front section of the *Times* and pretends to read it.

"But a baptism isn't just throwing water on the kid. It's a commitment to raise him Catholic. You can't bend the rules . . ."

"Oh really?" Rob drops the paper. "Is that why the church is packed with people who've had divorces and abortions? You kill someone, no problem. You go into the little closet with the sliding door and promise not to do it again. But get divorced? Nope, that's bending the rules. These are the values of Catholicism? Forget it."

"But I say the same thing all the time. I don't want to raise the child Catholic either."

"Yes, mule. Yes, stubborn ass," Rob says. "You don't have to change your mind, you're always right. With you it's just a matter of how long you have to wait before someone else agrees."

"How many things have you finally told me I was right about?" Alex says triumphantly.

"How many things have I finally given up trying to explain to you? Because you are a mule."

Alex laughs and throws a piece of bagel at him, signaling that the subject, still unresolved, can be closed.

Rob goes to work on the breakfast dishes. Alex has trained him in dishwashing methods as she has trained him to pick up his dirty socks from the floor. She will not accept the label of "nag"; she believes the word was created by men to describe women who ask them to do something perfectly reasonable that they don't feel like doing.

Alex grew up with the unnegotiable rule that you couldn't leave the house until your bed was made. (She took it upon herself to make her college roommate's bed along with her own until the roommate got the hint.) She stores a Dustbuster in the trunk of her blue Honda Accord to keep the interior free of nettlesome particles, and avoids riding in Rob's sports car because it is cluttered with debris. She refuses to hire a cleaning service, though she and Rob could easily afford it; in her opinion, no one other than her mother could possibly meet her exacting standards of housekeeping.

As Rob toils in the kitchen, Alex goes into the living room and lies down on the beige leather couch, feeling nauseous. The room is immaculate and oddly colorless, rather like the waiting area in an office suite, with its well-made but unobtrusive seating, a blue slate and white marble coffee table with nothing on it, not even a smudge, and vertical Levolor blinds in the same neutral shade as the walls. The only personal touches are the Christmas tree, Rob's piano against one wall, a jungle of tall plants against another, and three limited-edition Erté lithographs of Oriental women dressed in Alex's preferred color combination, red and black.

Rob enters the room and sits in the French blue armchair, studying Alex with concern.

"I wish I didn't have to watch you being sick," he says plaintively. "I wish you would let me hold your forehead when you throw up."

Alex tries to assume her usual feisty tone, which she knows will reassure him. "You like me being sick. I'm so much more malleable and sweet."

Rob looks relieved. "It's hard for you to be a tough executive when you're on your knees puking. You can't give your usual orders."

"If I have to hug a dirty toilet again because you didn't clean it, you're going to pay."

"Yes, I know," Rob says. "I'm sure that when you're in labor, every time you feel pain you'll grab me by my balls, so I can enjoy each contraction right along with you. That's what you want—a fully shared experience, right?"

"Right," says Alex.

**MONDAY, DECEMBER 18**
**Cape Cod**

ARAH IS DISGUSTED WITH HER OBSTETRICIANS BUT FEELS TOO FAR along in her pregnancy to switch. She has a double ear infection that makes her dizzy and a sinus infection that prevents her from sleeping. Yet the doctor in the practice who was on duty last week, when she went in with these complaints, refused to prescribe antibiotics. He was the same man who wouldn't give her painkillers when she was in labor with Ben, simply because, she guesses, he is a sexist asshole who likes to torture women.

Today Sarah calls her doctor's office again. "I can't breathe," she says to the nurse, "and if this goes on for two more days I'll wind up in the emergency room." The nurse gives her an immediate appointment with a different doctor in the practice, who writes out, in about ten seconds, a prescription for ampicillin; he says he'll put her in the hospital if the antibiotics don't work. That's all Sarah wanted from the first guy—to take her seriously enough to help her. She has never felt so sick in her life. It's the Christmas selling season, and she hasn't been able to work for a week.

Her due date is April 4, but Sarah hopes she'll be early, for her mother-in-law's sake as well as her own. Sarah loves and respects Michael's mother, Margery, who is strong but not pushy, self-confident but not arrogant, and who has never pressured Sarah to be someone other than who she is. The first time they met, when Michael took Sarah to the family home in Palm Beach, Margery handed Sarah a set of satin sheets. "Dear," she said, "I hope you'll be comfortable," and led Sarah and Michael to the guest room, even though they weren't married. Sarah's mother wouldn't have let them stay in the same house, let alone the same bed—a flagrant hypocrisy, Sarah thinks, given her mother's track record of multiple husbands and extramarital affairs. When Sarah married Michael, Margery said gently that she hoped Sarah would one day decide to convert to Judaism, but it would be her decision to make, in her own time and her own way. Sarah would never have converted if Margery had taken the more demanding approach her own mother would have favored.

She knows it's hardly Margery's fault, but *why did she have to get cancer now, in the middle of this horrible pregnancy?* Sarah feels heartless thinking such things, but she can't control what comes into her head. It would be just her luck to have Michael away in Palm Beach, caring for his mother, when she goes into labor. It's bad enough to have to carry a child by yourself for nine months. Sarah does not want to go through the delivery alone, too.

**Christmas Day**
**Westchester**

OR SIX YEARS, TESTS HAVE INDICATED THAT ALEX'S PLATELETS, which clot the blood, are routinely in the below-normal range. The condition is called idiopathic thrombositic purpura (ITP). She mentioned it to her obstetrician, Carl McAllister, at her prenatal checkup three days ago. The doctor said he was concerned that her condition might make a vaginal delivery dangerous to the baby. If the fetus gets ITP through the placenta, he explained, it might bleed within its brain when the head slams through the birth canal. A scalp sample can be taken as the baby crowns to determine whether or not it has the condition. If the test is positive, Alex will have to have a cesarean.

"Fine," she told the doctor. "I don't care how the baby comes out, as long as it does." In truth, Alex would just as soon be given general anesthesia. She's not one of those women looking for a supposedly fulfilling "natural" experience, who agitate for birthing rooms with wallpaper, soft lighting, a midwife, and no drugs. Alex, who thinks of herself as a scientist, finds the cold stainless steel and chrome of an operating room far more reassuring.

She called Rob at work to fill him in on her meeting with Carl (both Rob and Alex refer to doctors by first names to signal their lack of awe for the medical profession) and mentioned that she still hadn't gained any weight. Rob started screaming. "Why in hell didn't you bother to mention the blood thing to him before now? And what is he going to do about the nausea? How is this child going to be strong if you throw up every nutrient you take in?"

"Stop being hysterical. I just happen to have the bad luck to get sick. It doesn't affect the baby."

"Bullshit. If you're going to build a house, you need cement and wood and stone and wire and nails, and you are building a person. Don't you get it?"

"Why won't you listen when I tell you that my mother and my sisters all vomited copiously during pregnancy, with no negative consequences? Why are you so irrational?"

"Why are you so cavalier? It's not like you can say, 'Hold on, God, let's have a twelve-month pregnancy so we have time to make mistakes.' There are only nine months, and mistakes can't be corrected."

"Are you accusing me of deliberately not taking care of my health?" Alex slammed down the phone.

Rob is sitting at the dining table now, studying Carl's bill for Alex's November 21 visit, which includes twenty dollars for drawing her blood. Apparently, he thinks, Carl didn't bother to read the results of this test, or he would have known about Alex's low platelets a month ago. Why only now is he talking about intracranial bleeding and cesareans? Rob wants to make sure that Carl has done a cesarean before—the man is only thirty-eight years old, after all—but in many ways he would prefer it to a vaginal delivery. He persists in believing that women were not designed to live long after childbirth. Rob can't picture God saying, "Hey, we'll have this huge thing come out of this small opening and then let the machine run indefinitely."

Alex needs to be more vigilant at overseeing her medical care, he thinks, because doctors can't be trusted. *"Attention must be paid"* . . . It's a line from *Death of a Salesman,* and Rob can't get it out of his head.

His cynicism about the medical profession goes back fifteen years to the Incident, which forever removed doctors from the sacred world in which he had once placed them. He had just completed his sophomore year in college and had a summer job as a gofer in the neuroradiology department of a Manhattan hospital. He befriended a patient, a young woman about his age, who had been diagnosed with a brain tumor. Rob was allowed to observe her surgery. In the operating room, he studied the X-rays mounted on a light box and watched in horror as a resident made a fatal error: looking at the same X-rays, the resident confused an EKG lead for a catheter and pushed it into the girl's heart. The next day she had a massive coronary and became comatose. She died a year later. Rob knew the resident had killed her, and there was nothing he could do about it. No one would believe him, a mere college kid, if he stood up in court and said he had witnessed something all the doctors would deny. Rob had planned to go to medical school, but when he returned to college in the fall he switched his major from biology to English literature.

He has never been able to forget what he saw in that operating room so many years ago—the sheer carelessness of it—and the memory reverberates loudly now that Alex is pregnant. *It is one of the many ironies of my life,* Rob thinks, *that I make my living off doctors.*

Alex knows that the Incident, which occurred the year before they met, has made Rob suspicious of anyone in a white coat. She comprehends why he feels that way but disagrees with his global attitude. *Why condemn an entire profession,* she thinks, *for the negligence of one resident?* Rob's unswerving paranoia directed at her doctors is making her pregnancy much more difficult. She fantasizes about packing him in a box, marking it *Do Not Open Until July 30* (a month after her due date), and mailing it somewhere—anywhere, as long as it's away from her.

Once she could tell Rob anything without fear of reprisal. Her style with other men had been to hide what she really thought, but with Rob she could be honest; she fell in love with him in part because of that. But with pregnancy, Alex is beginning to think that she must revert to her old ways. To control his hysteria, she will have to censor herself.

ARIA LEAVES HER OFFICE AT FOUR AND BEGINS THE TWO-SUB-way trek home, never pleasant on days when your stomach's jutting out and your legs ache and you have to stand because there are no empty seats at rush hour and you're too proud to accept someone's rare offer to exchange places (always, Maria has observed, made by women, never by men).

An hour later she walks into her third-floor, one-bedroom apartment. Mounted in the entryway is Joe's trophy head of the buck he shot a few years ago in the Catskills; samples from his baseball cap collection are propped on its antlers. Maria's passion for Betty Boop, whom people say she resembles, is evident in the kitchen, where cardboard cutouts and miniature dolls representing the cartoon character are scattered on counters and walls. A small Christmas tree twinkles against the living room window. Presents for Joe's daughter, Cheryl, are still piled underneath; she was sick on Christmas Day and couldn't come over.

The baby will have to sleep in Joe and Maria's mauve-and-gray bedroom; the crib will go against the wall where their bicycles and Maria's collection of stuffed animals now rest. The apartment is too small for a family of three. By July 1991, when the lease is up, Joe and Maria hope they'll be able to afford a bigger place, possibly in a safer, more affordable city.

Joe is sprawled on the couch watching the local TV news. Just off the basketball court, he's still in athletic clothes. He is built like a bullet, with a solid, compact body, a thin mustache, and a military-style crew cut.

He jumps up to pat Maria's belly and tousle her hair. "It's a mess," he teases her. "You need a trim, babe." Maria wrinkles her nose, feigning annoyance. She gives him a hearty kiss and joins him on the couch.

"Cheryl is coming over tonight to open her presents," Joe says. "Let's surprise her with a real feast, Chinese takeout."

"You're feeling pretty good about her these days, aren't you?" Maria says.

"Yeah," Joe says. "Thanks to you."

Maria is pleased by the acknowledgment. She tries to be sensitive to her stepdaughter's concerns, assuring her that she will always be her daddy's little girl, no matter how many half-siblings enter her life. Cheryl has responded by calling Maria "Mom" and by showing Joe more affection than she has in a long time.

Joe wants desperately to be close to Cheryl, but his role as her long-distance disciplinarian has caused friction between them. He respected his own mother's steely ways of parenting: she instilled in her children the importance of good manners, neatness, and reverence for their elders, and wasn't averse to using a belt when words failed to establish her authority. Joe wants the same respect from Cheryl, but his firmness has in the past made her resent him—*run* from him. Last year, just after Joe and Maria married, they offered to have Cheryl live with them, but Cheryl said no. Joe was hurt, and was convinced that she rejected him because she knew he would be strict with her and wouldn't let her get away with everything, like her mother does. Since then, Maria has helped to bring father and daughter together, blunting Joe's hard edge when he overreacts to something Cheryl does or says and convincing Cheryl of his need for her love.

Sitting on the couch with Joe, Maria wonders why she feels so good. "Where," she asks him, "are those hormones that are supposed to make you crazy?" She tells Joe about last week's office Christmas party, where her boss hovered over her, treating her like an invalid, asking if he could get her something to eat or drink, as if she were unable to fend for herself. "I told him no thanks, and he said, 'But you're pregnant, you're supposed to nag and give orders and let yourself be spoiled.' I just stared at him and said, '*Why?* Pregnancy is not such a terrible thing.' And I'm telling you, he stared back at me like I said I was the Virgin Mary or something. Do *you* think there's some-thing wrong with me?"

"Hell no," Joe says. "Having a baby . . . it's the greatest thing in the world."

OB AND ALEX'S ONCE ROBUST SEX LIFE HAS DWINDLED TO A near standstill because of Alex's nausea. This troubles Alex, primarily because it seems wasteful not to take advantage of their remaining months of freedom. Still, there's been no lack of intimacy. They sleep like spoons, snuggling so close they end up using only half of their queen-size bed.

Today, for instance, they lie there until 2 P.M., talking to "the Ba-bies." (They're pretending Alex is carrying twins so she'll never have to go through pregnancy again.) When Alex says she's in the mood for bacon, Rob races to the grocery store and then to the mall. He buys a new glass blender (he thinks, for no particular reason, that glass will make Alex's milkshakes taste better than plastic does), a stovetop grill for the steaks and hamburgers Alex has recently craved, and a twelve-inch pan for making large omelettes. When he returns, he prepares eggs, hash browns, bacon, biscuits, orange juice, and a milkshake, into which he sneaks an egg for extra nutrition. "Protein is cement, cal-cium is brick, vegetables are wood, and everything else is wire and nails," he says, explaining his theory of baby building.

This week, Rob plans to quit his job. He has already accepted another, with better hours and more opportunity for growth. He'll give two weeks' notice, though he has already cleared his desk out and replaced his Rolodex cards with blanks in case he is told to leave immediately. Some people might find it foolish to make a job change when your wife is four months pregnant, but Rob—in an attempt to quash his belief that he is destined to be unlucky—repeats to himself over and over, like a mantra, *You can make any decision succeed or fail, depending on what you do with it.*

**JANUARY—JUNE, 1990**

**THURSDAY, JANUARY 4**
**Westchester**

 LEX SELLS SYNTHETIC FIBERS TO TEXTILE COMPANIES IN THE South and Northeast, but she is more than a salesperson; her chemical-engineering background enables her to advise customers on technical procedures for making fiber into fabric. She travels two weeks out of every month, three or four days at a stretch, and works from home the rest of the time. Customarily, she attends corporate meetings in which she is the only woman. On sales calls, she coaxes prospective clients, usually male, into multimillion-dollar contracts through an orchestrated amalgam of skilled listening and scientific acumen. Alex thinks of it simply as *playing up to their interests, like dating.*

When she was nine years old, she changed her name from Alessandra to Alex. This infuriated her parents; when friends called asking for Alex, they would say, "No one by that name lives here." But the name

Alessandra seemed simperingly feminine and therefore *vacuous,* a quality Alex loathes in women. Now thirty-four, she has proved to herself that she can compete and win in the business world as well as any man without having to look like one. She paints her fingernails and toenails (in shades of red, never pink), applies lipstick for business (again, shades of red), and brags that the tiny bikinis she wore in college still fit. Nonetheless, even in pregnancy Alex won't allow anyone, including Rob, to assist with her luggage. She doesn't want to appear dependent, weak.

To her surprise, she is finding that pregnancy, the ultimate expression of femininity, can be an asset in her professional life. Yesterday she met with a female executive of a textile company who could throw hundreds of thousands of dollars her way if she wanted to. The meeting wasn't going well until Alex excused herself, explaining that she was experiencing second-trimester nausea. The executive, who has a twenty-two-month-old daughter, instantly softened. Soon they were discussing the conflicts of being a working mother and the difficulty of finding good child care. By the end of the meeting, Alex had a new client.

This morning Rob tells the Babies he's quitting his job, but in the afternoon he calls Alex at home to report that he hasn't quite gotten up the nerve. He has made many job changes, but this is the first Alex regards favorably. He'll shorten his commute by thirty miles a day, his responsibilities are clear, and the people he'll be working with seem competent. Alex hopes the change will calm him. Between his anxiety over her pregnancy, his poor diet (midnight bingeing, no breakfast, too much coffee), his excess weight (thirty pounds since college), and, most offensive, his smoking (he chews peppermint gum to cleanse his breath, which doesn't fool her), she could accuse *him* of not taking care of himself, a charge he now levies against her.

Whenever Alex is in Rob's car and spots a cellophane wrapper the size of a cigarette box, she tells him, "I'll bring a date to your funeral, and I promise it will be someone you don't like."

ULIET ARRIVES PROMPTLY FOR HER 10:30 A.M. PRENATAL CHECKUP
with Dr. Bernstein, resigned to the fact that he rarely runs less
than forty-five minutes late. She has equipped herself with
magazines but does not read; instead she studies the other
pregnant women in the waiting room, many accompanied by their
husbands. Sam is home with the flu, so Juliet has brought a notebook
to record the details of her conversation with Bernstein. She and Sam
returned from their trip abroad three days ago and she is anxious to
find out how her pregnancy fared. She tried to be cautious, though she
did clamber in and out of small boats when they were cruising the Nile
and occasionally joined in with the Sudanese dancers.

Bernstein performs the exam at 11:30. When Juliet is dressed, she
follows a nurse into his office. The doctor, a genial man in his mid-
forties with an unpretentious manner that Juliet finds refreshing, informs her, to her relief, that he has found no change in her cervix.

"If it starts to open," Juliet asks, "can you catch it before it goes
bad?"

"We hope so. We'll be looking for something out of the ordinary,
like cramping or regular contractions. We'll see you more than most
people because we anticipate that kind of thing in DES women."

"What about the belt?" Juliet refers to a home device designed to
monitor contractions in women at risk for premature labor.

"You're too early for that. It would be after the amnio."

"After we had sex on the trip," Juliet says, "I bled a little bit, and
the next day too."

"That's going to become more of a problem, because you'll also
contract after sex. You're probably not going to be able to have it
much longer." Bernstein is sympathetic; he sees the disappointment on
her face.

"So you recommend that we stop having sex when?"

"The difficulty with DES women is that the uterus doesn't grow in the normal way and is more irritable—more likely to contract—when the baby gets to be a substantial size. That's coming up pretty soon, at about twenty weeks."

"So even if you see no change, I should stop having sex then?"

"Well, I hate to say this, but it's your first pregnancy and we don't know how it will play out. It would be best to eliminate activities we know can stimulate contractions."

Frustrated at his vagueness, Juliet laughs. "Okay, okay . . . and one other thing. One of my books says that if you're at all at risk for premature labor, you shouldn't take childbirth classes."

"We'll talk about that down the road," Bernstein says.

"So what I should be concerned about now is cramping?"

"For that, bed rest and lots of liquids. Any bleeding can be due to cervical effacement and I would need to take a look. If it's on a weekend, put your feet up and wait until I can see you."

After their meeting, Juliet heads for a nearby coffeeshop, where she consumes a hamburger and a green salad. She dreads the day when Bernstein will say she can't have sex. The idea of forced celibacy seems untenable: Juliet has always been libidinous, and pregnancy has made her more so. During the bleeding episodes early in the first trimester, when she and Sam had to be chaste, she had an uncomfortable sensation of congestion in her genitals and frequent erotic dreams that resulted in strong and sometimes painful orgasms. She began to wonder if it was more dangerous for her not to have sex than to have it.

She has a recurrent thought that shames her: *I need it, and if it does something to the baby, I can't help that.*

**SATURDAY, JANUARY 6**
**Cape Cod**

 ARAH SPENT THE FIRST DAY OF THE NEW YEAR IN THE EMERGENCY room, complaining about her inability to breathe and the incessant coughing that prevents her from sleeping. The staff doctor examined her, diagnosed her condition as allergic sinusitis, and prescribed codeine to help her sleep. He advised her to consult an ear, nose, and throat specialist and sent her home. Sarah has never had an allergy before; she can only conclude that she must be allergic to pregnancy itself.

Michael tried and failed to get Sarah an immediate appointment with a well-known ENT specialist, so yesterday she saw the family internist. He confirmed the emergency room doctor's diagnosis. Sarah's bedroom, the internist said, should be thoroughly vacuumed and the head of her bed raised on an incline of four inches. That night Michael took the bed apart, vacuumed all its surfaces, and brought bricks from the basement to prop it up. Sarah was grateful for his efforts on her behalf, which allowed her to sleep without the aid of codeine. But the congestion and cough linger. She can't shake the fear that if she continues to be sick, her baby will be harmed.

They leave for Palm Beach a week from today. Michael is ambivalent about taking his family with him: his attention will be split between Ben, Sarah, and his mother, and all three are demanding. However, having his wife and son there will give Margery something to focus on besides her illness. She adores Ben, and Sarah's belly will remind her that her first granddaughter is on the way—something to live for. This will be their last visit until after the birth. Sarah will soon be too pregnant to travel, and Michael can't leave her alone on the Cape with Ben.

There's no concrete prognosis from Margery's doctors, and Michael hasn't pressed for one. If it's bad, he doesn't want to know.

**SUNDAY, JANUARY 7**
**Westchester**

 OB STARTS HIS NEW JOB NEXT WEEK. HE EXPECTS IT TO BE AN improvement, but it's not what he really wants—to be a lawyer or a journalist. Still, he tries to remind himself, *Take care of business first and pursue your dreams on the side instead of the other way around, which always gets you into trouble.*

Rob has had two incapacitating bouts of depression—a confluence, he believes, of chemical imbalance and disastrous career moves. The first occurred when he was twenty-five, living with Alex and working as a paper salesman, which his father said was beneath him. Rob came up with an idea for a business that seemed certain to succeed. He wanted to restore a famous 1930s movie studio that had been shut down for years, reopen it, and rent it out for film production. His father backed him; together they invested thousands of dollars. The venture failed, the money was lost, and Rob was fired from his full-time job, since it became clear to his employers that his attention was elsewhere. For two months afterward, while Alex went off to work as a lab technician, Rob sat in the chrome and red leather barber chair in the apartment they shared in Brooklyn, staring out the window, a coffee cup and a brimming ashtray beside him. Alex begged him to get psychiatric help, but he refused. Eventually a friend convinced him to work for her. That arrangement didn't last, but neither did the depression. Rob was soon hired to sell medical equipment.

Five years later, after Alex and Rob were married, he had another episode. This time, again at Alex's urging, he saw a therapist, who put him on medication for a brief period. Alex did her best to be supportive but was confounded by the concept of mental illness, which meant little to someone from a blue-collar Italian family with no interest in dwelling on the inner life or on roads not taken. She felt as if she were watching someone who's drowning three inches away from the side of a swimming pool. She couldn't understand why Rob didn't reach out and save himself. Alex was sympathetic then, but over the years she has grown angry; his depressions, in the end, amounted to such an enormous waste of time, his and hers, and she is weary of what she calls his worthless routine, which leads to unrealistic fantasies. He wants to be a lawyer, a journalist, anything but a salesman—*so what?* Alex could just as well say that she wants to be an actress, but that's not the life she chose, and she's not going to change direction now.

This morning at breakfast, watching Rob daydream (Alex knows that's what he's doing when he puts his bagel and newspaper down on the table and looks out the window into nothing), she thinks, *Okay, he's been good to me these past months while I've been sick. But I've paid my dues. I don't have to get down on my knees and thank God he's my husband fifty times a day, which is what he seems to expect.*

STRIKING VIEW OF THE MANHATTAN SKYLINE IS VISIBLE THROUGH the window of Sam's office on the twenty-first floor. He sits with his back to it at his desk, where everything is arranged in neat piles, including the bound galleys of his new book on capital punishment.

Sam's slightly stooped posture, slender but decidedly unathletic build, high forehead, and salt-and-pepper beard lend him a scholarly air. He wears jeans, as he does on most office-bound days, and doesn't bother cutting what's left of his hair unless he has to appear in court or on TV. Although he can be sulky when he is not the center of attention, he comes across as amiable and unassuming. His sixties-style social consciousness and deceptively laid-back attitude is yoked to a very up-to-the-minute yen for fame.

He is supposed to be preparing for a complicated conference call but is thinking about Juliet's body. Sam is a gardener—he loves to watch things grow—and nothing has seemed as powerful or compelling as watching his wife swell and change shape. When he sees her naked, he is reminded of the Cycladian fertility goddess sculptures at the Metropolitan Museum, primitive carvings that are almost all belly, with nearly invisible heads and feet. Juliet's belly symbolizes to Sam the visual representation of the reproduction of life; it is both stirring and erotic. Yet he's not as upset as she is about the likely cessation of their sex life after the twentieth week of pregnancy. She can't masturbate because orgasm irritates the cervix, but Sam has no intention of relinquishing that option—even though to do so, he thinks, would be a rather romantic gesture of solidarity.

Sam has become much more protective of Juliet since the day in Egypt when they were walking over difficult terrain and she slipped and fell, and he thought to himself, *I should tell her to be more careful. If I can't carry the baby myself, I should at least watch out for it.* On the trip he stared raptly into the windows of toy stores and children's clothing boutiques. Before Juliet became pregnant, the only merchandise that attracted him was food, but now he looks for ways to connect to his child-to-be, growing in Juliet's body but not in his.

They left Egypt to celebrate their third anniversary, on New Year's Eve, in Venice, one of their favorite cities. At a restaurant there, Juliet allowed herself a glass of champagne to accompany dinner in front of a blazing hearth, and they talked about what it will be like to travel with a baby. Juliet's mother had sent a fax to their hotel: *"Hoping 1990 will be wonderful for the three of you."* Reading it, Juliet and Sam had the same dismayed reaction. *Who wants it to be the three of you?* It sounded like a crowd, like your kid brother was going to tag along with you for the rest of your life.

Sam's age is beginning to worry him. He turns forty-four next month, which makes him older than the average man having his first child, and he's sorry that he won't have more time to know his off-spring. His father and his father's father both died at sixty-three of heart disease. Sam's father knew that his family history put him at risk but refused to have a physical exam, even when he began experiencing chest pains. Sam was twenty-four when his father died and still resents him for not trying to forestall his demise by seeking early medical attention.

Ever since Sam turned forty, Juliet has hounded him to have a full physical. Now that he will soon be a father himself, he is determined to do so.

### SUNDAY, JANUARY 14
#### Westchester

 N THE ROAD LAST WEEK, ALEX HAD A BREAKTHROUGH IN NAU-sea management. She ate an apple before going to sleep, another in the morning, and drank a glass of tomato juice or strongly diluted grape Kool-Aid every hour. She didn't throw up or get cramps once. When she weighed herself upon her return, she had put on two pounds, her first gain in sixteen weeks of pregnancy.

Alex told a few of the customers she knew well that she was expecting. One, a man with two kids, was jubilant, nattering on about how the best part of having children was developing a new appreciation for your spouse. Alex didn't buy it, though she kept her skepticism to herself. Another customer, a born-again Christian, asked if she planned to have amnio. When Alex said yes, the woman paused, then said, "Of course you wouldn't have an abortion, would you?" Alex replied, tactfully but evasively, that she wanted all the information she could get before making such a decision. "The Lord doesn't give you burdens you can't bear," said the woman. Alex nodded, thinking, *How do people come by these Pollyanna-ish attitudes?* She finds it puzzling that anyone would choose to continue a pregnancy knowing that they're carrying a genetically defective baby. If faced with having a Down Syndrome child or no child, ever, she would choose no child. A new series on TV this season, *Life Goes On,* is about a Down child, and Alex considers it socially irresponsible. The show's glossy perspective seems far from the medical and emotional realities.

Alex expects a healthy baby, but if the facts are otherwise, she will have an abortion—though she has no illusions about that, either. Before she and Rob were married, she got pregnant accidentally (she and Rob always played Russian roulette with birth control, which is why she's pregnant now) and aborted the baby. It was the only logical decision; neither of them was ready for parenthood. But Alex was surprised at how it traumatized her. After the procedure, she kept sobbing. It felt so odd—as if she were outside of herself, observing the tears of a stranger.

**WEDNESDAY,**
**JANUARY 17**
**Manhattan**

OE LEAVES WORK AN HOUR EARLY TODAY TO RIDE HOME WITH Maria. He doesn't like her traveling alone on the subway when she's pregnant, and he was alarmed when she called him earlier in the day and said she felt dizzy. It turns out she simply wasn't eating well: coffee for breakfast, a knish off the truck at eleven, and no time for lunch because she had to go to the bank. "To hell with the bank," Joe says to her on the way home. "If it's your lunch hour, you should be eating." He always brings her plates of fruit and glasses of juice, urging her to eat. "Get with it," he commands. "Stop acting like a fussy little kid."

Maria's pregnancy has made Joe acutely aware of his obligation to provide for his growing family. He wants to release her from having to work; he believes, and she agrees, that a child is best raised by its mother. Joe fears the care of strangers; there's too much in the news about abuse in day-care centers. He wants to settle down in a nice house in a clean, relatively crime-free environment. So he is seriously considering a transfer to Florida. It won't be easy to get one. The postal service is automating; jobs for mail handlers and clerks are being phased out. Still, he's planning to drive down to Florida in March with some friends, résumé in hand. He knows he makes a favorable personal impression, and he wants to meet post office managers face to face.

Impending fatherhood has made Joe even more upset than he might have been about a crisis in his family. His sister-in-law, who lives with his brother upstate, in Lake George, gave birth to twins three months ago. One was born with a respiratory disease. Next week this tiny baby will have open-heart surgery at a local hospital; there's only a 50 percent chance he'll make it. Joe wants the operation done in Manhattan, where medical care is better, he believes. But he can't convince his brother or sister-in-law, and is annoyed by their apparent nonchalance over a life-or-death situation. Though the baby was born sick, his mother took him out all day on errands in icy weather, which seems to Joe almost criminally irresponsible. He doesn't understand people like that. There's no such thing, Joe thinks, as being too concerned about your children.

HE TEMPERATURE HOVERS BELOW FREEZING, BUT ALEX WEARS only a jeans jacket over a sweater and black leggings and has moccasins on her feet. She sits in the waiting room of a prominent medical center, filling out forms in preparation for amniocentesis. She is relieved that Rob's work prevented him from being here. His persistent anxiety over medical procedures would only vex her.

She completes the forms and is ushered into a small office, where a genetic counselor studies her family history questionnaire. "I see here," the counselor says, "that your husband is Jewish and you are not. Tay-Sachs is essentially a Jewish genetic disease because Jews tend to marry each other, but we have also found non-Jewish carriers. To be on the safe side, I recommend the test. You're Italian, so your risk for Tay-Sachs is between one in a hundred to one in three hundred. If it turns out to be positive, we'll test your husband, because in order to pass on the disease you'd both have to be carriers."

Alex is quick to pose a question that signals her grasp of the subject at hand. "So it's recessive?"

"Yes," the counselor replies with a nod of approval. When the interview concludes, the counselor has another pregnant woman and her husband join Alex for a slide show. Alex thinks the presentation soft-soaps the risks of amnio, which she has assiduously researched. Afterward, she goes into the "procedure room." She declines the doctor's offer of Novocain, knowing that it causes a burning sensation likely to be more uncomfortable than the needle itself. The doctor, a stranger to Alex, draws amniotic fluid from her belly; there is a slight sensation of pressure. Alex returns to the waiting room and is observed for a half-hour before she is allowed to leave.

She'd like labor to be as easy and painless as this was, but she knows better.

T OM DIDN'T ALWAYS PLAN TO OWN A GAS STATION. HE TOOK accounting courses in high school, thinking he might work as a CPA in some large firm. But after graduating, he began to assume more responsibility at the station and found he liked being his own boss. The idea of going to work for someone else stopped making sense. When his father told him he wanted to sell the business, Tom said, "I'm your buyer."

He knows now he would have been miserable as a CPA: he lacks the temperament for a desk job. Tom's idea of relaxation is constructing a new porch or cutting grass. He has never taken even a half-hour for lunch; he'll consume a bag of potato chips and gulp a Coke standing up. (He is careful to pay for the chips and soda, which he gets from the small concession stand on the premises. He owns the place, but he doesn't want his employees to think he places himself above them.) *The nature of this business,* Tom has often thought, *is to keep runnin'*— which suits his own revved-up metabolism.

But now there is nowhere to run. The station was shut down three days ago, as ordered by the EPA, pending the replacement of the underground tanks. Tom has nothing to do but stare at the gaping hole in the ground, feeling bored and scared and helpless. He assumed that after a week he'd be back in business, but the gas leak contaminated the soil, requiring special hazardous-waste trucks to haul the dirt away. It will be a month or more before he can reopen. He has rented a small space a few miles away to do repair work, which should generate enough income to keep his mechanics on salary. But he can't pay his other employees and will probably lose them.

Tom has always been an optimist, but now he seems to have lost all hope. If he is forced into bankruptcy . . . the prospect is bewildering. The gas-station business is all he knows. It's been his consuming passion for half of his life, the source of his identity. He takes pride in that sign over the door of the office, where his name and his father's

are engraved: *Tom and Chip Wright, Proprietors.* He is completely invested in earning and maintaining his customers' respect, dedicated to
perfecting his operation down to the marigolds that bloom in pots
between the gas pumps. Last year the station was praised in a local
consumer magazine. To Tom, that meant everything.

He doesn't want to burden Erin with his troubles; she has enough of
her own. When he straggles home after a depressing day, he finds her
bent over her homework. The new semester started and she's taking
six credits, going from her eight o'clock class straight to the office,
putting in a full day, driving home, studying. He should have dis-
suaded her from signing up for this overload, but for weeks he's been
unable to talk, for fear of what he might say—*I'm going under, I'm not
going to make it*—things she doesn't need to hear.

Erin got her period again. They must have made love at the beginning of the month, while she was ovulating—otherwise she wouldn't
have hoped to be pregnant—but he has no memory of it. Sex, like
everything else, seems to be on permanent hold.

## THURSDAY, JANUARY 18
### Manhattan

J ULIET LIES ON AN EXAMINING TABLE IN A ROOM OF THE MEDICAL
center where she will give birth. Sam stands by her head, his
hand resting on her bare arm, looking at the fetus on a monitor screen. A sonographer, beginning the work that will conclude with an amnio, takes a femur measurement. It confirms Juliet's
calculation that she is between the eighteenth and nineteenth week of
pregnancy.

Dr. Bernstein studies the sonographic picture to identify a pocket of
clear amniotic fluid. "Here's the cord," he says to Sam and Juliet, his
finger outlining it on the screen. "The placenta is on the back wall of
the uterus, which makes it easier to get the fluid out."

Sam is nervous. "Is there any danger," he asks, "if the baby moves
while you're trying to get the fluid?"

"Not really. It's like trying to poke someone at the bottom of a swimming pool. If you don't have enough fluid it's harder, but that's not the case here."

Juliet's placenta is low and almost covers the cervix. At this stage in pregnancy, the doctor explains, 50 to 60 percent of women appear to have a low-lying placenta. The incidence of this near term, which would mean a diagnosis of placenta previa, a dangerous condition, is only one in 250.

Bernstein unwraps a large needle from its plastic covering. "Take it easy, okay?" he says to Juliet. "This may feel a little cold." Sam takes Juliet's hand. She is unflustered, but he battles the urge to shut his eyes. Needles, even small ones, make him queasy. He forces himself to watch the needle going into his wife's belly. It will be good practice, he thinks, for the sights of childbirth.

Juliet grimaces as Bernstein withdraws the amniotic fluid. "I can definitely feel the pressure," she says. The procedure is over quickly. She wants to be sure the fetus hasn't been adversely affected by the needle, so she asks Bernstein to turn on the monitor. This time, Sam thinks he notices a penis between what appear to be the fetal legs, but he says nothing. Juliet doesn't want to know the sex, and if Sam finds out he'll be unable to withhold the news from her.

"The heart is beating; the baby's fine," Bernstein says. He helps Juliet into a sitting position. "You take it easy today, kiddo. Put your feet up, drink fluids. If you have any bleeding, cramping, fever, just call. I don't anticipate any problems, by the way."

When Juliet leaves the examining room to dress, Sam asks Bernstein again about the low placenta. "Don't worry," the doctor says. "The overwhelming likelihood is that it won't be a problem."

"And if it is?" Sam asks.

"We'll put her on complete bed rest. We'll look at it again at twenty-eight weeks or so."

"And in an extreme case?"

"We'll do a section. That's the worst thing. And thirty percent of people deliver that way anyway."

Juliet emerges from the dressing room. Sam takes her arm and leads her to the elevator.

"It really hurt," Juliet says.

"Like a sticking pain or a cramping pain?"

"A sticking pain—like something going right into you."

"If it were me, I would have thrown up."

"Were you actually watching it?"

Sam pauses. "Yeah," he says proudly.

**THURSDAY, JANUARY 18**
**Palm Beach**

S ARAH CAN'T BELIEVE HER CONTINUING BAD LUCK, WHICH SEEMS to encompass everyone around her. Last Saturday, ten minutes before leaving the Cape for Palm Beach, she learned from her obstetrician that her blood test for gestational diabetes, routinely given to women in late pregnancy, was positive. Next week she will have to undergo a more protracted test to confirm the diagnosis.

Today the Palm Beach doctors tell Michael that his mother has a maximum of eight weeks to live: they have found lesions on her brain. Margery has declined further treatment, so the hospital plans to release her on Tuesday. The Coens will return to the Cape in two days, as scheduled. In a few weeks, Michael will fly back to Palm Beach alone.

After Michael speaks to the doctors, he is tearful. Sarah holds him in her arms, rocking him as if he were a child. After a while he suggests that she take Ben to the beach. "I need to be alone," he says. Sarah understands this need; she recalls the death three years ago of her beloved grandmother, and how devastated she felt. She kisses him softly and leaves.

Methodically, willing himself not to feel, Michael uses the phone by his mother's hospital bed to arrange for round-the-clock nursing care so Margery can die at home, as his father did fourteen years ago. Between calls he gazes at his mother, dozing under the influence of morphine. He reflects on the period surrounding his father's death.

Michael dropped out of college at Antioch after two years because he was more interested in doing drugs than earning a diploma. He moved to Miami to work as a cook in his brother's restaurant, and later managed a second establishment his brother opened. By then Michael's cocaine habit was out of control. The restaurant failed and Michael blamed himself—he was too young, and too wired, to do the job. At that point his father's cancer was diagnosed as terminal. Michael moved back into the family home in Palm Beach until his father died six months later. Now it's happening with his mother, but Michael can no longer rely on the emotional oblivion that drugs provided him, and he has his own family to tend to. He can't leave his pregnant wife and his son on the Cape and move in with his mother.

This, Michael realizes, is what people mean by "the sandwich generation." *You've got your parents dying on one end and your kids being born on the other.*

### SATURDAY THROUGH WEDNESDAY, JANUARY 20–24
### Palm Beach/Cape Cod/ Palm Beach

N THEIR WAY TO THE PALM BEACH AIRPORT, SARAH AND BEN and Michael stop at the hospital. Margery is floating on morphine, but she knows who they are. They laugh and talk and hug; to Sarah it seems magical, as if Margery is no longer sick. After a while Sarah takes Ben out of the room to give Michael a few minutes alone with his mother. He takes Margery's hand and says he's nervous about leaving her. "It's time for all of us to be brave," Margery tells him, which is exactly what Michael needs to hear.

The Coens fly north into a snowstorm; it is evening before they reach their house. As they enter, drained and exhausted, they hear the phone machine recording a message from Michael's brother: Margery will not live through the night. Michael picks up the phone in mid-message and listens as his brother instructs him to get to Boston in time for an 8:30 A.M. flight to Palm Beach. He is too stunned to say anything more than "okay," and hangs up.

Sarah looks at his bleary eyes and strained posture. Concerned, she issues counterinstructions. She reminds Michael that there is a blizzard outside; he will have to leave the house well before dawn to make that plane, and she won't allow it. "You've got to have one night's sleep or you'll fall apart," she tells him. Then she says, with firm conviction, "Your mother will not die until you get there." She calls Michael's brother and informs him that Michael will take a later flight. She and Michael briefly discuss the wisdom of her accompanying him and who will take care of Ben if she does. Sarah wants to go—she knows Michael will need her support—but she is worried, being seven months pregnant, about the physical and emotional strain of returning to Palm Beach under these circumstances. Michael doesn't know what he thinks; he is too overwhelmed. He calls Sarah's obstetrician, who makes the decision for them by advising against Sarah's traveling.

Michael sleeps through the night. He calls his mother as soon as he wakes, expecting to learn that she is dead. But Margery answers the phone. Michael says he's on his way. "Good," she says.

He arrives in Palm Beach on Sunday night and relieves his brother at Margery's bedside at 7:30 on Monday morning. Sarah was right: his mother has waited for him. Three hours later, she is gone.

Snowbound and heartsick on Cape Cod, deeply frustrated at having to be separated from her husband during a time of profound mutual need, Sarah feels completely alone. She's stuck here with a *monster,* Ben, who has told her repeatedly that he hates her, and there is a baby inside of her who might be defective. Her second test for gestational diabetes, taken on Monday, confirmed the positive results of the first. Her obstetrician puts her on a 1,200-calorie diet as a precaution; the condition can result in overly large babies, posing complications during a vaginal delivery. He says he'll arrange for an extensive ultrasound examination in Boston to evaluate the size of the fetus, and assures her there is no reason for alarm. Only 5 to 6 percent of women with gestational diabetes, he says, give birth to defective fetuses. *Great,* Sarah thinks. *I'm bound to be one of those women.*

She tries to call Michael on Wednesday morning, but the line in Palm Beach is busy for hours. She becomes angry; the anger distances her from her grief over Margery's death and her sympathy for Michael. She feels she has been abandoned. The Coen family, together in Palm Beach, has shut her out. When she finally reaches Michael, an hour before the funeral, she is furious. "Why haven't you called me?" she demands. "Why did I get a busy signal all morning?" Michael says listlessly that he no longer knows whether it is day or night, which further enrages her. She tells him the diabetes news, knowing that she ought not to burden him with it until after the funeral, knowing that she's being a complete bitch.

Sarah's brother and father live nearby, but she dislikes her brother and won't confide in her father, the eternal adolescent. Her best friend, Lauren, recently moved to Boston; Sarah's relationship with her mother is hopeless; Margery is dead; and in some awful way, Michael feels dead to her too.

*I have no one,* she thinks.

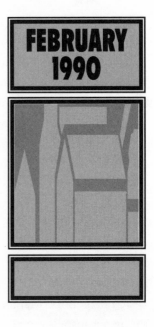

**FRIDAY, FEBRUARY 2**
**Cape Cod**

ICHAEL FLEW HOME FROM PALM BEACH EXACTLY A WEEK AGO, mourning his mother, fearing for his unborn child. He was greeted by a livid wife and an anxious, clinging son. It felt like going from one hell to another.

Before leaving Palm Beach he had asked Sarah to arrange for a babysitter so they could go to Friday night services at temple upon his return, but she was unable to. He went alone, thinking it would comfort him, and he was right. Ben's pediatrician, Esther Levin, was there; after the service, Michael asked her about gestational diabetes. Esther has been practicing pediatrics for twenty years and said she has yet to see a baby adversely affected by it. Michael drove home feeling restored. But in the kitchen he saw the sarcastic note Sarah left for him: "Good night, I'm in bed. I thought your first night home you'd want to spend with me."

Since then, Michael has grieved for his mother silently. He falls asleep with the TV headphones on, alone in the guest room, and wakes in the middle of the night disoriented, thinking he's in Palm Beach. He lies awake for hours with all the questions he never asked his mother running through his head. He wishes he knew more about his father, who lived off the family fortune that Michael's grandfather, a Russian immigrant, built from nothing.

Michael's parents never fought, perhaps because they led separate lives, even sleeping in separate bedrooms. When Margery wasn't doing volunteer work for Hadassah and the local library, she was in the living room, reading novels at the rate of five a week. His father spent most of his time in the den, watching TV—Jack Paar, Art Linkletter, Phil Silvers, *The Price Is Right.* They were together only at dinner, served by the live-in maid.

With just one domestic employee and a comfortable but not lavish two-story home, the Coens lived more modestly than their Palm Beach neighbors. Margery ran the household. She paid the bills out of the generous allowance provided by the family trust, set the rules of behavior for her sons (Michael's brother, nine years his senior, was already away at prep school by the time Michael was a toddler), and dispensed permission and punishment as needed. Michael's friends received BMWs or boats as birthday and graduation gifts, but Margery insisted that he pay for such luxuries himself. He earned the money to buy a motorcycle by working summers on the maintenance and construction crews for the family hotel and real-estate businesses.

Michael's father, uncomfortable in the role of authority figure, treated his son like a peer. Together they went to the beach, rode bikes around the lake, and indulged in the rituals Michael's father had designed to give shape to his otherwise idle days. Their favorite was the 10 A.M. hunt for the mailman. Father and son would get in the car with an unopened bottle of cold ginger ale and a cigar; when they spotted the postal truck, Michael would hand over the soda and the stogie in exchange for the mail. At times Michael was embarrassed that his father didn't get dressed in a jacket and tie and go to an office like his classmates' fathers did, but there was ample compensation: Michael was his dad's best friend.

The good times ended when Michael was entering adolescence. His father was diagnosed with diabetes, which triggered a depression so severe that he was hospitalized and given shock treatments. Florida allows you to get a learner's permit at fourteen, so Michael ferried his mother, who hated highway driving, back and forth to the hospital, five hours each way. They would visit Michael's father in a place where mirrors were made of plastic and patients weren't allowed to wear belts. After a year or so, Michael's father returned home, but he was never again Michael's jovial older buddy. Instead he stood in Michael's bedroom doorway every morning, sighing and sobbing. Life at home became unbearable.

Margery approved of Michael's decision to go away to prep school in Massachusetts, where he soon added marijuana and LSD to his diet-pill habit. But no matter how far he traveled or how many drugs he took, he could never obliterate the vision of his father weeping in the doorway, broken beyond repair. He fears that he will one day inherit his father's sickness and inflict it on his own children. Already Michael is conscious of uncomfortable parallels. He shares his father's dependence on a routinized existence; his fantasy of quitting his job and staying home resembles the rudderless life his father chose . . .

Michael doesn't share these thoughts with Sarah, assuming she won't want to hear them. *Somehow,* he thinks, *going back for the funeral without her put distance between us in more ways than one.*

## SATURDAY, FEBRUARY 3
### Westchester

ESTERDAY, AT THE ATLANTA AIRPORT ON HER WAY HOME FROM a grueling business trip, Alex spent the forty-five minutes before her flight regurgitating breakfast and lunch in the ladies' room. When she came out of the stall, she spotted a woman changing her infant daughter in the lounge area. Alex went up to her and said, "Please don't take this the wrong way, but could I hold your baby, just for a minute? I'm pregnant and I've just gotten sick again and I'd like to know there's some reward for this." The woman laughed. She told Alex that she had been sick all the way to term, and assured her that the end result was worth every bad moment. "You don't believe me, do you?" she added, observing Alex's dubious expression.

Early this morning, a woman calls with the amnio results. Rob happens to answer the phone. The woman says the fetus is negative for Down syndrome and spina bifida.

"What else could you have tested for?" Rob asks, mostly out of curiosity.

"Lots of things," the woman replies, "but unless there's a family history of a certain genetic disorder, we don't go further." Rob thinks, *You idiots don't know how to build a practice—if you can bill for it, why don't you do it?*

He tells Alex he missed the Babies while she was gone; he doesn't think it's fair that she gets to be with them all the time. Alex says she feels movement, but Rob glides his hand like a stethoscope over her belly, covering every inch, and feels nothing. He is frustrated.

When Alex is clothed, her pregnancy is imperceptible. But when she is naked, Rob can see her belly protrude. Her nipples look lush, much darker than before, which pleases him. He finds her more beautiful than ever.

### SATURDAY, FEBRUARY 3
#### Manhattan

ODAY SAM ADDRESSES AN APPRECIATIVE, OVERFLOW AUDIENCE OF prominent business people and actors (he recognizes Susan Sarandon, Ron Silver, and Sean Young). He thinks his speech is superb, and afterward the admiring comments confirm his evaluation. On the subway home, he waits for Juliet to praise him, but all she does is complain about someone in his firm who made a disparaging comment to her during the reception.

Sam is wounded by her lack of attention, so when they get off the train at Fourteenth Street he stalks ahead of her instead of holding her arm and watching out for potholes. Then he hears her cry out. He whirls and sees her lying in the gutter outside St. Vincent's Hospital.

Racing to her, full of guilt and fear, he blurts his first panicky thought: "Did you miscarry?"

"No, you dope," Juliet says sharply. "I sprained my ankle."

He moves her to the curb and cradles her head in his hands. "Do you want to go to the emergency room?" he asks.

"No," she says. "Get a cab and take me home."

Sam lifts her into the taxi and helps her hobble up the four flights of stairs to the loft. He spends the rest of the day contritely carrying her from the bedroom to the bathroom and back, fetching whatever she asks for, cursing his own narcissism for jeopardizing her safety.

With a belly swollen by pregnancy and an ankle swollen from the sprain, Juliet feels like a hog. She's sure Bernstein will soon order her to go on complete bed rest and is angry with herself for being so clumsy, ruining what would have been her last few weeks of freedom.

**TUESDAY, FEBRUARY 6**
**Cape Cod**

ARAH WALKS INTO HER DOCTOR'S OFFICE AND THROWS THE 1,200-calorie diabetic diet menu on his desk. "This is for pygmies," she exclaims.

The doctor peers at her from behind his glasses and says, "What do you mean?"

"This isn't enough food for a midget, let alone a pregnant person. Your office seems to be having trouble dealing with this."

"Didn't you give her the blue menu?" the nurse asks the doctor.

"No," the doctor replies, "the black one."

The nurse puts her hands on her hips and says, with an indignation that matches Sarah's own, "I've told you a hundred times, the blue one is for pregnant women."

Sarah is further emboldened in the presence of this unexpected ally. "I went to Boston for that sonogram last week, in case you don't remember ordering it"—Sarah hopes at least to raise the guy's eyebrow with her taunt, but his face is impassive—"and the staff nutritionist there told me that at twelve hundred calories a day I may have harmed the fetus or myself. I want to know what's going on. If you can't handle my pregnancy, send me to someone who can."

"I can handle it," the doctor says with an edge to his voice. He pulls out the report of Sarah's ultrasound exam in such a hurry that Sarah is sure he's trying to reestablish his authority.

"Everything looks normal," he begins. "There's fluid where it should be, there doesn't appear to be any problem with the heart, and the fetal size is just slightly larger than normal. It looks like you'll have between an eight-and-a-half- and nine-pound baby, and I won't let you go over your due date."

"Look," Sarah says combatively, "I've already told you, I won't be induced because I have a violent reaction to Pitocin," a drug that makes the uterus contract, which Sarah was once given. "I want that written on my chart."

By the end of their meeting, Sarah's doctor looks sheepish.

More women should try yelling at their obstetricians, Sarah thinks later with satisfaction. *If you can scare them, you can control them.*

**WEDNESDAY,
FEBRUARY 7
Manhattan**

AM, STILL PENITENT, TAKES THE AFTERNOON OFF TO MAKE THE medical rounds with Juliet. At 12:30 they see an orthopedic surgeon, who gives Juliet a removable plastic cast she'll have to wear on her ankle day and night for six weeks. At 3:00 they settle in Bernstein's waiting room, still excited about the amnio results they received on Monday; the baby is normal. At 4:30 the nurse calls them into an examining room. Sam, having recently read a piece in the *New York Times* about men who can't figure out where to stand during their wives' prenatal exams, positions himself by Juliet's head so he and Bernstein won't both be staring into her crotch.

Afterward, Sam and Juliet sit down in Bernstein's office. The doctor pulls out the genetics report. Juliet thinks, *I'd better warn him that we don't want to know the sex,* but she doesn't say it. Bernstein leans across the table and tells them offhandedly that the baby has an "insignificant chromosomal abnormality." This unnerves them; the geneticist who called on Monday didn't mention any abnormality. They ask Bernstein to explain. He seems flustered. "There's nothing to worry about," he says, but they're not satisfied and continue to ask questions.

Finally the doctor leans forward and says emphatically, pointing at the report, "Look, it says right here, *it's a normal baby girl.*" He pauses when he sees Juliet's stunned face. Then it dawns on him. "Oh, I wasn't supposed to tell you that," he says, apologizing. "It's okay," Juliet says, hiding her fury.

Then Bernstein tells her that for the next few weeks she should restrict her activity *(a pathetic joke,* she thinks, *considering I'm already crippled).* In a month, he adds, she should plan on staying in bed. Juliet doesn't ask about having sex, because she doesn't want to hear him say not to. Sam, who watched a TV program Friday night about babies born so prematurely they suffered severe defects, asks when the baby will be safe. If it's born at twenty-eight weeks, Bernstein explains, there's a chance of survival; at thirty-three weeks the odds are good.

Juliet has never seen a doctor as often as Bernstein and finds it annoying that he doesn't seem to remember who she is from one visit to the next. Though she likes his lack of pomposity, she's angry at him for his oh-so-casual comment about a chromosomal abnormality so minor that the geneticist didn't even mention it, and for his blithe acknowledgment of the baby's gender. Sam defends him, saying that the doctor allowed them to go to Egypt when everyone else warned them not to, and reminds Juliet of the bad things that *didn't* happen— the baby doesn't have Down, Juliet could have broken her leg instead of spraining her ankle. She knows Sam's right, but still . . .

As Sam listens to Juliet's complaints—her body blowing up on her, the discomfort that interrupts her sleep, the constant trips to doctors' offices only to sit for hours in crowded waiting rooms—he concludes that carrying a child is a lot to ask of someone under the best of circumstances. But the unexpected news that he is having a daughter has buoyed him; it makes the pregnancy less of an abstraction.

Last year, a woman on his staff went into premature labor at six months and insisted on naming the baby, even though it died three days after birth. At the time Sam couldn't understand why anyone would give a name to a fetus, but now he believes he would do the same thing. He has put his stomach up against Juliet's; he has felt the baby kick his own flesh. From the rhythm of her movements, he *knows* her. She is already a person. She deserves a name.

**SATURDAY,<br>FEBRUARY 10<br>Westchester**

LEX'S GROIN HURTS SO MUCH THAT SHE CAN'T ROLL OVER ON her side or her back. She says it's just ligaments stretching to accommodate her growing uterus, but it frightens Rob to see her in this much pain for this long—she has been talking about it for three weeks. He feels increasingly powerless.

In her zeal to get Rob to lose weight, Alex has ruined one of their favorite weekend activities, taking long drives while sharing a pound of pistachio nuts. Today she rations them out one at a time. *This,* Rob thinks, *is definitely not what God had in mind when he invented pistachios.* Alex tries to distract him by reviewing her recent research on strollers. Double wheels front and back and an adjustable height, she determined, are essential qualities, but she wants to shop around for the best prices. This leads to an ancient argument between them: Rob thinks she's excessively frugal, always willing to spend precious time rather than a few extra pennies, and she thinks he's so lazy he squanders money.

This morning, washing Alex's belly in the shower, Rob feels the Babies move for the first time. The sensation is that of a swimmer coming to the edge of the pool and kicking off in the other direction. He can't wait to meet this swimmer; he imagines it will be like meeting the most famous person in the world. He has a suddenly overwhelming sense of protectiveness toward Alex and her belly (he thinks of them as separate entities that just happen to be physically attached). When Alex is away on business, driving rented cars on strange roads and making three plane connections in a day, he worries about accidents and crashes. When she is a passenger in his car, he controls his tendency to speed by reminding himself that two people's lives are in his hands.

Today he listens to Alex's tales of her last trip, how she convinced the male executives of several Fortune 500 companies to give her their business. He asks after the Prince of Monaco—their private little joke. Rob once told Alex that she has so much control over him and is so devious that for all he knows she could be flying off to tryst with the prince instead of meeting with her clients. He does not consider this scenario to be outrageously far-fetched. Alex always describes to him the men who try to flirt with her when she's on the road. Her tone is teasing, but her message, however subliminal, is threatening: *I am financially independent and sexually desirable, and I don't need you.* The message has never been lost on Rob.

He finds her tales of flirtation interruptus flattering; that other men consider her attractive validates him. Still, he never really stops expecting her to leave him for someone else—someone with more money, more power, more height, more hair.

**SATURDAY,
FEBRUARY 10
Washington–New York
Metroliner**

S AM FORCES HIMSELF OUT OF BED AT 5:30 A.M. TO TRAVEL TO Washington for a board meeting of one of the political organizations he represents. After the meeting, he shares a cab to Union Station with his firm's controller, Brian Moss, who is returning to New York on the same train. Sam had thought of Moss as a cool, removed money man, but now finds himself in an animated dialogue about fatherhood with him. Moss has a four-month-old daughter; he tells Sam that when he goes home from work and his baby smiles at him, all the catastrophes of the day dissolve. Sam has heard this kind of stuff from men for years and has discounted it as hyperbole, until now.

Moss, Sam learns, is married to a struggling New York actress and has the same concern as Sam: will his wife allow herself to become consumed by motherhood in lieu of a satisfying career, and if so, what marital problems will it create?

When Sam came of age in the 1960s, women were starting to voice resentment about being burdened with the major responsibility for child-rearing. He sided with them, thinking, *Women have a right to their own lives and shouldn't have to stay home if that's not what they want.* But the reality of his life now is that Juliet doesn't have a steady job and he does, and someone's got to go out every day and earn a living. He'll do his share of the chores, but the possibility that he and Juliet may end up in a traditional arrangement—Dad works, Mom stays home with the kid—seems almost painfully ironic. He has no problem with her being a full-time mother if she can feel *whole* that way, but he wonders if she can.

During their second and rockiest year together, when Sam still thought of Juliet as a little volcano, she anguished over whether she was ready, at nineteen, to be tied down to one man exclusively. Meanwhile, Sam grappled with the fact that she wasn't what he thought he was looking for—a woman who had figured out what to do with her life. He soon decided that it didn't matter; on every other level, she was the woman he wanted. She still is. But her competitive nature combined with a paradoxical lack of self-confidence has kept her in a frustrating state of professional lockstep. There's no telling what will happen once she has a child, he thinks.

**TUESDAY, FEBRUARY 13**
**Queens**

OMORROW IS VALENTINE'S DAY AND CHERYL'S BIRTHDAY. JOE should be celebrating love and life but instead is haunted by thoughts of death. Two weeks ago, his tiny nephew died in surgery.

Joe and Maria went to Lake George for the funeral. Joe couldn't bear for his pregnant wife to see a dead infant lying in an open casket, so she took care of his brother's two older sons and the surviving twin at home while Joe attended the service. He left the viewing room when his brother and sister-in-law said they were going to hold the baby one last time. They asked Joe to do the same, but he found the idea horrifying. He played with the baby's hand as it lay in the coffin; that was as much as he could stand.

Joe and Maria shopped for baby furniture on Sunday. Joe felt a rush of excitement when he spotted a carriage for twins—*the ultimate great thing, to get two babies at once*—until he remembered his nephew. He choked up and had to walk away. The thought is always there: *It could happen to me, just as it happened to my brother.*

When he's not being morbid, he's agitated. Today he calls Maria at the office, where she has a million things demanding her attention, and starts going on about the blinds he wants to order for the living room. He's enumerating prices and describing fabrics and colors, instructing her to write the information down that instant, not listening when Maria says she's busy. "Do whatever you want," she finally tells him, and hangs up. Maria guesses that he's all riled up over unimportant things as a way of dealing with sorrow, but she wishes he would be more direct about it.

She's under so much pressure at work that every day feels like a nightmare. The woman who took over for her while she was on vacation last month made so many mistakes that Maria has to spend precious time cleaning up the mess. She has been unable to accomplish other tasks during the day and has been lugging work home with her, but each night she is too tired to face it.

Maria can't wait until May, when her maternity leave begins. Her boss thinks she won't come back after the baby is born. She keeps telling him she will. She has no choice.

J ULIET CALLS THE GENETICIST TO ASK ABOUT THE CHROMOSOMAL abnormality mentioned by Bernstein. The geneticist uses the term "benign variant"; it is not associated with any problem, she explains, only with inconsequential physical details inherited from the mother or father, like pointed ears instead of round ones. So Juliet has been thinking of the physical oddities the baby might inherit. For instance, the men in Sam's family have a heavy bone projection over the eyes that she and Sam call *the Neanderthal,* which would be unattractive on a woman.

Recently, they had dinner with her father and his new wife, a woman several years younger than Juliet. When Juliet announced her pregnancy, her father said, "Oh, well, we've waited a long time for that," and changed the subject. His reaction was in character, which is to say, he had no reaction. He didn't even ask when the baby is due. As always, his lack of interest angered Juliet. Strangers stop her in the street and ask when she's due, but her own father couldn't care less. The rare times that Sam exhibits her father's worst qualities, acting detached or self-centered, as if she doesn't exist, are the times that most infuriate her.

Juliet is sure Sam will be an excellent father; her doubts about parenting are confined to herself. She's impatient with human frailties and intolerant of stupidity, and fears inflicting these traits on a child. Sam is more flexible and conciliatory—sometimes for strategic reasons. (It amuses Juliet that people often think she's the bitchy one, whereas in private it's the reverse. Sam considers it a sport to take people apart; Juliet doesn't.) He is also less sensitive than she is. If someone slights him, he shrugs it off, figuring that the person was in a bad mood that day. But Juliet carries grudges and is easily wounded. She hopes she won't be destroyed when her child gets to the inevitable "I hate you, Mommy" stage.

When Sam repeats what Brian Moss said on the train—"You fall in love with your daughter, and it's this perfect love because there are none of the conflicts you have with your wife"—Juliet is upset. "Why are you telling me this?" she says. The unwanted revelation of the baby's sex has aroused preemptive jealousy in her. *Maybe he'll fall so in love with this little girl,* she thinks, *that I'll feel abandoned.*

She can't imagine losing the baby now. She'd heard the heartbeat, she'd stared at the Polaroid taken during the amnio, but until she felt movement, her child was still not quite real. Now there is a palpable physical closeness that is astonishingly intense. When Juliet and Sam have intercourse, she is aware of all three of them together, inside the same place at the same time. It adds a novel edge of poignancy to lovemaking.

This week, now that her ankle is stronger, Juliet will shop for maternity clothes. If she winds up in bed for three months, she doesn't want to entertain visitors in the same old nightgown. She imagines herself like some queen bee, lying on her back getting bigger and bigger, with people fanning her brow and carrying in her meals on trays, her entire function in life suddenly reduced to reproduction. The image is comical, and disturbing.

**THURSDAY,
FEBRUARY 15
Cape Cod**

 T THE RECOMMENDATION OF HER OBSTETRICIAN, SARAH SEES A diabetes specialist who puts her through a third glucose-tolerance test and concludes that she does not have gestational diabetes. If this were happening to another person, Sarah would find it hilarious.

After her appointment with the specialist, she goes to the obstetrician's. "I'll never believe anything any doctor tells me again," she says, adding that the specialist not only doubts that she has diabetes but says that her blood-sugar levels aren't high enough even to suggest it. "It might be a good idea," Sarah says sharply to the obstetrician, "for you guys and this specialist to get together and make sure you're using the same scale, considering you're in the habit of referring patients to each other." She enjoys the look of embarrassment on the doctor's face.

She and Michael haven't slept in the same bed for two months, but last night they made love. Sarah couldn't refuse him. For Valentine's Day he sent her a dozen red roses, secretly arranged for a sitter, surprised her with dinner at her favorite restaurant, and gave her a card with a handwritten message: "Roses are red, violets are blue, sugar is sweet, and your husband is horny."

Ben has been impossible, whining and throwing tantrums and telling Sarah he's going to kill the baby. A friend of hers with a master's in child psychology thinks his behavior is a result of stress in the household over Margery's death; she gave Sarah the name of a family therapist. Sarah wants to meet with the therapist as soon as possible. Before the new baby arrives and she gets postpartum depression, as she did after her first pregnancy, she wants to be told that Ben's behavior is normal, given the circumstances.

Sarah expects her depression to be worse this time because her best friend, Lauren, won't be around to help her through it. The timing of Lauren's move to Boston a few months ago couldn't have been worse. Michael told Sarah that they could move too, maybe to Washington, D.C., where Sarah has always wanted to live, and in the summer they could rent a house on the Cape and Sarah could stay there with the kids, and . . . *The kids,* she thinks. *Plural.* It sounds so strange.

**SATURDAY, FEBRUARY 17**
**Queens**

OE, IN HIS KNICKS JACKET AND SWEATPANTS, AND MARIA, IN white leggings, white boots, and faux-fur–lined white parka, pick their way through rows of baby furniture at a store in Flushing. As Maria compares prices with identical items she has seen elsewhere, Joe's mind wanders. Last night he dreamed about his nephew's death. In the dream he went to the hospital for a checkup, and a nurse called him into a room where two babies slept side by side in a double crib. Also in the room was what looked like a plastic beer barrel but was really a small casket. In it was a black baby doll.

Maria looks up from her price list and takes in Joe's morose expression. "Babe," she says quickly, "look at this lamp—we saw it in the city for $125 and here it's $69.99." Her strategy works. Joe turns his attention to the business at hand, figuring out how to get the most for the $1,000 they've budgeted for furniture. They don't believe in buying junk that won't last, especially since they plan on having more children, so they'll invest in the best they can afford and put it on layaway.

They stop to admire a crib with a white eyelet canopy, brass trim, and painted pearls on round knobs on top of the posts. Nearby is a matching carriage, changing table, and child-size coat rack. The elaborate ensemble, which reminds Maria of something *Dynasty*'s Alexis Carrington might own, is far out of their price range. In the end, they buy from a place on Long Island that Joe's coworkers insist has the best deals. The white crib they choose has brass trim and rounded posts like the Alexis Carrington model. With the matching changing table/dresser, the bill comes to $825. The Reyeses put down a deposit of 20 percent and leave the merchandise on layaway.

Before finalizing the purchase, Joe suggests that they buy a different model, also white, that converts to a junior bed. Maria says no. "A white crib is okay for either sex, but I don't think a boy who's five or six will look good in a white bed," she explains. "And I *know* we're having a boy."

**FEBRUARY 20**
**Southern Maryland**

 ODAY IS ERIN'S TWENTY-EIGHTH BIRTHDAY, BUT WHEN HER alarm goes off at six her first thought is *Pregnancy test*. Her period is five days late.

Tom is still asleep in the four-poster bed, so Erin pads quietly over the rose-colored carpet into the adjoining bathroom. She rips the cellophane off a pregnancy test kit and follows the instructions:

urinate into the little cup, mix the urine with a chemical, squeeze the mixture into the designated container. It takes one minute for the test to register pink (positive) or white (negative). Erin props the container on top of the toilet seat and steps into the shower stall, directly opposite the toilet. A minute later, with the water still running, she opens the door to glance at the container. The color is definitely pink. Her initial glee is quickly replaced by ambivalence.

Slowly, she turns off the faucets, wraps a towel around herself, goes into the bedroom, and nudges Tom.

"Happy birthday," he mumbles, his eyes closed.

"Well," Erin says tentatively, "I'm pregnant."

Tom instantly opens his eyes, sits up, and hugs her hard. Erin doesn't hug him back. "What's wrong?" he asks.

"I guess I'm a little anxious," she confesses.

That night, Erin writes in her diary: *I'm finally pregnant. Tom is overjoyed; me, I have mixed emotions. Me, the worrier, is already concerned about everything from being fat to college educations.*

For Tom, it's the best news in weeks. The station reopened Saturday, but the five-week shutdown depleted his cash reserves, drove away regular customers, and forced him to borrow more from the bank. Getting through the rest of the year without going under, he knows, will not be easy.

Tom's usual approach to trouble is, *change what you can change immediately and put the rest aside until you can deal with it.* But the events of these past months had brought him to despair. He needed something to keep him fighting. Now he has it. A baby. A reason to go on.

**WEDNESDAY,
FEBRUARY 21
Westchester**

ESTERDAY, AT THE DIRECTION OF HER OBSTETRICIAN, ALEX consulted a hematologist about her blood condition. Expecting a simple immunological screen, she was alarmed when the doctor performed a bone-marrow biopsy—an invasive procedure in which the bone is anesthetized through the hip and the marrow is drawn with a needle larger than the one used in amniocentesis. Alex, aware that such tests are given when there is reason to suspect cancer, asked the hematologist if that was the case with her. He said no; he wanted to determine the cause of her low platelet count. Either her body wasn't producing enough to begin with, or the platelets were being destroyed.

Rob, who worked late last night, didn't notice the large bandage over Alex's left hip until this morning. "What did that guy do to you?" he says, his tone panicky. He is incensed that the hematologist gave her no prior warning, agitated that Carl was either not aware of the hematologist's intentions or kept them from Alex, and annoyed with Alex for seeming so casual about all of it. Alex's brother has lymphoma and her father died of cancer. Rob assumes that her lack of concern is a pretense. She knows as well as he does what bone-marrow biopsies are supposed to test for.

When Rob arrives at his office in New Jersey, he phones Carl. Another doctor in Carl's practice, Bob Wilder, takes the call, explaining that Carl is on vacation. Wilder says he doesn't know why the hematologist performed the biopsy: "You're asking me something that's out of my specialty."

"In that case," says Rob, "doesn't it seem strange that you'd refer your patient when you don't know what's going to happen to her?"

"If you take your car to a transmission specialist and there's something wrong with the brakes," Wilder comments, "he sends you to a brake man."

Rob finds this unendurably patronizing. "Thanks for enlightening me," he says mockingly, and hangs up. Next he calls the hematologist. The receptionist asks Rob's name and his wife's, puts him on hold for what seems like hours, then tells him to check back after 2:00. At 2:10 Rob calls and is again put on hold. Finally the nurse tells him the doctor is "unavailable." *No wonder,* Rob thinks, *these guys get sued.*

Compared to the matter of Rob's working hours, Alex considers the biopsy inconsequential. When she and Rob first discussed the prospect of his moonlighting as a consultant, they agreed that he would do the work on Saturdays—a sacrifice that precludes ever going away for the weekend during these last unencumbered-by-baby months. But so far the consulting has consumed every weeknight, sometimes until 2 or 3 A.M., and not just all day but nearly all night on Saturday, which kills Sunday because Rob spends half of it sleeping. Rob's defense is that he will earn an extra $4,000 a month to go toward the house they hope to buy. But in Alex's view, money isn't worth sacrificing your health—or your marriage—for. They barely see each other now, between her traveling and his moonlighting. When they do, they spend too much time arguing about her medical condition and his chronic failure to tell her when he's going to be late. "You'll yell if I call and you'll yell if I don't," Rob says, "so why bother?"

When they were dating, Alex wouldn't tolerate his lack of promptness. If he was delayed more than half an hour and didn't call, she simply took off. But now they live together, and on these winter nights when she's pregnant and queasy, she's not going to drive on icy streets just so he can come home and wonder where she is. All she can do is yell.

**SATURDAY,
FEBRUARY 24
Cape Cod**

 NOW FALLS GENTLY OUTSIDE THE SLIDING GLASS DOORS OF THE kitchen, where Michael fixes a hamburger for Ben and Sarah pursues an argument about his boss that began last night.

"I'm still mad at you for not sticking up for yourself," she begins.

"I did," he says stiffly, "but not in your way. I don't want to get into it again."

"Your mother just died and your wife is about to give birth, and suddenly this asshole is pressuring you to work a forty-five-hour week. I would have said, 'Oh, so you're going to reprimand me for not working five more hours a week, and I've been here ten years and maybe if I'm lucky I can expect a raise in another five, and you think I'm going to sit here and take this shit?' "

"This is ridiculous," Michael says, noisily loading the dishwasher.

"Whatever you told him, it won't get you a raise and it won't make him treat you better. I've dealt with a lot of bosses, and—"

"You're upset because I'm still working there after ten years, that's the bottom line."

"I don't like to see an employer take advantage of you. You're too good for that, but you don't realize it because you're so demoralized."

"I see it very differently," Michael says. "I see it as a place to be my own boss, with little or no supervision. I go in, I do my work, I go home. It leaves me a lot of time for my family, which is what we both want."

"You should tell him to fuck off."

"I would tell him to fuck off if I had another job. I'd tell him, 'It's been nice, but I'm leaving in two weeks.' "

"I wouldn't care if you got fired. You'd realize how much you have to offer. You could open a business for yourself."

"What business?"

"A cooperative buying business. I'll tell you who could use your help right now, it's [a produce market], which is run so Cape Coddy. The food isn't fresh; they don't know what they're doing."

Michael sighs and glances at his watch. "It's time for Ben's bath," he says, thinking, *Anything to end this pointless discussion.* He disappears down the hall while Sarah continues to seethe. She thinks that Michael won't admit he's dissatisfied with his job because he's afraid he'll be rejected if he looks elsewhere, and he hates any kind of change. She is disturbed by the way he is handling his mother's death, retreating deep within himself where she can't reach him. She knows her hostile behavior last month didn't exactly invite openness, but she can't retract it now. The more he withdraws, the more frustrated she gets.

An hour later, at a restaurant, Michael studies the wine list and orders a bottle of California chardonnay. Sarah allows herself one glass; she figures that nothing can hurt the baby at this point. She and Michael discuss names for their daughter. Michael wants Margery, after his mother, but Sarah prefers Gabrielle or Hannah. They're trying to come up with a compromise that begins with *M*.

"Margot Gabrielle?" Michael ventures. "Margot is pretty close to Margery."

Sarah shrugs without enthusiasm, but leans forward when Michael, his tongue loosened by the wine, begins to talk about his mother. "I miss her a lot more than I missed my dad, and I wasn't prepared for that," he says. "Images of her in good times keep going through my head." Sarah waits for him to say more, but he drops the subject. "I'm nervous about having another kid because it will mean double the work," he says, "but I don't talk about it because I'm afraid you'll fly off the handle."

Sarah ignores this. "I hate your boss," she says. "It sticks in my craw."

"I'm in management. I understand his thinking."

"And *I*," Sarah says indignantly, "haven't been in management?"

"Not upper management." Michael pours more wine. He wants to be done with this topic. "I'm trying to figure out what will happen with an infant in the house, how to deal with the night wakings and the diaper changing on top of doing stuff for Ben and still not take attention away from him or show him I'm overwhelmed. Maybe you could go back to being a buyer, making real money, and I could stay home."

"But I'd have to travel two weeks out of every month."

"You'd love that."

"I never misled you," Sarah says, suddenly defensive. "You knew from the beginning I didn't want to get stuck with child care. I've already worked it out: I'll leave the baby with Kim [Ben's sitter] on Tuesday, Wednesday, and Thursday afternoons."

"But what we haven't worked out is the morning stuff, getting Ben dressed, the baby dressed . . ."

"I think the man should pay for the woman's having to carry the baby."

"Yes, I know," Michael says. "For the rest of his life."

OE BOUNCES AROUND THE CROWDED WAITING ROOM OF MARIA'S obstetrician, striking up conversations with pregnant strangers and their husbands. Maria is smiling as she watches him, flattered and charmed by his exuberance. For days he has been talking about the moment when he'll hear the baby's heartbeat for the first time.

The nurse summons them to the examining room, where Joe persuades the obstetrician, Dr. Spiegel, to hold the fetal monitor against Maria's uterus for a full five minutes. After the checkup, Maria quizzes the doctor about painkillers. Spiegel says he believes that a woman in labor should be made as comfortable as possible, but there are many variables, such as the position of the baby and the duration of labor, that dictate the amount and type of appropriate medication. Maria says she's afraid of pain, but Joe wants her to refuse all drugs for the baby's sake. Spiegel calls a halt to their debate. "There's no point," he says, "in getting into it now."

Joe and Maria stop for a pasta dinner on their way to a Knicks game. At the restaurant, he fills her in on the details of his scouting trip to Florida next week, which she fully supports; they agree that he needs to make personal contact with the managers of various post offices.

Maria doesn't mention her dismay over the length of the trip. She hoped it would be only five days, from Monday to Friday, but it doesn't make financial sense—Joe will save eighty dollars by staying over on Saturday night. Being without him for what amounts to two weekends would not have bothered Maria in the past. Pregnancy has changed that. She feels ever more dependent on Joe's physical presence. She hates to admit it.

### THURSDAY, MARCH 1
### Westchester

HE HEMATOLOGIST REPORTED TO ALEX LAST WEEK THAT HER bone marrow is producing enough platelets but her body is destroying them. Her platelet count has dropped slightly; the doctor said the decline is caused by the physiological stress of pregnancy. (About 8 percent of all pregnant women experience this.) There is no cause for concern or for a cesarean, he explained, unless her count dips drastically in the coming months. Alex urged him to be frank with her about risks and options, to be as technical in his explanations as needed.

"Usually," the doctor said with some surprise, "patients accuse me of being too clinical."

"You'll never hear that from me," replied Alex.

Later, Alex looked up ITP in one of her medical books and learned that the mortality rate caused by intracranial bleeding during a vaginal delivery for infants who inherit their mother's condition is 12 percent. She considered this frightening statistic inapplicable to her but promptly hid the book. The last thing she needs is for Rob to stumble on the same information.

It is Alex's twenty-third week of pregnancy. Tonight, flying home after a four-day business trip, she sits next to a woman traveling with her eight-month-old daughter. The woman brags to Alex about her fabulous nausea-free pregnancy. In the middle of her monologue the baby throws up. Alex is astonished that the woman doesn't get upset; she just wipes herself and her daughter off with a wet towel, saying, "Oh, Olivia, you must feel terrible," and apologizes to Alex. Alex, assuming that the woman will want to change her baby's clothes, asks if she can help. The woman says casually, "I'll change her when I get to my friend's house."

Arriving at anyone's house with a baby stinking of vomit—Alex can't imagine it.

**FRIDAY, MARCH 2**
**Manhattan**

ULIET ARRIVES FOR AN APPOINTMENT WITH BERNSTEIN PREPARED to hear him prescribe bed rest. Instead he tells her that her cervix and the baby's size are both as they should be. "You're doing well," he says. The inconsistency of his opinions from visit to visit confuses her, but she trusts his judgment. Suddenly she feels confident about the pregnancy.

When Sam hears about Bernstein's turnaround, he wonders if the doctor has been setting them up for the worst so that anything short of it will seem like a gift. If that is Bernstein's strategy, it has worked: Juliet has been giddy ever since the appointment. Sam, however, is more cautious. He knows that if the baby is born now, at the beginning of the twenty-fifth week, it will almost certainly die, and it's like contemplating his own death. He tries not to dwell on it, but every time there's a false alarm—for instance, the gas pains, mimicking contractions, that Juliet felt the other night—it reminds him of how tenuous her pregnancy still is. At least once a day he asks himself, *Can we make it to twenty-eight weeks? Thirty-three weeks? How long before I can stop worrying?*

Sam turned forty-four on Wednesday. He doesn't care that his beard is flecked with gray or that the top of his head is bald. (When he started losing his hair a few years ago, he was upset until a friend told

him, "Sean Connery looks even better without hair," and Juliet remarked afterward that Sam is beginning to resemble the actor.) He
feels good physically, his book will soon be out, he loves his wife, he's
going to have a baby.

Still, he is apologetic about his happiness. He believes it's a residue
of the sixties mentality, in which happiness was considered a serious
character flaw; you were supposed to maintain a sense of existential
woe at all times. If you didn't believe, or at least say, that life was
meaningless, the assumption was you were shallow and boring. But
except for when his first marriage was unraveling and when he had the
crisis over his academic career, Sam has never been able to work himself up into much of a depression. *So I'm shallow and boring,* he thinks.
*So what.*

**SATURDAY, MARCH 3**
**Cape Cod / Plymouth**

ARAH, THIRTY-SIX WEEKS PREGNANT, WAKES IN THE MORNING
with chills, aching bones, and a fever of 101. She sleeps most
of the day. At 5 P.M. she tells Michael she's having contractions. He calls the obstetrician, who says it must be the flu.
Sarah goes into the bathroom and runs water in the tub. She remembers from Lamaze training that if you sit in a warm bath and the
contractions get worse, your labor is real. (Many doctors would dispute
this advice. If your water breaks while you're in the bath you won't
know it, and if too much time elapses between rupture of membranes
and delivery, you run the risk of infection.) She's on her hands and
knees in the tub, trying to decide, when Ben enters the bathroom.
"Mommy, are you okay?" he says anxiously.

"Yeah," Sarah says, "I'm okay. The baby is going to come out
soon."

"Can I watch?" Ben asks.

*There's no way I can communicate with a three-year-old at this moment,*
Sarah thinks. From the continuing intensity and regularity of her contractions, she knows the labor is real. "Call Karen!" she yells downstairs to Michael. (Karen is a friend who has agreed to take care of Ben

when Sarah goes into labor.) Michael rushes to the bathroom to find his wife doubled over in the tub and his son standing by, looking confused. "We have to leave for the hospital right away," Sarah mutters.

Michael calls Karen and follows Sarah's terse instructions. He parks Ben in front of the TV, warms up the car, and puts a quilt, a pillow, and a towel on the back seat in case Sarah gives birth on the highway. He runs back upstairs, dries Sarah off, helps her into a terrycloth robe, slides her feet into slippers, and throws things into an overnight bag. (He's so nervous that when Sarah tells him to include a pair of black ballet shoes, he packs two left shoes.) Sarah has to have a bowel movement, which she remembers happening just before she went into labor with Ben. Afterward, she grabs a bowl and a roll of toilet paper in case she has diarrhea in the car.

"What's that for?" Michael asks in a dazed manner.

"It's to put over your head after I shit in it," Sarah says between clenched teeth. She resents always having to think for both of them whenever there's a crisis, because Michael's mind goes blank.

At 5:45, with Ben's macaroni and cheese still sitting half-cooked on the stove and Karen in place, Sarah and Michael get into the car. He guns for the hospital in Plymouth, the speedometer climbing to ninety. Sarah is naked under her robe and the temperature outside is below freezing, but she's burning up. She rolls the window down and leans out between contractions, which are so acute they make her clutch the safety bar above her head and scream.

They make it to the hospital, normally a forty-five-minute trip, in half an hour. Sarah demands medication, but the nurses say they can't give her anything without the doctor's permission. Sarah keeps yelling, "Where is the goddamn doctor!" When he shows up just before seven, Sarah says just one word: "Demerol."

"I have to examine you first," he says.

"Well, then, hurry up." She is nine centimeters dilated but gets the Demerol.

The nurses wheel her into the delivery room, where the doctor breaks her water. It is a definite green, signaling some kind of fetal distress that caused the baby to make a bowel movement. (This happens in about 18 percent of vaginal births.) The fetal monitor shows the heart rate has dropped from 180 to 70, another indication of distress. Michael can't stop shaking.

He begs the doctor not to do an episiotomy; after Ben's birth, Sarah couldn't walk for days. But Sarah knows her baby is in trouble. She whispers gently to Michael, "If he has to cut, let him cut." The doctor tries to stretch her with his fingers but in the end has to make a small incision. He tells Sarah to push as hard as she can. After two and a half pushes, he yanks the baby out. It is 7:29 P.M.

Sarah immediately feels great; her flu, or whatever it was, has left her body along with the baby. But when she looks at the obstetrician she feels terror. His face is white and strangely still. Michael senses that something is wrong and starts plying the staff pediatrician with questions, but he's working on the baby and doesn't answer. Sarah takes Michael's hand and holds it in both her own. "Let him work," she says.

Michael is quiet after that, but keeps thinking, *Why doesn't my daughter cry, she's supposed to cry.* He and Sarah watch, frozen, as a team of doctors quickly place tubes down the baby's throat to suction out the green feces, called meconium, before the baby has a chance to breathe it. They put a tiny oxygen mask over her nose and mouth and squeeze an air bottle, and finally Michael hears a gasp and then a weak cry. He feels relieved, but then he sees the team remove his daughter, now emitting strange mewing sounds, from the room. He remembers being told when he and Sarah toured the hospital that under normal circumstances newborns are not separated from their parents immediately after birth. *These must not be normal circumstances,* he thinks.

The pediatrician returns in fifteen minutes to explain that the baby has a fever (he does not mention that this is quite rare in a just-delivered infant) and they need to perform some blood tests to identify the infection causing it. He says they've put her under an oxygen mist, a normal procedure after suctioning, to soothe her upper airway, which is raw and sore from the suction tube. Michael spends the next few hours wandering in and out of the nursery, watching his daughter, worrying.

At 12:30 A.M., Sarah tells Michael to go home and get some sleep.

He looks out the window and sees a thick blanket of fog. "No," he says. "I want to stay with you." But Sarah is adamant that he should be well rested to face the morning.

Michael gets home at 1:30, takes a shower, straightens the sheets on the bed, and gets in. He lies there in the dark, thinking how nice it is to be in his own bed again after months in the guest room. Then he remembers that Sarah lay ill in this bed all day. He bolts out, hoping to avoid her germs—he can't afford to get sick—and goes downstairs to the guest room. He sets the alarm for 5:30. He wants to be back in Plymouth as early as possible.

His daughter is four weeks premature. She weighs five pounds, thirteen ounces. Her name is Hannah Marguerite.

Just before Michael falls asleep in what will be Hannah's room, he thinks, *I never got to hold her.*

### SUNDAY, MARCH 4
#### Plymouth/Boston

I N THE NURSERY, AROUND 3 A.M., THE DEVICE MONITORING HANnah's vital signs emits a warning signal: she has stopped breathing. The condition, called apnea, is not unusual in babies born quite prematurely, but at thirty-six weeks' gestation it may be due to infection. The nurse on duty turns the baby on her side and pats her back. She starts to breathe again.

At 7 A.M., Sarah learns that a medical team is going to airlift her daughter by helicopter to the neonatal intensive care unit at Tufts–New England Medical Center in Boston. There is still no diagnosis, but the fever remains. Sarah calls Michael a few minutes later, just as he's about to leave the house. "You'd better get here right away," she says. "They're taking her to Boston." Michael doesn't ask questions. He runs to the car.

In the hospital, Sarah waves away her breakfast tray, explaining to the nurse that today she is having her tubes tied. "Forget about that for now," the nurse says briskly. "Eat." For once Sarah does as she's told.

When Michael arrives, he and Sarah go to the nursery. Their

daughter lies listlessly in an incubator with tubes running in and out of her tiny body, her skin bruised from innumerable blood tests. The nurses urge them to stroke her, but they are afraid of jarring one of the tubes. Her condition, they are told, is "stable but guarded." *Is that good or bad?* Michael wonders.

Sarah is reeling from the first migraine of her life, a result of the stress of the past twelve hours coupled with her characteristic refusal to reveal painful emotions. She is intent on maintaining a steely self-control; the migraine, like the ulcer she had as a child, is the price she's paying for it.

A medical team enters the nursery to stabilize the baby for the flight to Boston. There are two nurses, a doctor, and a large apparatus that resembles an elaborate tool kit. To Michael it looks like the set of a TV show about medical emergencies. The Coens are asked to leave the room while someone inserts an oxygen tube in the baby's throat in case she stops breathing on the helicopter, where the confined space would make resuscitation difficult. Sarah stiffens at the thought; Michael starts to cry. The TV show he thought he was watching has turned horribly real.

An hour later, Hannah is ready to go. Michael and Sarah kiss her forehead gingerly and say goodbye. They stand back as the team places the baby in a heated incubator, puts the incubator on a gurney, and wheels the gurney into an ambulance. Sarah and Michael, accompanied by the staff pediatrician and Sarah's obstetrician, go into a room with a window that faces the helipad. The Coens stare through the window, tears streaking their cheeks. It is the first time throughout this ordeal that Sarah has permitted herself to cry.

The ambulance backs up to the helicopter. The gurney is loaded. The helicopter takes off. Hannah is gone.

Michael waits for his tears to stop and turns to the pediatrician. He wants to know why Hannah has to go to Boston. "If her condition gets worse," the doctor says, "she needs to be someplace where they specialize in neonatal care." Michael wants to see this "someplace" for himself, to counteract the terrifying sensation of watching the helicopter lift his newborn daughter into the unknown. He is aware, of course, that she is going to Tufts–New England Medical Center, but *where* in the center? What floor? Will there be other babies there? How many? Will she be lying on her stomach or her back? Who will take care of her? *Who will hold her?*

In the afternoon he goes to Boston, an hour's drive from Plymouth. His visit with Hannah is brief; he has to get back to the Cape, pick up Ben from Karen's, give him dinner, somehow try to explain what's going on . . . But Michael finds it reassuring to see his baby settled in a brightly lit ward with her own nurse, and to hear that the doctors have so far ruled out spinal meningitis and central nervous system disorder.

Back in Plymouth, Sarah's migraine is worse. She has taken Percocet and Tylenol with codeine, but the painkillers have no effect. When Michael calls from the hospital in Boston, describing the unit as brightly lit, Sarah thinks, *That'll be just great for my migraine.* It's easier for her to maintain her composure if she keeps her thoughts focused on herself. Once she permits herself to contemplate what might happen to her daughter, she will collapse.

Tonight she has a stream of concerned visitors, including her rabbi and his wife, her father, and her sister, who has driven to Plymouth from her home near Boston. Sarah is grateful for the distractions, but her head is still exploding. At midnight the nurse gives her a shot of morphine. The pain goes away, and Sarah sleeps.

Michael is too agitated to close his eyes for long. His mind is stuck in one groove: *I can't lose my daughter after losing my mother.*

### MONDAY, MARCH 5
#### Plymouth/Boston

 HEN SARAH WAKES UP THIS MORNING, THE LEFT SIDE OF HER face is partially paralyzed, possibly from the migraine. Her obstetrician tells her to stay in the hospital an extra day and see a neurologist, but she refuses. "Just get me out of this fucking place," she says. "I have to see my daughter." The doctor agrees to discharge her. Sarah arranges for her best friend,

Lauren, to pick her up at 2:30 and drive her to Boston; she'll stay at Lauren's until Thursday and return to the Cape for the weekend. Ben will spend the week at Kim's, leaving Michael free to commute back and forth to Boston. Sarah knows that Ben must be feeling confused and abandoned, but she can't worry about him now.

By 11 A.M., Sarah has already spent two and a half hours on the phone by her hospital bed, trying to locate an electric breast pump in Boston that hasn't already been rented. She wants Hannah to have breast milk because it might help her body fight the infection, though it will have to be given through a feeding tube. Sarah's persistence with the yellow pages finally yields a pump. She's glad the search took so long; it kept her mind off Hannah.

She arrives at the Tufts–New England Medical Center at four and is soon holding her daughter for the first time. She struggles to keep her emotions in check. *There's no point in getting too attached,* she tells herself, *until I know the prognosis.*

**TUESDAY, MARCH 6**
**Boston**

HE NEONATAL INTENSIVE CARE UNIT IS ON THE SIXTH FLOOR OF the Floating Hospital section of the medical center. Signs outside its entrance stipulate that no one with a cold may enter except for the babies' parents, who must wear a mask; children under sixteen are not allowed at any time; parents may be accompanied by no more than two other people. Inside, each heated incubator is labeled with a multicolored cardboard sign decorated with a drawing of Winnie the Pooh announcing *Look Who's Here!*, with the name and birthdate of the inhabitant. Rocking chairs are plentiful; the nurses encourage parents to relax with their newborns and not be afraid to hold and rock them.

Hannah, wearing only a diaper, is sleeping on her stomach on the pad of thick lambswool that lines the incubator. An IV drip of phenobarbitol to keep her tranquil and prevent seizures or unnecessary movement, which would expend precious energy, is inserted in a vein in her scalp, which has been partially shaved. (Newborn heads are full of veins, making them a good site for intravenous medication.) Her face is under an oxygen hood. A cord wrapped around her toe connects to a machine flashing two numbers, indicating oxygen saturation rate and heart rate. A plastic container inside her diaper collects urine for testing. More wires extend from leads taped to her back and the top of her left thigh. A nurse periodically measures her belly to assess any swelling, which might indicate infection.

At noon, a nurse wheels Hannah away for a CAT scan to determine whether an abnormality in her brain caused the apnea episode that occurred within hours of her birth at the hospital in Plymouth. Sarah rushes into the unit a few minutes later, upset about just missing her. She knew that the CAT scan had been scheduled and had intended to arrive beforehand, but Lauren had car trouble on the way. Sarah's face is still partially paralyzed, but she won't see a neurologist. She can deal with only one crisis and one set of doctors at a time.

Hannah is returned to the unit around 1:30. Sarah sits next to the incubator, watching a nurse attach electrodes to the baby's head in preparation for an EEG. An IV line of antibiotics is now running through Hannah's hand, and her arm is strapped down in a tiny splint so it doesn't move. Sarah stares at the needles moving up and down on one of the monitors and wonders what they indicate. A nurse explains that they record the REMs of Hannah's sleep. She shows Sarah the chart: here the baby cried, she snored, she stretched—nothing abnormal.

Later, around three, while Sarah discusses Hannah's case with a medical student, Michael calls the unit. A nurse leads Sarah to the phone.

"I won't be able to come tonight," Michael tells her. "There's a blizzard watch."

Sarah erupts. "You'll go to the ends of the earth for your mother, but not your daughter!" *How can he even consider leaving me alone with this?* she thinks, choking back tears. "Fuck your job, you're leaving in ten minutes. If there's a blizzard, fine. You've got four-wheel drive. Get in your car. I need you here, *now!*" She slams down the receiver, shaking.

A few minutes later, the unit's primary nurse introduces Sarah, calmer now, to the neonatologist, a woman about Sarah's age named Dr. Isaacson. Sarah admits to the doctor that she's distraught, partly because she doesn't know whether Hannah is getting better or worse. The doctor assures Sarah that her daughter is steadily improving. There is no indication of neurological problems, and the nature of her infection has just been identified. It's called listeria, an extremely rare disease caused by bacteria that is often food-borne (the doctors determine later that Sarah probably contracted it from eating unpasteurized goat cheese the day before going into labor) and can severely affect newborns, debilitated or elderly people, and those with depressed immune systems. If the bacteria are passed through the placenta from mother to fetus in utero, which generally occurs in the third trimester, it is usually fatal to the fetus if not treated. Dr. Isaacson credits the staff pediatrician at the hospital in Plymouth with saving Hannah's life. By luck or instinct, he gave her the right antibiotic to fight the bacteria without knowing the diagnosis.

Sarah feels faint and sinks into a chair. She had thought that Hannah might die, but when none of the doctors mentioned it, she put it out of her mind. Now it hits her hard. "Are you all right?" Isaacson asks gently. Sarah swallows and nods.

"Most parents," the doctor continues after a moment, "want to know if development will be normal. At this point I can't tell you that. The infection may or may not have some long-term effects—"

"I don't care," Sarah interrupts, recovering her wits. "All that matters is she's not going to die."

"You are the only parent who's ever told me that," Isaacson comments admiringly.

Sarah checks her watch: 4 P.M. Lauren will be waiting downstairs. She hastily thanks the doctor and rushes out of the unit, her legs feeling rubbery. *Hannah is going to live.*

Michael is standing in Lauren's driveway when they arrive. At first Sarah is happy to see him, but his stupefied air soon upsets her. *I'll have to keep being the strong one,* she thinks, *and I don't know how much strength I've got left.* To conserve it, she doesn't tell Michael about her conversation with Isaacson, which she is sure will only make her dizzy again.

"I've got to pump my breasts," she says, disappearing into the guest room.

Lauren takes in Michael's bewildered expression. "You need a drink," she says. She leads Michael into the kitchen, produces a bottle of Pouilly-Fuissé, and pours both of them a glass. Then she fills him in on Hannah's diagnosis, which Sarah explained to her on the way home.

Michael listens intently but doesn't comment. He sips the wine, thinking of something Sarah once said to him: "If I ever had a baby with problems, I would give it up for adoption." *It's one threat,* he thinks, *that she doesn't seem willing to carry out.* Her behavior toward him these past few days has vacillated from loving to beastly, but he forgives her the worst of it. He is amazed at her high level of functioning in the midst of this emergency. *If she can pull it off only by attacking me,* he muses, *it's worth it.*

Sarah and Michael eat dinner hastily, eager to get to the hospital. They arrive at 9:30. When they reach the sixth floor, Sarah points to the bank of pay phones outside the unit. "I have to make a call," she says. "Why don't you spend some time with her alone?" Michael enters the unit prepared for the worst but is pleasantly surprised. The lights are low, no babies are crying, and the angry red blotches on Hannah's skin that Sarah had described are gone; the baby's flesh is soft and pink because a nurse has just given her a moisturizing bath. When Michael last saw his daughter, on Sunday, there were tubes running out of her mouth and an oxygen hood over her head. Now there is only an IV lead in her hand and monitor hookups taped to her feet.

A nurse comes over and tells Michael that Hannah is doing well. "Do you want to hold her?" she asks. Michael is reluctant. "Come on," the nurse says, leading him to a rocking chair and placing Hannah in his arms. He is nervous at first, but the nurse tells him to relax. When he does, he realizes how wonderful he feels—almost *high,* as if he is on the best drug in the world. Sarah was brutal to him on the phone today, but now he blesses her for making him come.

An hour passes, but Michael has no awareness of time. He rocks his daughter and kisses each mark on her scalp where the tubes were attached. At one point she opens her eyes and looks straight at him. It is the first time he has sensed that she will be okay.

Sarah waits outside the unit, watching Michael through the glass. She wants to give him a chance to get comfortable with Hannah. At 10:45 she enters, taking her turn in the rocking chair as Michael stands by. A nurse comes over and says that Hannah is doing so well she might be moved to the "step-down" unit, reserved for babies who are no longer in critical condition. This news makes Sarah apprehensive. She wishes the nurse hadn't said it, in case it doesn't happen.

At midnight Michael and Sarah place a little stuffed rabbit in the incubator and kiss their daughter goodnight. They say little in the car, but the silence feels intimate.

The next morning Michael returns to his office on the Cape and Sarah resumes her vigil at the hospital. She hovers over Hannah's incubator, trying to resist the urge to hold her. The nurses have wrapped the baby in blankets in an attempt to raise her body temperature without using warming lights; Sarah doesn't want to disturb Hannah's cocoon. The nurses encourage her. Soon she has her swaddled baby tight within her arms.

Dr. Isaacson comes in with good news. They're weaning Hannah off the phenobarbitol and she's responding well to the antibiotics. The doctor confirms that she has improved enough to be moved out of intensive care in a day or so.

Sarah calls the head of the agency who arranged months ago for a baby nurse to come to her home for the first two postpartum weeks. She explains Hannah's condition and requests someone experienced with premature babies. The man seems taken aback. "We don't really have anyone like that," he says. "Maybe you should try elsewhere." Sarah hangs up in despair. Her anxiety mounts whenever she tries to imagine bringing Hannah home; every time the baby sneezes, she panics. She knows she will need help.

Later that night, in an hour-long phone conversation with Esther Levin, the family pediatrician, Sarah learns that listeria is so rare that in all her years of practice, Esther has seen only three cases in newborns. Sarah thinks, *Why* my *child?*

ESTERDAY, WHILE ROB WAS ON LONG ISLAND WORKING AT HIS second job, Alex vacuumed and did laundry and changed the bed and scrubbed both bathrooms. By the end of the day, she was so exhausted she made a revolutionary decision: she will hire a cleaning lady. It irks her to pay someone to do something she can do so much better herself. But she is too pregnant to be lugging a vacuum around, Rob is never home to help, and the idea of just letting the house go is unacceptable.

Rob and Alex waste an hour this morning arguing after Alex tells him that she'll be seeing the hematologist every two weeks to have her platelets monitored.

"Nobody," he screams at her, "has told you that eating's important, isn't that amazing? Bone marrows are important, monitoring the platelets is important, but no one says eating is important."

"You're making things up. Stop being hysterical."

"Look, I'm upset because the people making the decisions are everyone but me, and I . . . feel . . . helpless."

"I understand you feel helpless," she says, "but can you understand that *I* feel miserable?"

Later, hugging the toilet, watching her breakfast come out of her, Alex thinks, *I could never be pregnant again.* She's approaching her sixth month and wants to destroy every woman who has ever told her how fabulous they felt during the second trimester. Alex threw up so much this week she has lost two pounds, information she has withheld from Rob.

*Why,* she thinks, *should I cater to his emotional needs when he seems oblivious to my feelings?* The first question Rob asks when he comes home, if she's still awake, is "Did the baby move today?" The first thing he does after asking that question is touch her belly, which Alex feels is not the same as touching *her.*

**E**RIN HAS NOTICED THAT HER WORRY LIST HAS LENGTHENED along with her uterus.

First on the list is her weight. She lost twenty pounds before she got pregnant and five more from nausea, but by the time she delivers she's sure she'll be enormous, with even bigger breasts (a selfish reason not to nurse, but a powerful one nonetheless). She worries about getting through the first trimester without miscarrying. She worries about getting through labor without dying from pain. She worries that her worrying will affect the baby in her womb.

But most of all, she worries that she will not be *a good role model.* If something—motherhood, for example—prevents her from earning her degree, how can she impress upon her offspring the importance of a college education she herself didn't have? Tom didn't go beyond high school either, but Erin exempts him from her own rigid standards. He is *business smart,* and his self-confidence alone, she thinks, will make him a good father.

Tom feels strongly that the best person to raise their child is a parent. He runs a twenty-four-hour-a-day, seven-day-a-week business, so it's not going to be him. He's been talking to Erin about her staying home for the first few years. He'll hire her as his bookkeeper, hooking up a modem to their home computer so she can communicate with the station. He'll try to be home more in the evenings, so she can complete her schooling. They'll lose her $40,000 annual income, but maybe the station will be in better shape by then and he can draw a larger salary.

Erin agrees with Tom that for her to stay home will save money otherwise spent on child care and be in the baby's best interests. Still, she has reservations. She's afraid that working for Tom won't be stimulating enough. Bookkeeping bores her, and she suspects full-time motherhood will too. When she accompanies Tom to banquets hosted by the oil company of which he is a franchisee, she meets husbands and wives who run stations together and thinks, *I want my own interests*. She likes her place in the white-collar world, removed from gas pumps and carburetors. Her boss's reliance on her feeds her fragile ego in ways she doubts parenthood will. And as much as she hates the long commute to her office in Washington, she thinks it is preferable to being *stuck out here in the sticks*.

It was a mutual decision to leave their friends in suburban Gaithersburg, an easy drive to Erin's office and Tom's station, and move to the home they now own in an unfinished rural development. Closer to D.C., they couldn't afford anything comparable to what they have here —a four-bedroom Colonial on a flat half-acre of land near the water, with access to a dock for Tom's twenty-one-foot powerboat. But now, less than a year after the move, both Tom and Erin wonder if they made the right choice. They're considering selling the house and moving north again in a tradeoff of space for convenience. In Gaithersburg they were surrounded by restaurants and ate out several times a week. Here they are surrounded by crops of corn and tobacco, and horses grazing in green fields. The friends they made in Gaithersburg are slipping away through lack of contact; the one neighborhood couple they've met here is about to move north.

Tom has always been somewhat of a loner and requires far less social life than Erin. But his commute to the station, slightly longer than hers —over an hour each way—is getting to him. He's afraid he'll never know his child. He imagines pulling his Ford Bronco into the driveway just as the baby goes to sleep and leaving in the morning before it wakes up.

*Scary* is the word that most often comes to Tom's mind when he contemplates life after Erin's due date, October 25. Already he has so little flexibility that the idea of being chained to the station and to child-care duties is daunting. But he plans to contribute as much as he can. He doesn't want to evoke the same feelings in Erin that caused their separation three years ago—she has no future, she is *nothing*. He already worries that one day his lack of curiosity will bore her and she'll leave him because of it.

Erin wants to see the world; Tom is content with taking the same vacation at the same place every year. He doesn't share her openness to new environments, new people, new ideas. If there's anything he wants, it's not stimulation. It's a little less pressure in his life.

**SUNDAY, MARCH 11**
**Westchester**

RIDAY NIGHT, ROB GOT HOME AT EIGHT FROM HIS OFFICE IN NEW Jersey and toiled at his computer from ten until four in the morning for his consulting job. At seven-thirty he went to Long Island to moonlight, arriving back home at one the next morning. He wakes at eleven today; by the time he and Alex get out of the apartment to look at baby furniture, the store has closed. Rob says he's sorry for ruining the day, which means nothing to Alex. Her parents always said that Americans apologize too much because they don't think before they act.

Rob's exhaustion from his now routine eighty-hour work week makes him ever more jittery about the pregnancy. Alex tries to be understanding, knowing that he considers himself unlucky and is always expecting disaster. But she is running out of patience. "My job," she shouts at him this afternoon, "is not supposed to involve comforting *you* right now."

Alex believes that if she has to throw up for nine months because of pregnancy, the least he can do is to stop smoking. She wakes up freezing every night because he opens all the windows to try to get rid of the odor. His smoking, his ridiculous hours, his compulsive eating —Alex can't keep even a jar of peanut butter, excellent pregnancy food, in the house for fear he'll consume it at one sitting—it's all part of the same thing, his inability to manage himself.

"The word *just*," she tells him, "is your biggest enemy. 'Just one more cigarette, just one more tablespoon, just a little more, just until the pressure's over'—that's a real good lesson to teach your kid, that immediate gratification is more important than long-term results."

"I'm planning to quit smoking," Rob says.

"When?"

"Soon."

"*When?* Tomorrow at three?" Alex doesn't want to hear about his future plans, which she puts about as much stock in as his telling her he'll be home on time.

*If he can't control himself,* she thinks, *the least he can do is stop dumping his baggage on me.* He's concerned about what she's eating, but not at all concerned about how he's aggravating her, which is bound to affect the pregnancy. And that angers Alex most of all.

**MONDAY, MARCH 12**
**Boston**

ANNAH HAS BEEN MOVED TO THE STEP–DOWN UNIT. HER course of antibiotics ends tomorrow; she will be released from the hospital on Wednesday. Sarah is pleased with her daughter's steady improvement, frightened about caring for her at home, and tense when she considers Ben, who was a *monster* all weekend. Esther, the pediatrician, explained to Sarah and Michael that Ben is angry with them for abandoning him to tend to Hannah, and they should expect his behavior to get worse when his new sister arrives. Sarah understands that the last week has been difficult for her son and she should be patient with him, but she is under so much stress herself . . .

Hannah's head is still bald; the markings from IV tubes remain visible. Dr. Isaacson says that she is now "just like any other newborn," but she looks gravely ill to Sarah.

Outside the unit, she feeds a quarter into the pay phone, still trying to arrange for a baby nurse. On Wednesday, the day of Hannah's discharge, Esther is going out of town. Sarah has no rapport with the other doctors in Esther's practice, and if she doesn't find a nurse, she'll be completely on her own. The thought is sobering enough to keep her from ranting at the agency that promised to send her someone. Instead she tries to be ingratiating. "Call back tomorrow," the agency tells her.

ARIA'S WEEKEND ALONE, WHEN JOE WAS IN FLORIDA, WAS DE-
pressing. She spent Saturday night sewing a cover for the
VCR because Joe complained that it was getting dusty.
She misses him so much that she would actually welcome
the chance to iron his uniforms. "Don't leave me like this again," she
said when he called that night. Joe told Maria he was lonely for her,
but his voice was exhilarated. "Hang on, babe," he said. "It's good I'm
here. There are some real possibilities." The post office manager in
Boca Raton, he explained, seemed impressed with him and asked how
soon he could relocate. "Are you ready to make the move?" he asked
Maria on the phone.

"I wouldn't hesitate for a second." She prays for the transfer to
come through. Joe said Boca seemed clean and tranquil, with "a nice
family atmosphere."

Maria's belly is so big now she's sure she'll give birth well before her
May 24 due date, which also happens to be her twenty-sixth birthday.
Her mother plans to fly up from Puerto Rico on June 3 to help her
through the first few postpartum weeks, but Maria thinks she ought to
come sooner.

She takes today off from work to be tested for gestational diabetes.
Everyone told her the sugary stuff you have to drink tastes horrible,
and because you can't eat anything beforehand, you spend the hour in
between drinking it and having your blood drawn feeling faint and
nauseous from hunger. But the test turns out to be no big deal. Maria
is done with it by 9:15, drives home, eats breakfast, and spends the day
cleaning the already spotless apartment. She wants everything to look
perfect for Joe's homecoming.

ODAY, JUST BEFORE HANNAH IS DISCHARGED, SARAH ASKS ONE OF the hospital neonatologists what special care the baby will need at home. "A father and mother's watchful eye," the doctor says. This strikes Sarah as an odd thing to tell someone whose newborn has spent ten days in an intensive care unit. "Can you be more specific?" she asks. As the doctor complies, she scribbles a list under the heading "What to watch for" on a yellow legal pad:

1. Acceptance of feeding
2. Course of weight gain
3. Detection of regurgitation
4. Abdominal distention
5. Frequency and character of stools
6. Changes in behavior (lethargy, seizures, hyperactivity)
7. Changes in color (jaundice, pale, blue)
8. Resp. problems (long pauses between each breath)
9. Check body temp.

At 2 P.M., Hannah receives her last dose of antibiotics from a very long needle, which makes her scream for five agonizing minutes. At 3:30, Michael picks them up. He and Sarah are too preoccupied with their respective anxieties to venture into a conversation during the two-hour drive home. Ben is still at Kim's; Sarah told Michael to delay picking him up until tomorrow because she needs a night to get herself and the baby settled.

Later, Esther Levin, the pediatrician, comes over to examine Hannah and assures Michael and Sarah that she looks fine. "A parent will know if a child is in distress," she says.

"I hope so," Sarah replies doubtfully.

Michael manages to get some sleep, but Sarah spends most of the night wide awake. Hannah lies next to her in a bassinet; each time she

makes a sound, Sarah peers at her nervously. For once, the lack of
sleep doesn't bother Sarah. She'll catch up on it tomorrow. The
agency finally came through with a baby nurse, who will arrive in the
morning. She costs a hundred dollars a day, and Sarah expects her to
be worth every penny.

**WEDNESDAY, MARCH 14**
**Westchester**

OB IS IN HIS CAR, DRIVING TO HIS OFFICE IN NEW JERSEY FROM A
meeting with a client that hasn't gone as well as he hoped
—in other words, *no one jumped on a table and said, 'God,
are we glad we met you.'* As he drives, he pictures the opening scene of *Death of a Salesman,* in which Willy Loman drags himself
into his house and says to his wife, who thought he was off on a sales
call, "I couldn't make it . . . I got as far as a little above Yonkers
. . . suddenly I couldn't drive anymore. I came back at ten miles an
hour." Rob envisions himself like Willy, disgraced and defeated, only
worse. In the play unfolding in Rob's head, there is a new character, a
hungry baby, who looks at him with sad eyes and holds an empty bowl
and starts to cry, and Rob says, "I didn't sell anything today, son; we'll
have to catch field mice or we won't eat."

He remembers telling the therapist he saw five years ago, during his
second depressive episode, about his fear of having children. Rob believed that once he became a father, he would lose his chance to
change his life—*all hope would end.* The therapist convinced him he
was wrong. But now, as he drives, the feeling assaults him once again.
*There is,* he thinks, *no more room for error, no more room for change.*

"Y OUR CERVIX IS STILL CLOSED, BUT IT'S SOFT," BERNSTEIN SAYS to Juliet after he examines her, "so I hope you have a lot of good books to read. You'll have to take it easy."

"Take it easy?" Juliet hopes he means only that.

"Yeah," Bernstein says. He doesn't offer specifics, so Juliet decides he is leaving the definition of "take it easy" up to her.

She has been using the monitoring device for two weeks now, long enough to conclude there is no relationship between activity level and contractions. She and Sam had sex a few days ago and the monitor registered only two contractions. (She transmits the recordings to a twenty-four-hour phone number, where they are analyzed by an obstetrical nurse representing the belt company.) Yesterday she was out shopping and walking for hours; at night the belt registered zero. She has been weaning herself off the Indian food she loves (spicy food can give you indigestion, and indigestion can bring on contractions), so last night she ate plain broiled fish, brown rice, and artichokes. This morning she records five contractions.

Now she lies on the couch, remonitoring herself, which she has been instructed to do whenever she gets a reading of five. She is drinking so much water, which prevents cervical irritability, that she badly needs to urinate, but she can't get up because the belt is on; this concerns her because a full bladder can cause contractions. There was an alarming twenty-four-hour period this week when the baby was unusually inactive. Juliet was relieved when she felt the somersaults start again, but the movement grew so pronounced she soon feared it would stimulate contractions. The more she worried, the more aggressively the baby kicked, as if in response to her mother's fretting. The idea that her anxiety could bring on labor made her even more anxious.

*There seems to be no limit,* she thinks, *to the Catch-22s of this pregnancy.*

HANK GOD FOR DESIREE, THE THREE-HUNDRED-POUND MOTHER
of five from Tobago sent by the agency. Desiree kept Hannah with her in the nursery from eleven last night to seven
this morning, giving Sarah eight blissfully uninterrupted
hours of sleep. Today she feels like a human being, able to endure with
good humor the breast-pumping routine, though her nipples are
cracked and sore. She is determined to keep pumping for at least a
month, or until Hannah's sucking reflex is developed enough to feed
directly from her mother, so the baby can get the immunities of breast
milk.

Michael and Sarah are continually on the lookout for a recurrence
of Hannah's symptoms, but Desiree is helping both of them realize that
Hannah is just like any other newborn, and the nurse's soothing presence has allowed Sarah to give Ben some attention. Last night he
refused to eat unless Sarah took him on her lap and fed him; she
indulged him without resentment.

Sarah feels that if she'd had a baby nurse when Ben was born, she
might have bonded with him from the beginning. He was extremely
colicky; for the first three months he screamed from morning to night.
Those difficult months might not have had such a lasting negative
effect on both of them, Sarah thinks, if someone like Desiree had been
around. Sarah decides that when Hannah and Ben have their own
children, she will give each of them a gift: a baby nurse for the first
two weeks.

Today Sarah finally sees a neurologist about her facial paralysis,
which is gradually going away. He finds nothing wrong—in fact, he
seems uninterested in Sarah. His questions are all about Hannah. Sarah
is so annoyed that she storms out of his office. Later she takes Hannah
to the pediatrician filling in for Esther, who says that Hannah's temperature, skin color, bowel movements, and heartbeat are normal. The
pediatric scale indicates she has gained four ounces on breast milk, but

the doctor advises Sarah to give her formula at night because it's more substantial. Again Sarah compares what she knows now to what she didn't with Ben: *If I had given him formula at night instead of breast milk, he might have slept more.* The reason he cried relentlessly, Sarah realizes, was simply that he was starving.

**SUNDAY, MARCH 25**
**Manhattan**

S AM SPENDS THIS BLUSTERY AFTERNOON BAKING BREAD. IT USED TO be his routine weekend activity in the 1970s, when he led the mellow life of a college professor. Suddenly he feels compelled to take it up again. It seems to approximate as much as anything can the experience of growing a baby.

He mixes his starter with yeast in a yellow ceramic bowl and consults his mother's recipe, adding safflower oil, eggs, and honey to the dough. He sprinkles wheat flour on a bread board so the dough won't stick and begins to knead, his favorite part—he finds it satisfying in some primordial way. After ten minutes or so, he transfers the springy dough to an oiled blue bowl, places a cloth on top, and checks his watch. In an hour he'll know if he grew his child successfully.

Sometimes Sam wishes he had the anatomy to carry a baby. He has always thought that God, or someone, made a gender tradeoff: boys go to war and girls go through labor. Given the choice, Sam would prefer the latter.

Juliet enters the kitchen and approaches the blue bowl. "Don't touch it!" Sam yells. "You're always trying to mess around with my cooking."

Juliet retreats, laughing. "Bread baking is a substitute," she tells him. "Once you have the baby, I bet you'll never make bread again. You're always going like this"—she forms a cradle with her arms and rocks it —"saying, 'Don't you wish we had a baby right now?' The answer is no. We don't want to rush things."

"I don't want the baby to be born early."

"But you're so impatient to hold her . . ."

"Two or three weeks ago, so were you."

"I was more nervous then, but now I'm content."

Juliet thinks about the mornings, when she lies quietly in bed and feels the baby waking up, starting to stretch. As the day wears on, she senses it responding to her moods. Carrying a baby, she thinks, is like the very best sex, an intense commingling of body, mind, emotion. She's sorry Sam can't experience it. She suspects he feels left out.

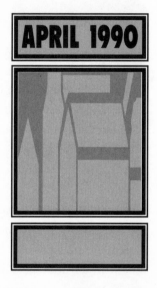

**TUESDAY, APRIL 3**
**Washington, D.C./**
**Southern Maryland**

RIN SHRUGS A SENSIBLE TWEED COAT OVER HER CALF-LENGTH shirtwaist dress and stands by her desk, examining her face in a makeup mirror. Pregnancy has caused an outbreak of acne, and the reflection does not please her. Her sedate clothes, large glasses, and slow, deliberate movements give her a solemn air, but her stunning full-throttle smile radiates warmth and pulls people into her orbit.

It has been a very long day in this corner of the world of municipal finance law, in which Erin's firm specializes. She worked frenetically toward a six o'clock deadline, executing minute details involved in closing a major bond issue. Now, as she retrieves her Honda from the underground parking lot of her office building, she thinks longingly of a soak in her bathtub.

She begins her commute home in heavy Beltway traffic with the radio tuned to an oldies station and her mind on her weight. She has lost five and a half pounds, which would be cause for celebration if she didn't happen to be pregnant. Her obstetrician is concerned that the baby may not be getting the nutrition it needs and says if Erin's weight doesn't stabilize over the next ten days, they'll "talk about it." She didn't elaborate, though she commented that Erin's nausea may be related to stress.

Erin's law firm is merging with another, and her hard-won designation as secretary/paralegal won't exist in the new corporate structure. Once again she'll be classified as *just a secretary*. Beyond the psychological impact of this change, there are practical concerns. Under the current plan she's entitled to eleven weeks' maternity leave at full salary and two weeks at 60 percent, to which she planned to tack on another three weeks of accumulated sick leave and vacation time. But it's unclear whether the newly merged firm will honor this, or cover the full costs of prenatal care, delivery, and hospitalization.

Erin's schooling is another problem. She didn't anticipate how much homework she would have, taking six credit hours. She tries to do it on her lunch hour, but there are so many interruptions she can't focus. At home, her concentration is no better because of her fatigue.

Around seven, she swings her car into the gravel driveway and parks in the two-car garage. The Wrights are the first tenants of this three-level Colonial, painted gray with red shutters. Inside, the house is airy, spacious, and spotless, thanks to Tom's meticulous cleaning. A few steps down from the smallish kitchen is the cathedral-ceilinged family room, where Tom and Erin spend most of their time. The room is inviting, with skylights, a ceiling fan, and a white linoleum floor meant to look like tile. There is a fireplace, with Erin's collection of sandstone English cottage miniatures displayed on the mantel, and a gallery of family photos mounted on the opposite wall. Upstairs are three bedrooms, two baths, and an open loftlike area that Tom will convert into an office, moving out of the room that will become the nursery. Erin's needlepoint—framed, signed, dated, and expressing sentiments like "Bless Our Home" and "Welcome"—is evident throughout the house.

Erin accepts a sloppy kiss from the dog, Clarence, and sits down in a cane and chrome chair at the kitchen table with a stack of newly delivered bills beside her. Because Tom lets them accumulate for a week or more and Erin wants to get them out of the way as soon as they come in, bill paying is her job. Tonight, however, she dreads opening her checkbook, which carries a disturbingly low balance. Tom has been unable to draw a paycheck for the past month. Lacking the capital to replace employees he lost during the shutdown, he has taken on the extra work himself, leaving for the station before Erin wakes up and returning home well after she does. She feels depressed whenever she enters her empty house, and by the time he arrives she is either weeping or fuming or both. *Tom and I had an awful argument,* she wrote recently in her diary. *He worked late again. I feel neglected and sick and* very *emotional.*

At eight, earlier than usual, Tom walks in. He removes his grease-stained running shoes at the door and goes straight to the refrigerator for a Lite beer. Then he kisses Erin on the cheek and slides into the chair next to her. Even sitting down, he is in motion, his foot tapping away underneath the table, his fingers drumming above it. He is six feet tall, taut and thin, with appealing hazel eyes set in a weathered face.

Erin is hungry, and neither of them is in the mood to cook. "Let's go out," she says, leaving the unopened bills on the table.

It takes twenty minutes over dark country roads to reach the restaurant, situated on a river that flows into the Chesapeake Bay. Tom orders a beer and fish and chips from the wisecracking waitress; Erin asks for a Coke and chicken teriyaki. This weekend they have an appointment with a realtor to discuss selling the house.

"It just kills me," Erin says, "to know how little we spent on this house and how big and nice it is compared to what we could get up there."

"Yeah. If I used the boat more I could justify staying here, or if I knew I'd be home three nights a week at five o'clock, I wouldn't mind the commute. I could probably make that happen if I set my mind to it." Erin greets this optimistic statement, which she has heard before, with a skeptical raise of her eyebrows.

"I know, I know"—Tom catches her look—"the business runs me more than it should. But when I'm just about out the door and a customer asks me something about a repair job, it's another forty-five minutes before I can leave. I don't want to be rude and say, 'Hey, I gotta go' to someone who's spending money on me. But I promise, it will change. I see myself working at this pace for ten more years, and when I'm forty I'll try something else."

"Ten more years at this pace and you'll be dead," says Erin.

"Okay, maybe not at this pace, but in this business. It's a lot of pressure, and I don't have a doctor's degree or a mansion to show for it, but I do have pride in my name . . ."

"I'm afraid that won't be enough," Erin says. "I'm afraid you'll go through an identity crisis like I did. For your entire adult life you've had the same all-consuming job and the same high-maintenance woman. You might want to chuck it all someday. You might want someone whose job is to take care of you and have dinner on the table every night, the way our mothers were with our fathers."

"What?" Tom isn't sure he heard her correctly. "I want you and whatever family we have." He can tell by her furrowed brow that she doesn't believe him.

Tom is perplexed by this leap in Erin's thinking, which seems to come out of nowhere. Though he tries to take her concerns seriously, her hypothetical scenarios have always confounded him.

OE IS PLANNING A SURPRISE SHOWER FOR MARIA. FOR FIVE HOURS, at a cost of $150, he has rented the gym in Brooklyn where he used to play basketball. He sent invitations to seventy people, plus kids, with a notation to the men to bring their basketball gear. He visualizes the men shooting hoops and the women sitting around exchanging war stories about giving birth, and his video camera set up on a tripod, recording the whole thing. He'll provide liquor and soft drinks; his women friends will contribute roast pork and barbecued chicken. He's so restless waiting for the baby that planning the shower is a welcome diversion.

He went through Lamaze training with his first wife, but forgot how unbelievably boring it is. The classes entail a lot of repetitive videos, like the one where you see fifteen kids being born, the same thing over and over with different faces. Joe smuggled his transistor radio to last week's class so he could listen to the NCAA basketball championships; as soon as the Lamaze teacher turned her back, he whipped out his earphones. Another husband noticed and whispered to Joe that he wished he'd thought of the same thing. At halftime Joe signaled the score to the guy, and the teacher caught him. Joe felt like he was in junior high, being discovered with a comic book hidden inside a history text.

After class he apologized to the instructor. She was more sympathetic than the teachers in junior high. "I'm just sorry for you guys, having to be here," she said.

**SUNDAY, APRIL 8**
**Westchester**

OU'RE AN IDIOT," ALEX SCREAMS AT ROB AS SOON AS HIS EYE-lids flutter open this morning at 10:30, "and I'm an idiot for marrying you!" He hasn't been home before 1 A.M. all week, and his denim jacket has been lying on the couch in the den for days. On an affront scale of one to ten, Alex rates this about a two, but hanging up the jacket matters more to her than his vaunted trips to the supermarket. This is typical of men, she thinks. They prefer the heroic gesture—*Look what I did, I went out in the middle of the night to get you pistachio ice cream*—to the simpler one of putting their dirty clothes in the hamper.

Last week Alex flew to Pittsburgh, rented a car, stopped for canta-loupe, a boiled egg, and chocolate milk, and headed for her first ap-pointment, in Morgantown, West Virginia. It was a ninety-minute drive, and by the end of it she was nauseous. She pulled into the first McDonald's she spotted from the highway and rushed to the bath-room, where she rid herself of her breakfast. Then she went back to the car and checked her watch; she had time for a quick nap. She reclined the seat of her luxury car and locked the doors. Just as she closed her eyes, someone knocked on the window. It was a woman who had seen her in the restroom. Could she get Alex water, she asked, or call anyone for her? No, said Alex, thanking her profusely for her kindness.

It has taken pregnancy for Alex to appreciate other women. Every time one of her doctors tells her that throwing up constantly is just bad luck, she thinks, *Obstetrics would be a lot more advanced if men bore the children.*

AM'S NEW BOOK IS IN THE WINDOW OF SEVERAL STORES, AND today it is prominently and quite favorably covered in the *New York Times Book Review.* Tomorrow is the official publication date; Sam's day will be filled with television appearances. He's fine when the cameras are on him—his nerves turn to ice —but today he's apprehensive. He counters his pregame jitters by baking Irish soda bread, which he hopes will distract him. But the mixing and measuring don't relieve his fear that no matter how good the reviews are or how articulate he is on TV, no one will buy his book.

It occurs to him that he's unusually concerned about the book yet strangely calm about the baby. Whenever Juliet tells him a new horror story, like the recent episode on *L.A. Law* in which parents kill a premature baby who is born with a serious intestinal obstruction and no eyesight, Sam fails to find it relevant. He refuses to give a moment's thought to any of the catastrophes Juliet envisions, even though he knows the two of them are more at risk than the average expectant couple. Yet he had a dream the other night: Juliet was pregnant with a second child, conceived because her first died. Sam doesn't need to consult a psychiatrist to realize that his subconscious has transferred anxiety over the baby into anxiety over the book.

This morning, showering together, Sam and Juliet get into a discussion about the whole oedipal conflict thing. They agree that it's not a big deal if the kid wants to sleep in your bed with you or catches you naked. When their child is older, Sam thinks it's probably better to explain that he and Juliet want to have sex and simply close the bedroom door behind them than to say nothing and lock the kid out. Sam believes he was more obsessed with sex as an adolescent than he needed to be because his parents were extremely modest and avoided the subject. Juliet was raised in a far more relaxed household. She thinks it's silly for Sam to worry about these things when he's years away from having to.

HE ATMOSPHERE AT THE COENS' IS UNREMITTINGLY TENSE. Desiree is gone, and Sarah is up every two or three hours at night to feed Hannah; her fatigue is taking its toll on everyone. Ben's behavior, obviously reflecting the stress, is at a nadir, putting Sarah over the edge. Yesterday, when she bent down to kiss him goodnight, he punched her in the face, causing her glasses to fly off. Sarah reacted without thinking: she slapped him hard on the cheek. She had never hit him like that before and regrets it now. Still, she believes her reaction was justified, if overly aggressive. "No child," she told Michael, who was aghast, "is going to live in my house and get away with that stuff."

Hannah requires and Ben demands constant attention, but Michael and Sarah can't share the burden equally because Ben wants nothing to do with Sarah when Michael is in the house. When Michael holds Hannah on his lap, Ben wants to be there too. It seems to Michael that with two parents and two laps, he ought to be able to let Sarah take Hannah so he can be free for Ben. But Sarah is determined for Ben to learn that from now on his father's attention will be divided between him and his sister.

Michael is depressed. He can't concentrate during the day; at night he sleeps fitfully and wakes unrested. He feels powerless, unable to minimize the animosity between Ben and Sarah. His instinct is to protect his son, which only enrages his wife. Hannah is the only member of the household who seems to be thriving. Michael is thankful for that, but whenever he looks at his infant daughter he thinks of his mother. He wishes Margery could hold her, just once.

Sarah says that he's been so withdrawn he ought to see a therapist, but Michael is chary of talking to strangers; he can barely talk about private matters with people he knows well. He fantasizes about having a wife who is gentle and patient enough to coax his feelings out of him, but that's not the wife he has.

He knows Sarah is difficult, yet he loves her. She's his companion, the mother of his children, the person who orchestrates his life, and . . . *There must be other things,* he thinks. *I just can't remember them right now.*

**M**ARIA DRAGGED HERSELF HOME FROM WORK ON THURSDAY TO discover that the dog had had diarrhea all over the entryway and kitchen floor. Joe was at softball practice, so Maria mopped up the mess herself. In the middle of this revolting activity, Joe called to say he would be going directly from practice to the basketball court. "You just played softball; why do you have to play basketball now?" Maria said, more plaintively than she intended.

"I'm stiff. I've got to work out the kinks in my knees."

"Oh, go do what you have to do." Maria hung up and started sobbing. *I'm pregnant,* she thought. *I shouldn't have to be scrubbing dogshit off the floor.*

When Joe got home he asked her to massage his knees. "Forget it," she said. "Don't bug me." She stomped off to her sewing machine. Working on the jumpsuit she plans to wear home from the hospital, she attacked the pattern with a vengeance, knowing that Joe wants her to wear something else. He ridicules the casual, funky getups she favors, calling them her "Michael Jackson look."

When Maria finished sewing, she went to bed without ironing Joe's uniform or saying a word, though her mind was racing. All week long he has given her lame excuses for not being around. On Tuesday it was a favor for his supervisor; on Wednesday he had to pick up someone's car in the Bronx. When he got home from these mysterious errands, he was so tired that he fell asleep on the couch with his earphones on. If Maria didn't know him better, she would wonder if he was fooling around on her.

Joe couldn't defend himself against her long face and stony silences. He couldn't tell her the truth, that he wasn't home all week because he was organizing her shower. He didn't really play basketball on Thursday; after softball practice, he picked up the stork-shaped vanilla cake with cherry filling he had ordered and dropped it off at a friend's house. He couldn't wait for Maria to find out what he had really been up to.

Maria wakes this morning knowing that she has to take Cheryl to a friend's birthday party (Joe's ruse for getting her to the gym) and dreading it. Running around in her very pregnant state with a bunch of twelve-year-olds does not sound like a relaxing Saturday. Cheryl, who knows the real story, gleefully plays along, asking Maria's advice about what to buy the phantom birthday girl and what to write on the card. Maria dresses way down, which seems appropriate for the supposed event, in white maternity slacks and an orange blouse. She ties her hair in a ponytail without regard to straggly ends. Joe can't ask her to take more pains with her appearance or she'll suspect something.

Maria enters the gym at 5 P.M. with Cheryl and Joe flanking her. Seventy people throw water on her. *"Surprise!"* they shout. As the women lead her to a white wicker throne draped in white lace and bows, with a white ruffled umbrella perched over it, she feels deeply guilty about her snippy behavior with Joe.

Next to the throne is a wishing well draped in yellow and white crepe paper, filled with gifts. Maria opens about five of them, exclaiming over each, before Joe can be dragged away from the basketball game at the other end of the gym. Sweating, he sits next to Maria in a matching throne. The women tie elaborate beribboned bonnets on both their heads.

Joe drinks a Budweiser and performs for the video camera, pretending to suck his thumb and make wailing baby sounds, while Maria unwraps more presents. They get three different car seats, a highchair, a playpen, a portable crib and changing table, a walker, a couple of comforters—enough merchandise to fill the van Joe has cleverly rented for the occasion.

"Babe," Maria says anxiously to Joe afterward, "I've been such a bitch all week. I'm so sorry, I didn't know . . . This was such a great thing for you to do for me."

"Don't worry about it." Joe beams. He feels like a hero.

**F**OR THE FIRST TIME IN MONTHS, MICHAEL IS ALMOST LIGHT-hearted. His boss has stopped pressuring him to work longer hours, and there is less friction at home. After the slapping incident, Sarah has been gentler with Ben, and, reiterating the family therapist's warning that she and Michael need to be equal players in Ben's discipline, she has convinced Michael to be more assertive when the boy gets out of hand.

Yesterday morning, Hannah was cranky from gas and Michael was trying to comfort her. Bereft of his father's attention, Ben threw a tantrum, kicking and screaming and pounding the floor. Instead of giving Ben what he wanted, Michael ordered him, in an angry voice that surprised them both (and elicited an approving glance from Sarah), to go into his room and close the door. Unused to such firmness from his father, Ben complied. For the rest of the day he was a model child.

Last night Michael and Sarah went to the movies. They saw *Pretty Woman*. Sarah found it sexy, but Michael was sad, watching it. He cried during the scene in which Richard Gere's character talks about how he hadn't seen his father for fourteen years and now he's dead. *What were the questions* he *never asked?* Michael wondered, forgetting it was only a movie. The scene reminded him of his eighteenth birthday, when he sat with his mother in the living room of their Palm Beach house. "I look in the mirror now and I see I'm old, but I'm still looking through eighteen-year-old eyes," his mother had said that day. Michael wishes he had told her how good it was for him to hear her express such optimism about life. He wishes he had asked her if she still felt that way even as she lay dying.

Michael credits his mother for instilling him with a sense that the glass is half full and is sorry that Sarah sees it as half empty. *If Sarah had a mother like mine,* he thinks, *it might have made all the difference.*

AM HAD TO BE IN WASHINGTON OVER THE WEEKEND TO APPEAR ON a national news show as part of the publicity campaign for his book. With Bernstein's approval, Juliet went along, though she was nervous that she would go into labor and wind up in a strange hospital, especially after she and Sam made love Saturday morning and the belt recorded four contractions. A limo met them at the train station to transport them to the TV studio and picked them up later for the ride to the luxurious, all-expenses-paid hotel, where they ordered an extravagant room service dinner. Juliet had four contractions again that night.

Today she has a 10:45 appointment with Bernstein. After he examines her, she notices a glint in his eye, as if he is finally justified in his predictions. "Your cervix has flattened out quite a bit," he says. "It's eighty to ninety percent effaced. Time to go to bed." The effacement, he explains, could be caused by contractions or by the pressure of the baby's weight dilating the cervix; with DES women, the cervix is more susceptible to such passive dilation. He mentions the option of treating Juliet with ritodrine, a drug that relaxes the uterus, as a precautionary measure, but she rejects the idea. Ritodrine also stimulates the heart. If she has to lie in bed while her heart is racing, the impulse to get up and move around, she fears, will be intolerable.

Juliet tells herself she shouldn't be depressed, because she has gotten away with so much more activity than she thought she would, but she's depressed anyway. A producer for an educational TV station she once worked for called last week to hire her for a free-lance project; the first Lamaze class is scheduled for tonight; Sam's book party is next Monday; her thirty-sixth birthday is May 1—and she won't be able to participate in any of them. Sam has a publicity tour in California and another in Washington over the next two weeks, but when he learns about Bernstein's decree, he threatens to cancel the trips. He doesn't want Juliet to be alone if something happens, or even if something doesn't. As much as she wants his company, Juliet tells him to go ahead for the sake of his book.

They've chosen their daughter's name—Lily—but have done nothing to get ready for her. They haven't bought furniture or cleaned out the spare room that will be the nursery. When Juliet considers that without Lamaze training she'll go into labor and not know what to do, she starts crying.

She's been crying a lot these past two weeks, even before today's bad news. She often wakes up in tears, feeling desolation and loss. She hears in her head the refrain of a melancholy solo from *South Pacific,* sung by the male lead character: ". . . this promise of paradise, this nearly was mine . . ." She has always identified this musical with her childhood; her father is French, and so is the character who sings "This Nearly Was Mine." When Juliet was a little girl, in the days when her father still paid attention to her, he would often take her on his lap and croon "Dites-Moi," the playful song from the first act that the leading man sings to his children.

In London two years ago, Juliet and Sam went to a revival of *South Pacific.* When the orchestra struck up the first chords of "Dites-Moi," Juliet cried. She and Sam had just started trying to conceive, and she was struggling with the idea that having a child meant you were no longer one yourself. Her feeling now is similar: because she is pregnant, she will soon lose her youth forever. She mourns the years of freedom with Sam and berates herself for having accomplished so little while she had the chance.

Juliet hopes the sense of loss will recede in the face of greater gain once Lily is born. However, when that happens, she expects to feel bereft. Right now Lily gives her little trouble and much pleasure, making her feel complete, yet still somehow innocent.

**TUESDAY, APRIL 17**
**Southern Maryland**

RIN AND TOM PLANNED A COZY DINNER OUT TO CELEBRATE their eighth anniversary tonight, but Erin has to work late. Instead Tom makes dinner at home—chicken on the grill, salad, and strawberries. They sit outside on the deck, Erin with a Coke, Tom with a beer, and toast each other. It feels good to be married this long.

Their sanguine mood reflects the easing of stress in various areas. They decided to forget about trying to sell the house, at least for the moment; Erin's nausea has abated; the station has been running smoothly, so Tom can pay himself a salary again. They spent Easter Sunday with both sets of parents and the talk was all about the baby, which gave them a comforting feeling of solidarity and support. Tonight they realize something about adult life: it takes only the slightest shift in a positive direction to make you feel that things are much better than they were.

Tom presents Erin with a basket of spring flowers to commemmorate the anniversary. Erin gives him a card with a handwritten message: "This is the last anniversary when it will be just us." The sentiment reflects her continuing ambivalence, which Tom doesn't share. *Yeah,* he thinks, without reservation. *I'm looking forward to that.*

**THURSDAY, APRIL 19**
**Westchester**

OB CUTS HIS WORKDAY SHORT TO GO TO THE SUPERMARKET IN preparation for Alex's return from Toronto. He buys everything he imagines she might want to eat—hot dogs and lamb chops and steak and potatoes and imported chocolate wafer cookies. In the store he spots a man shopping with a cute little girl perched in the cart, and it occurs to him that he is no longer hoping for a son; he doesn't care what sex his baby is. One advantage to having a girl, he thinks, is she would be more likely to visit you when you're old. The disadvantage is that Alex very definitely wants a girl—she says she feels better equipped emotionally to mother someone of her own gender (despite her oft-stated preference for the company of men)—and if she gets one, Rob doubts he can convince her to have a second child.

Alex, meanwhile, endures a harrowing journey home from Toronto. Her flight to New York is delayed; her luggage is the last to come off the conveyor belt; she misses the car she booked to take her to Westchester. When she walks into the apartment several hours later than expected, Rob is eager to show her the amply stocked refrigerator. Alex shows mild interest in his purchase of dishwashing detergent but notices nothing else, swallows a lamb chop, and goes to bed at eleven. At one she throws up the lamb chop and moves onto the pull-out couch because of Rob's snoring.

Before falling asleep, she remembers the dream she had in Toronto: she woke up in her childhood room in her parents' house and reached down to touch the baby in her belly, but her belly was flat. She ran into her parents' bedroom. Her own crib from infancy was there against the wall; inside it was Alex's baby, who seemed to be a girl. The baby wore a cartoonish oval hat and an aqua outfit, and she was laughing. Alex's parents sat in bed watching the baby's antics and laughing with her. Alex sensed something wrong about her father's being there but didn't realize in the dream that he has been dead for eight years. He seemed utterly himself, a strong, warm man who laughed with every muscle in his face. Alex woke up smiling. It was the nicest dream she has ever had.

During her absence, Rob continued his grueling schedule—a full day at his office in New Jersey followed by a late night at the consulting job on Long Island. He didn't want to be home anyway. It was lonely there without Alex to yell at him, and he missed the Babies so much he felt a physical ache.

Last night he stopped at his mother's house to approve the inscription for the stone to be placed on his father's grave. His mother was stoical, but Rob cried. He couldn't stop thinking that a mere six months ago his father was there with them. Sitting in the living room of his parents' house, he recalled his father's acute sense of the unpredictable unfairness of life. *When death means you will never see your son become a father,* Rob thought, *it is the ultimate unfairness.*

JULIET, NOW ON BED REST, IS LIVING OUT HER QUEEN BEE FANTASY. She lies on the couch all day with a seltzer bottle filled with tap water, a jar of Tums, a cup of herbal tea, and a stack of books within reach. In her inactive state she is easily preoccupied by a new and troubling thought: what if her daughter doesn't like her?

She is aware that many people find her abrasive and difficult to get along with; she can be inflexible, intolerant, impatient—qualities basic to her personality. She knows a lot of mothers whose daughters can't stand them because their personalities don't mesh. *It's one thing to choose a husband or a friend,* she thinks, *but you can't choose your child, and your child can't choose you.* In the beginning, she knows, her daughter will need and want her, but as the years go by, will they wind up in family therapy because they can't get along? What if Lily prefers Sam?

A few years ago, Juliet's younger brother, David, told her that when they were kids he found her intimidating and very hard on him. David went on to detail a litany of bad feelings he accumulated over the years. Juliet had thought their relationship was mutually fulfilling and was jolted by what he said, though his tone was soft and reasonable. His criticism wasn't of her behavior or of any specific action she took or didn't take; she experienced it as an attack on her personality, her entire self. The revelations upset her in the way she imagines a woman would feel upon discovering that her husband has been cheating on her: all the while she was stupidly thinking everything was fine.

Friends have asked Juliet if she's nervous about labor, but she's more fearful about motherhood. Even if labor is horrible, it will end. *Pain doesn't kill, after all, and it's not the nineteenth century,* Juliet thinks. *Nobody dies anymore in childbirth.*

ARAH IS *PSYCHED*. MICHAEL PUT A NEW RÉSUMÉ TOGETHER—NO small accomplishment, she thinks, considering his defeatist attitude. He has always felt that no one would hire him for a top position without a college degree, though Sarah has told him often that experience counts for more than any diploma. But only when Michael saw an ad in Sunday's *Boston Globe* for a food-service job based in Boston that said "college degree preferred, but will look at experience over education" did he believe her. With surprising swiftness, he called the company that ran the ad. He has an interview scheduled for tomorrow.

Michael turned thirty-seven on April 22, which has a great deal to do with his aggressive pursuit of new employment. He realized he was edging close to forty having reached a professional dead end. He works for a company in which there is little opportunity for further advancement. He has put in ten years there and can't see staying for another twenty.

Sarah supports his efforts to move on for a variety of reasons, some of which are admittedly selfish. She would love to settle in Boston, where there's more cultural stimulation, more restaurants, more baby-sitters, better stores, and her friend Lauren. But she also thinks it would be good for Michael to realize he has options; he can tell the boss she loathes to fuck off and be all the better for it. She has advised Michael for years that the only way to make more money is to move around, but until now he insisted (falsely, she thinks) that he wanted to stay where he is.

Michael is basking in Sarah's praise for his decisiveness, but he's so nervous about the interview he has bitten off his fingernails.

**SUNDAY, APRIL 29**
**Manhattan**

HERE ARE FEW THINGS JULIET RESISTS AS MUCH AS BEING THE center of attention, but here she is, in apricot silk pants and a peach blouse, presiding over her baby shower before an audience of twenty assorted family members and friends. Still on bed rest, she doesn't move from the living room couch. Sam, who has trouble containing his impatience when not the center of attention, fidgets next to her.

Juliet's friend Donna, a magazine editor and the mother of two children, offers the first toast. "You've had your moment in the sun," she says to Sam, raising her champagne glass in his direction, "and it's over. No one will ask about you again, only about the baby." Next Juliet's mother, Felice, pays tribute to her daughter's "patience and good humor in conception and now in confinement." Like Juliet, Felice eschews cosmetics and wears her hair loose and unstyled. She is dressed in pants, a tank top, and black Reeboks. In contrast to her comical manner and casual appearance, Sam's mother is reserved and ladylike in a print dress and stockings, her hair neatly twisted into a bun.

After the gifts are opened, Sam regales the guests with anecdotes about his book party last week in Los Angeles, where many Hollywood celebrities turned up. He refrains, however, from describing the long flight home. Staring out the airplane window, he had fixated on one thought: if the plane crashed and he died, would Juliet name the baby Samantha, after him, instead of Lily? It was the first question he asked Juliet upon his return. To his dismay, her answer was no.

N THURSDAY, ALEX SAW YET ANOTHER DOCTOR IN CARL'S practice, Frank Lindeman, who told her that the baby weighs about three and a half pounds, large enough to survive if she gives birth prematurely. Alex described her continuing nausea, as she has to each of the doctors. She expected him to say what everyone else has: there's nothing to be done about it. Instead he suggested that she stop taking her prenatal vitamins for five days. The vitamins contain iron, which makes some women sick. Alex was perturbed that none of the other doctors had made this connection. Lindeman also explained that the recurrent stabbing pain in her groin is caused by the cord of muscle that extends from the sides of her belly into her groin. Throughout pregnancy, he said, women can feel anything from an electrical jolt to a charley horse anywhere from their navel to their knees.

When Rob takes Alex to the airport today, she jumps out of the car and starts lifting her luggage out of the trunk. Her insistence on maintaining an "I'm pregnant but so what" attitude disturbs him—he's afraid she will endanger herself or the baby—but it is also amusing because it's *so Alex*. Before he has a chance to dissuade her, a skycap rushes over. "You're pregnant," he says. "You shouldn't be doing that." He grabs the bag from her.

*Good,* Rob reflects, *let someone else argue with her for once,* though he worries that people are looking at him and thinking, *Schmuck, why are you letting your pregnant wife carry her own luggage?* The truth is, he can't control her.

ARIA DRIVES HOME ON THE LONG ISLAND EXPRESSWAY WITH shooting pains in her groin and cramping in her stomach. Her fingers are so swollen she can't wear her wedding band. Still convinced she'll deliver early, she is tearing through the final preparations—getting things organized at work for her temporary replacement, cleaning the apartment, editing her list of baby names, and choosing homecoming clothes feminine enough to satisfy Joe. (She finally agreed to wear a blue-and-white-striped sleeveless cotton dress in place of the jumpsuit she was making.)

Maria reaches her building at five. She opens the door of the apartment and groans at the clutter. Baby paraphernalia is piled against one wall of the living room, blocking access to the dining table. In the bedroom, the new dresser is filled with layette items; the crib is there but is still not assembled. Maria thinks it's bad luck to put it together before the baby is born.

Joe, who has been in the basement retrieving laundry, enters the bedroom with a pile of clothes in his arms. Two of his fingers, sprained during a recent basketball game, are taped together. He wears a *Top Gun* T-shirt, and a beeper is attached to the waistband of his black denim jeans in case Maria goes into labor while he can't be reached by phone. He drops the clothes on the bed and fingers the hem of Maria's homecoming dress hanging nearby. "You have to look good," he says. Maria rolls her eyes.

A friend of his, Joe tells Maria, got him a ticket to the Knicks-Celtics game at Madison Square Garden next Wednesday.

"That means you'll come home with a sore throat from yelling, and you'll be exhausted the next day," Maria says.

"Why don't you come?" Joe counters. "If you give birth at the Garden, I bet they'd give us free season tickets."

"I'm sure we're having a boy, but last night I dreamed it was a girl," she says. "I was sitting down, and the baby pushed against my belly. I saw an imprint of her face on my skin. She came out, and she had a lot of hair and a pink barrette."

"Well, I dreamed I was playing basketball and telling the guys I had a boy. I guess it's just wishful thinking."

They've agreed to hire Maria's sister-in-law, Tracy, to care for the baby at her home during the week. Maria isn't completely happy with this solution; Tracy is a chain smoker, has thyroid problems, and is often sick. Joe thinks the most important thing is that she's part of the family; he doesn't trust strangers. He wishes Maria could stay home, and she agrees, but they can't afford it.

*So be it,* thinks Maria.

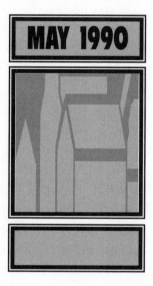

**MAY 1990**

**WEDNESDAY, MAY 2**
**Southern Maryland**

 OM CLUTCHES ERIN'S HAND, LISTENING INTENTLY TO THE SOUND of his baby's heartbeat, staring at the fetal heart monitor as the obstetrician moves it over Erin's uterus. He can remember feeling this degree of elation only once before in his life—the morning of February 20, when Erin announced she was pregnant. He marvels at the sheer technology of this moment and can't stop thinking of unromantic analogies to auto mechanics.

Afterward, the doctor mentions her concern over Erin's weight; the scale registers a two-pound loss, making a total of seven. The doctor orders a sonogram to determine whether the baby is growing properly, though she tells them reassuringly that Erin's uterus is the right size for this stage of pregnancy. Tom, who usually doesn't fret about things beyond his control, is deeply concerned. Hearing the heartbeat makes the pregnancy real to him, and fraught with danger. Erin, who usually worries about everything, is untroubled. Her weight loss, she thinks, is connected to her prepregnancy diet and the better eating habits it induced, and she attributes her feeling of tranquility to the unusual amount of attention Tom has recently lavished on her.

He took both days off last weekend, a singular event, and made no plans: "I want to be with you," he said. On one of the days they went out on the powerboat and dropped anchor in their favorite cove. They devoured a picnic of chicken and potato salad and talked about the baby, Erin's office merger, and their respective families, rehashing events large and small of the past month—a luxury they rarely have time for. Then they were quiet, their thoughts drifting with the waves. Later they agreed that those few hours of pacific companionship were exactly what they needed to armor themselves against the stress of daily life.

*I ought to get a normal job,* Tom reflected. *This must be what normal people do. They spend their weekends relaxing.*

**WEDNESDAY, MAY 2**
**Cape Cod**

ICHAEL'S INTERVIEW IN BOSTON WENT OKAY, THOUGH HE HAD second thoughts about the job when he was shown the office in which he would be working, a small basement room—a cubbyhole compared to what he's used to. Before the meeting, Sarah coached him about how to handle the salary question: "Don't name a figure before getting a sense of what they're willing to pay, and don't underprice yourself." But Michael doesn't think straight when he's nervous and managed to do the opposite on both counts. He thinks he'll be called back for a second meeting and tells himself that just getting his résumé together and practicing his interview skills was worth the trip to Boston. Nonetheless, he feels deflated and is more withdrawn than usual.

"I spend the day with an uncommunicative infant," Sarah complains. "When you get home, I want to talk, but you won't say anything."

"I bust my ass at work," Michael says. "At home, I want to veg out."

"It's not that simple. You've been unapproachable since your mother died. It would help you to talk about it."

"You wouldn't understand."

"That's not true. I know what it's like to watch someone you love die. I went through it with my grandmother, remember? That was three years ago, and I still miss her." Sarah pauses, feeling a rush of sympathy for Michael. "Don't shut down," she implores him. "That makes it worse."

Michael says nothing.

**FRIDAY, MAY 4**
**Manhattan**

T HE SURFACE OF SAM'S DESK AT THE LAW FIRM IS ARRANGED JUST so, reminiscent of the household in which he was raised, where nothing was ever out of place. He remembers the first time he walked into the apartment in which Juliet grew up, where two dogs were yapping maniacally and piles of clothes, books, and papers cluttered every available surface. It took many years and a great deal of bickering before he and Juliet reached a reasonable compromise between her slothfulness and his insistence on order.

With a new and far less manageable source of chaos about to enter his life, Sam has worried intermittently that this old marital conflict will reassert itself. But as he reflects on an incident that occurred during Juliet's baby shower, he feels newly confident. One of the guests' kids, a four-year-old girl, grabbed a piece of chocolate cake and stomped it into the living room rug. At first Sam blanched, but then he decided it wasn't a tragedy and laughed it off. He hopes he'll be equally tolerant of his daughter. Now he fears his biggest problem will be overinvolvement. Where, he wonders, is the line between maintaining a constant interest in your child and being controlling?

**FRIDAY, MAY 4**
**Queens**

AT MARIA'S APPOINTMENT ON TUESDAY, DR. SPIEGEL TEASINGLY presented her with an ideal labor scenario: "Begin contractions around 5 P.M. on Sunday. Come in to the hospital at five Monday morning, four centimeters dilated. By seven I'll be done with my rounds and you'll be further along. By ten I'll deliver you. I'll still have time for my regular patients and I'll get a good night's sleep." He told her not to go into labor on any of the next three Fridays because he won't be on call those weekends. "Very funny," said Maria.

Joe is upset that Spiegel might not be the doctor who delivers the baby. He doesn't understand why Maria can't just tell him to come in, even if he's not on call. Joe is certain she's about to go into labor any second; he almost gave up his ticket to the Knicks game tonight to stay home. It was the first time Maria had to urge him to go to a game.

She has stopped trying to choose a girl's name because she is certain she's having a boy. She and Joe have agreed to name him either Luis Joseph or Joseph Luis, to be called Luis. Her bag is packed with the blue-and-white dress, two nightgowns in different colors—so that each night Joe visits her in the hospital she'll be wearing something new— and white sandals. (Maria's choice was pink Keds, but Joe hates the look of sneakers with a dress.) Still, the apartment is not clean enough for Maria to sit down without feeling anxious. If she goes into labor and comes home to the place in its current state, she knows it will depress her more than any amount of postpartum blues.

She has had a lot of cramping and her blood pressure is low. Spiegel thinks the drop in pressure is due to dehydration; drink more water, he advised. Maria does whatever he tells her to. She wants to get on with it. She wants to bring her baby home.

HE WOMEN IN BERNSTEIN'S WAITING ROOM CHATTER ABOUT talk-show hostess Kathie Lee Gifford's return to television after maternity leave (skinny as ever, everyone complains, after only six weeks.) You'd have to be pregnant to know or care about Kathie Lee's travails through gestation, labor, delivery, and now breastfeeding and sleep deprivation. Certainly Juliet, whose taste in television runs more to *Nightline,* would have dismissed perky Kathie Lee in days past, but now she is grateful that the show happens to be on during the hour in which she monitors her contractions.

She was outraged by the prudish and judgmental conduct of child-care guru T. Berry Brazelton, a guest on Monday's show. Poor Kathie Lee described how she developed mastitis, a painful infection of the breast, and had to give up nursing. Brazelton interrupted her to say that many women persevere despite the infection. When Kathie Lee protested—"It was just too painful; my nipples were *like this"*—and tried to show what she meant with her hands, Brazelton sucked in his breath as if he found her demonstration offensive. Juliet crossed all books by Brazelton off her postpartum reading list.

She can't help identifying with Kathie Lee; Juliet is so anxious to nurse that she fears something will prevent her from it. Soon after Brazelton's appearance, she dreamed she was in the middle of a murder mystery in which children were scattering body parts, most notably pieces of nipples.

Juliet also learns today, from listening in on conversations in the waiting room, that the odds of getting Bernstein to deliver her baby are slim. She doesn't think it matters who does it, as long as the delivery is vaginal. But if she has to have a cesarean, it will be frightening to be cut open by someone she has never met.

ARAH'S TUBAL LIGATION WAS PERFORMED YESTERDAY IN PLYM-
outh, at the same hospital where her children were born. She
refused anesthesia until she saw her doctor in the room—she
wanted to make sure that no other surgeon would substitute
for him without her knowledge. Her doctor appeared as she de-
manded. The last thing she remembers hearing before losing consciousness was him saying, "You are a pain in the ass."

Michael was beside her in the recovery room when she woke up,
and he brought her home. For the past twenty-four hours he has taken
care of both kids, made the meals, and done the laundry, while Sarah
lies helplessly in bed. She feels blessed that he is her husband.

Her incisions, one above her pubic hair and the other through her
navel, are more painful than she expected, but the freedom she now
feels is ample compensation. She was told not to have intercourse until
she stops bleeding from the surgery, in two or three weeks; after that,
she told Michael, they can have sex every night if he wants.

Her session with Ben and the family therapist a few days before the
ligation was edifying. The therapist placed Sarah in a chair in the back
of the room so Ben could interact with him as if she weren't there. He
drew a picture of a boy with a sad face. "What makes you sad?" he
asked Ben.

"When Mommy spanks me. But I know when Mommy spanks me,
she still loves me."

"Why do you get spanked?" the therapist questioned.

"Because I don't want to get dressed." Ben turned to face Sarah.
"Right, Mommy?" Sarah nodded, thinking, *He understands more than I
give him credit for.* She feels that she and Ben have begun to comprehend
each other for the first time.

At this moment, lying in her king-size bed with a spring breeze
wafting through the window and a belly button swollen to three times
its normal size, Sarah concludes that having her tubes tied has done
wonders for her outlook.

LEX NEVER BUYS WOMEN'S MAGAZINES, SINCE SHE CONSIDERS them vacuous, but she sometimes reads them on airplanes, where they are supplied for passengers. En route from Toledo to Pittsburgh today, she scans an article in *Glamour* about how to treat your man. The piece says that in his twenties a man wants a wide variety of sex; in his thirties, he looks for reassurance that he can still conquer the world; in his forties, he realizes his time is valuable and he must learn his limits. Rob's behavior, Alex deduces from the article, is typical of his age group—he works ungodly hours and will not listen when she tries to talk sense to him. Since all he has done with the consulting job is lower his hourly rate by putting in twice as much time as he contracted for, Alex has advised him to go back to the company and tell them to hire more personnel, increase his salary, or lower their expectations. "It's not the right time," Rob keeps saying.

She thinks of the crack in his car windshield, which he hasn't gotten around to fixing in two months; his tiny office at home, such a mess that his shoulders tense when he enters it; the wad of toll receipts sitting for weeks on top of the toilet bowl in the second bathroom, the one he uses. Alex used to clean it, but the day she noticed the toll receipts she thought, *Why am I bothering?* They have two bathrooms, after all. She shut the door and hasn't entered it since.

ARAH'S DOCTOR REMOVES HER STITCHES AND PRONOUNCES HER ready for sex. "I think I'll tell my husband we can't do it for another few weeks," she says. The doctor laughs. "I don't want to get in the middle of *that,*" he says. He assures her that she can't get pregnant, but Sarah finds it incredible that after only ten days she can be completely healed with no chance of conceiving.

If not for fear of pregnancy and the restrictions two children place on spontaneity, Sarah would welcome sex. She misses Michael's tender lovemaking. And since he has been so uncommunicative, she misses him in general.

Michael finally wrote to the company in Boston asking about the status of his job application. The letter elicited a return phone call. He was told that no decision had been made, though the company was considering reinstating the person who was supposed to vacate the position. It wasn't a blanket rejection, but he no longer feels hopeful.

He puts their house on the market. Summer is the big selling season on the Cape, and if he can get $225,000 or better, he'll take it. Sarah is enthusiastic, as she is for any action that preserves the sense that her life is not at a standstill.

**MONDAY, MAY 14**
**Westchester**

 HE FILMS ROB SEES TONIGHT AT THE FIRST LAMAZE CLASS CON-firm his view that vaginal birth is not only unnatural but anatomically impossible. The huge head, the tiny birth canal, the gyrations—he can't imagine that the FDA would approve God's idea of childbirth. "The conception part seems okay, Lord," he can hear the FDA man saying, "but do you really want to pass a twenty-one-inch-long, nine-pound object through a ten-centimeter opening?" And God would answer, "Hey, I've been up for six days. I'm taking tomorrow off. I'm not working on this thing anymore."

Alex has a vaginal infection and is dismayed that it means no sex for a while. Rob, however, is relieved. Intercourse has come to seem strangely isolating, as if he is in one corner of the room and Alex is in the other, a thick wad of flesh separating them. Rob pictures the baby getting crushed, like those old horror movies when someone's imprisoned in a room and the walls move in.

The last time they made love, Alex was physically uncomfortable and Rob was distracted by thoughts of the baby being flattened. Afterward, he said, amusing Alex, "Can you believe this used to be our reason for *living*?"

**TUESDAY, MAY 15**
**Queens**

EX IS BECOMING A PROBLEM FOR JOE. DURING INTERCOURSE HE thinks of the baby; with each thrust he fears his penis will strike its head and hurt it. *If I'm going to get this scared,* he thinks, *it's not worth it.*

A female colleague who had a baby a few months ago confided in Joe that since the birth, her husband will not make love to her or even talk to her. Only the baby interests him. Joe told Maria the story; her reaction, which seemed paranoid, surprised him. "What are you trying to tell me?" she said. He hastened to say he's sure his coworker's problem is irrelevant to them.

Joe has revised his opinion about Maria's going into labor early, but this morning he urges her to quit work immediately instead of on Friday as scheduled. He wants her to rest. Her hands are numb, her legs are tired, she says she can't wait to go on leave, but every time Joe says, "Just do it already, what's another day or two going to matter?" she ignores him. She promised her employers she'd stay until the eighteenth, and Maria does what she says she will.

Joe is a happy man. Lamaze is over; he won't have to sacrifice any more Knicks playoff games unless Maria gives birth on one of those nights. He's about to receive another incentive award from the postal service. And for the rest of his life, he'll celebrate throughout the month of May: Mother's Day, Maria's birthday, and, he hopes, the arrival of his child.

**TUESDAY, MAY 15**
**Manhattan**

ULIET SAFELY PASSES THE THIRTY-THIRD WEEK OF PREGNANCY. Bernstein says she can now be as active as she wants, except for sex. "It would be best to hold off until you're at thirty-six weeks," he tells her. "After that, assuming you're not dilated, it's okay."

Juliet remembers the story of one of Sam's coworkers, a woman who had a cervical stitch and took ritodrine to prevent premature labor. She made it to term. At her final prenatal appointment, her doctor loosened the stitch so her cervix would open when labor began. He told her to go home and have sex with her husband. She did, and immediately went into labor. If the onset of labor can be controlled to that extent, Juliet thinks she and Sam should make love on Saturday morning, June 2. She'll be in her thirty-eighth week, her mother will be in town, and, most important, Bernstein will be on call. They could leave for the island a month later and stay through the end of September. (Sam plans to take three months off.)

During the private Lamaze session at home last night, Juliet made detailed notes on how to evaluate the color of her water when it breaks; the various stages of labor; which entrance of the hospital to go to and what to bring; the types of pain medication available. As the teacher spoke and Juliet scribbled, Sam wondered what will happen if she goes into labor at nine o'clock on a weekday morning, when it's impossible to get a cab in their neighborhood. Does he call the police? An ambulance? Assuring swift transportation to the hospital, he decided, seems to be one of the few things a husband can offer.

Sam can't make sense of Juliet's often-voiced fear that he and Lily will somehow leave her by the wayside. His relationship with Juliet has always been based on a great deal of interaction, and Lily, in his view, will be just one more thing to interact over. Nor is he concerned that motherhood will leave his wife with no emotional energy for him. He doubts she can get everything she needs from a baby. The one danger,

Sam thinks, is that they will both become so wrapped up in family life they won't maintain connections outside of it.

They've bought a stroller, a car seat, a changing table, and a rocking chair, and they're interviewing a pediatrician next week. They're as ready as they'll ever be.

**SUNDAY, MAY 20**
**Westchester**

ATCHING ALEX INDULGE IN A HOUSE-CLEANING FRENZY, ROB assumes it's part of the "nesting instinct" that supposedly seizes women near term. He wishes he had a similar technique for gaining control over his environment. If he did, maybe he wouldn't worry about things like the umbilical cord becoming wrapped around the baby's neck. Alex has a first cousin whose infant died that way.

This morning Rob takes a walk and sees a dead chick lying in the road; later in the day he drives past a hearse. Both encounters make him fear for his unborn child. Alex refuses to make such morbid associations. "Nothing can go wrong with the pregnancy at this point," she says.

But Alex's dream life is less rational. Recently she had a nightmare about Jennie, her best friend from childhood, who committed suicide by throwing herself in front of a train three months after giving birth. People attributed her death to postpartum depression, but looking back, Alex thinks that signs of disturbance in Jennie were present when they were teenagers. They used to walk home from school together on a route that took them over a highway. When they got to midpoint on the overpass, where the roar of the traffic below was at its loudest, Jennie would scream with abandon. Alex sometimes screamed with her, just to be companionable, but always felt silly doing it. She still remembers the exultant look in Jennie's eyes.

Alex thinks about Jennie often these days, but doesn't consider her fate personally relevant. Alex feels immune to the combination of unlucky hormones and skewed outlook on life that, she guesses, must have led to Jennie's suicide.

ANNAH'S NAMING CEREMONY YESTERDAY, A RELATIVELY RE-cent innovation for Jewish baby girls meant to parallel the briss ritual for boys, was chaotic. Ben clung to Michael; Lauren's son screamed to sit on her lap while Lauren, acting as Hannah's godparent, was holding Hannah. Afterward Sarah served mimosas and bagels, cream cheese, and smoked salmon. As she predicted, her relatives gobbled up the fish. "WASPs," she told Michael, "consider smoked salmon exotic."

Michael has decided that if he is offered the Boston job, which seems increasingly unlikely, he will turn it down. He didn't like the basement office and thinks his current position offers more autonomy. Sarah approved of his decision to send his résumé out to Boston headhunters.

They had sex last night for the first time in months. Sarah feared it would hurt after such a long abstinence, but it didn't, and not having to worry about birth control made her feel more relaxed, more romantic. Later they cuddled and whispered and fell asleep in the same bed. This afternoon, Michael sends Sarah twenty-four long-stemmed red roses.

Tonight he comes home to what feels like a very good dream. Instead of his usual frantic cooking after a nine-hour workday, with a whining toddler, a screaming baby, and a complaining wife nipping at him, he is greeted by Sarah's neatly set table and fully prepared meal. *Other men,* Michael realizes, *must take such things for granted.*

ARLY YESTERDAY MORNING, MARIA'S FIRST DAY OF FREEDOM from work, Joe's car was stolen. Instead of getting last-minute prebaby errands out of the way, Maria spent the day with Joe dealing with the police and the Department of Motor Vehicles. Today she goes into the city and waits an hour to see Dr. Spiegel. She learns that she is 60 percent effaced but not dilated. If she hasn't gone into labor by early next week, Spiegel will perform a fetal stress test. Concerned because Spiegel won't be on call this coming weekend, Maria tries to get Joe to make love to her this afternoon to bring on labor. He begs off. He has a bad headache, he says, and is depressed about the car theft.

Later he snaps at her for forgetting to take meat out of the freezer for dinner. "You're going to be a housewife, you're going to be taking care of a kid," he tells her. "You've got to remember these things."

"Just because I have a kid doesn't mean I'm going to cook every night." Maria is offended by the implication that she'll have nothing else to do while on maternity leave.

Joe apologizes, blaming his outburst on due-date jitters. When the countdown gets to zero, his coworkers tell him, it drives you crazy.

ODAY BERNSTEIN SAYS THAT SAM AND JULIET'S BABY IS "READY to go," but he won't predict when labor will start. "If you go past your due date after all my warnings about premature labor," he tells Juliet, "I'll be mortified."

Juliet and Sam traveled up the Hudson River last weekend to attend an outdoor benefit for one of Sam's pet causes. It was Juliet's first venture out of Manhattan since going to Egypt in December. The weather was perfect and everyone was dancing, including Juliet and

Sam. People said to her, "My God, it must be a really big baby," but Juliet, who has gained close to forty pounds, didn't feel self-conscious. She was amused to approach a group of people and watch them part for her from twenty feet away, as if they saw this huge whale coming. "When I was eight months pregnant I felt so ugly," her friend Donna told her later. "I wanted to hide from the world, and you're *dancing* in front of it."

Juliet is regularly recording five contractions and thinks she may be close to labor. She would like one more week to practice her Lamaze breathing, but it's not necessary. Sam says he knows the exercises by heart, and Bernstein estimates Lily's weight at six and a half pounds. It can happen tonight or two weeks from now; either way, Lily will be fine.

Following the Lamaze teacher's instruction to bring evocative pictures to the labor room—"focal points" to stare at and help manage the pain during contractions—Juliet goes out today to buy some art postcards. She selects fluid landscapes by Matisse and Gauguin that project serenity, and scenes involving mothers and daughters in loving embrace. One card depicts St. Francis receiving stigmata from an angel. This especially attracts Juliet, for reasons she does not understand.

### FRIDAY, MAY 25
### Southern Maryland

I T'S THE START OF THE MEMORIAL DAY WEEKEND, A SLOW DAY AT work. Erin takes a real lunch break—a brief walk followed by iced tea, a chicken sandwich, and French fries at a restaurant near her office. She wears a black-and-white checked suit from her prediet "fat closet." At nineteen weeks she still isn't showing, but her postdiet clothes are tight and her maternity clothes look wrong because she doesn't have a real belly yet. She thinks she looks hideous and is especially dismayed by her expanding bustline.

With school out for the summer, she wakes at seven instead of six and has time to watch *Good Morning, America*. But the leisure hasn't calmed her roiling emotions. Tom's hours have again lengthened. His excitement over the pregnancy reassures her of his love, but his prolonged absences make her edgy. She looks forward to her sister Molly's visit tomorrow, a workday for Tom. Erin thinks of Molly, thirteen years her senior, as her surrogate mother. ("Great," Molly said when she learned Erin was pregnant. "I'm going to be a grandma.") Molly offered to be in the labor room with Erin and Tom, but Erin declined. She wants to share the experience with just her husband.

At work, she feels devalued and dispensable; the new management's attitude seems to be *If you don't like it, quit.* She wonders if she's the only one who feels that way. Is it just that she's pregnant and prone to exaggerate things even more than usual? But there are such silly new rules, like getting docked for pay if you're ten minutes late. Her boss has often remarked that it's terrible how some women go on maternity leave with no intention of returning yet say nothing until they've collected their benefits. Erin once agreed that that was unconscionable, but now she's tempted to do the same thing.

Tom's dominant concern at the moment is Erin. Almost every night this week he has come home to find her crying about work. He fears that her misery is hurting the baby. Erin, he knows, is not a quitter, but he doesn't think any job is worth this much anguish. He tells her that if she continues to suffer like this, he will tell her employers she's leaving, and to hell with her benefits.

**TUESDAY, MAY 29**
**Westchester**

 OB PAYS HIS FIRST—AND, ALEX SAYS, HIS LAST—VISIT TO ONE of her doctors. Carl turns out to be the lucky fellow. Rob ignores Alex's warning ("This is the guy who's going to do the episiotomy, so we want him on our side") and becomes combative. "Do you think the vitamins made her sick?" he asks Carl. Alex knows Rob wants an outright apology from Carl for ignoring her nausea; she thinks this is not only undiplomatic but beside the point. "I think the pregnancy made her sick," Carl hedges, "but the vitamins probably didn't help."

Alex quickly changes the subject to pain medication. The Lamaze instructor said that you can't get an epidural if you're too far along in labor; she doesn't want Carl to wait until it's too late. "Don't worry," Carl says, "we'll make you as comfortable as possible." Rob interprets this to mean that Alex can have whatever she wants; Alex thinks Carl evaded her question.

On Sunday a prospective buyer was scheduled to arrive at noon to see the condo, which Rob and Alex have recently put on the market. Rob got home from work at four in the morning and was still asleep at eleven. Alex literally threw icewater on him. She wanted him to clean his messy work station. The buyer came early, and the first room he wanted to see was Rob's cubicle, still a wreck. Later Rob spent an hour in there, accomplishing nothing. When Alex checked on him and found him playing a computer game, she threatened to go on a hunger strike. Rob responded by shoving a piece of paper under her nose. It was a song he wrote for her when they were courting, set to the music from *Annie;* it's about what he will do around the house *tomorrow, tomorrow, tomorrow.* Alex had to smile. *How can I be pissed at this person?* she thought. *He's not malicious; he truly believes nothing is important enough to change until . . . tomorrow.*

Last week Alex completed her final trip until September. It will be her longest hiatus from business traveling since she was twenty-one, and it feels strange. She arrived in downtown Jacksonville and was greeted by a large sign mounted in the lobby of her client's office building. "Welcome, Alex della Croce—Big Mama," it read. Alex was moved by the client's thoughtfulness, but when the client mentioned during a conversation about health habits that he knows four people under the age of forty-five who had major heart attacks recently, she felt panic. She doesn't want Rob to die.

**WEDNESDAY, MAY 30**
**Manhattan**

WO MONTHS WITHOUT SEX (NOT COUNTING MASTURBATION): it's the longest Sam has gone in twenty years. Friends tell him the more pregnant your wife gets, the better other women look. This hasn't been true for him.

He finally had a full physical exam. There was no sign of heart disease, but the doctor said that given his family history, he should have a checkup every year.

At work, Sam is in a holding pattern, which makes him anxious. The promotional activity centered on his book is over. There's no point in taking on a new case or cause because he plans a three-month leave. This calculated winding down of his professional life makes him fear that he'll never be able to plug back into it. He is by nature methodical, a man who sets goals, reaches them, and sets new ones. Now he has none ahead of him. He keeps thinking, *Let's get on with it.*

**WEDNESDAY, MAY 30**
**Westchester**

OB ADMIRES HIS WIFE, WHO LIES FETCHINGLY ON THE CREAM leather couch wearing a blue robe, her red nails adding a vivid touch. The tableau is graceful and harmonious, words he could never apply to his own saturnine frame of mind. He sold nothing this week, and he is frightened.

He has always been burdened by an excess of empathy, which makes him see the other guy's point of view too readily, at his own expense. And he is both tormented and bolstered by the certainty that he was meant for something better. Rob wants what money can buy—the best ski gear, a state-of-the-art stroller for his child, a four-bedroom Colonial in a classy neighborhood. But doing what he has to do to make that money is odious to him.

Alex believes that the point of working is to earn a paycheck, not self-fulfillment. Rob is convinced this attitude frees her to enjoy what she does and to be successful at it, a combination that eludes him. She expects nothing except financial reward; he expects everything else. It depresses him that people don't care if he's smart or if he can make them laugh, only how many dead presidents are in his pocket.

When he was younger, much younger, and still thought he was destined for great things, he assumed he would achieve without trying to. In those days he identified with McMurphy in Ken Kesey's novel *One Flew Over the Cuckoo's Nest,* a poetically iconoclastic character who was exempted, by virtue of his specialness, from the quotidian grind, from dotting the *i*'s and crossing the *t*'s. But now Rob sees himself as Willy Loman—*a sad sack, a schlepper.*

Rob doesn't need Alex to tell him he should quit smoking and lose weight. He's worried about having a heart attack, he really is, but keeps forgetting to do anything about it. He wakes in the morning with every good intention. Then he gets bored while driving to a client's office, or nervous just before a pitch, and lights up a cigarette or stuffs himself with food or both.

Alex warns that she'll have his tombstone engraved (in Arabic!) with this message: *Here lies a schmuck.* She promises to raise her fatherless child in an atmosphere devoid of classical music, literature, art—any of the influences Rob thinks essential for the prevention of idiocy. Beneath her threats, he knows, is real concern, and he is touched by it. He'll shape up. Tomorrow.

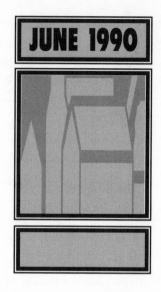

**FRIDAY, JUNE 1**
**Queens**

*ES, I'M STILL HERE.* MARIA IS SICK OF SAYING THAT TO ALL THE people who call expecting to hear a newborn gurgling in the background. She has dragged herself through every shopping mall in Queens hoping to jostle the baby out of its seemingly locked position. She feels as if she'll be pregnant forever and is furious with herself for going on maternity leave too early. If she had waited, she'd have three more weeks' pay now, and three more weeks to be with the baby on the other end.

Spiegel's exam on Tuesday revealed little progress, but he didn't suggest inducing her. Maria was relieved; she heard that contractions stimulated by Pitocin are more painful than natural ones, and still hopes, for the sake of Joe and the baby, to get through the birth without drugs.

On Wednesday her mother arrived from Puerto Rico. Maria's sense of humor hasn't totally left her—she was able to laugh about worrying that her mother would miss the birth. Now she fears that her mother will return home without seeing her grandchild.

Joe tries to amuse himself by following Maria around with his video camera, filming her last days of pregnancy, but gets upset when she won't clown around. Last night he forced her to walk with him through the neighborhood for hours. Later, hoping to bring on labor, they had sex—another exercise in futility.

### FRIDAY, JUNE 1
### Manhattan

J ULIET PACKS UP HER BELT THIS MORNING AND SAYS GOODBYE TO the obstetrical nurse who interpreted her numbers and counseled her whenever she needed it. When she hangs up the phone, she feels sad. *Now I'm like everybody else,* she reflects. *There will be no belt to tell me when I'm going into labor.*

She and Sam toured the hospital Wednesday night. Juliet thought the labor and delivery rooms resembled torture chambers. She was distressed when she asked what the nursing staff does to comfort a crying baby. "We ignore it," she was told, "unless it's very prolonged. Then we give a bottle of water." Juliet's books say newborns should be held immediately; instead, it sounds like they're abandoned.

The lack of physical self-consciousness that characterized most of Juliet's pregnancy has suddenly turned to disgust. She looks at her expanding hips and thighs and thinks, *My God.* When her weight hit 170, she instructed Sam to stop her if she seems to be eating too much. But when she asked for ice cream the other day and he started to tease her about it in front of friends, she bridled. "Get off my back," she told him.

Sam has a desperate urge to sample every cuisine and see every movie in New York because he's afraid it's his last chance. He and Juliet have been out every night this week, indulging in Indian food and Italian food and southwestern food, followed by one mediocre film after another. They had sex last weekend at Sam's urging (he pointed out that Bernstein was on call), but Juliet found it painful, awkward, and quite unproductive in terms of stimulating labor. As for Sam . . . he prides himself on not being, as he puts it, an insensitive male boob. If Juliet doesn't have a good time, well, he doesn't either.

S ALEX WALKS DOWN THE STREET TODAY WEARING SNUG WHITE leggings, she hears a car approaching slowly from behind, and then an unmistakable wolf whistle. She turns her head as the car passes to see three young men ogling her. She wishes fervently for a photograph of their faces the moment they realize she is a very pregnant matron. She enjoys the encounter and wastes no time telling Rob about it.

Rob is sure he'll be fired any minute; his sales record has been abysmal lately. His conviction, Alex thinks, is an expression of desire. Somehow he *wants* to be fired—he thinks it will release him from misery.

"It's no wonder you're not selling," Alex commented yesterday when he arrived home at 6:30 A.M. after working all night at his consulting job. "You start out every week in your main job exhausted. Don't you realize it has to affect your performance?" She threatened to call Rob's second employer herself and announce that he's quitting. But in Rob's current state, dominated by his vision of a sad-eyed, starving baby, with the word *failure* hammering against his brain, he feels too insecure to give up the income.

Alex has a hammering pain of her own, although hers is in her uterus. Carl says it's false labor. If the pain is rhythmic, he explains, it is the real thing; if it is severe and incessant, accompanied by a rock-hard stomach, it signifies an abruption, in which the placenta detaches prematurely from the uterus, dangerously compromising the blood supply to the fetus. Alex, who feels increasing affection for and trust in Carl as her pregnancy progresses, confides in him her aversion to one of the doctors in the practice. "I do my best to be clinical and impartial in my observations," she explains, "and the last thing I expect from a physician is a patronizing attitude. But that's what I got from him."

"Many pregnant women *like* to be patronized," Carl says. "They want to know only that we'll make their problems better. Obviously, you're not one of those women." Alex is mollified.

Last night Rob interrogated the Lamaze instructor about the placement of the umbilical cord. At one point Alex took his hand in hers. "You want a guarantee that everything will be all right," she whispered, "and there is none." *He doesn't seem to grasp,* she thought, *that there is nothing preordained about life.*

**WEDNESDAY, JUNE 6**
**Manhattan**

TODAY JULIET WRITES A LETTER TO HER UNBORN CHILD. "DEAR LILY," it says, "now it is only two weeks before you're officially due . . . My body is huge, my knees are strained, my groin muscles are stretching and my hips are turning out in preparation for your birth. I have an awful hunger to see you, to meet you, to get to know you. It's like carrying on a long-distance, vague and muffled relationship for nearly a year with someone you're fated to marry, and the moment of actual meeting is rapidly approaching. Only this event is even bigger, because marriage can be legally rescinded and our connection will last a whole lifetime. The suspense is riveting.

"At times I am also filled with fear—fear that something will go wrong during your birth, that something will be wrong with you, that I won't be a good mother, that our relationship will sour, that I'll feel forever trapped by overwhelming maternal responsibilities. Becoming a mother is a tremendous leap into the darkness . . . but you're taking an even greater leap, into life itself, and it's one you've had no choice about whatsoever. I hope that neither of us ever regret it . . ."

**WEDNESDAY, JUNE 6**
**Manhattan**

AT 5:30 A.M., AFTER JOE HAS LEFT FOR WORK, MARIA WAKES UP IN pain. In the bathroom, she sees she is bleeding vaginally, a sign of labor. She times her contractions: seven to ten minutes apart. She calls Spiegel. He says to come to the hospital when her contractions are five minutes apart or her water breaks.

Maria beeps Joe at work. He is gleeful. They arrange to meet at the apartment of a relative on the Lower East Side, not far from the hospital. Maria and her mother get there at eleven, and when Joe shows up soon after, everyone starts placing bets in rapid-fire Spanish on the time of delivery.

By two o'clock Maria is in so much pain that Joe decides to take her and her mother to the hospital. Spiegel's exam an hour later reveals that she is only three centimeters dilated, but he doesn't send her home; he tells Joe to march her around the courtyard. With every step, Maria protests—she's nauseous, she wants to sit down, the contractions are killing her—but Joe keeps her moving. At 4:30, an obstetrical resident examines her and says she's between four and five centimeters dilated. The resident admits her.

At 6:45, Joe leaves Maria moaning in the labor room to order Chinese food for his mother-in-law, who sits patiently in the guest lounge on the labor floor. He returns ten minutes later to find Maria screaming, "I can't take this!" She flings her head so violently that she bangs it on the bed rail. "*Please*," she begs him, "get someone to help me!"

Watching his wife in agony is wrenching, but Joe hardens himself to her cries. He thinks, *I've given up so many Knicks games to learn this breathing, so breathe already*. Both he and Maria still hope to get through the birth without drugs; the Lamaze techniques will have to suffice. Aloud, he says, "Babe, you've waited nine months, don't give up now, screaming will only use up your strength. *Breathe, baby, breathe*." He says it firmly, over and over, until Maria stops cursing and focuses on the breathing, which gives her some sense of control. Later she thinks, *He actually took charge of my mind*.

Spiegel arrives around nine and asks Maria if she wants medication. Joe pleads against it. Maria declines an epidural but accepts Demerol; it offers little relief. Spiegel explains that her cervix is very narrow. "I'll do my best to deliver you vaginally," he says, upsetting Joe with the prospect of a cesarean. Between ten and midnight, Maria is in transition, with no epidural to blunt the searing pain. Joe's eyes fill with tears. He whispers to no one, "I'm sorry."

By midnight Maria is fully dilated. Spiegel tells her to start pushing. The doctor works closely with her, pulling the baby down with each push, but the head doesn't descend to a point where delivery is feasi-ble. At 2:30 he says, "I think you'll make it, but just in case, we'll prep you for a section." Joe murmurs in Maria's ear, "Oh baby, don't give up now, we've come this far, to have a section . . ." His ankles are swollen and his bad knee is bothering him. He sits down for a mo-ment, dejected, wanting to sleep. But he tells himself, *I have to stay strong for her.* He stands up and resumes his soothing patter. "This will be over in a few minutes, think about holding the baby, think about seeing it smile at us . . ."

The nurses get Maria ready for a section, shaving her pubic area and ordering blood as a precaution. At 3:20 A.M., Spiegel tells Joe and Maria they'll go into the delivery room, where he'll try to pull the baby out with forceps. Joe is alarmed: a forceps delivery, which he associates with brain damage, seems even less desirable than a cesarean. Spiegel explains that forceps are commonly used. "It's our best chance to avoid a section," he says. Joe has confidence in Spiegel, but he is scared. Maria can see the fear in his eyes. As she is being wheeled to delivery, she forces herself to smile. "Don't worry," she says to Joe. "It'll be okay." He wants to give her a medal for bravery. Friends have told him that women get nasty in labor, but Maria has yet to be anything but a trouper.

When they get to the door of the delivery room, Joe hangs back. There is so much frantic activity in there that he doesn't want to get in anyone's way, and he's leery of actually seeing the forceps in Spiegel's hand. He puts on the scrubs the nurse gives him and lingers outside, quelling the impulse to flee. *I can't abandon her at a time like this,* he thinks. When a nurse beckons him to enter, he goes into the room.

Maria pushes—once, twice. Spiegel places forceps on the baby's head. With the third push, it's over. The time is 4:38 A.M.

Joe hears someone say, "You've got yourselves a son."

N THE LOFT, AT 3:15 P.M., JULIET'S WATER BREAKS. SHE HAS NO contractions, she has no pain, and she laughs out loud when she thinks about her mother calling her at eleven this morning from a wedding in upstate New York. "Now promise," Felice said, "you won't go into labor until I get back tomorrow night, will you?" and Juliet replied, "Okay, Ma." She leaves a message with Bernstein's answering service and laughs again when she gets a call back from Fred Fischl, the doctor on duty. When Fischl wonders why she's laughing, Juliet says, "Because you're going to deliver my baby and I've never met you." She composes herself enough to ask if there is anything she shouldn't do (no baths, no sex) or should do (walk around). Fischl tells her to call him later with a progress report. If she hasn't gone into labor by morning (90 percent of women do so within twenty-four hours of their water's breaking), he'll induce her.

While Juliet giggles, Sam sits on the toilet. He's had diarrhea ever since her water broke. He's confused and nervous but not, or at least not yet, unable to function—that is, assuming he can get out of the bathroom sometime in the near future. He has to go out, buy some food and some blank tapes; he wants to bring music to the hospital, the soundtrack of *South Pacific* for sure. He thinks, over and over, *My life is going to change completely.*

By 9:30 they've taken a walk, watched *A Man and a Woman, Part II* on the VCR, called Juliet's mother and brother, rechecked Juliet's packed hospital bag to be sure the "focal points"—the art postcards she chose with such care—are in place, and consumed the turkey sandwiches Sam picked up at the local deli. (Fischl didn't tell Juliet to avoid eating, but she learns later that it's not a great idea. Food sits in your system for twelve hours, and if you're lying on your back in a labor or delivery room and vomit, you run the dangerous risk of aspirating your meal.) They check in with Fischl, who says he'll see them in the morning unless her labor intensifies, in which case they should go to the hospital.

Sam and Juliet snuggle on the living room couch to watch another movie—*A Man in Love,* with Peter Coyote and Greta Scaachi. Juliet, who has yet to feel a single contraction, is still laughing.

RIN, AT TWENTY-ONE WEEKS, IS NOW IN THE SECOND TRIMESTER, which everyone says is magical. For once everyone seems to be right. The nausea is gone; she has abundant energy; she has adopted a Zen-like, wait-and-see attitude about her job.

The Wrights had a crash course in parenting on Friday night at Erin's ten-year high-school reunion. Although Tom graduated three years ahead of her, he knew a lot of people in her class. Everyone at the reunion seemed to have kids already, and almost all said their once-carefree lifestyles had vaporized. Tom expected this, but had thought of it in vague terms—less spontaneity, fewer dinners out, less sleep. Now he was hearing about babies who cry inconsolably from six to ten every single night, ruining even the simplest microwaved dinner; about having your sleep interrupted every two hours for countless weeks; about couples who haven't had the time or energy to conduct a dialogue, let alone make love, for months; about infant ear infections and raging fevers, so terrifying to inexperienced parents, that set off renewed cycles of sleeplessness and anxiety. Whenever Tom's expression revealed dismay, his tormentors hastily said some variation of "But it's all worth it," as if to reassure themselves as much as him. *Scary,* Tom thought, as he had early in Erin's pregnancy.

Erin was preoccupied with the subject of weight gain. After her slow start she has put on pounds quickly, three in ten days, and it has thrown her into panic. She asked all the women the same questions— how much did you gain, how long did you take to lose it, how did you stand being so fat for so long?

ULIET AND SAM WAIT IN VAIN FOR RHYTHMIC CONTRACTIONS TO begin. Just after midnight, she is in so much pain she has trouble talking, but she isn't sure she's in labor. Sam insists they go to the hospital and find out. The resident on duty there is, Juliet thinks, a complete jerk. He says to her, "I thought you were coming in the morning, what are you doing here now?" as if she has somehow screwed up his evening. He examines her grudgingly and says that she is dilated no more than one centimeter. "Go home," the guy says indifferently. "Take a walk, go to sleep." Get lost, in other words.

By the time Sam and Juliet climb the stairs to the loft, it is 2:30 A.M. Juliet considers taking a shower but is too uncomfortable. She lies in bed with Sam and dozes off for maybe fifteen minutes before she is awakened by strong contractions. When they're about three minutes apart, at 5 A.M., she and Sam return to the hospital. The same obnoxious resident examines her and finds no change, but this time he tells them to stay. Fischl arrives at 7:30 and determines that Juliet's labor isn't progressing. He puts her on Pitocin to stimulate contractions. She is not yet dilated enough for an epidural.

During the difficult hours from 8 to 10 A.M., when Juliet is in excruciating pain, Sam's eyes are continually wet; he can't stop his tears. At one point Juliet asks if he's crying. "No," he says. "My eyes must be watering because I'm so tired." He doesn't want her to think he's upset, because he's not. He is simply overwhelmed by the magnitude of what he sees and feels. The analogy he made as a teenager between men going to war and women having babies now seems laughable. The latter is incomparably more noble, more strenuous, and more dramatic. Now he thinks the aggression that drives men to make war is compensation for the experience of giving birth, which is forever denied to them.

By ten o'clock Juliet is three centimeters dilated, and Fischl orders the epidural. Juliet is grateful he doesn't make her wait longer. She is already exhausted, and though the breathing techniques are helpful, she is concerned about her endurance. Sam is asked to leave the room while the epidural is put in place, a procedure that is not pretty to watch: a hollow needle is plunged into Juliet's vertebra and a catheter is threaded through it, bathing the nerve roots coming out of the spine in anesthesia. The process requires Juliet to sit up and remain motionless through several contractions, which is torture. But once the medication kicks in, after twenty minutes, the pain disappears. When Sam returns, Juliet is smiling. "This is the difference between heaven and hell," she says. She feels good enough to be solicitous of *him*. She strokes his cheek; she tells him she is sorry for what *he* is going through. Her tenderness very nearly breaks him.

At eleven Sam swallows a couple of aspirins and a carton of orange juice in the lounge on the labor floor and exhales a long, pent-up breath. The word that sticks in his mind is *awesome*. The process of labor has so far been primitive and uncontrollable, like going for a ride on a wild horse and not being able to get off. It astonishes him that anyone would submit herself voluntarily to this terrifying ordeal. *Any man who lacks respect for women,* he thinks, *need only watch someone in labor.*

Sam goes back to Juliet. At 11:30, Fischl examines her; she is at five centimeters. The doctor says he'll keep her on the epidural until she's fully dilated and ready to push, which, he predicts, should be sometime before eight. In the labor room are the tapes Sam made and the "focal points" Juliet bought, but she never unpacks them from her bag. They seem completely irrelevant.

Juliet dozes while Sam skims the Sunday *Times*. He considers the near future with delight. He has no commitments for the next three and a half months and looks forward to spending the time with his wife and baby, snug in the island farmhouse with the ocean view, doing anything Juliet wants him to. *There is no demand she could possibly make,* he thinks, *that could come close to equaling what I have asked of her in having this baby.*

By five o'clock Juliet is fully dilated, but the baby's head is still high in her pelvis. Fischl takes her off the epidural; if she feels the contractions, she'll be able to push the baby down more effectively. Then he leaves to attend to two other patients in labor. As the drug ebbs away, Juliet feels escalating pain. At some point she screams: it feels as if her insides are rupturing. During Fischl's absence, Sam holds one of Juliet's legs and a nurse holds the other. They work with her, telling her to push when the contractions begin, to breathe when they subside. Sam is exhausted from watching Juliet in agony.

At eight Fischl returns to examine her and finds the baby has made no progress. He orders the nurses to prepare Juliet for a section, diagnosing her condition as cephalopelvic disproportion (CPD), meaning that the baby's head is too big for the pelvis—one of the most common reasons for a cesarean. Fischl says the delivery itself will take about twenty minutes, and then he'll need an hour to finish up. Juliet is relieved. After twenty-three hours of labor followed by three hours of pushing, it is clear to her that the baby is going nowhere on its own.

They wheel Juliet to the operating room while Sam puts on scrubs and hurries to a pay phone to call their mothers. He tells each of them that Juliet is about to have a section and he won't be back in touch until it's over. Then he enters the OR, a setting that seems spooky, unearthly. The lights in the operating room are so bright, the gowns of the medical people so blue, the instruments so silver, sparkling and cold. Juliet's arms are strapped to the table. She is shivering. A curtain is suspended above her waist on a U-shaped frame to block the lower half of her body from view, but Sam, standing by her head, catches a reflection in the window behind the curtain. He feels as if he's hallucinating.

Juliet's lower body is numb from the renewed flow of the epidural (used as a local anesthetic during cesareans so the woman can remain conscious), but she is in a state of acute mental awareness. With her arms strapped down, the sensation of helplessness is frightening. *You can deal with this,* she tells herself. But she begs Sam to stay close to her. "Talk to me," she says. He feels blank. He touches her arm and tells her he loves her. *She must be terrified,* he thinks. *She's never been operated on before, and here she is, awake.* She mutters to Sam, "I feel pressure . . . they're cutting me . . ."

At 9:31 Sam hears someone say, "Nice big girl," and then there is this astonishing sound, deep and resonant like a musical instrument: his daughter's cry. He sees the baby then, emerging from behind the table in the arms of a nurse. He thinks she looks about as healthy as anyone can with blood all over her. He watches as the nurse places Lily on the warming table. He feels relief well up from his gut.

But then Juliet's color starts to change, to pale. She becomes agitated. Sam hears someone, probably Fischl, yell, "Give her a shot of Methergine!" This is a drug that contracts the uterus. Juliet misunderstands; she yells back, with the indignance Sam has always loved, "I don't need Methedrine!" Sam turns to one of the anesthesiologists and asks if everything is okay, but if there is an answer, he doesn't hear it. There are too many voices now, sharp and urgent. "Nurse!" Fischl shouts. "Wipe my forehead!" and someone else demands blood and platelets, and suddenly several nurses run into the OR. Through the reflection in the window, Sam sees blood-soaked towels piling up on the floor. He turns again to the anesthesiologist.

"What's going on?" he asks.

"Your wife is bleeding," she replies, "and they're trying to stop it."

Normally the uterus contracts within minutes of delivery, shrinking down like a deflating balloon and allowing the placenta to separate spontaneously. But Juliet's uterus doesn't contract, probably because of prolonged labor and subsequent overdistention, possibly because of her history. (In DES women, the capacity of the uterus to expand and contract efficiently can be limited.) Her uterus fills with blood and swells instead of shrinking.

When the Methergine doesn't work, Fischl holds Juliet's uterus in his hand and massages it to try to get it to contract. To Juliet, the massaging feels like a brutal assault. *He's trying to put my organs back into my stomach,* she thinks, *and they won't fit.* The massaging doesn't help either, so Fischl injects Pitocin and prostaglandins (other drugs that aid contraction) directly into the uterus. They have no effect.

It occurs to Sam that he is holding his daughter, but he can't remember anyone putting her in his arms. He stares down at the swaddled bundle and thinks, *She is cute and I wish I could fall in love with her, but I can't feel anything, I'm too worried about Juliet.* He hears someone say, "Get the baby," and a nurse takes Lily away. He tells himself not to feel terrible for being so grateful. *There will be lots of time with her later,* he rationalizes. *Juliet's the one who needs me now.*

A nurse grabs Sam. "You have to leave," she commands, hustling him out of the room. She doesn't tell him that Juliet's blood pressure has dropped precipitously from loss of blood volume and the effect of the epidural. "There's too much going on there," she explains to Sam in the hallway outside the OR. She runs off and returns shortly with a glass of orange juice for him.

"Is my wife going to die?" he asks.

"Oh, no," the nurse answers.

"Will she lose her uterus?"

"I don't think so. The doctor will be out soon to talk to you. In the meantime, why don't you go look at your baby?"

Sam trudges to the nursery and stares bleakly at his sleeping daughter behind the glass. A placard taped to her bassinet gives Juliet's and Fischl's names, Lily's weight (eight pounds, one ounce), height (twenty inches), time and date of birth. *What difference does it make?* Sam thinks. *If Juliet dies and I have to bring this kid up on my own . . .*

He fears he will not survive if he loses Juliet. *She is so integrated into my life,* he reflects. *The baby is nothing to me yet, she seems secondary, out of the loop.* He remembers Juliet saying to him, a month or a lifetime ago, "I'm worried that labor will be painful and the baby might not be okay, but at least I'm not worried about dying." *This can't be happening . . .*

Sam gropes in his mind for a comparable experience and remembers the time ten years ago when the plane he was on took a nosedive and he was sure it would crash. The panic was instantaneous; there was no time to think. But there was also no time to feel. Now the sense of love and loss threatens to overwhelm him.

Inside the OR, Juliet curses her alertness, wishing she were less conscious of the agitation around her, inside her. She had a panic attack once while scuba diving but got herself under control quickly. That terror was nothing compared to what she feels now. Here, unlike the scuba-diving experience, she has no control.

Someone tells her that they're going to give her general anesthesia and comes toward her with a mask. She wants to fend it off, but her arms are strapped down. She thrashes, trying to free herself. Although some part of her wishes for oblivion, she is convinced that once she goes under she will never wake up. *If I'm going to die,* she thinks, *I want to know I am dying.* She pleads for Sam's return, but the anesthesiologist puts the mask on her. Juliet's last thought before losing consciousness is an angry one: *People aren't supposed to die in childbirth in the last decade of the twentieth century.*

Sam paces the hallway outside the OR. Fischl emerges. He explains the cause of Juliet's bleeding. Sam asks if she will lose her uterus. The doctor says he thinks he can save it.

"If there's a choice of risking her life or her uterus," Sam says, "you'll take her uterus, won't you?"

"Of course," Fischl says, "but there are other steps we can take before a hysterectomy."

At that point Sam looks over Fischl's shoulder through the glass, into the OR. He sees people clustering around Juliet's head. He is sure her body has stopped functioning and they're trying to resuscitate her.

"What's going on in there?" he asks, his voice shaky.

"They're giving her general anesthesia. She's upset and uncomfortable, and there's no time to talk her through it. We have to attend to the bleeding." Fischl says he's called in Dr. Martin, the chairman of the department of obstetrics and gynecology, who is experienced in the two procedures open to them before deciding on a hysterectomy. The first involves tying off the hypogastric arteries, the main source of blood to the uterus. If that doesn't stop the bleeding, they will pack Juliet from below. They'll run a gauze pad through the uterine cavity to apply pressure from within and thereby get the uterus to clamp down, much as one applies a Band-Aid to a cut finger. (A generation ago, when Pitocin and other contracting agents were not available, packing was more commonly used, but few doctors today are familiar with the technique. As it is, the chance of a woman hemorrhaging after a cesarean and requiring such drastic measures to stop her bleeding is remote—about one in a thousand.)

Fischl goes into the OR and Sam resumes pacing. *I don't give a damn if I never have another kid,* he thinks. *I have my one kid now, I have no right to demand more than that from life. What in the world is there to gain by saving her uterus and taking the chance she might bleed to death?* He fears he's disintegrating. He needs someone to lean on. Juliet's mother and brother are just a taxi ride away . . . *No.* First he must find out if Juliet is going to live. He can't share the burden of his fear with anyone, because it won't help—it's like being on an airplane. Having Juliet in the seat next to him doesn't stop him from seeing death staring through the window. He'll either crash or he won't; no one can convince him that everything will be okay until it is.

Sam sees a man in street clothes running down the hall, coming toward him. The man doesn't seem to notice Sam as he hurries past and ducks into the OR. It is Dr. Martin, the head of the department.

Seconds later, a medical resident emerges. Sam says, "What's going on?"

The arterial ligation helped stanch the blood, the resident explains, but Juliet's uterus was still ballooned out and bleeding. "They had to pack her. Now they're closing her up."

When Dr. Martin leaves the OR, Sam pounces. "What's the prognosis?" he asks.

"Reasonable," the doctor says curtly, and continues down the hall.

*What does that mean?* Sam thinks angrily. A reasonable chance she'll keep her uterus? A reasonable chance she'll live?

Just before midnight, a nurse tells Sam that Juliet is awake and wants to see him. Sam rushes into the OR. Juliet's eyes are bugging out of her head. He has seen her like that once before, on a bad drug trip in 1973.

She grabs his hand. "Am I going to die? Am I going to die?" she asks, in a weak, wailing tone he can't identify with the Juliet he knows. Sam sees that she's not sure whether he's her ally or her enemy. She seems to be in isolation, in some kind of netherworld, where you have no anchor and you trust no one. He has to comfort her enough so she will let him into her world, but whatever he says has to be convincing. And he doesn't know the answer . . .

"No," he says, looking directly at her. "No, you're not going to die." He smiles.

"Why are you smiling?" she says angrily. "They almost killed me."

There it is: her *life force*. The real Juliet has returned. She is saying, *They're not going to get away with doing this to me, I'm not going to die—they* meaning the doctors, life, God. Sam is vastly relieved.

"I'm smiling," he says, "because I'm happy to see you."

Juliet is wheeled to the recovery room as Sam walks beside her, holding her hand. He needs to call their mothers, but Juliet won't let him leave her field of vision. Finally she agrees if he will summon Kathy, a nurse who has been with her throughout the evening. Kathy appears and Sam makes his calls. He doesn't ask anyone to come to the hospital, but after hanging up he realizes again that he needs support. He calls Juliet's brother, David, and gets his wife. She says David is already on his way, and at 1 A.M. he arrives. Sam embraces him, sobbing against his shoulder.

Sam leads David to Juliet. She is hooked up to a series of monitors that gauge blood pressure, heart rate, and urine output; she is exhausted beyond endurance. David kisses her and lies down on the gurney next to her. Sam says he's going to get some sleep in the lounge but David should wake him if anything happens. Drunk with fatigue, he lurches into the lounge and falls onto a couch. He is out for the next five hours.

When Juliet's blood pressure crashes in the middle of the night, medical personnel flood the room. David goes to get Sam. He sees Sam is sleeping and decides to let him rest.

### SUNDAY, JUNE 10
#### Westchester

T 10 A.M. ROB AND ALEX ATTEND THE UNVEILING OF HIS FATHER'S gravestone. Rob had been tense for days beforehand, rebuking himself for not being a good son. Even in death he cannot accept his father for what he was—a man who toiled for years without ever becoming financially successful, a man who could and should have been a renowned academic but instead peddled stocks and bonds—and wonders if his offspring will judge him with similar disdain. Rob would rather have his son say, "My dad doesn't make much money, but that's because he's a writer," than "My dad makes OK money, but he's only a salesman."

Later Rob and Alex tour the maternity ward at the hospital with their Lamaze class. The teacher encourages the women to load up with fluids in the last weeks of pregnancy, saying that hydration keeps the uterus from getting irritated and sending out signals of false labor. "You're not drinking enough fluids," Rob accuses Alex.

When the teacher stops the class outside a labor room and delivers a lengthy explanation about what goes on inside, Rob grows concerned that Alex is standing too long. He asks if she wants to sit down. "No," she says. "There aren't any chairs, and it's not just me with a special need. There are four other pregnant women here."

He asks a second time, and a third. "Look," Alex says, exasperated, "if you have a question, ask it once. If I give you a decisive answer, assume that's correct. Don't think I'm being polite."

"You're not going to let me help you in labor. You're such a martyr."

"If you feel that way, don't come."

In the labor room is a small metal stool with a swivel seat, presumably to accommodate husbands. One of the women in the class points at the stool and says, "But this looks so uncomfortable."

Alex laughs. "You're a very sweet wife," she tells the woman. "I wouldn't give a rat's ass about how uncomfortable my husband was at that point." Rob stares at her as if she said the cruelest thing in the world. But her comment, Alex points out later, is proof that she will not be a martyr. "I'll worry about myself," she tells him. "You should do the same."

AM SPENDS THE MORNING STUDYING THE MACHINES THAT MONI-
tor Juliet's vital signs. Her heart rate is twice normal, and her
blood pressure, which was stabilized last night with another
transfusion, is again erratic. With her condition so volatile,
he's concerned about what will happen if she hemorrhages during the
unpacking of the gauze, scheduled for this afternoon. Sam knows that
in that case the doctors will perform a hysterectomy, which will require general anesthesia; he also knows that anesthesia is dangerous if
your vital signs are unstable.

Sam hears talk that Juliet may be moved to the intensive care unit.
"Is she in critical condition?" he asks a nurse.

"The critical care specialist will examine her," she says. "He'll make
the decision."

The specialist is the first doctor to offer them any reassurance. "I've
seen much worse," he tells Juliet. "You'll be okay." Both Sam and
Juliet are impressed by his quiet competence and humane manner. He
changes the mix and doubles the quantity of the intravenous fluids.
Soon Juliet is stabilized.

Emotionally, she's a wreck. She doesn't think she'll make it through
the unpacking. *Either I'll hemorrhage during the unpacking and die,* she
thinks, *or I'll have a heart attack during the hysterectomy and die.* She can't
envision any other possibility. In the early afternoon, she starts to sob.
"I want to see my baby," she says to Sam. "It may be the last time."
But when Sam brings Lily to her, Juliet turns her head away. *I'll die
without ever knowing her,* she thinks. *I can't bear it . . .*

At 3:30 the procedure begins. Juliet is again strapped to a table, a
curtain concealing the lower half of her body. She is surrounded by
people—Fischl, the critical care specialist, anesthesiologists, assistants,
residents, nurses—too many people. She feels embarrassed, on display.
"Are all of you planning to watch this?" she asks in a sharp tone.
Quickly everyone but Fischl, two residents, and Sam leaves the area.

Juliet's legs are up and apart, bent at the knee. Her knees begin to shake; she leans one against Sam. Fischl says to put the other one against him, but she resists. She loathes this man. She is sick of hearing him say repeatedly, "There were buckets of blood last night . . . I've never seen so much blood." She is furious that he never communicated with her directly, never once asked her how she felt. Bernstein, she is convinced, would not have been so alienating—but Bernstein is out of town. Once again her life is in Fischl's hands.

The unpacking is excruciatingly slow. With each second, Juliet expects to gush blood and be rushed into the operating room. Sam stands by her side, rubbing her forehead and occasionally wiping it with a damp cloth, while Fischl pulls the gauze inch by inch, stopping for several agonizing minutes between tugs. During these intervals he makes small talk with Sam, which drives Juliet crazy. Sam returns the patter. *That's Sam,* Juliet thinks irritably, *always trying to get along with everyone.* When Fischl says to Sam, "You look really tired; you must not have had any sleep," Juliet is so enraged she pulls off her oxygen mask and says, "He's had a hell of a lot more sleep than I have." She wants Fischl to acknowledge her, but he never does. He keeps talking about his heart palpitations and how awful last night was. At one point, Sam bends down to kiss Juliet's forehead. "I'd do that too, dear," Fischl says, "but I'm all tied up now." Juliet thinks, *Is that supposed to be a joke?*

Fischl said the procedure would take no more than twenty minutes, but it requires forty-five. When it's over, Juliet collapses into tears. She did not hemorrhage. She still has her uterus. She is alive.

She is taken on a gurney to the recovery room, where a private-duty nurse awaits her. The nurse gives Juliet a sponge bath, gently cleaning the dried blood caked all over her body. She brushes Juliet's hair, massages her back to ease the pain from so many hours of lying flat, and tells Fischl that Juliet needs to rest and should be moved to a quiet room of her own. Fischl arranges for one of the labor rooms. There Juliet asks for Lily and holds her for the first time. When Lily is returned to the nursery, Juliet sleeps. Sam beds down for another night in the lounge. Fischl told him that if the next twenty-four hours pass without incident, Juliet will be "out of the woods." Sam won't leave the hospital until those twenty-four hours are up.

By Tuesday Juliet is able to nurse Lily, even though her arms are hooked up to IVs and she has to lie on her back. The critical care specialist comes by. "I won't be seeing you anymore," he tells her, "because you're not sick enough."

Sam goes home that night. He is unable to think, or to feel anything but exhaustion. He showers and gets into bed. Within seconds he is asleep.

**FRIDAY, JUNE 15**
**Queens**

IGHT–DAY–OLD LUIS NAPS IN HIS CRIB, DECORATED WITH SEVERAL "It's a Boy" helium balloons. The parental bed is outfitted with Joe's homecoming gift to Maria—white shams, pillowcases, sheets, quilt, and dust ruffle, which she has wanted for a long time. As soon as Luis was born, Joe decided to surprise her with them. He thinks Maria deserves everything in the world.

Maria wonders, as she did throughout pregnancy, where her hormones are hiding. There were a few weepy moments in the hospital, usually when she had no visitors, but other than that she has not felt depressed. She's not even tired: Luis sleeps five hours at a time, from 11:30 to 4:30, which is about as much uninterrupted rest as she has ever gotten. Other than a few headaches, and vaginal swelling from prolonged pushing which makes it painful to sit, she has no physical complaints.

She and Luis have taken easily to nursing, and Maria is unfazed by other elements of newborn care, such as bathing and comforting, that are daunting to many first-time parents. The combination of her unflappable personality and her experience with infant nephews and nieces has already made her a confident, competent mother. Joe is openly proud of her.

He slides a tape into the VCR. He never tires of watching the videos he made of the end of pregnancy and the beginning of parenthood. There's Maria on May 20, with Joe's voice in the background narrating her every mundane move—doing laundry in the basement, taking Nico for a walk, touring the maternity ward. The postpartum segment begins with a shot of Maria on her hospital bed, holding up Joe's gifts to Luis—tiny Air Jordans and a Mets outfit—and speaking directly into the camera: "It was well worth it after twenty-two long hours. He looks like his daddy." There's one-day-old Luis, drooling, and Joe saying, "God bless you, my little athlete" as he tries to fit the Air Jordans onto his son's feet. There's Maria holding the baby, a small bundle in a receiving blanket, while Joe says, "They wrap 'em here like little burritos." On homecoming day there is Joe, in slacks and a crisp white shirt instead of his usual sweats, dressing Luis and wrapping him expertly in a fringed white blanket, joking, "And here's our brand new burrito, uh, baby." There's a long take of the new family walking to the car, driving on the highway, arriving at the balloon-framed front door of the apartment, and finally a closeup of Joe's face, grinning widely, saying, "I'm the happiest man in the world, and the greatest woman in the world is behind the camera . . . I love you." Maria's voice echoes, off camera, "I love you, too."

## WEDNESDAY, JUNE 20
### Cape Cod

 ITH HANNAH DOZING IN HER CAR SEAT, SARAH DRIVES HOME from an overnight visit to Lauren in Boston. A delicate diamond and sapphire bracelet adorns her wrist, a gift from Michael to commemorate Hannah's birth. Sarah glances at the bracelet as she drives. It is, she thinks, the best thing anyone has given her.

Ben's behavior has improved, thanks to the intervention of the family therapist, who recently allayed Sarah's fear of being a lousy mother for putting Ben in day care at four months. (Ben, the therapist assured her, is smart and well adjusted.) The partial facial paralysis she experienced after Hannah's birth, never explained, is gone. She weighs eight pounds less than before she got pregnant; her breasts are again small and pert, now that she's stopped nursing; the tubal ligation has made an appreciable difference in her attitude toward sex. She feels unusually content. *What it comes down to,* she thinks, *is I have resigned myself to having a family.*

Hannah wakes just as Sarah pulls into her driveway. Inside the house, Sarah settles her daughter on the floor with some toys and rushes around rinsing bottles, preparing formula, and carting a load of laundry down to the basement. Her contentment has suddenly left her. *Why is it,* she thinks, *that as soon as I walk into this house I get irritated?* When Michael and Ben arrive at 5:30, she is sitting on the upholstered bench in the kitchen, feeding Hannah.

"Say hello to someone," Sarah says to Michael, thrusting the baby at him. "She has a poop."

Michael makes no effort to reach for his daughter. "You take her," he says.

"*You* take her," Sarah says, more forcefully. Michael changes Hannah's diaper and returns her to the kitchen floor. Sarah offers him a glass of wine, which he refuses.

"I'm tired," he says.

"I'm tired too," she says.

"There was a thunderstorm here last night and the power went out," Michael explains. "I went to sleep at eleven and the dog woke me at two. The second storm scared Ben—he woke me at five. I told him to pretend the thunder was a drummer boy in the sky. He went back to sleep, but I kept wandering around the house, trying to find a flashlight because the power went out. Basically I got three hours."

"I didn't get any more than that. Lauren's kid was up at one, screaming his head off, and Hannah was up at four."

"Well, of course I couldn't possibly be more tired than you, ever," Michael says. "I can never work more or have any less sleep than you. Your life is one hundred percent harder than mine."

Sarah turns to Ben. "Are you happy to have me home?" she says.

"Yeah. Did you miss me?"

"I missed you."

"Why?" Ben asks.

Sarah pauses. *Why?* "Because," she says, disconcerted, "you're my little boy."

Michael asks Ben whether he wants noodles or rice for dinner, annoying Sarah. She doesn't see why a four-year-old should dictate the menu. Ben mumbles "noodles" and begins to toss his Ninja Turtle up and down, trying to touch the ceiling. Michael goes outside to the deck and lights the barbecue. When he returns, Sarah puts Hannah in his arms. Michael sits on the bench with the baby on his lap as Ben shoots his Batman gun near her ear and Sarah hauls another load of laundry down to the basement. Michael places Hannah on the floor and pulls a Pyrex dish of fresh salmon fillets, which he has marinated in teriyaki sauce, from the refrigerator. Sarah reappears. Michael takes the fish outside and grills it while Sarah dishes up noodles and steamed zucchini. At 6:30 the family sits down to dinner, which lasts eleven minutes.

By nine o'clock Ben is asleep. Michael unloads the dishwasher while Sarah watches *How to Marry a Millionaire* on TV in the living room, holding Hannah on her lap. Michael enters the room and moves toward a chair. "The clothes are on top of the dryer," Sarah says quickly. Michael backs away from the chair and goes down to the basement. He brings the laundry basket into the living room and folds the clothes, dividing them into four neat piles, one for each member of the family. The minute he finishes, Sarah says, "Take your daughter." Michael puts Hannah to sleep in the bassinet upstairs and returns to the living room, hoping to watch TV. But Sarah has other plans for him.

"You're going to bed right now," she says flirtatiously. "I need someone to cuddle with." Michael eagerly follows his wife upstairs, his arms full of folded laundry.

**WEDNESDAY, JUNE 27**
**Queens**

 OMEN ASK MARIA SO OFTEN IF SHE'S DEPRESSED THAT SHE'S starting to feel concerned that she's not. Maybe their husbands aren't as helpful as Joe, who seizes every opportunity to be with Luis. *If anything,* she thinks, *he is too involved.* He gets home from work, hugs Maria, and runs to his son. If

Luis is sleeping, Joe wakes him up with hundreds of tiny kisses, ignoring Maria's plea to let him sleep.

Joe can't get over how different his life is now from the early days after his daughter's birth, when he was unhappy in his marriage. He appreciates being part of a family more than he did then; he is aware of an aura of love and affection sheltering him and Maria and Luis. When he sees his son at Maria's breast, it puts him *into another dimension*. He finds it gripping to watch his child feeding directly from its mother, never having to touch anything artificial. And yet . . . he's not sure if Maria is happy.

When Joe asks her tonight why she's been acting distant, Maria is nonplussed. "What?" she says. "I don't know what you mean." She tries to be a good wife, making dinner every night, keeping the apartment spotless. Other than a spat here and there about what Luis's cries really mean or why Joe shouldn't wake him or how Maria feels tied down by nursing, she thought they were getting along well.

"The minute I come home, you jump up and start the chores," he says. "Why don't you want to be with me?"

"The only time I can get anything done, unless he's napping, is when you come home and take him. And I don't want to interfere with your time with him."

"You're so withdrawn. I wish you would talk to me." He doesn't ask if she's depressed; he believes if you don't talk negatively, you don't think negatively. But he's sensitive to what can happen to women after they give birth, especially if they're used to an active life outside the home and find themselves housebound all day with only a baby for company.

"Nothing is wrong," Maria says.

Later Joe goes on a rampage looking for his pistol. He can't remember where he hid it, and he needs it to go skeet shooting this weekend. He pulls clothes out of closets and paws through dresser drawers, frantic. When he finds it, he goes into the bedroom to tell Maria, who is nursing. Joe stands at the foot of the bed and puts the unloaded pistol to his head, mocking himself. Maria starts to cry. "Why do you have to do things like that?" she exclaims. Her reaction is uncharacteristically emotional. *What's with her?* Joe wonders. Is she mad because he threw stuff around? Scared by his clowning with the pistol? He sits down on the bed.

"You're giving the kid teary milk, babe," he says. "Give me a smile, talk to me. Let me help you."

Maria turns the corners of her mouth upward. "I'm okay," she says. "Sorry. I don't know why I got so upset."

*I know why,* Joe thinks. *The postpartum blues.*

**FRIDAY, JUNE 29**
**Westchester**

LEX, THREE DAYS SHY OF HER DUE DATE, IS LONELY IN A WAY she's never been. She can no longer travel, which means she now spends her time at home, waiting for Rob. She has lost the sense of intimacy she had with him throughout the pregnancy, which usually transcended their frequent arguments. They literally never see each other now. Alex's loneliness makes her angry— she hates feeling emotionally dependent on anyone—and her anger makes her less tolerant of Rob's existential gloom.

Her anxiety over the briss issue has been mounting. Alex doesn't care about the "five thousand years of tradition" Rob uses as his argument; it's irrelevant to her. She doesn't care when he says it's for his father. His father is dead. Even if he weren't, it's Rob and Alex's decision—no one else's opinion or feelings count. She already went through hell with her own parents because she insisted on living with Rob, knowing the hurt and mortification she was causing them. She refused to be dictated to then, and it makes no sense to be dictated to now—from the grave, no less.

She admired the "About Men" column in last Sunday's *New York Times Magazine,* as she does anything that tells her generation that it hasn't reinvented the wheel. Alex's male acquaintances seem unjustifiably smug about their parenting compared to their fathers': *We diaper! We mix formula! We know Lamaze! We're right there in the labor room!* But in reality, as the column pointed out, the older generation of men traveled less and worked shorter hours; they were home in time for dinner, lawn mowing, a game of catch. To Alex, those activities have more to do with wholesome family life than any amount of hands-on care. She's sure Rob will be happy to change diapers, but she would rather he made an appearance in the house while the kid is still awake.

If she ever gives birth, that is. Alex is tired of waiting, and not just for Rob. She's only a centimeter dilated; it's possible she won't go into labor for another two weeks. The kid is stuck inside her. She's taken to calling it *Crazy Glue*.

### FRIDAY, JUNE 29
#### Manhattan

ULIET SITS UP IN BED, EATING A STRAWBERRY POPSICLE. SHE HAS been home for nearly two weeks. She's still exhausted, and anemia has left her with little energy—it could be a month or more before her blood levels return to normal. She has a great deal of back pain (from the epidural needle and from lying for hours on the operating table), and her stomach is still sore from Dr. Fischl's pounding on her uterus. But she hasn't been depressed. She's too happy to be home with her harrowing ordeal behind her.

Her mother, Felice, has been here every day to care for Lily so Juliet can rest. Sam and Felice have been so efficient that Juliet has yet to change a diaper. Lily wakes in the middle of the night, but Juliet doesn't have to get out of bed. Sam brings the baby to her for nursing.

Juliet expected to enjoy breastfeeding, and she does. In the hospital she was anxious about her milk coming in; her breasts never became engorged. But a nurse showed her how to manipulate her nipples to determine if she had milk, and when it came gushing out, she relaxed.

Sam enters the bedroom with Lily in his arms. Juliet unbuttons her white cotton nightgown, trades her Popsicle for the baby, and guides Lily's mouth to the nipple. Lily latches on aggressively. Sam licks Juliet's Popsicle absently; his eyes are on his wife and daughter. He is envious. He wishes he could be the one to give nourishment.

His current concern, with Juliet out of danger, has turned again to his work—will he be restless without it this summer? Juliet says he'll adjust quickly; she's already impressed at how he's taken the baby's disruption of his sleep in stride. For the eighteen years they've been together, Sam has insisted on eight or nine undisturbed hours. When he didn't get it, he complained of headaches, and that his day was shot. Now he's up and down all night and says, to Juliet's amazement, that it doesn't bother him, not at all.

JULY—
DECEMBER
1990

**JULY 1990**

SHOPPING IN THE MALL FOR A MINICAM, ROB MOVES THE BRISS discussion into a new phase. "It's just a way for me to apologize to my father for being a bad son and not respecting him," he tells Alex. "If we don't do it, I'll feel terrible."

"Okay," says Alex, glad to hear the "five thousand years of history" line replaced with a more personal plea.

Her due date, July 2, passed without a single contraction. Rob wants the baby to be born tomorrow, as he is entranced by the idea of having his child's birthday on the Fourth of July, forever to be celebrated with fireworks. But it frightens Alex to contemplate a holiday delivery. She imagines the least senior nurses on duty at the hospital, the newest member of Carl's practice on call. She remains as motionless as possible, hoping to avoid labor.

Rob's former secretary gave them their first baby present: an infant car seat. Today Alex belts it into her Honda, thinking, *This change is permanent, like losing your virginity. From here on in, the answer will always be "Yes, I have a baby."*

**SATURDAY, JULY 7**
**Manhattan**

ONSIDERING THE TRAUMATIC CONDITIONS OF HER BIRTH," Lily's new pediatrician says briskly to Sam and Juliet, "she's doing quite well." They're too shocked to ask the doctor what he means. Lily lies naked and screaming as he examines her. "She has quite a little temper, doesn't she?" he says. *What does he expect from a newborn?* Juliet thinks. His manner is too businesslike for her taste, but he does return her calls quickly, and his office is only a block and a half away.

When Lily is inconsolable, usually from gas, it upsets Sam to run through all the prescribed routines—rocking and burping and feeding and singing and holding—and still be unable to soothe her. Since diapering is his job, he felt responsible when she was constipated for three days. It made him so anxious that he yelled with joy when she finally made a mess. He is amused by how little it takes—*poop on a diaper!*—to get him excited these days.

He got the bill from the hospital: $10,000 for Juliet's care, including $800 for six units of blood and a bargain $500 for the critical care specialist. Juliet is assembling a scrapbook for Lily and debating whether to include the hospital bill, or her notes about October's bleeding scare on the island. She doesn't want her daughter burdened with guilt over what her mother went through.

Whenever Juliet looks at Lily, she wishes the moment could be frozen; she fears she will never risk having another child. Sam tries not to think about the aftermath of Lily's birth, but memories of it hit him at odd times, while walking to work or meeting with a client or taking a shower, and he feels suddenly overpowered by them.

Juliet had her six-week postpartum checkup three weeks early, because she wanted medical clearance to leave town for the summer. After the exam, she grilled Bernstein.

"Was I officially in critical condition?"

"Whenever you need several units of blood and your pressure is down and you have to have your hypogastric arteries ligated, yes—but the definition is kind of loose. You're young and healthy and can take a lot."

"My blood pressure kept dropping, even after I had the transfusions."

"When they fill you up with blood, it's not like filling a gasoline tank. A transfusion replaces volume, but you still have to metabolize it and dilute it, and that takes time."

"One of the residents said, 'I think they should give you more blood, but it's not my decision.' I asked him why they wouldn't give me more and he said, 'I guess they're worried about AIDS.' Should I be worried about that?"

"No," Bernstein said firmly. "But nobody likes to give blood products, it's foreign matter. The less we have to put into you, the better."

"So there's no point in my getting tested for AIDS?"

"There really isn't; the blood you got is very well screened. Nothing in this world is absolute, but would I bet on this? Absolutely."

"You said in the hospital that if I ever got pregnant again, you'd do an elective cesarean with the prospect of a hysterectomy if anything went wrong."

"I don't know." Bernstein paused. "I've been thinking about it a lot."

"You've been thinking it's too dangerous for me to try to have another baby?"

"No, not at all. My question is whether I should try to deliver you vaginally or not. You were fully dilated, but the baby didn't come out. I just had someone in labor this morning who had that happen with her first child, but the second one, today, came out naturally."

"But you said if you delivered it vaginally, it could be much more dangerous."

"Did I say that? Then I've revised my position. As I've read through the reports and thought about you, I think that reaction was more of an emotional thing for me. I want to be there the next time."

"Well," Juliet said, "that's another consideration. I might feel more secure with a doctor who tends to be around more than you."

"There was a woman in the waiting room today, I've delivered all four of her children." Bernstein seemed defensive. "I wanted to announce it to everyone."

"But part of what made the experience so traumatic was having this guy Fischl, who I didn't know, who said things to me he shouldn't have, like 'For the next couple of days it'll be touch and go.' I interpreted that as meaning I might die."

"You weren't close to dying at any point. I think 'touch and go' meant a hysterectomy, and from our point of view, a hysterectomy in someone your age is scary. What you went through is rare, it's unnerving, and you want to be reassuring, but—"

"But goddammit, Sam was reassuring, the nurses were, the anesthesiologists were, the critical care guy was. Fischl could at least have told me I wasn't going to die."

"You weren't going to die." Bernstein looked at her sympathetically.

Juliet reminded him to write a prescription for a new diaphragm. "I don't want to get pregnant right away, in any case," she said, laughing.

**SUNDAY, JULY 8**
**Westchester**

N THE HOURS BEFORE DAWN, ROB AND ALEX FIGHT BITTERLY. ROB promised to be home from his consulting job at midnight; when he staggers in just before 4 A.M., Alex is waiting in the study. She attacks him with a litany of criticisms ranging over the twelve years of their relationship. To Rob it's like watching a bee flit from flower to flower, from one of his flaws to another. (He is impressed by her memory of every misstep he has ever made.) It reminds him of Alex's mother, who often calls to complain that none of her children come to visit, though they were there yesterday and will be there tomorrow.

Alex keeps it up over his pleas to lower her voice so she won't alarm the baby inside of her. Rob doesn't want to further arouse her ire by reacting; he wants this tirade to be over, he wants desperately to sleep. But every time she seems to be winding down and he makes a move toward the bedroom, she comes at him with renewed force. He feels like a prisoner of war under torture. Finally he snaps; he goes over to the bookshelf and pulls it down, hurling volumes all over the place.

"Let's get divorced," Alex yells, scooping up her car keys. "You can keep the baby." She bolts out of the apartment.

Rob has to stop her. Once she drives away, her stubbornness will prevent her from ever returning, even if she wants to. He follows her to the eerie darkness of the underground garage, where she is about to get into her car. To prevent her from leaving, he apologizes, feeling like a character in a Kafka novel *(What exactly is my crime, madam?)*. She continues her assault. "The only reason I stayed with you was I couldn't admit I'd made the wrong choice," she says finally, confirming what Rob has often suspected.

By 6 A.M. her rage is spent. She sleeps in the bedroom, Rob in the living room.

Now it's 3 P.M. He's still in the living room; she's still in the bedroom. Rob knows they won't speak unless he makes the first move. *She must know she's been unreasonable,* he thinks, *but I have never heard her say "I'm sorry" about anything.* He doesn't see why it matters that he came home at four instead of midnight. He has to do his job. *It's not like this has been going on seven days a week for five years; it's only been three months. It's not like I was out drinking, gambling, chasing women . . .*

He will be nice. He will ask if she wants a pizza or a sandwich or something, anything; he will go out and get it. As always, he will be the one who bends. He often tells people, "Alex married an invertebrate, so bending is no problem."

Alex refuses the pizza and the sandwich, but Rob goes out anyway, for an aimless drive up the Taconic Parkway. His thoughts drift to the umbilical cord, which he hopes is not wrapped around the baby's neck.

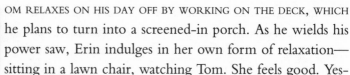

**SUNDAY, JULY 8**
**Southern Maryland**

OM RELAXES ON HIS DAY OFF BY WORKING ON THE DECK, WHICH he plans to turn into a screened-in porch. As he wields his power saw, Erin indulges in her own form of relaxation— sitting in a lawn chair, watching Tom. She feels good. Yesterday they went to a wedding where people said nice things to her, such as "You're so far along and you don't even show."

Erin has decided to nurse, though according to her sister Joanie, who recently had a baby, breastfeeding is a surprisingly complex venture. Erin listened to Joanie talk about hand versus electric pumps, different styles of nursing bras and breast shields, Playtex liners versus Evenflo nipples, whether or not to supplement with formula, and if so, which brand, and does the powdered kind smell better than the liquid ready-to-serve variety . . .

Next Sunday the Wrights leave for a week's vacation. Erin likes to lie on the beach all day with a stack of magazines, but she has heard that pregnant women should avoid the sun. She asked her obstetrician, who told her to be careful about her body temperature going up too high. "Go in the water a lot," the doctor said, "and use an umbrella."

Tom is nervous about taking time off. He's short a mechanic, and summer is a busy season at the station. With reluctance, he will put his bookkeeper in charge. He trusts her under normal circumstances but is not confident about her ability to manage a crisis.

He views the vacation not as a pleasurable break but as a hurdle. Something to get over before real life starts.

NE SHORT MONTH AFTER LUIS'S BIRTH, MARIA FEELS EVERY-thing is back to the way it was—her sleep, her body, and her sex life. She knew you're not supposed to have sex until six weeks after giving birth, but she doubted she could hold out that long and knew Joe couldn't. Last week a girlfriend brought her a magazine article proclaiming that the six-week rule is a myth; it was all the excuse she needed.

That night she and Joe made love. *I hope I won't start bleeding,* Maria thought as they began; *I hope it won't hurt.* She didn't bleed and it didn't hurt. She was close to orgasm when Joe ejaculated. His climax was nothing short of staggering—comparable in intensity to what he felt the very first time he had intercourse. Considerately, he continued to move inside her, but she stopped cold, suddenly worried they shouldn't have done it without a doctor's okay. "You owe me one," she teased him.

They haven't received the insurance money for Joe's stolen car. He takes hers to work, leaving Maria without transportation. She can do a few things in the neighborhood while pushing Luis in his stroller, but it's frustrating to have an entire summer off without access to a car. She has yet to go to the beach or even to her sister's pool. She's done nothing but clean the apartment.

Joe's carelessness about picking up after himself bothers Maria more now that she's home. Today he comes in from playing basketball, removes his sneakers, and shoves them under the dining table. "Do you think those sneakers are going to walk by themselves?" Maria asks. "The maid's gone home for the day."

"You're being a nag."

"If I don't clean, you say I don't do anything, and if I do clean, you tell me I'm ignoring you, and if I ask you for help, you say I'm a nag, so I can't win." She has a new appreciation for full-time housewives. She never realized how much work is involved in staying home all day.

Joe senses that Maria feels imprisoned. He knows he ought to be more helpful, but when he gets home from work after a day that starts at 4 A.M., even putting a sock in the laundry hamper seems a major undertaking.

A LEX'S CONTRACTIONS BEGIN WHILE SHE AND ROB ARE WATCHING *The Bourne Identity* on TV. When the contractions settle into a pattern, coming every five minutes and lasting forty-five or fifty seconds, she leaves a message with her obstetricians' service. Dr. Lindeman, who is on call, gets back to her within minutes. He remembers instantly that she is an ITP patient and tells her to go to the hospital even though her water hasn't broken. (Rob proclaims Lindeman a "class act" for his attentiveness.)

Rob is anxious, but Alex is calm. They may as well finish watching the movie, she tells him. When it's over at 10 P.M., she turns the answering machine on, checks Rob's wallet for the list she prepared of twenty people to call after delivery, and applies lipstick. They leave the apartment.

In the hospital, it comes as news to both Rob and Alex that she can't have an epidural. The anesthesiologist is concerned that the needle might cause a vein to bleed into her spinal cord; because of her low platelets, she might not clot. She has a shot of Demerol instead, which makes her doze between contractions. Rob is focused on the doctors, the doctors are focused on Alex, and no one is watching the monitor closely enough to tell her when to start the Lamaze breathing. Alex wakes from her Demerol-induced nap when the contraction is spiking and can never get on top of the pain, which is more extreme than she ever imagined. "Make it stop, make it stop," she moans to Rob. It is so unlike Alex "I can handle this" della Croce that he is shocked.

Alex knew her doctors would take a scalp sample from the baby to determine whether it has inherited her blood condition (if the test is positive, they will not deliver her vaginally), but she never told Rob about it, knowing it would agitate him. The scalp sample turns out negative, but it is not the kind of surprise Rob enjoys—some guy pricking his baby's head before the poor thing is even *born*.

Alex does not dilate beyond five centimeters, and the medical team can't help matters by giving Pitocin to stimulate contractions; again, her blood condition makes administration of the drug risky. The baby is too large for her pelvis, and its head is in a problematic transverse position. After fifteen hours of useless labor, the doctors perform a cesarean. Without the option of an epidural, they have to give her general anesthesia. Alex is thrilled; she can't wait to be knocked out.

According to hospital policy, husbands cannot witness deliveries requiring general anesthesia. (Watching the doctors insert an endotrachial tube, through which the anesthesia is given, into the mouth of one's wife tends to produce panic in expectant fathers—not what the medical staff wants to deal with in the midst of surgery.)

"Listen," Rob says to the head nurse, "I can understand if you don't want me here while you're putting her out, but I'm going to be here for the delivery." The nurse insists on following the rules. Rob maintains a reasonable tone so as not to be dismissed as a crazy, interfering husband. "The only difference between a cesarean with anesthesia and without anesthesia is anesthesia," he says. "So I'll stay away for that, but I'll return for the surgery." The nurse capitulates.

During the delivery, Rob's eyes are trained on the anesthesiologist. He thinks back to the Incident, to the woman who didn't make it because *some fuckin' second-year resident didn't know how to read a fuckin' X ray*. Rob wants this guy in charge of Alex's life to watch the dials, hook up the right bottles, turn the right screws. When they open Alex up, Rob sees the umbilical cord—wrapped around the baby's neck.

The baby is fine: a strapping nine-pound, three-ounce boy. The birth is recorded at 12:31 P.M., July 10.

Rob will not let his son out of sight until he personally sees someone put the baby's ID bracelet on. *I don't want to learn thirty years from now,* he thinks, *that someone else went home with my kid.* He follows the baby out of the OR and into the nursery. He watches a nurse attach the bracelet, and reads it: Alex's name is on it. Then he studies the placards taped to the other bassinets, which confirm his giddy suspicion that his son is the biggest baby in the nursery.

With Alex settled in a private room, Rob goes home briefly to shower and make all the calls on Alex's list. He adds a twenty-first: to the *mohel* who will perform the briss.

**MONDAY, JULY 16**
**Westchester**

I T IS ALEX'S SECOND DAY HOME. SHE'S CONCERNED THAT HER cesarean scar may never fade enough for her to wear her briefest bikinis but is otherwise unperturbed. When her cousin, an early visitor, calls her "the calmest first-time mother I've ever seen," she is flattered. Alex attributes her equanimity to her sense, from the moment of birth, that her son, Daniel, is *independent* of her. Though she has yet to experience the rapture other new mothers have described, she hasn't felt their anxiety either.

Alex is more puzzled than ever by the concept of postpartum depression. She muses about Jennie, her friend who committed suicide three months after giving birth. *How could anyone have a healthy baby,* she wonders, *and be depressed?*

At night Rob leaps out of bed the instant he hears Daniel cry, lifts him out of the bassinet, and hands him to Alex for breastfeeding. (Rob refers to her breasts as "the diner" or "the Left Bank and Right Bank cafés.") He wonders if it's common for men to be jealous of their wives for being able to nurse; he certainly is. He begs Alex to pump her breasts so he can feed Daniel himself from a bottle, but, she reminds him, the pediatrician says to wait two weeks until the baby gets used to nursing. Besides, Alex finds pumping cowlike and tedious, while breastfeeding is rewarding. She'll have only two months of it before she has to wean Daniel and resume traveling, and she wants as much closeness with him as possible.

Rob already feels that his values have changed. Something that didn't exist a week ago is now all he thinks about. He drives slowly; he's in no hurry to get anywhere but home. He feels serene for the first time in memory. One of his clients, a forty-five-year-old man, has a nine-month-old from a second marriage. He tells Rob he's cut down on the patients he sees so he can be home more with his son. Rob feels the same; he has decided to quit the consulting job. He doesn't want his son to grow up practically fatherless.

In the hospital, he and Alex argued about Daniel's last name. Rob lobbied hard for della Croce. When he was young, kids called him "weenie" and worse; he doesn't want his son to be taunted. But Alex insisted on Weiner. She refuses to break the tradition of giving a child its father's last name. "You chose to see your name as a handicap," she said to Rob, "but you could have chosen to let it toughen you. My parents spoke broken English; as a result, I speak English very well." Still, Rob remained in conflict.

When Alex handed him Daniel's birth certificate and told him to make a decision one way or the other so he could fill it out, Rob called his older brother, Jack, as a last resort. Rob, who finds his brother condescending and often nasty to him, is not in the habit of asking Jack's advice. But Jack has a ten-year-old daughter; maybe, just this once, he could be helpful . . . Rob told Jack he wants his son to love him and is afraid he won't if Rob gives him a crummy last name. Jack said that a child doesn't judge you on external things—how successful you are, how big your house is, what last name you have. What matters is how much time you spend with him, how you treat him.

After Rob got off the phone, he picked up the birth certificate. On the appropriate line, he wrote *Weiner*.

### MONDAY, JULY 23
### An island off the New
### England coast

**S**AM HAS DISCOVERED THE SECRET TO POSTPARTUM ADJUSTMENT: Take the first three months off and make no plans. If you don't have to get up and go to work, the lack of a full night's sleep is bearable; with both spouses around, you spell each other. You don't argue over who does what when or have to coordinate intricate schedules. Working, Sam realizes, is what complicates family life. He does spend two hours a day on the phone with his office, but Juliet's mother is on the island with them; she watches the baby if Juliet wants a nap while Sam is busy. (They've taken to calling her "Saint Felice.") Having your mother-in-law living with you for weeks on end could be a problem for some people, but not for Sam, who considers Felice excellent company.

He knows he and Juliet are luckier than most new parents, being able to create this idyllic island world where the most complex issue they confront is who will take the garbage to the dump: Sam alone? Sam and Juliet? Sam and Felice? Everyone? *But it shouldn't be a matter of luck,* he thinks. *It should be written into the Constitution that every new parent should be given three months' paid leave.* Juliet wonders if their luck is some form of karmic compensation for the horror of Lily's birth.

They've had a few houseguests, but generally their days are disturbed only by Lily's occasional crying and the birds chirping outside. They sleep in the double bed upstairs, with the baby next to them in the bassinet. Lily wakes once around 4:00 A.M., and after Juliet nurses her, everyone goes back to sleep until 7:30. Then the three of them lie together in bed for another breastfeeding session. Sometimes Sam dozes off, but usually he peers over Juliet's shoulder, hoping to catch one of the baby's smiles. After an hour or so, they get up. Sam dresses Lily, and everyone, including Felice, goes for a morning walk, with Lily carried by Sam in the Snugli. They drive to the beach and take turns swimming, go to town for the newspaper, return to the farmhouse for breakfast. Sam makes his calls and Juliet reads the paper while Lily kicks her feet on the blanket they've placed on the living room floor. After lunch, Juliet naps. In the late afternoon they take another swim. The only frenzied time is just before dinner, when Lily gets cranky. Felice and Sam take turns rocking her while Juliet cooks; she often eats with the baby attached to her breast. Sometimes Sam and Juliet have sex, usually in the morning before Lily is awake. They're often racing to finish before the baby starts to cry, but it never fails to be satisfying. The only problem with sex is that they keep forgetting about birth control. Sam will be about to enter Juliet when one of them will say, "Get the diaphragm!" and they shudder at the thought of accidentally conceiving and having to face a second catastrophic delivery.

To Sam's surprise, he doesn't miss professional life. Sometimes he fears he'll *fall behind the eight ball,* but when he picks Lily up and plays with her, the fear abates.

Juliet's apprehension that she would be deprived of Sam's attention after Lily's birth has proved unfounded. She does get less of it—for instance, he used to rub her back at night and now he often doesn't (they're exhausted or trying to put Lily to sleep)—but she isn't envious.

This morning, Juliet is in the bathroom and hears Sam down the hall, cooing to Lily. "What are you doing?" she calls out.

"Making love to my daughter."

"That's not allowed," Juliet says, but she is laughing. It is the kind of exchange she once imagined with dread, but in reality, she finds it endearing.

At times the hospital experience comes back to her—the nerve-wracking sensation in the OR that something had gone wrong, the anesthesiologist looming over her with the mask, the forty-five minutes while Fischl unpacked her uterus. But these memories have been recast as a bad dream from which she has finally awakened.

**MONDAY, JULY 23**
**Westchester**

LEX CRIES SO RARELY THAT SHE CAN NEVER REMEMBER WHEN the last time was, but just before the briss last week, her eyes welled with tears. She had the terrible sense that she was delivering Daniel up to be slaughtered. Her mother had to take a tranquilizer for the same reason.

The women—Alex, her mother, and her mother-in-law—did not witness the actual event. They sequestered themselves in the study, where Alex's mother made her swear (in Italian, to prevent Rob's mother from understanding) that she hadn't converted to Judaism and the child wouldn't be raised Jewish. Alex's mother knows that Daniel won't be raised Catholic either, but as she said to Alex, "If he can't be ours, then he can't be theirs either." Alex reassured her. She wasn't going to start worrying about what will happen when Daniel approaches the age for bar mitzvah.

Meanwhile, Rob and his brother were in the bedroom with the *mohel*. Daniel cried as the *mohel* manipulated his foreskin, and for a moment Rob was upset with himself for letting the *mohel* give Daniel the ritual taste of Manischevitz on a piece of gauze; maybe he gave him too much. ("This is why Jews have an aversion to alcohol," he joked to Alex later. "Have a drink and get your dick cut off.") During the ceremony, as the *mohel* recited the Hebrew prayers, Rob thought of how pleased his father would have been. He was glad he had held his ground with Alex.

Before Rob had a chance to quit the consulting job, he was fired. His employers told him that they need someone who could work full-time. Rob agreed but felt rejected. He wanted it to have been *his* decision. "Either way, it's nothing but good news," Alex said. "You accomplished what you wanted to financially, and now you can watch your kid grow up."

He rarely leaves the house before 9 A.M. on weekdays now and is home by 6:00 or 6:30. Alex doesn't ask why he couldn't have arranged these hours before. *The baby,* she thinks, *is obviously more compelling to him than I am.*

Rob envisions his future with Daniel—the two of them walking in the park, going to the batting cage, involved in Little League. Maybe Daniel will like to play the piano, and maybe he won't. Rob is confident that he'll be able to share his child's interests, whatever they are. His jealousy over Alex's nursing makes him guard the only territory he can carve out for himself—diapering. Rob would prefer Daniel to associate him with something other than shit, but has no choice.

The women in the household laud Rob's diapering technique but criticize him for not holding Daniel's neck securely enough. Rob feels this is unfair.

"Why do you see it as undermining you rather than offering constructive suggestions?" Alex says. She quotes an old Jewish expression to him: "If three people tell you you're dead, then lie down already."

"He's going to be twenty years old and you'll still be telling me, 'Do this, do that.' You're treating me like some caricature of the boob father, and I don't like it."

"If you're not doing something right, one of us will tell you. The baby is more important than your feelings."

Still, Rob secretly likes having his and Alex's mothers around, alternating as live-in babysitters. They iron his shirts, cook his meals, do the laundry, tend to Alex, and leave him free to spend every minute with Daniel. Rob complains about how awful it is having to go to work, but Alex insists that it will be worse for her when she resumes traveling. Already she's thinking about how emotionally difficult it will be to wean Daniel.

Her weight is back to normal, but her belly is like Jell-O from having her stomach muscles cut during surgery. Last night, lying in bed, thinking about how her scar measured ten inches in the hospital, she mourned the passage of her youthful body. *Having a cesarean,* she realized, *is visible evidence that you will never be the same again.* This morning she measures the scar and finds it shorter: her stomach must be tightening up, probably helped along by the contractions caused by nursing.

Rob quit smoking. Alex was slightly annoyed when he told her, "Daniel is the best reason I've ever had for wanting to live."

**THURSDAY, JULY 26**
**Cape Cod**

HE WEATHER HAS BEEN OVERCAST AND ODDLY COLD FOR LATE July, no good for taking the kids to the beach. Sarah's mother is visiting (not, thank God, as the Coens' houseguest), and she and Sarah are not getting along. Yet for reasons Michael can't fathom, Sarah hasn't taken out these frustrations on him. Instead she has been unusually solicitous, doing more of the morning chores, even urging him to leave for work before Ben wakes up and whines for Daddy. They make love at least once a week, an astonishing frequency.

Sarah credits her good humor to a book she's reading: *When You and Your Mother Can't Be Friends.* It has convinced her that she's not alone —the author wrote that no one she interviewed got along with her mother. The book also helps her to feel empathy for Ben, who has just begun swimming lessons. The first day he went into the water only to ankle height; the second day he clutched Sarah as he stood in water to his waist; today, as they leave the house for the swimming lesson, he falls in the driveway and scrapes his knees on the gravel. Chlorine on his raw skin will hurt too much, Sarah knows, for him to go in at all. She remembers her own terror when learning to swim, and her mother's impatience with her. Sarah doesn't want to push Ben the way she was pushed.

The other night Michael watched Sarah doze in a thin white night-gown on the couch upstairs and felt aroused; he began to fondle her breasts, waking her up. He expected her to be furious, but instead she smiled. She allowed him to pick her up and carry her to bed, like a bride.

**SUNDAY, JULY 29**
**Southern Maryland**

 OM HAD TO SPEND ONE DAY OF VACATION SOLVING A CRISIS AT the station. He returned to the beach the same night. Over-all, he kept his worrying about business to a minimum and concentrated on fishing and sunbathing, often thinking, *This is the last vacation for years without having to deal with a kid.* He and Erin went out to dinner a few times, but otherwise pursued separate activities; Tom fished and Erin read on the beach. He enjoyed the time off and thought Erin did too.

He is startled when she tells him, now that they've been home for more than a week, that she felt lonely and distanced from him on vacation, and still does. "You always seem to want to be by yourself, never with me," she says.

"Okay, so I'm a rotten husband." Tom is resentful that she seems to begrudge him his solitude. *Maybe I was being selfish,* he thinks, *but in the course of the year there's very little time devoted to Tom Wright.*

"It's not that," Erin says carefully. "It's just that I'm tired and emotional, and you have to make a little more of an effort toward me."

"I wish you had let me know about this sooner. It's not fair to wait until you're ready to boil."

Erin acknowledges his point, and Tom admits that he is also to blame. He has left the responsibility for planning for the baby mostly in her hands, and regrets it. He never intended to be one of those men who dump everything on their wives. Later, when Erin says she's going out to shop for nursery wallpaper, Tom tells her he wants to come, more from a desire to be a nice guy than from genuine interest. But once they start looking at samples, he realizes he likes being involved—it gives him a sense of excitement about the future.

They go out to dinner with Erin's sister Joanie, visiting from California with her three-month-old son. Erin is impressed by Tom's confident way of handling the infant. When the baby starts to cry in the restaurant, he volunteers to take him outside, where, to his surprise, the baby quickly calms down. *This isn't so scary; this isn't so terrible,* Tom thinks. *You can still go out to dinner, and if the kid fusses, you just take a walk.*

### MONDAY, JULY 30
### An island off the New
### England coast

 OR A WHILE JULIET THOUGHT SHE HAD DEVELOPED THE DREADED mastitis, which Kathie Lee Gifford had described on TV months ago. Hard, painful lumps materialized in one of her breasts, which became significantly engorged. She checked one of her books and determined she had a blocked milk duct. The treatment, she read, is to nurse your baby for as long as possible, apply hot compresses, and take Tylenol. Juliet kept Lily on her breast almost all day. By evening her nipple was sore, but there was no more blockage. The nursing marathon contributed to her bemused sense that she has ceased being a person; she is merely an appendage connected to a breast.

This morning Lily wakes up cranky. Sam talks to her, sings to her, changes her, burps her, and soon has her gurgling happily. He feels a rush of pride no less intense than when he wins an important case.

Sam feels sad thinking of all the men, including his own father and most of his friends, who never had the opportunity to spend uninterrupted months watching their babies see the world unfolding around them. Juliet feels sad thinking of all the women who give birth and are left alone with week-old infants when their husbands return to work. The women have no one with whom to share these blissful moments that will not come again.

**THURSDAY, AUGUST 2**
**Queens**

ARIA DEVOTES THE DAY TO ACQUAINTING TRACY, HER SISTER-in-law and Luis's future babysitter, with Luis's needs—the difference between his hungry and tired cries, the preferred temperature of his formula, how he likes to lie with his blanket against his cheek. By the time she returns home it is already 4 P.M. Mindful of her new housewifely role, she sacrifices a planned workout at the gym to fulfill Joe's request for a shrimp dinner. Joe is napping, so Maria puts Luis in his swing and shells the shrimp. Her hands are full of breadcrumbs when she hears the baby crying. Since Joe is now in the bathroom shaving with the radio on, unable to hear Luis, she has to stop her preparations and go to her son.

"A little help from you would be nice," she says sharply to Joe when he emerges.

"What's wrong?" Joe takes Luis from her. "You always have a face on. It's not like you."

"I don't have time to joke around like I used to."

Joe stares at her baggy shorts, her old T-shirt, her hair tied back in a sloppy ponytail.

"Every day I see you like this," he says, "looking like that cleaning woman Carol Burnett used to play on TV."

"What am I supposed to do, wear a dress and makeup every day?" Maria glares at him. "I can't even take a shower unless someone's here to watch the baby. Even if he's asleep, I won't. I'm afraid he'll choke or something."

"What's wrong with looking decent? It would make you feel better."

"You don't think I do anything."

"I don't think you're enjoying your time off. You have a car now" —he bought a used station wagon a few weeks ago—"but you still say, 'I wish I'd done this, I wish I'd done that.' "

*"We* haven't done anything at all this summer," says Maria.

Joe points to Luis. "Oh yes we did," he says.

He can't figure out what seems so different about her. *She used to be so gung-ho . . .* Is it that she's not going to an office? In the old days he'd get home first, and she'd come in from work nicely dressed and accessorized, hair combed, makeup on.

Maria thinks that more living space would ease her irritability and the tension that has arisen between them. But there's a freeze on hiring throughout the postal system, which makes a transfer out of New York unlikely, and Joe's research on subsidized low-income mortgages here in the city told them that their combined income is too high to qualify—yet he also learned it might be too low to finance a place in a decent neighborhood through a regular bank mortgage.

Joe is depressed about this housing paradox, but his personal troubles seem insignificant compared to world events. The Iraqi army has just invaded Kuwait; U.S. troops will soon be sent to the Persian Gulf. Joe is afraid for his brother, Tony, a U.S. Army staff sergeant stationed in Georgia. Tony is the only one of Joe's four half-siblings with whom he feels deep affinity. He and Maria have chosen Tony as Luis's godfather. The idea of Tony's dying in a foreign war without ever meeting his nephew haunts Joe. It makes him fear that his family is slipping away.

**MONDAY, AUGUST 6**
**Westchester**

 EAVE HIM ALONE, ROB, HE'S SLEEPING." ALEX WATCHES ROB, still in his bathrobe at 8 A.M., hovering over Daniel's crib.

"He just moved, he's up," Rob says, reaching over the Styrofoam baseball bat and ball nestled inches from Daniel's head.

"No, he's not, he twitched in his sleep."

"I didn't get to hold him enough yesterday."

Alex rolls her eyes, but her tone is affectionate. "That's because yesterday you played baseball for five hours."

Rob backs away from the crib. "Yeah, I know—'You weren't the one strapped down to the table screaming, so you have no rights.'" They laugh at the line, which has become Alex's defense for everything.

This is her first day of full-time motherhood. As much as she enjoyed being pampered by her mother and mother-in-law, she wants her house and her baby to herself; there is so little time remaining. In another month the mothers will return. Alex begins seeing local customers after Labor Day and resumes life on the road in October. She doesn't want to dwell on what it will be like to be away from Daniel. There's no point. Traveling is the only way to do her job and she can't afford to quit, though she honestly wouldn't mind being a housewife. She derives satisfaction from the mundane rituals of baby care—sterilizing bottles and pacifiers, bathing Daniel, folding his clothes. She likes having time to rearrange cabinets and clean the Levolor blinds one by one.

Alex often thinks of Carl, her obstetrician. She wasn't prepared to feel such a sense of loss. She misses their stimulating conversations, which were rarely confined to Alex the Patient. She remembers his telling her about women who would come into his office with birthing contracts in hand, spelling out exactly how they wanted their deliveries managed. "They want control, but you can't possibly give it to them," Alex commented, basking in the pleasure on Carl's face, which seemed to say, *You really comprehend what we go through.*

Once she and Carl discussed the new edition of *Our Bodies, Ourselves.* "It's completely out of touch with modern obstetrics," Alex said.

"People who subscribe to that kind of philosophy are not the people I'd want as patients," Carl agreed. "They start out with a basic lack of trust in the relationship." Alex knew he was telling her that she was exactly the kind of patient he wanted.

Reviewing these conversations, Alex realizes that Carl's was the only voice of reason she heard in her last months of pregnancy. *No one ever talks about this,* she thinks. *Do other women miss their obstetricians once it's over, or is it only me?*

Now Daniel is making real wake-up noises. Rob scoops him out of the crib, carries him to Alex, and watches her nurse with jealous impatience. When she's done, she hands Daniel to Rob and goes off to make coffee. Rob grins as he holds his son against his chest, the baby's tiny mouth pressed against a cloth diaper slung over his shoulder. The burping routine, Rob thinks, is more thrilling than box seats behind the dugout at Shea Stadium.

"Why didn't anyone ever tell me this was going to be wonderful?" Rob says to Alex, who has reappeared in the bedroom with two mugs of coffee. "All I ever heard about was how much work it is."

"They were trying to prepare you for the worst," Alex says, "something you of all people should be able to appreciate." She opens a plastic container of crisp cookies, called *pizzelles,* that her mother has baked for them, and removes two thin wafers. "If I had only known that a baby would make you into a person instead of a temple of doom, I would have had one a lot sooner."

Alex is astonished by the change in Rob's attitude since Daniel's birth. He wakes with a smile on his face, smiles all weekend, smiles when he comes home from work. "What am I, chopped liver?" she says when he sweeps by her, going straight to Daniel. But she thinks her envy is a reasonable tradeoff for Rob's happiness.

N HER NIGHTMARE, JULIET IS HEMORRHAGING. "HELP ME, HELP me," she pleads, but no one hears. She wakes at 3 A.M., her breasts painfully engorged, her body covered in sweat. She nudges Sam awake and tells him she has a fever. "No, you don't, go back to sleep," he says, wanting to go back to sleep himself. Juliet begs him to fetch the thermometer. He does; it registers 101.5.

Today the fever is gone, but Juliet has another blocked milk duct. She keeps Lily on her breast for nine hours straight. Then she hands the baby to her mother.

"Let's go into town," she says to Sam. "I need a drink." She pauses, then adds, "Now I know why parents are always saying stuff like that!"

ICHAEL, WHO PUT ON FIFTEEN POUNDS DURING SARAH'S PREG- nancy, has been following the Weight Watchers diet for ten days. The shift from eating whatever he wants to eat- ing almost nothing puts him in a curmudgeonly mood. His problem, Sarah believes, isn't the diet but the way he distributes calories. He saves up everything for dinner, an approach she finds gender-specific. "You don't eat right because you're a man," she tells him, "and men have no common sense."

The weekend they've planned in Nantucket a few weeks from now will be their first time away from the kids in nine months. It will cost them $100 a day in babysitting alone, but Sarah says she doesn't care if it's $1,000 a day. "We need to be alone," she tells Michael, who is too hungry to care.

Michael is nervous about their decision to renovate their house instead of sell it. He wonders if it's foolish to sink $75,000 or more into building an addition; they may never get it back on a resale, and he worries about depleting his trust fund. The way they live, he calculates it will last another five years, ten years at most, and in bleak moments he fears that Sarah will leave him when the money runs out. She knows he has taken care of the kids' educations but has otherwise shown no interest in discussing financial matters; he does the planning, she does the spending. *What will happen,* Michael thinks, *when there's nothing left to spend?*

He's upset about Hannah. He can't soothe her or even get her to take a bottle from him. She wants only her mother. Michael, who thinks of himself as the more maternal parent, feels rejected.

"Now you know how frustrated I was with Ben, when you were the only one who could calm him," Sarah says. She is sympathetic to Michael's distress, but can't help feeling somehow vindicated.

**SATURDAY, AUGUST 11**
**The coast of Maine**

RIN'S FETUS STOPPED MOVING, ALARMING HER. HER BOOKS SAID if you're more than thirty weeks pregnant, as she is, a prolonged absence of movement can indicate trouble. On Thursday, after twenty-four hours without a flutter or a kick, Tom took her to the hospital, where a sonographic exam revealed that the baby was fine. Erin's doctor told her there was no reason to cancel their weekend in Maine, a reunion with Tom's family.

Erin asked if the doctor could tell the baby's sex from looking at the sonogram. Yes, the doctor said. It's a girl. Erin was openly delighted but Tom didn't react. She wondered if he was disappointed. Driving through southern Maine, she asks him. He admits to hoping for a boy, but says he was so relieved to learn that the baby is alive that he no longer cares. Still, when they stop in Freeport at the L.L. Bean store and browse through hunting and fishing gear, Tom says in a regretful tone, "I guess I won't be buying any of this for our daughter."

"Girls can do whatever boys can," Erin says, reminding him that her father took her hunting, fishing, and boating.

The news of the baby's sex makes parenthood seem real and leads to newly specific discussions. In the car en route to Bar Harbor, site of the family reunion, they decide to call their child Kaitlin Ann—the first name a traditional Irish one in honor of Erin's heritage, the second after Erin's mother. When they reach the motel, Erin makes Tom read an article in a parenting magazine about how men can help their wives cope with postpartum blues and how women can soothe husbands who feel left out once the baby is born. Later, at dinner, she voices her fear that responsibility for child care will be 99 percent hers.

"I'll be more active than you expect," says Tom. "I bet I'll feel more neglected than you'll feel burdened."

They talk about how to handle finances if Erin doesn't return to work, how to approach potty training, even how to tell their daughter about sex. The conversations give Tom a renewed feeling of unity with Erin. He has a sense of things falling into place.

### SATURDAY, AUGUST 11
### Upstate New York

OE AND MARIA DRIVE TO THE BASEBALL HALL OF FAME IN COOPERS-town. There Joe holds Luis, dressed in his tiny Mets uniform and cap, on his lap inside Yogi Berra's clubhouse locker while Maria snaps their picture. They then spend hours looking for a vacant motel room. They're ninety minutes away from Lake George when they give up and decide that they may as well drive to Joe's mother's house and sleep there.

Early the next morning Joe's brother Tony calls, sobbing. He's going to the Persian Gulf and wants to see his family before he leaves. Joe tries to work out the logistics. The lowest plane fare available to Tony's army base in Georgia, he learns, is $258 round trip. Joe can afford one ticket, but his family seems to expect him to pay for everyone. "I look like the bad guy here," he says to Maria privately. "They want to go and I don't have the money to send them."

"Look," Maria tells him, "you're not God, you're not made of money." Joe calls Tony back and gets his wife, Theresa. "Tony is too broken up to talk," she says. Joe explains the situation to her. In the end the family decides that between them all, they can scrape together only enough money to send Joe's mother and stepfather.

Back home, Joe watches the news reports obsessively, saying to Maria, "I wish I could go with Tony." She tries to calm him: "It's the career he chose, you can't do anything about that." But Joe is fixated on the thought that Tony will die and Luis will be deprived of knowing him.

Maria attempts to cheer him by putting on makeup and his favorite dress. "Do I still look like a housewife?" she asks coquettishly, expecting compliments. Instead he tells her she needs a haircut.

**MONDAY, AUGUST 20**
**Westchester**

 LEX HAS HER POSTPARTUM CHECKUP AND IS SHOCKED BY HOW much the pelvic exam hurts. Carl says estrogen levels drop while a woman is nursing, affecting vaginal lubrication. She is reminded of what other women have told her: a friend saying that intercourse still hurt eighteen months after the birth of her child; her sister-in-law saying that she didn't even try having sex for ten months. Alex, who has been vacillating between desire and lack of interest, now wonders if she'll be able to make love at all. But she figures nothing can be as agonizing as labor, the yardstick by which she now measures all physical pain.

Rob has been doing well at work; his sales are way up. But as his client roster lengthens, so do his hours. He often gets home after eight, leaving Alex alone to endure Daniel's cantankerous period, from six to eight. Tonight Rob makes a rare appearance at 6:30. After fifteen minutes of Daniel's nonstop screaming, he demands that she call the pediatrician. Alex glowers at him. "If you read the fucking books," she says, "you'd know it's normal. In a month he'll be out of this phase." Rob looks at her suspiciously. She can almost hear him thinking, *There you go again, being cavalier, denying there's a problem.*

A new object hangs over Daniel's crib—a medallion with a cross, an anchor, and a heart, respectively symbolizing faith, hope, and charity. It's a good-luck charm to ward off the evil eye, known in Italian as *malocchio*. Alex's father bought several of these charms in Italy twenty-one years ago, for his grandchildren-to-be. Alex was only thirteen at the time and unaware of her father's purchase until a day ago, when her mother presented her with one of them.

Sadness is not an emotion Alex readily feels, but for a moment, watching the medallion swing over the crib, she almost weeps. Daniel is the only one of her father's ten grandchildren he didn't live to see.

**THURSDAY, AUGUST 23
An island off the New
England coast**

LIGHT RAIN FALLS BEYOND THE WIDE, UNCURTAINED LIVING room window of the farmhouse. Juliet nurses Lily on the couch in front of the window while Sam works on his latest domestic project, replastering the dining room ceiling. Lily pulls herself off Juliet's breast and stares up at her mother, forming contented little *o*'s with her mouth. Juliet laughs.

"She makes me feel like Greta Garbo and Robin Williams rolled into one," Juliet yells out to Sam. "I've never had this kind of absolute love from any human being."

Sam climbs off his ladder and hurries into the living room for his share of Lily's adoration. He sits close to his wife and daughter on the couch and mimics Lily's *o*'s. The baby rewards him by grabbing his beard.

"A couple of days ago," he tells Juliet, "I was jealous, watching you nurse her for hours. It surprised me. It was this feeling that you were so involved with her, you could do without me . . . you couldn't care less if I was there or not. You have just so much energy, and the baby is going to get it first."

"You weren't very sympathetic when I was in pain from the blockage," Juliet counters.

"I'm not very sympathetic to anything in the middle of the night. If you woke up and said, 'I'm dying,' I'd probably say, 'Okay, now go back to sleep.' "

"Well, I guess you make up for it. I've seen you hold and rock her when you're talking about some really complicated legal issue with someone on the phone, even while she's crying. If I had a job like yours, I couldn't take care of the baby at the same time."

"But you can't tell a baby to shut up," Sam says magnanimously, enjoying Juliet's praise.

"You never say to me, 'I have to work, you take care of the baby.' "

"That wouldn't be fair."

"Fair, schmare! You have a job. I don't."

"But this is a period when I'm *supposed* to be with the baby. If I feel like doing something else at the same time, she still comes first. I'm not going to put her down just because I'm talking to some famous dildo in Washington. Besides, I like telling someone, 'The baby's crying, I have to get off the phone.' It's a way of saying there are more important things in the world than all this professional bullshit."

"That's because you're a man. If you're a woman and you say that, people think you're not serious about your career or you're not successful enough to hire a babysitter."

"Yeah . . ." Sam's interest in the conversation flags; Lily is smiling at him. He holds out his arms to her.

**WEDNESDAY,
AUGUST 29
Southern Maryland**

 HE PAST FEW DAYS HAVE BEEN DIFFICULT ONES FOR ERIN. ON Saturday a bee stung her hand as she sat in the back yard watching Tom work on the porch, and an allergic reaction sent her to the emergency room. The next day she felt a craving for sex—for intimacy, really. Tom was more than willing to oblige but lost his erection as soon as he entered her. Erin can count the times this has happened in the twelve years they've been lovers: exactly twice, when he'd had too much to drink.

"This isn't working," Tom said, pulling away from Erin and lying back against the pillows.

"What do you mean?"

"Maybe I've had too much to drink."

"Come on, you know you haven't had anything to drink today."

"I'm afraid I'm going to hurt the baby."

"Trust me," Erin said, "there's a nice cover in there, you're not going to penetrate it." But he had given up. Erin went into the bathroom and looked at herself in the mirror. She returned to bed crying. "I'm ugly and fat," she said. "You don't want me."

Tom tried to reassure her. "It's not you. But I can't stop myself from thinking there's a baby in there, watching us. I never thought that before."

"I look grotesque."

"Not to me. Maybe your stomach is a little bigger, but there's a good reason for it." Tom saw he was getting nowhere, and Erin decided she will not instigate lovemaking again.

On Monday she was too depressed about the failed sexual encounter to go to work. She felt better that night; she talked to a friend who told her that *her* husband wouldn't make love to her for the last five months of her pregnancy because he feared hurting the baby. And a section about expectant fathers in one of Erin's books mentioned this as a common concern. Tom's explanation, she began to think, might be truthful.

In the shower Tuesday morning, Erin felt an odd protrusion on her labia. She got out, sat on the toilet seat, and held a hand mirror up to her genitals. The reflection revealed an alarmingly swollen vein. Erin called her obstetrician, who told her it was a varicose vein; one in five women, she said, experience this late in pregnancy. She advised Erin to put her feet up whenever possible, soak in a warm bath or use a compress, and avoid heavy lifting as well as intercourse and orgasm. Any of those activities, the doctor said, could cause the vein to rupture. "We can't have sex anymore," Erin told Tom, relieved to have a medical excuse to avoid any more failures.

Today, driving home on the Beltway, Erin considers a heartening piece of news. To her surprise, the law firm agreed to shorten her workday by two and a half hours, beginning September 10. She thought they'd refuse her request on the grounds of setting an unwanted precedent. The new hours, from 10 A.M. to 4:30 P.M., should ease the fatigue of her final two months of pregnancy. Her employers also approved the four-day work week she requested when (if) she returns from leave in February.

Erin and Tom again discuss her working as the station's bookkeeper. Tom is convinced it's a good idea, but Erin remains ambivalent. She fears making mistakes that might cost the station a lot of money—and, more significant, she fears disappointing Tom. She once prided herself on her relentless attention to detail but recently has been careless, and often finds herself apologizing profusely to her boss, Philip. He always assures her that her work is beyond reproach, adding that his wife also complained of forgetfulness during the third trimester. "It goes with the territory," he says. His words are soothing, but Erin thinks, *If your boss happens to be your husband, even one slip-up would be too many*. Even if she is faultless, she still envisions conflict. If they run the station together, how can they go on vacation at the same time? Suppose she tries it for six months and doesn't like it; will Tom be angry, or hurt? When she voices these concerns, Tom says blithely, "We'll work it out." Maybe, Erin thinks, she *does* worry too much about hypothetical problems, as he often tells her, but he doesn't worry enough.

Tom has been home by seven almost every night lately; sometimes Erin walks in to find he has already made dinner. "Am I demanding too much from you?" she asked the other night, feeling guilty.

"Don't be ridiculous," he said. "You and the baby are my first priority. I don't want to act like I did before, centered on work and myself and not on us." *What is going on here?* he thought. *First she tells me to make more of an effort; now it bothers her.*

The fathers in the neighborhood tease Tom mercilessly about Lamaze, which begins in two weeks. "Bring lots of pillows," one man says, "because you're going to be sound asleep." Another expresses an attitude that Tom finds selfish and dumb: "Hey, you get your wife pregnant; that should be enough. Why do we have to do all this other stuff?" Tom agrees with Erin that the classes will be an opportunity for them to meet other couples going through the same thing they are, which will make what lies ahead less *spooky*. As for the birth process itself, well . . . He likes the idea of having something so powerful that they can share forever.

**THURSDAY, AUGUST 30**
**Queens**

"Y OU'RE NOT GOING OUT IN *THAT*," JOE SAYS TO MARIA, STARING at the miniskirt she wears. Friends of theirs are getting married this weekend, and Maria is on her way to the bachelorette party at Chippendale's, a nightclub featuring male strippers. Maria makes a face and retreats to the bedroom. She appears minutes later in the same skirt, pulled down over her hips to make it look longer.

"You're like a teenager going out on a date, trying to fool her parents," Joe says. "The minute you get outside you'll hike that skirt up again."

Maria laughs. "Babe," she says, flouncing out the door, "you're so old-fashioned."

"Have a good time," Joe calls after her. He means it, though he *is* old-fashioned. He doesn't like to see his wife, or his daughter for that matter, in provocative clothes, and he suspects that when girls—even those with children—get together for a night on the town, it's *cuckoo*. But he's more concerned about the expense of the evening than the length of her skirt. It will cost twenty dollars just to get into Chippendale's; whatever Maria drinks will be extra. Joe is suddenly conscious of every penny they spend, because they've found a house to buy.

It's on a cul-de-sac in a racially mixed area of Queens (Joe didn't want an all-white neighborhood, where he suspects people might give a Hispanic family a hard time). It has three bedrooms, a full basement, a separate dining room, a large yard, and is semiattached to Maria's brother's house, giving them access to a pool. The place needs work, but Joe can do most of it himself with assistance from relatives. The price is $140,000. They need a 10 percent cash down payment; they've got $6,000 in the bank and will have to borrow the rest from family and friends. Depending on interest rates, their monthly housing costs will jump from $700 to about $1,200. The purchase will force Maria to return to work on September 10, three weeks earlier than planned. She is sad to be deprived of that time with Luis but sees no point in self-pity. The fact is, they need her paycheck.

If they buy the house, the commute into Manhattan will be fifteen minutes longer for both of them. To be on time for work at 8:00, Maria will leave home with Luis at 6:30, drop him at Tracy's, and get on the subway. Joe, whose day is over at 2:30, will pick the baby up in the afternoon and take care of him until Maria returns at 5:00.

Whenever Joe looks around their tiny apartment, he feels relief. Once they become homeowners, he will have fulfilled his duty as head of the household, providing his family with space and security. Joe's relief, however, is tempered by nagging skepticism. The deal, he reminds himself, could always fall through.

**THURSDAY, AUGUST 30**
**Cape Cod**

ICHAEL AND SARAH'S WEEKEND ON NANTUCKET WAS GREAT while it lasted, which wasn't long enough. They ate and drank so much that Michael gained back the few pounds he lost on Weight Watchers. They shopped in the island's arty boutiques, toured the galleries, and indulged several times in what Sarah considered wild and furious sex. They talked about how much harder it is to have two kids than one. "You have to have a really strong marriage to survive it," Sarah said. "I think ours is strong enough." Michael was shocked, and heartened. "You *do?*" he said, musing about how a simple change in environment has a remarkable effect on his wife.

To Sarah, the weekend accomplished what she hoped. It reminded her that when they're alone together, their natural compatibility (and her sense of humor) reasserts itself. Although she missed her children more than she expected to, she tells Michael they must get away from them every three months from now on; it is critical, she says, to the health of the marriage.

Since their return Hannah has been sick, waking several times at night, and Sarah is back to her sleepless, cranky self. She says the weekend renewed her faith in the marriage, but Michael doesn't see what difference it made, in the end.

**MONDAY, SEPTEMBER 3**
**Westchester**

HE POSTPARTUM HONEYMOON IS OVER. LIFE IS BACK TO WHAT Alex calls *S.O.S.*: the same old shit. Rob is smoking again. His eating is out of control, which means that Alex has to hide desirable food (with little success). He won't make time for the most minor household repairs, like the light switch in the den that got disconnected eight weeks ago. Alex could do these things herself, but why should she? She already juggles her work, the housekeeping, the errands, and full-time care of the baby, while Rob does nothing once he gets home other than play with Daniel. He seems to think his willingness to change diapers should earn him a Nobel Prize, but Alex feels differently. *It's okay to play the '50s husband if you're the sole wage earner and your partner is happy playing the '50s wife,* she believes, *but that scenario doesn't apply to us.*

Lately Rob has been talking about getting a law degree and moving to the country, where he would be a small-town attorney doing wills and real-estate deals for $10,000 a year. He says he wants to be respected, like Atticus Finch in *To Kill a Mockingbird.* Alex has heard this before. Years ago Rob got as far in his fantasy as taking the LSATs, but he didn't score in the highest percentile and gave up on law school, saying that he would only be able to get into a second-rate one. Now he wants to try again, which tells Alex that although parenthood may have lightened his gloom-and-doom outlook, it hasn't affected his Peter Pan–like refusal to face the facts of adult life.

"You were so damn smart in college," she says this Labor Day morning. "You could dance around everyone with your flypaper memory, get A's without studying. But you can't do that as an adult. That's why I'm pissed off when I see you overeating and smoking— why are you doing it if it doesn't work? You think I hound you about trivial shit, you think people who keep appointment books and to-do lists are stupid lemmings, but those things are what would keep you from tottering on the edge."

"How am I supposed to argue with you?" Rob says. "You're smart enough to be able to misunderstand almost anything in a coherent fashion. You think this is about me being childish. But it's really about your life not being perfect."

"All I can see ahead of us is this long road of arguing about bullshit, and I won't put up with it for the next thirty years, or until you have a heart attack and die, whichever comes first."

Rob sighs. The holiday dawned sunny and warm; he wanted a family stroll in the park. Instead he has to listen to this harangue. "You probably wish you had married Jeffrey," he says, referring to her ex-fiancé. "You would have been the wife of a rich doctor."

"Oh, *please,*" Alex says. "You know I never wanted to be *paid for.*

When I say I want you to be successful, I mean I want you to be happy with what you do."

"You lucked into a good situation. I didn't."

"If that's true, it's because I plugged away at a job I hated in order to get a better one. The harder I work, the luckier I get, but all you see is the luck, you don't see the work. And speaking of work, I've made more changes in my lifestyle than you to accommodate the baby. I'll compromise on sleeping, I'll hold Daniel while I do the laundry, even though I'd rather sit down and watch TV like you do."

"Just tell me what it is you want done."

"But that's the point. We're supposed to be partners. I don't want to tell you, and you shouldn't want to be told. That's bad for our marriage."

The argument ends when Daniel wakes from his nap. Rob takes his stroll—alone. Alex nurses the baby and thinks about her father, who didn't play the *male idiot role* Rob has adopted, though he was of an older generation and a macho Italian besides. Her mother arranged her life to suit her husband, who wanted her home when the children arrived from school. But he assumed his share of domestic responsibility without being told to. He washed Alex's face each morning, using his bricklayer's hands so gently that Alex didn't feel the roughness. He helped in the kitchen: he baked the Christmas cookies, washed the salt off the anchovies, grated cheese for pasta, prepared the Sunday lamb by cutting slits in the raw meat and filling them with parsley and garlic. He was always respectful and solicitous of Alex's mother; in countless ways he demonstrated how he valued her. If only Rob would do the same.

Rob continues to show no interest in sex. When Alex asks about it, he makes jokes. She scrutinizes herself naked in the mirror: her stomach, she judges, is still soft, but otherwise her body looks good. She can't imagine that Rob doesn't think so. *But when your husband doesn't want to make love to you,* she reflects, *it's impossible not to take it personally.*

**MONDAY,
SEPTEMBER 10**
**Southern Maryland**

T YESTERDAY'S BABY SHOWER GIVEN FOR ERIN BY HER SISTER Molly, there were beautiful flowers, delicious food, lavish gifts, and people telling her she looked great, which Erin badly needed to hear. The gift that meant the most was Molly's. It is a child's rocking chair that once was Erin's. When Erin was ten, Molly had her first child, and Erin gave the chair to her baby niece. Molly refinished it and painted it in a whimsical style. Now it has come full circle.

Today is Erin's first shortened workday, at the beginning of her thirty-fifth week of pregnancy. She arrives home at five, naps until six, and spends the next three hours at somewhat of a loss. She doesn't know what to do with the open-ended time she yearned for, so she worries. How will she know she's really in labor? Will she make unnecessary trips to the hospital? Or will she fail to arrive in time? Will her labor be so quick she won't get an epidural? So slow that the doctor will take her *off* the epidural, causing God knows what kind of pain? How much bigger will her breasts get if she nurses? How guilty will she feel if she doesn't?

The baby's room is ready—wallpapered by Molly, painted by Tom. When the work is done, Tom stands alone in the center of the room, staring at the crib he assembled. *In another month,* he thinks, *there will be a baby in it.* He tries to picture this, and fails.

**FRIDAY, SEPTEMBER 14**
**Queens**

ARIA'S FIRST WEEK BACK AT WORK WAS A STRUGGLE. ON SUNday she was depressed and weepy, thinking about being away from Luis. On Monday morning she dropped the baby off at Tracy's and couldn't stop kissing him, talking to him, dripping tears all over him, though he was asleep. She arrived at her office looking forward to nothing but a paycheck. Her coworkers gave her a warm reception, with doughnuts and bagels and a hand-lettered WELCOME BACK sign. That helped, but she was so anxious to get home that her heart raced all day. She entered the apartment at five, calling for Luis, and found him in the bedroom with Joe. Luis saw her, dropped his bottle, and giggled; Maria cried. *When he takes his first steps, says his first words,* she thought, *I'll be at work.*

She has so many chores to do at night that she has little chance to play with her son before his 8:30 bedtime. She is envious of Joe for getting off work at 2:30 and having two uninterrupted hours with him.

It looks like the house deal will go through, which both elates and frightens them. The extra $500 a month in real-estate costs on top of the $260 for Tracy's babysitting services has forced Joe to reduce his weekly Lotto investment from $14 to $4, to consider canceling his beloved cable TV service, and to scrutinize the phone bills, which have been stratospheric this year because of all the family crises.

Joe wonders why he has committed himself financially to staying in the New York area when what he really wants is a town where the living is easy enough to allow Maria to stop working and have another child by the time Luis is two. *Don't start doubting the decision now,* he tells himself, *or you'll end up spinning in circles.*

### MONDAY, SEPTEMBER 17
### An island off the New
### England coast

N A DREAM, JULIET'S SUNGLASSES AND EYEGLASSES BREAK. SHE TRIES to put them back together with a needle and thread but instead sews her nipple to Lily's ear. She interprets this dream quite literally as an expression of fear that she will fasten herself ever closer to Lily and be blind to the rest of life.

Juliet's favorite time of day is the cozy early morning nursing hour. Her second favorite is when she wakes from her afternoon nap and

Sam brings Lily to her. The baby greets her with an eager smile, the reaction fathers get all the time when they come home from work, Juliet assumes. *If you're together constantly,* she thinks, *there is never a moment when you rediscover each other.* If she hires a part-time babysitter in the city, she will be away from Lily enough for them both to experience rediscovery—enough, but not too much. Juliet remembers women friends with careers telling her about how hard it was to go back to work full-time when their babies were three months old and no longer colicky, just as it was starting to be fun. Juliet is grateful for her privileged life, which allows her to enjoy the best of both worlds, being away from and being home with her child as she pleases. She is also guilty about being able to hire a sitter without having to earn a paycheck, about having two homes when some people have none . . .

Sam is going through his own mental winding-down process as they enter the final two weeks on the island. *It's no wonder,* he thinks, *why couples fight more when they have a kid.* Even in this relative paradise, there's a fair amount of parental irritability. How bad will it get when they return to the real world?

**WEDNESDAY,
SEPTEMBER 19
Westchester**

 CIGARETTE BURNS BETWEEN ROB'S FINGERS AS HE SITS IN HIS car, puzzling over his lack of sexual desire. *I'm tired . . . there's no time . . . everything is so baby-oriented now . . . there's something about the nursing; Alex and Daniel seem like an indivisible unit.* Once Daniel is weaned, Rob thinks, he'll feel differently. But now, when he sees the baby at Alex's breast, she seems so *beautiful, almost virginal . . . like a shrine, and you shouldn't violate a shrine.* Alex's breasts, always a major part of their lovemaking, are now part of the shrine. He can't imagine touching them. It would be like defiling something holy.

His need for her is emotional, not physical. He cherishes their intimacy when the apartment is cold and they're in bed, cuddling for warmth. Even when they're naked, pressed against each other, he doesn't feel aroused. His love for Alex overwhelms him, it's a more powerful love than he has ever felt, yet somehow it leaves no room for desire. He knows she's upset, but there's nothing he can do.

Last night *Field of Dreams* was on television. Rob has seen it three or four times and always cries. *"If you build it, he will come"*—a passion for baseball shared by a father with a son who becomes a father. Rob last saw the film just before Daniel was conceived. When the character played by Kevin Costner says to his father, "Dad, do you want to have a catch?" Rob remembers thinking, *If she gets pregnant, if we have a son, my son and I will have a catch.* Now that those *ifs* have become reality, the movie has taken on a new dimension. *Now I have a son,* Rob thought, watching the TV screen; *now we will have a catch.* There were tears in his eyes. "The first time we saw this," he told Alex, "I never thought I'd be lucky enough to have a son."

These are the things he thinks about. Sex is part of another century, another life.

**THURSDAY,
SEPTEMBER 20
Cape Cod**

UTUMN HAS BEGUN, BRINGING WITH IT THE GLOOMY VISTA OF the coming Cape Cod winter. But Sarah is keeping herself too busy to get depressed. She's setting up a crafts bazaar, planned for mid-October, for one of the businesswomen who hired her as a consultant. The pay is minimal, but the project is rich in side benefits: it puts Sarah in touch with talented people and utilizes her artistic and organizational strengths. She's putting in ten hours a week on another consulting job, for a woman who hand-paints silk fabrics. She's serving on two synagogue committees. She's taking a weekly art course, for which Michael is happy to pay $200 in tuition. He knows that Sarah never wants to be, as she often puts it, one of those boring people who can only talk about their kids.

Tonight is her first art class. Michael hugs her as she leaves the house. "This is a big moment," he says. "I'm really proud of you." His excitement touches her, but she won't reveal it. "I'm only going to school," she says. Michael stands in the doorway watching her drive away, wondering if she really feels so nonchalant. He'd be anxious about his performance.

When Sarah gets home, the kids are asleep and Michael is in the guest room watching TV. She joins him there and says she wants to make love. *If that's all it takes to put her in the mood,* Michael thinks afterward, *I've got to get this woman out of the house more often.*

**FRIDAY, SEPTEMBER 21**
**Westchester**

IGHTER, TIGHTER, TIGHTER!" ALEX STANDS MOTIONLESS IN the middle of the study, directing her mother, who is binding her breasts with a wide ribbon of elastic. Not wanting to traumatize Daniel by removing herself and her breasts from him at the same time (she begins traveling in two weeks), she stopped nursing yesterday—perhaps too abruptly. She is still full of milk, which makes it painful to lie on her stomach or to tolerate a shoulder belt against her chest. None of her books on breastfeeding said anything about how to stop the process, so Alex called Carl for advice. He recommended using ice packs and wrapping a sheet or pillowcase as tightly around her chest as she can stand.

With the binding in place, Alex feels she's having a heart attack. She can't breathe, move, talk; pain shoots through her body. Finally she gestures to her mother: *take this thing off.* Liberated, she collapses on the couch. Now she knows why turn-of-the-century women bound up in bustiers to slenderize their waists were always in need of smelling salts.

She couldn't enjoy the final days of nursing because she so regretted having to stop, but she seems to be suffering more than Daniel. He sometimes turns his face to her chest when he's hungry, but he doesn't cry, and without being subject to every asparagus stalk his mother consumes, he has less gas.

Alex is moving ahead with plans for Daniel's baptism. She has to stick to what she told Rob—if there is a briss, there will be a baptism —and she doesn't want to disappoint her family, particularly her brother Giovanni, who will be Daniel's godfather. Giovanni has lymphoma, and Alex hopes the responsibility bestowed upon him at Daniel's christening will give him a new reason to live; the della Croces take godparenting seriously. During the ceremony she and Rob will have to agree (or at least go through the motions of agreeing) to raise Daniel as a Catholic. Her uncle, a priest, could officiate, but Alex won't allow it. She can't bring herself to lie to him.

On September 17, Rob turned thirty-five. It is also Alex's mother's birthday. Usually they celebrate together with a cake inscribed with both of their names, but this year Alex decided to surprise Rob with his own—a Carvel ice cream concoction, his favorite. When the first cake appeared on the table with just his mother-in-law's name on it, Rob looked stricken. "Did you forget about me?" he whispered to Alex. He was so upset that Alex almost told him about her surprise, which was in the kitchen. Instead she said, "Rob, don't make a scene."

When the cake came out, covered with flickering candles, Rob cried. He looked at Alex and at Daniel. He thought, *This is the happiest I've ever been.*

### THURSDAY, SEPTEMBER 27
### Southern Maryland

SO FAR, THE LAMAZE COURSE IS INFORMATIVE BUT DULL. THE BEST part was the hospital tour, which allowed Tom to rehearse in his mind certain details (which parking lot to use, which door to enter) and Erin to worry some more.

Today at work a staff meeting is called. Erin is nervous—has she done something wrong?—but when she enters the conference room, people yell, "Surprise!" It is another baby shower, with food, drink, gifts, and every one of the law partners is present. Erin is remorseful about all her recent complaining.

The gas station business has slowed considerably, because of a combination of the conflict in the Gulf, the sluggish national economy, and the time of year (dry, temperate fall weather doesn't cause profitable car problems). But Tom is, strangely, at peace. He feels, as parenthood approaches, that he and Erin are in sync, working together toward a common goal. They are a team, helping each other, which makes the bad things better and the good things great.

**THURSDAY,
SEPTEMBER 27
Westchester**

 *OMETHING IS OVER,* ALEX THINKS AS SHE STARES AT HER shrunken breasts. With the drying of her milk comes a profound sense of finality. Her physical connection to her son, which began with conception, is forever broken. Next week she goes on the road. She looks forward to being a businesswoman once again, admired for more than her ability to measure formula, but she wasn't prepared for the emotional hardship of combining work with motherhood. *It would be so much easier to be either Tarzan or Jane,* she realizes, *instead of pieces of both.*

Alex finally mentions the baptism to Rob, expecting resistance. She gets none. He knew she'd go through with it after he forced the briss; he has had two months to resign himself to it.

She was surprised the other night when he said he wanted to make love. Deciding that this was no time to ask *Why now?* Alex opened the drawer of the rosewood nightstand, where condoms are stored. There were none.

"I promise," Rob said, lying on the bed, "it will be safe."

Alex sighed. She hated to miss the opportunity—*who knows how long it will be before he'll want to do it again?*—but she would not risk another accident. "That's how this whole thing started, remember? You said it would be safe, I got pregnant, and that was the end of our sex life."

"I'll control myself."

"Sure."

He shrugged. "Okay," he said. He got under the covers and went to sleep.

**MONDAY, OCTOBER 8**
**Manhattan**

 AM DEVOTED THE WEEKEND TO PARING DOWN THE CONTENTS OF the living room closet, which was cluttered with junk Juliet has accumulated over the years. When he was done, he admired his work. The coats were neatly hung, the hangers lined up in the same direction. The top shelf contained only items still in use. The floor was completely cleared and swept.

When Sam gets home tonight, Juliet is exhausted from her day alone with Lily, depressed because she interviewed yet another sitter she doesn't like, and sad because she put Lily down to sleep in a crib instead of the bassinet for the first time (another sign of the end of Lily's infancy). Wearily, she looks in the refrigerator, wondering what to make for dinner—it's her turn. She goes into the living room to ask Sam what he wants and finds him staring into the closet. On the floor is a shopping bag filled with clothes for Lily, hand-me-downs from relatives that are still too big.

"I just emptied out this goddamn closet and you're starting a new pile of junk," he explodes. "Why do you always have to dump everything wherever you please?'' He grabs the bag and throws its contents around the room.

"You're acting like a lunatic!" Juliet is sobbing. "I've spent all day with the baby, I'm tired, I put something in the closet, and you act like I'm trying to kill somebody!" She runs into the bathroom, slamming the door.

The force of her response—she almost never cries when they argue —makes Sam stop flinging. He feels abject. He knows he overreacted idiotically.

He goes into the bathroom. Juliet is in the tub, still crying. He apologizes repeatedly. "I'll fix dinner," he says.

"Forget it. I'm going to bed."

"Don't go to bed, please don't," he implores her. He hates to end a fight with one of them going off angry and alone. "I went berserko, I'm sorry. I was an asshole." He is so penitent that Juliet, who normally would torture him with silence for a while, agrees to stay up. She finishes her bath while Sam goes into the kitchen and heats some leftover ratatouille. He sets the table. The food is waiting when she comes in; the fight is over. They discuss the need to hire a babysitter.

Juliet is stalling. She feels guilty about having help because she's not working, and in some way she is loath to give up time with Lily. But she is also desperate for time to herself. Her mother comes downtown for a few hours each week to relieve her, but other than that there's no respite until Sam gets home. By then Juliet is so tired she can barely move, talk, or think. She can't engage in lively dialogue, *any* dialogue, with Sam. She has no time to read, and when she doesn't read she feels empty. Sam will mention the Gulf crisis or the federal budget, and Juliet has no opinion at all, which she finds terrifying. She didn't feel this way on the island, where there was no discrepancy between their daily experiences. Now Sam goes off to work and returns home with gossip and ideas and news, and Juliet fears she has nothing to offer him in exchange.

"That's horseshit," Sam tells her. "You have a ludicrous fear of being boring. You still do twice as much reading as I do. Maybe we talk more about the baby and less about politics than we used to, but that's because the baby's more interesting than the other crap. You don't need to read more. You need to hire help."

"I don't know if we should spend the money when I'm not bringing any in."

"Stop feeling guilty about that. If we don't get help, you'll go crazy, and that won't do wonders for our relationship."

A sitter won't increase the quantity of their time together, but Sam expects it will enhance the quality. He can tell from the phone conversations they have during the day that Juliet's patience begins to run out around noon or one o'clock; he thinks they should get a sitter from one to five, four afternoons a week, so she won't be at breaking point when he gets home. He has to go to Europe later this month. If they don't line up help before then, Juliet will have the baby all day and night, which will be too much.

The morning after their fight, Juliet gets her period. She is shocked. She didn't expect it to happen while she was still nursing. She feels her body is telling her something she's not ready to hear: *it's time to reproduce again*. She continues to wonder if she's abnormal. The same thing that kept her from getting pregnant for so long, that almost killed her in childbirth, that gave her blocked milk ducts, also made her period begin too soon.

During her postpartum checkup in July, Bernstein predicted that her menstrual flow would be reduced because her arteries are tied. But she bleeds heavily. The fear that began a year ago on the island and peaked after Lily's birth is once again aroused: *I will bleed until I die.*

### MONDAY, OCTOBER 15
### Westchester

 LEX COMPLETED HER FIRST POSTPARTUM BUSINESS TRIP WITH mixed feelings. Her clients seemed thrilled to see her and exclaimed over pictures of Daniel. Many of the men confided that their wives were still overweight years after giving birth, yet here was Alex, slim as ever. She felt smug. But at night, alone in her hotel, she missed Daniel.

Years ago she stopped leaving Rob her itinerary; he used to call her incessantly wherever she was, running up huge phone bills, for no specific reason. Though he said he did it because he missed her, Alex thinks he wanted to check up on her. Having a baby hasn't made her feel that she should be more accessible to her family. If something happens to Daniel when she's three plane rides away and can't get home for hours, she thinks, there's nothing she can do but worry herself sick. So she still doesn't leave her phone number, but now she calls in twice a day instead of every other day. Whenever she called during this trip and Rob answered the phone, he eagerly enumerated the unique and charming moments of life with Daniel, telling her how happy the baby was—as if to say, *He doesn't need you.* Alex returned home in no mood to share her son with anyone. "I haven't seen him in days," she told Rob repeatedly. "Now go away and let me hold him."

While Alex was gone, Rob showered Daniel with new toys, mobiles, and a Bugs Bunny sweatshirt with a hood and two big floppy ears. For himself he bought a box of fudge-covered Oreos and ate them openly and at leisure. Without Alex around, life was much less structured and a lot more fun. But it horrified Rob to think of how many Oreos he would consume and cigarettes he would smoke, and how fast he would go broke buying things for Daniel, if her absence was permanent.

**TUESDAY, OCTOBER 16**
**Southern Maryland**

ESTERDAY ERIN WASTED HER FIRST DAY OF FREEDOM FROM work worrying that she would be two weeks overdue and go out of her mind waiting. She is amused when her water breaks at nine this morning, one day ahead of her due date. Her contractions are mild, no worse than menstrual cramps, so she drives herself to Washington, parks her car in the office garage, and meets Tom on the street. They walk the few blocks to the hospital. Erin admits to being nervous, but Tom, resolving to show her nothing but confidence, keeps his anxiety to himself. By two o'clock they're in a labor room and the contractions are getting stronger, but Erin is only three centimeters dilated. Her doctor wants to delay giving her an epidural because it may slow down labor, which would be risky since Erin's water has already broken, so she is given an injection of pain medication, which only makes her woozy.

The nurse recommends an enema to help stimulate contractions; Erin agrees. Then she is told to roll her nipples between contractions. This has an astonishing effect: by four o'clock she is seven centimeters dilated and gets the epidural. Once it kicks in she feels nothing. She watches the needle on the monitor peak with each contraction and frets to Tom about forgetting to shave her legs. "Don't worry about it," he says with a laugh. "They're going to see everything anyway."

The rough part begins around seven o'clock. Erin is fully dilated and the doctor tells her to start pushing, but Tom can see she's pushing more with her face than her pelvis. Gently, he tells her so. But the epidural has numbed her; she can't feel the contractions. The doctor decides to take her off the drug. "If you do that," Erin screams, "I'll kill you. I've got a gun in my purse." No one pays attention.

The doctor tries to manipulate the baby's awkward position in the birth canal. Its head is large, making a quick delivery difficult. Tom and the nurse hold Erin's legs up in the air as the doctor presses rhythmically on her uterus. The pain is excruciating. "I'm giving up," she howls at one point. "I want out of here." The doctor smacks her lightly on the hand with a rolled-up newspaper. "There's no way you'll get out of here without having this baby," she says impatiently, "so let's get on with it."

Tom keeps his eye on the monitor so he can direct Erin's breathing and applauds every push. When the doctor points out the baby's head to him, he shouts encouragement: "I can see it, we're almost there." Erin doesn't believe him. She hates him, her doctor, everyone in the room.

After an hour and a half of pushing, the doctor says she'll try forceps. Tom scrubs his hands, puts on a gown, and follows Erin and the medical team into the delivery room. The doctor has second thoughts about forceps; the head isn't in the right position. She screams at Erin to keep pushing. Finally, at 8:45, Kaitlin Ann Wright is born. Soon she is in her mother's arms, and Tom and Erin are crying.

Around midnight, Tom drives to his in-laws' house nearby for a brief sleep. It occurs to him that not once in fifteen hours did he think about the station.

**SUNDAY, OCTOBER 21**
**Manhattan**

ILY'S FIRST WEEK WITH THE NEW BABYSITTER WAS DIFFICULT FOR both mother and child. On Day One, Juliet forced herself to sit in the studio apartment one floor below the loft that Sam rented for her to use as an office. Feeling purposeless, she counted sixty minutes before allowing herself to check on Lily. On Day Two she ran errands for three hours and felt no better. Both nights Lily woke at 3 A.M., after months of sleeping through. Juliet checked *What to Expect the First Year* and learned that a new sitter can sometimes disturb babies, causing them to revert to old sleeping patterns.

On Friday, the sitter's day off, Juliet woke with flu symptoms. She struggled to play with Lily, feeling awful. She had looked forward to Saturday, envisioning the family at large in the city, relaxing in cafés, browsing through the farmer's market, taking in a museum or two. But she was too tired and ill to do anything but sleep, leaving Lily in Sam's care.

As the day wore on, Juliet grew tense. She and Sam had to go to her brother's birthday party at night; they hired a college student to babysit for the first time. Juliet was overcome with anxiety: how would Lily take to yet another new face? She wanted to be sure the baby was asleep before they went out, which would probably make them late for the party. "If she cries, she cries; what's the big deal?" Sam said. "If we're late for the party, so what? No one will think less of you."

"I don't care what anyone thinks." Juliet was annoyed at his nonchalance. "I'm just worried about her." As it turned out, Lily fell asleep before the sitter came and didn't wake up even when Sam and Juliet brought friends back to the loft after the party.

This morning Sam's family is due for a visit. A half-hour before they arrive, Lily dirties her diaper. Sam and Juliet have an agreement that he will be in charge of diapering on weekends. "You have to change her," Juliet says.

"I don't have time." Sam is curt. "I have to clean the house." Since he did this already, yesterday afternoon, Juliet figures he wants to relieve some kind of anxiety by indulging in one of his obsessional things.

"But it's your job," she says.

"*It's my job?* That's ridiculous. You should be able to see when I'm busy and you're not. If Lily takes a shit during that time, you should just change her and not ask me. Who do you think has been with her since five-thirty this morning? I spent two and a half hours with her while you lay around in bed!" For several mornings in a row Sam has gotten up with Lily, and here it's Sunday and he works hard all week and Juliet has a babysitter to assist her and he never gets a break . . .

"I'm with the baby eight hours every day," Juliet says, though she knows it's true only on Fridays.

Sam storms off while Juliet takes Lily to the changing table in the bathroom. She thinks, *How dreary, how unoriginal—a who-does-what argument that millions of couples with babies have.*

Minutes later Sam accosts her. He has just found two new bags on the floor of the living room closet. "I keep cleaning it out and you keep putting things in," he yells.

Juliet has Lily in her arms. She wants to raise her voice but won't, because loud tones startle the baby. In frustration, she starts to cry. "Don't scream, can't you see it upsets Lily? Just shut up. Don't even try to talk to me," she says.

The buzzer rings: Sam's family is here. Juliet hastily composes herself. She welcomes their guests warmly, Sam follows her lead, and the day proceeds without incident. After everyone is gone, Sam and Juliet take Lily to a café. As the baby lounges in her stroller, her parents discuss the fight calmly. Sam apologizes for his tantrum, adding, "But you were so tense on Saturday about the sitter, and I tried to relax you. When I was tense because of my family coming, you weren't at all understanding."

"That's true," Juliet concedes, "but you were an asshole."

"I know . . . but ever since we've gotten back from the island you've been picking on me. I don't think you appreciate how much I do. It's a lot more than most men, and you don't give me any credit. Look at Jim, look at Terry [the husbands of Juliet's friends], they do absolutely nothing."

"Yeah, but I didn't marry them, I married you. It's good what you do, but you *should* do it. I don't feel I have to give you credit all the time for what you should be doing anyway."

"I've been getting up with the baby all week long, and I'm exhausted."

"Well, if you mind doing that, you should tell me. Don't save it up for an explosion."

"When you said, 'It's your job'—I think that's the worst thing you could have said."

"But I thought that was our agreement."

"Can't you trust that I'll do 'my job' whenever I possibly can? Does it have to be some written contract?"

"Okay. But you shouldn't say, in effect, *How dare you ask me, I've already taken care of the baby for two hours.*"

Juliet agrees to be less critical and never to say "It's your job." Sam agrees to stop throwing tantrums whenever he sees a bag out of place and to refrain from raising his voice around Lily. They conclude that the combination of being back in the city and having a baby has left them with less emotional resilience, and subsequently, less tolerance for each other's annoying habits.

*SAD ROUTINE*—THAT'S HOW JOE BEGAN TO THINK OF LIFE AT home these past weeks. Maria would walk in at five. They'd talk for a few minutes about nothing, exchanges characterized by missed signals and prickly coldness. She would go into the bedroom with Luis. Joe would sit in the living room in front of the TV, feeling like he and Maria were *slipping into darkness*, into separate rooms, separate thoughts, even separate TV screens. He was scared by the way things were going. He has always resisted the advice of friends who told him to hire a babysitter one night a week and go out with Maria, saying, "New parents need to be alone together." Joe never felt that need, and Maria agreed. They are away from Luis all day; why should they leave him at night? But Joe began to wonder if his friends had a point.

One night he asked Maria to watch a ball game with him instead of retreating to the bedroom. She complied. After a while he got up to take the dog out. In his absence, Maria changed the channel to another program.

"Why did you do that?" Joe said when he returned. "I want to see the game."

"Fine." Maria stomped off to the bedroom. Joe followed her.

"Come back in here with me, babe, come and watch the game," he pleaded. But Maria was stony.

"You're so selfish—we can only watch what you want to watch. Why should I sacrifice my program just to sit with you? It's not fair." She fixed her eyes on *her* TV screen. He went to the living room. When his game was over, Maria was asleep.

She complains about his lack of help, but Joe has been drowning in paperwork for the house deal and she hasn't shown the slightest interest. It's hard for him to make phone calls during the workday; he has to use a pay phone on the street. He asked Maria to call their real-estate lawyer today from her office.

"Did you talk to the lawyer?" Joe says tonight.

"No," she snaps. "I had a few other things on my mind." She realizes instantly that her tone is all wrong. She feels contrite that she hasn't managed this small task.

Joe grows quiet. She has been critical of him for weeks and he has been taking it silently, but now he has to defend himself. "You're always telling me I never help you out," he says, "but when you come home there's nothing you need to do with the baby, I've fed him and changed him. I do a lot of other things too. I've kept the wheels in motion with the house, and you can't even make one phone call. All you do is act like you don't want me around. I feel like we're drifting apart."

"You're right," she says, surprising him. "I'm the one who hasn't been helpful. I'll look at the applications. I'll make time for you and the baby."

During the rest of the evening Maria tries to demonstrate that she values Joe's help and his company. She sits down with him instead of scurrying back and forth from the ironing board to the kitchen sink. She familiarizes herself with the mortgage application, makes a note to call the lawyer first thing in the morning, plays with Joe and Luis instead of washing clothes.

Joe has been complaining lately of her lack of interest in sex (it's not that, she tells him, she's just so tired with work and baby and chores), so tonight she gets into bed beside him and nuzzles his shoulder invitingly. Before he can respond, she is snoring.

"I couldn't believe it," Joe says the next morning, amused.

"Why didn't you wake me up?" Maria feels bad, but Joe shakes his head and laughs. He knows they're okay again.

LEX AND ROB MEET WITH THE PRIEST THEY SELECTED TO PER-
form Daniel's baptism. "Yes," Rob says, looking directly
into the priest's eyes, "we will raise the child Catholic."

"It's probably less blasphemous for me to do the lying,"
he tells Alex later, "since your god, not mine, is involved."

"You mean only you will have to go to hell for this?" she says. They
both find the concept hilarious.

Alex's immediate family will be at the baptism next week. Rob
doesn't want to tell his mother about it, but Alex says she's bound to
find out and will be even more upset that it was kept secret. Reluc-
tantly, Rob agrees to inform her. Alex is sure he'll wait until the last
minute.

Last month she thought they were close to resuming a sex life, but
Rob has shown no further interest. Alex wonders if he's punishing her
for harassing him about smoking and overeating, or for planning the
baptism, or because she makes more money than he does. *It has to be
some kind of power trip,* she decides. She remembers what happened
years ago, in September 1977, to be exact. She was living with her
parents after her college graduation; Rob had another semester to go.
Because Rob and Alex's mother have the same birthday and Alex
couldn't be in two places at once, she told Rob she would spend the
day with her mother and celebrate with him later. She visited him on
campus for the following four weekends, and each time he refused to
sleep with her. It was Alex's first inkling that sex could be used as a
weapon, and she was startled. She had never confused sex with other
things, never offered it as appeasement nor withheld it as punishment.

Her reunion with Daniel tonight after three days on the road is
upsetting. She walks in the door and holds out her arms to him; he
stares at her, clinging to Rob. *He doesn't know who I am,* she thinks
sadly, *and there's nothing I can do about it.* She rationalizes his behavior: *If
he recognizes me, it would mean he misses me—he would be suffering in my
absence.* She tells herself, *It's better this way.*

DORNING THE WRIGHTS' FRONT LAWN IS A FIFTEEN-FOOT wooden stork with pink high-top sneakers painted on and a message: "Kaitlin Ann, October 16, 1990, 8 lbs., 2 oz." It is a group gift from several of the neighbors.

Inside the house are two minimally functioning new parents who have yet to master what Erin's books describe as switching the baby's clock: Katie sleeps most of the day and is up every two hours at night. Tom, who got up with the baby at five and then put in a full day's work at the station, sprawls on the couch, eyes bloodshot from fatigue. Erin spent the night with Katie on the reclining chair, so as not to disturb Tom's sleep, and is still there now, nursing. Occasionally she winces; she has a large hemorrhoid from pushing and lingering soreness from her episiotomy.

"I know someone who calls these first three months the fourth trimester," Erin tells Tom. "Now I know what she means."

Katie, sated, pulls away from the breast. Tom takes her upstairs to change her diaper, cooing as he goes. Erin stays in the chair and blesses Tom for his helpfulness. She is relieved that she's not still pregnant and grateful for all the family support they've had. Molly, her parents, and her in-laws have been around to help them through this first postpartum week. But Erin looks forward to being on her own. She wants to get into her *mother role* without interference.

She feels more normal by the hour. She weighs one pound less than at the beginning of pregnancy. She has yet to fall in love with nursing, but it's going better than she expected, and the lack of sleep isn't so terrible since she doesn't have to go to work. Yesterday she managed to get her hair cut and do the grocery shopping, though her father insisted on driving. He's of the old school: new mothers, he believes, are invalids.

Tom returns with the baby and sits down on the couch, rocking Katie in his arms. Erin wants to talk about her behavior during labor and delivery, which she is embarrassed to recall as belligerent.

"You did fine," Tom reassures her. "I was expecting almost anything, but the worst thing you did was tell the doctor you had a gun. I still can't believe how she stuck her hand inside you and tried to turn the baby around like you were just a bunch of pliable parts." He shakes his head. "I mean, a car you can do that to, it's designed for it, but to treat someone's body that way . . ."

"I could never have gotten through it without you."

Tom seems self-conscious. "I just did whatever I could," he says, and changes the subject.

### TUESDAY, OCTOBER 30
#### Cape Cod

 HE COENS' THIRD SET OF HOUSE PLANS, SCALED INTO SIMPLER lines with less square footage, finally met with the approval of the town planning board. Tonight Sarah decides that she doesn't want a bigger house, she wants a bigger city—Boston, Washington . . .

"Fine," Michael says, calling her bluff. "Let's move. You could get a real job that pays well. I'll stay home with the kids."

"You're being unrealistic. You'd have to do something. What if I couldn't support the family?"

"Don't worry about it."

"But if we moved and I couldn't get a job I liked, you'd throw it in my face."

"No, I wouldn't."

"You don't pick up after yourself. I'd have to come home to a messy house. And if we made that kind of change, you'd have a nervous breakdown."

"There's a lot about me that seems to bug you," Michael says with unusual directness, "but there's nothing about you that bugs me, have you ever noticed that?"

Sarah doesn't respond. She is thinking that she once perceived herself as a *happy-go-lucky person,* and now . . . *What do I want?* She's not sure. *A city, any city. A challenge.*

She finds it unbelievable when Michael says the best thing about his job is that it's easy. Sarah can imagine doing the same thing day in and day out only if you enjoy it. When her kids are older, she tells herself, she'll start her own business, but now it wouldn't be fair to them. The idea of separating from Hannah, whose exuberant, affectionate personality is beginning to emerge at seven months, particularly disturbs her. Sarah thinks of her daughter as her salvation. If Ben were her only child, she believes, she would always have maintained a negative attitude toward motherhood. Still, she remains in conflict, her desire to be released from the tedium of child care warring with her conviction that her kids need her. *It's my selfishness fighting my sense of responsibility,* she thinks, *and Michael doesn't understand because he's a man.*

Sarah was transfixed by a recent Oprah Winfrey show featuring a specialist in marital communication. She fantasizes about having this man treat her and Michael. *Our problem is simple,* she believes. *Our communication stinks.*

**TUESDAY, OCTOBER 30**
**Queens**

T HE FIRST BANK THE REYESES APPROACHED FOR A MORTGAGE turned them down. Their outstanding debts plus the monthly house payment will add up to 38 percent of their income, two points over the maximum allowed. Joe reapplied elsewhere and was told that he and Maria have to pay off at least $3,000 of their debts in order to qualify. He feels stymied, but Maria takes a more definitive view: forget the house. Everyone says real-estate prices will drop further; she doesn't want to overpay for a place that two banks have told them they can't afford.

"Look," she says to Joe tonight, after the second bank rejected them, "maybe there's a reason for all these obstacles. Maybe it's not meant to be."

"But we've put so much effort into it, and we've already gone to contract."

"So what? I'd rather pay the lawyer and lose that money now than go into hock and lose more later."

"We made a deal, we should honor it. We've made Richard [the seller] wait so long . . ."

"Tough luck. We tried to make it work, and if we're not eligible, it's not our fault. If he wants to sell so badly, he can lower the price by $10,000."

"But this apartment is driving us crazy. Luis is almost ready for a walker. Where's he going to go? There's no floor space."

"We'll clear things out, try to make it more comfortable, just until the lease is up in July. Then we'll rent a two-bedroom, maybe on Long Island."

"Okay," Joe says. "But I'm going to call Richard, see if he'll drop the price."

Instead of calling, he sits glumly in front of the TV with Luis on his lap while Maria makes baked ziti for dinner and does the dishes. She stays up past midnight sewing Luis's Halloween costume; he will be a jester, with bells hanging from his sleeves and hat.

The next morning she is sick and feverish with a violent stomach flu. She can't get out of bed to take Luis to the sitter or to go to work. Afraid to hold the baby or play with him in case she's contagious, she keeps him in his crib. But he cries so much that she has to call Joe at work. He rushes home at noon.

Joe dresses Luis in the jester's costume and takes pictures. Maria feels terrible: by getting sick, she thinks, she has ruined her child's first Halloween.

**WEDNESDAY,
OCTOBER 31
Southern Maryland**

 RIN IS IN A MINOR PANIC. TOM FORGOT, FOR THE FIRST TIME IN memory, to carve the Halloween pumpkin. *We are so spaced out these days,* she thinks, carving the pumpkin herself during Katie's afternoon nap. Tom is working late; she'll have to contend with hordes of candy-seeking kids.

Getting into her *mother role* has been a pleasure. There are frustrating moments, but Katie is so alert (something Erin didn't expect in the first month) that she's already good company. The house is quiet, and Erin is free to play with the baby without worrying about anyone else's needs. The week's major outing was to the pediatrician's, which allayed Erin's fear that she might not have enough milk: Katie has gained a full pound. The doctor said that Erin can now introduce her to a bottle, so she ordered an electric breast pump.

When the doctor pricked Katie's heel to get blood, the baby let out a harrowing yelp and continued to scream inconsolably for the next hour and a half. Erin was so unsettled that she broke down in tears for the first time since Katie's birth. *If someone as emotional and oversensitive as me has only one crying jag,* she thinks, *this whole postpartum depression thing has got to be greatly exaggerated.*

Erin's boss calls today to see how she's doing. He offers news of her colleagues and says he can't wait for her to come back. She is flattered and enjoys hearing the office gossip. She misses her colleagues, though she doesn't miss working.

When Tom is with Katie it thrills her; Erin reads the adoration on his face for this baby they created together. Tom's love for his daughter is an extension of his love for her, and Erin feels passionately in love with him. *It goes on and on,* she thinks, *like some enchanted, unbreakable circle.*

 ICHAEL AND SARAH, MINUS KIDS, ARRIVE IN NEW YORK, CHECK into a midtown hotel owned by Michael's family, dump their luggage, and taxi to Hatsuhana for the kind of sushi wizardry, Sarah assures Michael, you will never find on the Cape. Back at the hotel they make love eagerly. Before going to sleep, Sarah thinks blissfully, *There is no baby here to wake me up.* At 1 A.M. she is disturbed by the sound of shower pipes rattling upstairs, and at 5:30 she hears what sounds like a jackhammer in the room but is actually a generator on the street.

"God hates me," she mumbles to Michael. "Instead of a baby he makes me listen to a friggin' generator."

Still, her mood is jubilant a few hours later, as she and Michael ogle $1,400 sweaters and $200 ties at Bergdorf Goodman Men on Fifth Avenue and then repair to the Waldorf, where Michael has a haircut and a beard trim. ("I wish this barber would move to the Cape," Sarah says afterward, approving of Michael's new look.) They reserved well ahead for lunch at the Union Square Café, which has an eclectic Californian-French-Italian menu and a wine list that impresses Michael, though he sends back his glass of chardonnay, telling the waiter that it tastes of cork.

Sarah sips her Campari and soda, listening to Michael grouse good-naturedly about having to pack for the trip himself. He believes that since Sarah has very specific ideas about what he should be wearing at any given moment, she should select his clothes (she usually does). But this time she gave him only general guidelines: bring one jacket, three pairs of pants, two ties, three shirts.

"It's something I think you should do for me," Michael says, spearing a raw oyster on a cocktail fork. "I do things for you." He looks at her with a loopy grin.

Sarah returns the look. "I don't think sexual favors and packing are in the same category," she says, stroking his cheek.

**TUESDAY, NOVEMBER 6**
**Queens**

 N A DEAL–SAVING GESTURE, RICHARD OFFERS TO PAY THE $2,500 IN points for the Reyeses' mortgage (assuming that one comes through) if Joe and Maria give him $50 a month against it. After the conversation, Joe sits down at the dining table to go over his figures again, feeling desperate and wanting to run away. If they can't afford to buy a house, he thinks, he will have failed his family.

Maria studies his hunched shoulders and feels compassion. "Why don't you go over the figures with me?" she says, pulling a chair close to him and sitting down.

For an hour they work with a calculator, and in the end conclude together they can't do the deal. Even if they qualify for the mortgage, they will be left with no reserves.

"Babe, I know how you feel. I know you want to provide for us," Maria says. "But we can't live like this, without money for winter clothes, for fixing the house, even for doctor's bills. If there was a medical emergency that wasn't covered by insurance, we wouldn't be able to pay for it. It scares me."

Joe hasn't thought of this before. "That's true," he says. "And it's not fair to deprive Luis of things. I wish I could always say, 'Buy what you need . . .' "

"That won't ever be possible if we're paying $1,200 a month for a house."

Joe calls Richard and tells him to find another buyer. Richard suggests that the Reyeses consider renting the house for a year, with an option to buy. Joe consults his lawyer, who says such an arrangement can be worked out, but first Joe should calculate where it would put him a year from now in terms of qualifying for a mortgage. Joe hangs up the phone, feeling hopeless again.

"I promise you," Maria says quickly, "something better will come up. That thing about God closing one door and opening another—there is a reason for everything."

*I'm glad I got her involved,* Joe thinks, less despairingly. *I need her.* "Okay, we'll let it go," he says. "These big decisions—I feel less alone when we make them together." He feels suddenly flush with money and love. "Get Luis ready," he says. "I'm taking us out to dinner."

FRIDAY, NOVEMBER 9<br>Westchester

OB ROLLS DANIEL ON THE BED AND "SPRINKLES" HIS LITTLE belly with "mozzarella" as the baby squeals merrily. The game, invented by Rob, is called "pizza-making."

Alex walks into the bedroom just as Rob begins to dress Daniel in a dinosaur outfit. "I want him to wear this," she says, pulling a plain blue sweatsuit from the dresser.

"But we're going to the Chinese place," Rob protests. "If he wears the dinosaur thing, the waitress will give us free wontons."

"You don't need any wontons," Alex says, replacing the dinosaur suit in the drawer. "The sweatsuit will be too small soon, and I want him to get some wear out of it."

As she puts the sweatsuit on Daniel, Rob notes how well coordinated his son is, how talkative, how expressive. "He's three to four months ahead of where the books say he should be in development," he brags.

Alex, ignoring him, ties a knit cap on the baby's head and slips his arms into a jacket. When they're ready to leave, Rob takes him from her; he loves to parade his son down the corridor, hoping neighbors will be around to admire him. They aren't, but when the family settles into a table at the Chinese restaurant, Rob is satisfied by the fuss the waitresses make.

Rob has had a turnaround at work, breaking sales records and earning the envy of his colleagues. Alex perceives a corresponding surge in his self-esteem. The proof: he has cleaned out his closet-cum-office at home, organized his briefcase, and, most remarkable, Simonized the interior of his car. Disorder is the rule, Alex observes, when Rob feels bad about himself.

As the waitress brings their order to the table, Daniel falls apart, rubbing his eyes and crying. Alex swallows a few bites of food and takes him for a walk around the restaurant. Rob fills his plate and contemplates the upcoming weekend with excitement. He adores getting up with Daniel at 6:30. They bathe together, drive to the store for the newspaper and fresh bagels, listen to Copeland on the stereo, and eventually rouse Alex for a late breakfast. Daniel has taken the place of everything Rob once considered important, including his job—which he believes has freed him to make a success of it.

And including sex. At some point it will be necessary, because Rob wants another baby—two more, in fact. Having just one child, he believes, indicates parental selfishness and lack of foresight: *you don't want to leave your kid alone in the world when you die.* He thinks about his own death often now, in the middle of the night, when he gets up in the morning, when he drives to an appointment. It will be from cancer, he's sure of it, though he hasn't quit smoking because he's *too weak.*

Rob consumes two helpings of everything before Alex returns to the table. He takes Daniel outside and smokes a cigarette while Alex picks at her orange-flavored beef. Her mood is sullen. The baptism was Saturday; since then, her mother-in-law has maintained a hostile silence towards her.

*How is it,* she thinks, *that my mother was able to accept that once I married Rob, everything thereafter would be a compromise, but Rob's mother refuses to do the same?* Her mother's presence at the briss, Alex believes, was her way of acknowledging Rob's place in the della Croce family, regardless of his background. Alex didn't expect her mother-in-law to attend the baptism, but nor did she expect to be treated like this: a subhuman species known as *the shiksa.* Rob says his mother will get over it, but when? Soon it will be Christmas. Alex is in no mood to do their usual hide-the-tree act in order to spare her mother-in-law's feelings. Alex thinks, *What about* my *feelings?*

 AM HID HIS TEARS FROM JULIET, NOT WANTING TO UPSET HER, AS he packed for his trip to Geneva. Although he controls his fear of flying enough to be able to get on a plane, his dread remains. There is always the chance that he won't come back.

The trip was productive but no fun. He worked eighteen-hour days and slept poorly. Each night in the hotel he opened a small picture album and stared at photos of his wife and daughter, kissing each of their faces repeatedly.

He returned last week to find Juliet and Lily sitting on the couch, waiting for him. He was so relieved to be alive he almost cried again. Lily smiled so broadly he thought she actually remembered him, which seemed unlikely considering she is only five months old. She looked different—bigger, more sure of herself, more *together.* Sam tried to envision her at fifteen or twenty and realized how old he'll be then, in his sixties—an alarming thought. On the other hand, he told himself, if he were any younger he wouldn't have the patience for parenthood.

Today Sam and Juliet take Lily to an Indonesian art exhibit followed by a Balinese puppet show at the Asia Society. Juliet delights in such cultural outings; Sam finds them tedious—or at least he used to, before Lily. With his daughter in his arms he loves the exhibit and the puppets simply because she is so entranced by them. Afterward they walk in the park, stopping at a café to stare at passersby, a mutual passion of Sam and Juliet's that Lily seems to have inherited. *It's just like the old days,* Sam thinks, *only we just move a little more slowly.* Five years ago it would have been too slow for him, but now it feels exactly right.

Sometimes Juliet is jealous when Lily flashes Sam one of the gleeful smiles she seems to reserve only for him. Sam insists the baby does this not because her love for him is greater but because he's a novelty, a fresh face after a day spent with her mother. Juliet has read this in her books and tries to accept it, but her jealousy dredges up an old insecurity: *Sam is successful and gets along easily with everyone, and I'm not so successful and not so easy, and maybe he would be better off with someone else, someone more glamorous, more accomplished, less difficult.* Sam's response to this has always been "Don't be ridiculous, you're the one I love." When he says it now, it has more meaning. Juliet sees the joy on his face as he plays with the baby and realizes she has done for him what no one else could do: she has given him Lily.

All things considered, Juliet believes that Lily has enhanced her existence rather than diminished it. Before she became a mother, she found it both wonderful and strange that she and Sam had been together so long, yet she was never bored. Now she looks back on their childless life and thinks, *We did the same things over and over; how could it have been as much fun as I thought it was, because it's so much more fun now?* They still do the same things over and over, but in Lily's company everything seems more eventful.

Juliet remembers how sad she felt during pregnancy, brooding over the loss of her youth, and knows that Lily's presence has actually meant the opposite—a *retrieval* of childhood. When she takes Lily on the carousel in Central Park, as her mother once took her, she squeals right along with her daughter, viewing the world through Lily's eyes.

Before Lily, Juliet often felt she wasn't truly engaged in whatever it is to be alive. Not having a real job, she had no ongoing contact with people; being so shy, she had difficulty creating connections on her own. She was isolated, even in the midst of her own parties, as if some part of her wasn't really there. That feeling is gone.

**FRIDAY, NOVEMBER 16**
**Southern Maryland**

RIN'S PARENTS COME OVER FOR DINNER. ONCE ERIN WOULD have focused the conversation on current news events, but now she finds herself prattling on about a TV commercial she saw featuring a cat with dentures. She stops in mid-sentence when she notices the look on her parents' faces, which she interprets as *Oh dear, her mind is going.* Erin fears this may be true. Lately she feels that she exists on a different planet, with an intellectual temperature below zero.

It's not that she doesn't enjoy motherhood. She has gotten the diaper-bag packing routine down and has conquered her anxiety about Katie crying in public, so she never feels housebound. And she has the pleasure of observing her daughter's development firsthand. Yet Erin is beginning to yearn for the bustle of office life, the contact with clients, the sense of belonging to the world. She's usually too tired or too busy to read the paper or *Newsweek,* which she once did religiously. When she does get the chance, she has trouble retaining information. If she doesn't return to that other world, the *real* one, her mind will indeed be gone.

LEX ACCOMPLISHED *A TRIPLE HOME RUN* FOR HER COMPANY
yesterday, amounting to a substantial and unexpected bot-
tom-line profit. All she asked for in exchange was one day
off to prepare Thanksgiving dinner. She's hosting it for her
entire family, plus Rob's mother and brother—a total of a dozen adults
and one baby—and is concerned that it will be a disaster.

Rob asked everyone in Alex's family not to mention the baptism for
fear of upsetting his mother, but Alex thinks it will be impossible to
control that many people and their off-the-cuff remarks. She wants to
say something now, today, to her mother-in-law, who is in the apartment watching Daniel, but Rob has begged her not to. "Let it slide,"
he advises, which to Alex is another way of saying *Be an ostrich.*

Alex has rehearsed her opening line to her mother-in-law: "I've felt
very uncomfortable since the baptism and I'd like to talk to you about
it." But, she suspects, there's a good chance that her mother-in-law
will refuse. When pictures of the baptism arrive in the mail, Alex
leaves the Kodak envelope on the coffee table. "They're from the
baptism," she tells her mother-in-law. "Do you want to see them?"
Her mother-in-law's response is . . . no response.

"My mother speaks many languages," Rob often jokes, "but she's
most fluent in guilt." Guilt has no place in Alex's vocabulary, but she
is wary of creating a permanent rift between Rob and his mother. She
knows that even as he pursues his policy of emotional containment,
Rob is this close to saying *fuck you* to his mother. Alex feels the same
way but tries to defuse the tension with seemingly mindless chatter
around the two of them. It's a technique she has used successfully in
awkward business situations, but it fails to relax her mother-in-law.
Alex is sure the woman sits at the dinner table listening to her small
talk and thinking, *Who is this idiot who married my son?* The Weiner
family reveres intellect, and Alex surmises she has been judged as lacking in it. No wonder Rob denigrates his profession: his parents made

disparaging comments, as if being in sales were somehow tawdry. Rob's brother, Jack, is a professor, which is almost better in their eyes than being God. To Alex there is nothing particularly relevant or admirable about having a Ph.D. She sees it as a form of masturbation. It serves you and no one else.

At first she was captivated by Rob's family. She presumed they had all the things her family had, plus what they didn't—a knowledge of culture. The Weiners seemed special then, but now they seem stupid. So what if they can quote Milton from memory and identify specific movements of Beethoven's symphonies? *What good is that,* Alex thinks, *if you make your kids feel bad about themselves?*

She will swallow her rage and endure the subtle criticism her mother-in-law now levies at everything, including the Thanksgiving menu. Today she asks Alex what she's serving.

"Pasta," Alex says, "and then turkey."

"But no one will eat the turkey. They'll be too full."

Alex wants to say, "The hell with you. Pasta is simply an appetizer, like matzoh ball soup." Instead she responds innocuously, "Oh, I think it will be all right."

She is angry—about her mother-in-law, about her sexless marriage, and about how Rob seems to think Daniel's mere existence should be enough to place her in a state of permanent happiness. Her only respite from anger is when she travels. Her job, she realizes, has become her escape.

**WEDNESDAY,
NOVEMBER 21
Cape Cod**

 ARAH ALWAYS ANTICIPATES THE HOLIDAY SEASON WITH DREAD. IT'S supposed to be a family time, and she ends up feeling she has no family. At Thanksgiving her brother and father, who live nearby, go to their respective in-laws'; her sister stays in Boston, her mother in Georgia, Michael's brother in New Hampshire. At Christmas, no one invites the Coens because they're Jewish. But this year Michael suggested that they make a traditional turkey dinner and invite their surrogate parents, an older couple who live on the Cape, to share it. Sarah, pleased, began paging through Michael's cookbooks for recipes. Christmas is still a problem, but at least Thanksgiving sounds family-like enough.

Since the weekend in New York, Michael and Sarah have entered a relatively mellow period. They moved Hannah downstairs to the nursery; Michael now sleeps in the marital bed. They're fighting less and having sex more—or at least they were.

It was one of those nights when Sarah wanted desperately to go to sleep but Michael was intent on making love. She accommodated him, and he rewarded her by bringing her close to orgasm. But then he had his own and rolled off her—unusually inconsiderate behavior from him.

"You are such a brat," Sarah told him angrily. "You force me into this and work me up and then leave me twisting in the wind." For two weeks she punished him. Today she decides it's been long enough.

### SUNDAY, NOVEMBER 25
#### Southern Maryland

T'S BEEN SINCE, WHAT, AUGUST?—TOO LONG WITHOUT SEX FOR Tom. In another week or so Erin will have her postpartum checkup; he hopes lovemaking will follow, and one more aspect of life will be back to normal.

Generally, the adjustment to parenthood has been easier than he expected, but then he expected the worst. He feels closer to Erin; their mutual enjoyment of Katie has brought them together in a new way. His fear during pregnancy of perpetual confinement to the house was unfounded. It's not like it used to be—they can't just pick up and go somewhere on a whim—but it's not at the other extreme either, especially since Erin is willing to supplement breastfeeding with formula.

Tom thinks everything runs more smoothly with Erin home. The house is clean, the grocery shopping is done, dinner is usually on the table when he gets home, and, most important, Katie is a happy baby.

He believes ever more strongly that Erin should stay home with her for a year or two, but he's not going to push it. If Erin feels she needs more stimulation than the baby can offer, well, it's her call.

Since eight this morning, when Erin left to spend the day with friends in Annapolis, Tom has been in sole charge of Katie. He had trepidations about it but didn't tell Erin. He feared that Katie wouldn't let him comfort her—wouldn't *like* him. He was wrong. She's had some fussy moments, but when he picks her up and rocks her, she stops crying. It gives him confidence, and a feeling of emotional connection to his daughter, that he could have experienced in no other way. With Erin around, he would throw up his hands at the first sign of trouble, assuming that a mother could calm an infant better than a father. He won't make that assumption again.

Tom knows many men who refuse to be left alone with their babies for any length of time. Now he understands why: *They never give themselves a chance.*

## SUNDAY, NOVEMBER 25
### Queens

ODAY IS JOE'S THIRTY-FIFTH BIRTHDAY. IN THE MORNING HE plays football with some guys in their twenties and receives the ultimate compliment from one of them: "Man, I thought you were twenty-four, twenty-five. I can't believe a thirty-five-year-old kept up with *me.*"

After the game Maria and Luis take Joe shopping for his gifts: a pair of shoes and a leather jacket. Joe models the jackets for Maria, as excited as a kid let loose in a toy store. He hasn't bought himself anything in months, since he was saving for the house they didn't buy. When he completes his selections, he tells Maria it's her turn. "Get yourself a full-length leather coat," he says. "It's an early Christmas present."

Joe and Maria traditionally shop together for gifts of clothing (their fashion taste is so at odds they're afraid to surprise each other). But Maria always includes something unexpected. Knowing that Joe wanted a Levi's jeans jacket, a purchase so straightforward she couldn't go wrong, she bought one during the week but forgot to get a gift box. So she waits until today, when Joe is in the shower, and puts the jacket on Luis, rolls up the sleeves, ties a red ribbon around the collar, and tucks a birthday card in the pocket. Joe is thrilled, as much by the presentation as the gift.

At night they splurge on a take-out dinner—barbecued ribs and all the fixings from Tony Roma's. Maria clears the plates and disappears into the kitchen. She comes out with an ice cream cake in the shape of a football, blazing with candles.

"I wish I could have thrown you a party, if only we had a bigger place," she says wistfully.

"Start planning for next year," Joe says, blowing out the candles with one vigorous breath.

**THURSDAY,
NOVEMBER 29
Manhattan**

 NTIL JANUARY, WHEN SAM HAS TO START TRAVELING AGAIN, HE feels he and Juliet are getting away with murder. They no longer spend entire Saturdays seeing one movie after another, but they don't feel deprived of each other's company. They go out by themselves one night during the week and one on the weekend. When they're home, Lily goes to bed before 8 P.M., which allows her parents to have a quiet dinner together. They have the rented studio downstairs, where Sam indulges his mania for order without causing marital flak (Juliet stays upstairs until he's done fussing) and where she works sporadically on a new novel.

Juliet still has trouble committing herself to her work but can't blame it on Lily; it's hardly a new problem. Work, or the lack of it, takes on varying degrees of importance at different times, and right now she feels it is imperative to accomplish something beyond what she calls the usual female relationship stuff—being a mother, wife, friend.

She misses just two aspects of prebaby life. The first is lying around

in bed in the morning with Sam, reading and making love and dozing.
The second is her flat stomach, toned by years of ballet lessons. She
remembers being a teenager and looking scornfully at her mother's
belly, thinking, *How could she let herself go like that?* and never taking
into account the fact that her mother had carried three children. Now
she looks at herself and thinks, *My God*.

**FRIDAY, NOVEMBER 30**
**Westchester**

OB PLANS TO BUY HIMSELF A HOLIDAY PRESENT: A LIONEL TRAIN
set he will add to each year, setting it up on the first night
of Chanukah. It will ultimately cost $2,500, an insane
amount of money. He can't rationalize such an expendi-
ture to Alex, so he'll lie, tell her it cost a couple hundred bucks. This is
why he refuses to merge their checking accounts, something Alex is
campaigning for. He doesn't want to ask her for permission to buy a
train set for himself, a toy for Daniel—or the diamond ring she has
wanted for a long time. He would buy her one now . . . if not for
the pearls.

Three years ago Rob gave Alex an exquisite strand of pearls for
Christmas. It had been a year in which he had nearly doubled his
income and she had gotten a new, lucrative job; he wanted to celebrate
their success by buying her something special. He selected the pearls
with great care. On Christmas morning he gave her the box and
watched excitedly as she unwrapped the glittery paper. She opened the
box and stared silently at the contents. Then she said to Rob, "Are you
some kind of fucking asshole? This money should have gone toward a
house. Do you know how expensive these are?"

"Of course I do, I bought them." Rob was devastated by her reaction and has not bought her a present since. Every Christmas he reminds her why.

Alex kept the pearls because she thought it would be rude to return
them, but now regrets it. She has worn them only once; her life never
calls for dressing up. When she's not in business clothes, she lives in
jeans and T-shirts. She knows Rob thinks she acted like an ungrateful

bitch, but she feels she was only being honest. *You're not supposed to stand on ceremony with your spouse,* she thinks, *only with the rest of the world.* She doesn't like expensive presents. In fact, the less gifts cost, the more she values them. Rob used to bring her charming little bouquets of flowers, not for a special occasion and not for much money. Alex loved that, but he won't do it anymore. He won't buy her anything at all.

**FRIDAY, NOVEMBER 30**
**Cape Cod**

T HE COENS, ALL FOUR OF THEM, LEAVE FOR A TEN-DAY VACATION in Florida tomorrow. Sarah is annoyed that Michael's brother and his wife, who were supposed to vacate the condo two days before their arrival, allowing a housekeeper to clean in between, have altered their plans, so their visits overlap. Michael is delighted to see his brother, but Sarah doesn't want to change sheets and clean bathrooms the minute she arrives. *This close-ness thing Jewish families have,* she thinks, *wanting to be on top of each other every second . . .* it's so different from the way she was raised. Such behavior would be viewed as rude by her family.

Sarah also learned at the last minute that Michael and his brother, presumably accompanied by their wives, plan to take Margery's ashes on a boat and sprinkle them over the Atlantic, as requested in Margery's will. Sarah tells Michael to count her out of the expedition. "This vacation is not supposed to be devoted to your family every minute of the day," she says. "If you want to spend your time with them, fine, but don't accept any invitations for me."

Still, it will be a relief not to worry about the cat, the dog, Ben's transportation to preschool, or Hannah's to the sitter. Sarah commends herself for hiring a teenage neighbor to accompany them to Florida. The teenager will babysit as needed (Sarah has never used her before, but assumes she will be competent enough) in exchange for plane fare and expenses, and will enable Sarah and Michael to go to a fancy hotel for a nightcap on a whim. Sarah wants time alone with her husband, even if she has to go to Florida and cope with his relatives to get it.

**DECEMBER 1990**

**THURSDAY, DECEMBER 6**
**Queens**

JOE IS IN THE LIVING ROOM WRITING A CHRISTMAS CARD TO TONY when he hears the news on TV: Bush warned Saddam Hussein to pull out of Kuwait by January 15 or risk invasion. Maria is changing Luis's diaper in the bedroom. She hears Joe cry out and rushes to him.

"It's over," Joe mutters. His tears fall on Tony's card, smudging the felt-tipped message he has started to compose.

"You can't say that. You've got to be positive."

But Joe stares bleakly at the TV, thinking, *All the boys out there—boys like Tony, just twenty-nine years old, with a wife and three young kids—they're going to be killed, they'll cast their shadows over the country, like the shadow in my dream.*

Last year, when Tony was stationed in Korea, Joe had the dream for the first time. He and his family were waiting in a strange house for Tony to return. It was dark outside the house; someone said, "He's home," but all Joe could see was an eerie silhouette. Joe went down to the basement of the house to fix some toys. Soon his mother and one of his brothers joined him there, crying; they realized that the silhouette was not Tony but the *absence* of Tony. Joe woke up from the dream in tears.

On several recent nights Joe has had the same dream. The elements vary, but each time he sees the silhouette of Tony, the negative of Tony—the symbol that he is gone.

Joe thinks of Tony, in a sense, as his twin: they anchor the family on two sides. They hold the poles, and a tarpaulin stretches between them, sheltering the family, keeping it together, warm and safe and strong. Joe wants that tent preserved for Luis and for his future siblings. If the dream comes true, there will be no Tony to hold up the other end. The structure will collapse.

**THURSDAY, DECEMBER 6**
**Southern Maryland**

 RIN'S POSTPARTUM CHECKUP CONFIRMED THAT SHE HAS FULLY healed. But tonight, when she and Tom try to make love, he can't sustain an erection. He blames it on using a condom for the first time in two years, saying he forgot how it interferes with sensation. He also comments that intercourse seems "weird, different somehow." Anxiously, Erin asks for specifics. "It didn't feel as tight," he says, and, "Gosh, I saw so much down there during delivery, the baby's head coming out and everything."

"If you had to push an eight-pound baby out, believe me, things would be out of place with you too," Erin says, thinking, *My ego is too fragile to handle this.* She assumed that if anyone had trouble with sex after childbirth it would be the woman, not the man. "Go find yourself an eighteen-year-old virgin," she adds, running to the bathroom to cry in private.

Tom feels frustrated. He can't make Erin understand that he's not being critical of her. His impotence is not her fault. Nor is it his: he saw his child come through the place that once gave him sexual pleasure. The moment he entered Erin, he envisioned the birth. The thought distracted him. He felt confused.

### THURSDAY, DECEMBER 6
#### Palm Beach

HE ATMOSPHERE HERE IS SO STRAINED, SO *UNVACATION-LIKE,* that Michael thinks they would all be better off at home. Hannah's sleep schedule is turned upside down. She won't nap in the day and wakes twice at night, which means Sarah is not only irritable and tired but a major b-i-t-c-h, according to Michael (who takes pains to spell out the word whenever Ben is within earshot). This morning Sarah tells Michael she wants to go home, so he grabs their return plane tickets and heads for the door, explaining that he's going to the airport to change their reservations. "There's no way I'm going to start packing right now," she says. "We're not leaving early." *I can't win,* he thinks.

Sarah asks if they can go somewhere nice for dinner on Saturday, their last night in Palm Beach and their only night alone; Margery's friends and relatives, Sarah reminds him, have been underfoot all week. Michael says sure. He doesn't say, "No, I can't stand being around you," which would be more truthful. The sad thing, he thinks, is they could be having a great time if only Sarah didn't have this attitude problem. Michael doesn't know why she insists on organizing each day's events and then frets about "having" to do so. Ben is happy going to the playground or hanging out at the pool; Hannah is too young to care; Michael defines "vacation" simply as not having to go to work. But Sarah seems to feel that a vacation with children is an oxymoron.

Sarah goes out for a manicure and pedicure today, which temporarily amuses her—she's the only person in the salon under the age of seventy-five. But by late afternoon, back in the condo, she's on edge again. She is so disappointed: nothing, including the teenager she brought from the Cape to watch the kids, has worked out the way she hoped. *The weather is cloudy . . . We're stuck on the eighth floor, so Ben can't run outside by himself . . . The sitter is a space cadet . . . Michael's family smothers us . . .*

Michael's brother and sister-in-law spent the first three days of the Coens' vacation sitting around the condo, endlessly discussing with Michael the dispersal of Margery's ashes and never deciding which part of the Atlantic was best—off Florida? Off Cape Cod? Sarah wanted to say, *For God's sake, just do it already.* As soon as they left, Margery's friends descended, hovering over the kids and expecting to be entertained. Every day Sarah has had lunch with a different Coen aunt because she's too polite to refuse their invitations, and the intimate dinners with Michael she envisioned have yet to materialize because she is afraid to leave *that brain-dead teenager* alone with Ben and Hannah. The girl now has the flu, leaving Sarah with *three* kids to care for, shuttling chicken soup to one, Ninja Turtles to another, diapers and bottles to the third.

The condo building has many rules to protect its elderly residents: no strollers, no playpens, no food at the pool. Yesterday Sarah sat in the shallow end with Hannah on her lap. Some blue-haired octogenarian came up and said, "Babies are not allowed in the pool, dear," looking disapprovingly at Hannah's diaper.

"She's not in the pool, she's on my lap," Sarah responded. "Not one bit of diaper is touching the water, *dear.*" The dowager backed away to huddle with a couple of her friends. They glared at Sarah. She glared back.

Sarah supposes she could view this horrible week as a lesson learned: two kids are harder than one, two kids in a strange place are worse than two kids at home, and if one of the two kids is an infant, you are a prisoner. It's their first vacation as a family of four. Sarah is determined it will be the last—at least until Hannah walks, talks, eats regular food, and is fully toilet trained.

EY," TONY WRITES ON AN OFFICIAL U.S. ARMY POSTCARD, "Do you think you could pack up Luis and ship him to me? I sure could use some good help around here . . . We're just waiting till the 15th of January to see what's going to happen. If anything does go down make sure you guys keep extra close contact with Theresa. Love Always." He signs it with his new nickname, "Brother Hollywood." *He's already a celebrity out there on the front lines,* Joe figures. *That's Tony—he makes his presence known wherever he is.*

Maria and Joe put together a Christmas package for him with cards from Luis, homemade chocolate-chip cookies, an audiotape Joe made of Tony's favorite songs, and a "certificate of merit" that Maria fashioned on the office computer. She signed it "from the grateful American public." Joe mails the box from work. As he watches it go down the chute, he thinks, *I wish I could pack myself and Luis inside.*

HERE'S BEEN A SHIFT IN OUR RELATIONSHIP THAT REALLY bothers me," Alex says to Rob. "Lack of sex is a big part of it. I have three brothers. I don't need a fourth."

"But we get along fabulously."

"I always get along fabulously with men, that's not a big deal. But if you think not having sex is not a big deal, you're mistaken." She waits for him to respond. When he doesn't, she adds, "I think we should plan a ski weekend, without Daniel."

"I don't want to leave him."

"Fine. We'll bring him. There are always sitters available at the lodge." Rob shrugs and wanders into the kitchen.

*It's as if his role as Daniel's father is the only one he's willing to play,* Alex muses. Rob tells Daniel all the time, "You're my best friend." It distresses her. He used to tell her the same thing.

Alex had an important discussion over the phone with her boss this week; she had to interrupt it twice because Daniel was crying. The third time she let him scream until she completed the call. She told Rob about it later, expecting sympathy. "You should have put your boss on hold," he said. "Daniel is more important."

Rob used to be forgetful about lighting Chanukah candles, skipping a few if not all of the eight nights. But this year he hasn't missed one: his mother is around. Yet he has refused to discuss the Christmas tree with Alex, though it has always been mounted and decorated by her birthday on December 10. "I don't want to upset my mother right now," he explains. *Everyone,* Alex thinks, *is more important than I am.*

And he won't make love to her. With each day, Alex grows more prideful, her attitude hardening: *If you don't need me, I certainly don't need you.* She will not sit around in silk underwear panting for him, just as she wouldn't wait more than half an hour for him to show up when they were dating. She will not buy condoms and leave them in some obvious place, hoping he'll get the hint—that would seem too needy. She has never gone this long without sex and has never had to beg for it. She spends her business life saying no to attractive men. *How ironic,* she thinks, *that the only man I'll accept is the one man who doesn't want me —my husband.*

"The next good proposition I get, I'm going to take the guy up on it," she tells him, eliciting nothing beyond a raised eyebrow. In truth, she wouldn't consider an affair on purely practical grounds—it would be stupid and messy and pointless. Still, she reflects, *if my marriage remains sexless for much longer, I can't imagine it will survive.*

Listening to Alex grouse about the lack of sex and his obsession with Daniel, all Rob can think is *How can you complain when you have this beautiful baby?* He rationalizes his lack of sexual desire as representing a common reversal of male-female roles that occurs over time in marriage. After a while, he maintains, there's little to drive the male sexual urge, especially once you've witnessed your wife giving birth, which removes one of the most important aspects of male arousal: visual stimulation. *When you've seen all these people handle her as if they're stuffing a Thanksgiving turkey,* Rob thinks, *the mystique is ruined.*

He couldn't help noticing how alluring Alex looked the other day, working out on the NordicTrack in only a hip-length T-shirt and sneakers. But instead of ripping off the T-shirt and taking her to bed, as he would have been compelled to do in the past, he felt inert. Maybe, he thinks, she's right about going away for a weekend. He now understands why there are so many advertisements for marital getaways in the Poconos. But it would mean leaving Daniel behind.

*Marriage is work, work is work, and sex is work,* Rob concludes. *Daniel is anything but.*

**THURSDAY,
DECEMBER 20
Queens**

T 4 A.M., AS JOE DRESSES FOR WORK AND MARIA SLEEPS, THE phone rings. It is Maria's mother in Puerto Rico, calling to say that Maria's dog died. Joe wakes Maria with the news. She's so upset she can't go back to sleep. She cries as she sits with Joe, drinking coffee. When he leaves, she starts ironing, not knowing what else to do.

Late in the afternoon, Joe learns that his brother's hardware store in Lake George burned down. "Why is all of this happening at once?" he frets to Maria. "We lose the house, your dog dies, my brother loses his baby and then his store burns down, Tony could be killed any day . . ."

"It's life," she says. "You get bad news and then things are good and then they get bad again."

"I guess," Joe says doubtfully.

Maria goes to the kitchen to make the burritos Joe wants for dinner. He's been so good to her she'll do anything he asks. Yesterday he agreed to do the marketing with Luis so she could finish her Christmas shopping, though he planned to play basketball. Most other men Maria knows would say, "No, I'm going out. You're the mother, *you* stay with the baby."

Joe tells Maria about the people who stopped to admire Luis in the supermarket. "You must be such a good husband and father to watch the baby and shop at the same time," they said. Maria is not indignant that no one would be impressed by a woman doing the same thing.

"You don't know how much I appreciate you," she says at dinner. "I tell everyone how lucky I am, how great you are . . ." She goes on and on, making him feel good.

Joe looks at the pretty Christmas tree in the corner, the display of holiday cards he arranged on the wall in the shape of a tree, the colored lights twinkling in the window, which Luis so loves. He thinks about the celebrations ahead—two tree-trimming parties this weekend, Luis's first Christmas Day, the New Year's Eve bash at Maria's brother's, Luis's baptism on January 6. Maria, he concludes, is right. Life gets bad and then it gets good, and as long as you have your family, you can survive.

**MONDAY, DECEMBER 24**
**Westchester**

 LEX WAS ON HER WAY TO HER BROTHER'S HOUSE ON DECEMBER fifteenth, thinking mean thoughts about her mother-in-law. Thanksgiving dinner went smoothly enough, but her mother-in-law continues to freeze her out of conversation, and Rob continues to delay installing a Christmas tree in the apartment. *That woman is controlling my faith, my house, my life. . . .* Alex was so distracted by anger that she lost control of the car and skidded into a tree. The car was totaled, though Alex was unharmed. The accident made an impression on Rob; the next day they bought a Christmas tree and put it up.

Alex assumed he told his mother, but as she dressed to pick up her mother-in-law for babysitting on the seventeenth, Rob mumbled from the bed, "You better tell her about the tree on the way over here so she won't walk in the door and have a heart attack."

In the car Alex said casually, "We've been putting up some holiday decorations," which was met with silence. When they reached the apartment (Rob, *the coward,* had left for work), Alex's mother-in-law didn't glance at the tree. Alex cloistered herself in the study. Soon she heard her mother-in-law in the adjacent bathroom, blowing her nose. *She's crying,* Alex thought, consumed with guilt and rage. She resolved not to look at her mother-in-law's eyes in case they were red.

A few minutes later there was a knock at the study door. "Alex, I have a cup of coffee for you," her mother-in-law said. Alex invited her in, astonished. Not only had the woman never brought her coffee before, not only were her eyes clear, but she was friendly, for the first time since Daniel's birth. Alex still has no idea what happened. Maybe her mother-in-law grew tired of her own behavior. Maybe eight nights of lit Chanukah candles softened her. *Who the hell knows,* Alex thinks. *I can't figure this family out.* Rob's mother has been a paragon of sweetness ever since. *We'll never have to hide the Christmas tree again,* Alex realizes with great relief.

Tonight Rob and Alex dress Daniel in black velvet pants, a red velvet vest, and a black bow tie and drive to Alex's brother's house for the traditional della Croce Christmas Eve fish dinner. At the table, Alex says to the fifteen-odd members of her family, "I can't believe that last year I was so sick from being pregnant I couldn't eat a thing, and here I am, stuffing my face."

"Don't worry," Rob announces blithely. "Next year you won't be able to eat again."

Alex shoots him a murderous look, but he avoids her eyes. *If he thinks I'll have sex with him just to get pregnant,* she fumes, *he is out of his fucking mind.*

FTER THEIR RETURN FROM THE VACATION IN HELL, MICHAEL stayed out of Sarah's way as she plunged into frantic Chanukah shopping. The holiday came and went. For a blessed few nights Hannah slept through until seven, offering Sarah a break from the fatigue that so affects her mood. One morning just before Christmas, as Michael was leaving for work, she ran to the door and threw her arms around him. He stiffened. *All of a sudden she decides to be affectionate,* he thought, *and I'm supposed to forget how nasty she's been, just like that?* Sarah sensed his resistance. "What's wrong?" she asked. He pulled her close.

That night Sarah suggested that they see a marriage counselor. She hadn't felt this much distance between them since Margery's death. "Maybe," Michael replied, but he considered the idea seriously. The next morning he happened to drive by the synagogue. Quite spontaneously he pulled the car into the lot and went in to talk to the rabbi, who knows the Coens well. Michael asked if he could recommend a good marriage counselor. The rabbi seemed surprised; he said he never suspected they had any real problems. "Why don't you see me?" he suggested. "It's part of my job to counsel members of the congregation." The idea sounded appealing; Michael has always felt comfortable with the rabbi.

He went home and told Sarah about the visit, expecting to be commended for it. But she said they should find someone else. "I'd feel guilty taking up the rabbi's time," she explained. "Other people need him more than we do." She attends a weekly class the rabbi leads for people who have converted to Judaism. After one recent class, she told Michael, she asked the rabbi how his counseling work was going. "The last six months have been unbelievable," he said. "People are coming out of the woodwork with marital problems." Sarah didn't relay this to Michael because it never occurred to her he would go to the rabbi when she mentioned counseling.

"Okay," Michael said. "The next move is up to you."

On Christmas weekend, Michael and Sarah took turns in bed with the flu. One night Hannah woke at 2 A.M. Sarah heard her crying on the monitor and went downstairs to check on her. The baby was burning with fever; the thermometer registered 103. Sarah brought her upstairs and phoned the pediatrician. The doctor on call was the newest and youngest member of the practice, which made her nervous. He advised her to give Hannah Tylenol. She did, but at 4:30 there was no change in the baby's temperature. Michael started to panic. All the memories of Hannah's first week of life flooded him. *What is wrong with her now?* he thought. *Will she make it?*

He called the doctor back at five to say he was taking Hannah to the hospital. The doctor met Michael there and gave the baby a shot of antibiotics. "Take her home," he said. "Just watch her." Michael called Sarah from the emergency room. "Screw that," she said, frightened that Hannah's condition might deteriorate. "I want her in the hospital. Tell that guy *he* can watch her."

Hannah spent the night in the pediatrics ward, and Michael picked her up in the morning. When they got home, Ben was at a friend's house and Sarah was resting upstairs. Michael put Hannah on top of the king-size bed with some toys. "Let's make love," Sarah said to him. Hannah's latest medical crisis invoked in her a sense, both cozy and frightening, that she and Michael were alone in the world—they have only each other. She felt suddenly close to him and needed to express it.

"It'll freak her out," Michael said, pointing to Hannah playing at the foot of the bed.

"No, it won't. She's not old enough." Michael was easily convinced, thinking, *Take it when you can get it.* They made discreet love under the sheets. Sarah was right—Hannah paid no attention.

Later Sarah took the baby to Esther Levin, their regular pediatrician, who looked intently at Hannah's eye, which was swollen and red. "I think she should go back to the hospital," the doctor said very calmly. "The eye tells me she still has an infection. I want to monitor it."

Sarah tensed. Hannah has been sick for eight weeks on and off, with fever, cold, flu, and now this—which, after another night in the pediatrics ward, was diagnosed as a strep bug common in babies. Sarah is convinced that Hannah's immune system was permanently impaired by the infection she contracted at birth, though Michael accepts Esther's less ominous explanation: it's winter, and kids under two, especially those with older siblings, are susceptible to everything.

Tonight Sarah and Michael are going ahead with their black-tie-optional New Year's Eve dinner party for twelve friends. Michael selected the wines and worked out the menu with Sarah: pasta with sun-dried tomatoes and goat cheese, followed by deviled crabs, salad, and peppered tenderloin of beef. He will cook, with Sarah acting as sous-chef.

Sarah considers the dinner a dry run for the elegant, intimate restaurant she hopes will be in their future. She envisions a reservations-only, weekends-only setup, with the best china and crystal and silver. Michael will supervise the kitchen and she will take care of decor and hostessing duties, which would please her because she loves to entertain. Michael is dubious about how profitable a tiny restaurant would be, but Sarah is optimistic. *It may be a pipe dream,* she thinks, *but it keeps me going.*

**MONDAY, DECEMBER 31**
**Westchester**

T IS 11 P.M. ROB AND DANIEL AND ALEX LIE IN BED TOGETHER. ONLY Alex is awake.

This is the first New Year's Eve in a decade Rob and Alex haven't spent with friends in Philadelphia. It seemed too burdensome to attempt the trip with a six-month-old. Today's major event involved the redemption of coupons Alex had clipped diligently, resulting in six boxes of diapers and a hundred jars of baby food. They had just dragged the bags into the apartment and deposited Daniel on the living room carpet when Alex noticed the baby starting to gag. She pulled him on top of her, reasoning that it would be cheaper to take a shower and change her clothes than to have him vomit all over the rug.

They went out for an early Chinese dinner with Daniel, who vomited again in the restaurant, this time on Rob. Back at home, they put the baby to bed and watched TV. During a commercial, Rob announced that 1990 is the first year he can remember looking back on without self-loathing. "My kid is spoiled rotten and my wife is spoiled rotten," he told Alex, "and I feel great about both of you." *Well,* Alex thought, *it's not sex, but it's something.*

Now, with Rob snoring and Daniel drooling into the pillow beside her, Alex realizes that New Year's Eve isn't what it used to be. It's not a question of better or worse. It's just not the same.

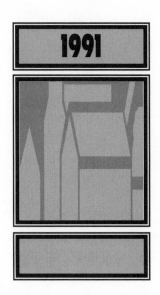

**1991**

### THURSDAY, JANUARY 3
#### Manhattan

THE CHRISTMAS TREE, DECORATED WITH SUCH TONGUE-IN-cheek ornaments as Sam's handmade crayon rendition of an angel transforming into a devil, still twinkles in the living room. For once, Juliet plans to keep the gifts Sam bought her: a suede purse, a silk shirt, and a necklace (all purchased with credit from the last gifts she returned). Sam likes the Escher-print tie she selected for him but isn't thrilled with the Dustbuster. Juliet thought it was the perfect idea for a man who hates litter of any kind, but Sam finds it insultingly unromantic.

For the first time ever, they stayed home on New Year's Eve, their fifth anniversary. They had planned to travel uptown early in the evening to attend a party given by Juliet's mother, then return to the loft to entertain another couple. But Lily fell asleep at five; waking her for a long subway ride in freezing weather didn't seem worth it. At six, the couple they invited canceled.

Sam lit the wood stove in the living room. He and Juliet ate caviar and oysters and drank champagne while watching a rerun of *An American Family,* the 1971 documentary about the Louds of Santa Barbara. Sam thought, *Here I am, married with child, at home on New Year's Eve.* He waited to feel depressed. He waited in vain.

On New Year's Day, Sam prepared brunch for various members of his and Juliet's families. As everyone consumed his specialty, crepes with fresh strawberries, he realized he felt more relaxed at this obligatory holiday event than in past years. The difference, he figured, was having Lily around. Babies (as opposed, Sam assumes, to sullen adolescents) make people feel good; when *your* baby is responsible, you feel good, too.

Juliet does not feel good. She feels envy and despair. A novel with a theme similar to one of hers was just published to glowing reviews. The holidays are over; it seems that everyone but her is returning to work. She feels *just barely alive, crawling through the mud.* She knows it's time to get involved in something beyond motherhood. The question is, what? Should she burn her novels, or try to be more aggressive about getting them published? Should she return to the screenplay she abandoned a few months ago? Should she go ahead with her idea to start a catalogue company in partnership with a friend? In her current mood there is only one answer: Don't bother. Failure seems inevitable. All she really wants to do is sleep.

**THURSDAY, JANUARY 3**
**Southern Maryland**

RIN'S LAW FIRM AGREED TO HER TERMS: SHE'LL WORK FROM 9 A.M. to 4:30 P.M., with Fridays off, at a flat hourly rate. She won't have benefits, but she and Katie can go on Tom's insurance plan. At twenty-four dollars an hour, her salary will equal what it was before.

Erin read the chapter on how to go about finding child care outside the home in *What to Expect the First Year* and placed an ad in the local paper. She got twenty-two responses. Today she eliminates all but nine candidates over the phone. Some live too far away, one has a pit bull, a few seem too transient, and one is too countrified, judging by her grammar and vocabulary. Erin schedules interviews with the women remaining on her list.

Christmas, she thinks, was awful. Fifteen people spent the long weekend at her house; Molly and Erin cooked and Tom cleaned, while everyone else sat around doing nothing. It's always that way, but this year, with a baby of her own draining her energy, Erin found it annoying. The living room was loaded with gifts no one needed, which suddenly seemed obscene. Next year, she thinks, they should make donations to charity instead of buying one another useless objects, and there should be a pot-luck buffet so she and Molly can relax with everyone else.

By the end of the long weekend, Erin couldn't wait to get everyone out of her house. *Now,* she thinks, *I need a vacation.*

### THURSDAY, JANUARY 3
#### Queens

 ARIA, IN AN APPLE–GREEN TRENCHCOAT BELTED OVER A BLACK turtleneck and pants, clutches the overhead bar on the subway train. Her eyes are riveted on her fellow passengers. Yesterday she noticed a man in the process of picking a woman's backpack; she stared the guy down, preventing the theft. Joe tells her not to take such risks, but she hates to stand by while one person preys on another.

She gets off the train one stop out of Manhattan, at Long Island City, where she has parked her car. She has to go to the store where she bought Luis's christening outfit and trade it in for a bigger size. The ceremony is on Sunday afternoon at her sister-in-law's house. Maria ordered the traditional favors: white ribbons printed with Luis's name and the date of the christening.

Months ago Joe and Maria had chosen Tony to be Luis's godfather, but since he's in Saudi Arabia they'll have to use a proxy, and Maria is against it. She believes the godparents need to be there in person for the honor to mean anything. "Tony will get the next kid," she said to Joe, unwittingly touching off his tears.

Joe's a mess. At midnight on New Year's Eve, he hugged and kissed everyone at Maria's brother's party and then grabbed Luis. "I want you to meet your Uncle Tony in 1991," he said, his voice breaking. Abruptly, he handed the baby to Maria and disappeared into the bathroom. When he came out his eyes were red, but he was composed. He apologized to Maria for losing control. She told him not to worry about it. "You're so good to me, you're always there," he whispered.

On New Year's Day he called Tony's wife, Theresa. She was sobbing. The January 15 deadline is approaching; her ten-year-old daughter is sleepwalking and having nightmares and asking why her daddy couldn't be home for Christmas; Theresa has no immediate family other than her three young children to lend emotional support. Joe revealed nothing to her of his own foreboding. Maria was proud of him, and amused when he used on Theresa many of the lines Maria has tried to no avail on him, such as, "You've got to think positive."

Maria exchanges Luis's outfit and completes the trip home. The small Christmas tree in the living room is decorated with football ornaments, red apples, candy canes, a silver-and-blue sign reading BABY'S FIRST CHRISTMAS, and a Polaroid shot of Nico, the dog. Joe's tree-shaped Christmas card display is intact against the wall.

Joe comes in from the bedroom with Luis in his arms. Maria reaches hungrily for the baby and covers him with kisses. Joe seems entranced by the affectionate tableau, unable to take his eyes off the two of them.

**WEDNESDAY,
JANUARY 9
Southern Maryland**

 ATIE'S NEW BABYSITTER, LORRAINE, IS A MIDDLE-AGED WOMAN licensed by the state (which makes Tom happy) and comes with glowing recommendations (most important to Erin). She lives a few minutes away, has a child of her own, and takes care of two others. She offered Erin a typed contract specifying her services, a professional touch that Erin appreciated. Erin will stop by to pick up the contract, she said, but she didn't say when because she wants to see how Lorraine operates when she isn't expecting visitors.

Today Erin arrives unannounced to find a large, clean house with a neatly kept yard. Inside, Lorraine and her five-year-old charge are on the floor, drawing with crayons. Erin is satisfied with the setup. Tom will do his own reconnaissance next week, on the pretense of returning the contract, and they'll leave Katie with Lorraine for a half-day trial run. When Erin returns to work on February 4, the Wrights hope they'll be adjusted to this new routine. Erin is nervous about leaving Katie but eager to resume her place in the real world.

Tom would like to escape that world. He is so caught up in it that he sees little of Katie; he leaves the house before she wakes and returns when she's about to go to bed. He often stares at the eight-by-ten picture of her smiling face mounted on the wall of his small office, especially when he's about to explode at an irate customer or a lax employee. *Her smile is so wide and happy,* he thinks, *just like her mother's.* Looking at it is usually enough to calm him down.

### SATURDAY, JANUARY 12
#### Westchester

I N MIDWEEK ROB AND ALEX FOOLED AROUND ON THE COUCH— *lots of kissing and heavy breathing,* Alex thought, *like teenagers—* but Rob had to finish a project on his computer. "No way will I settle for a quickie after all this time," Alex said without rancor. Rob laughed and went off to his cubicle.

Today is Saturday. No one has to work. In the morning, a broker shows the condo, which is still on the market, to a client; Alex makes sure it's in impeccable condition. After the broker leaves, she can relax (the house is clean), meaning that Rob can too. Outside, a thick blanket of snow from yesterday's blizzard makes staying in desirable. There is nothing to do but play with Daniel and loll around.

At night, after Rob rocks the baby to sleep, he and Alex watch

*Internal Affairs* on the VCR. They start necking. *Finally,* Alex figures, *this is it.* But there are still no condoms. They are restricted to oral sex . . . but it's better than nothing.

"Do you want to start a streak?" she says afterward.

"Don't make a big deal about it," Rob says solemnly, thinking, *The more you talk about sex, the less you do it.* He remembers the Jon Voight character in *Midnight Cowboy,* who brags about going to New York to be a stud and then is impotent with his first female client.

"Why did it take us so long?" Alex persists.

"Absolutely everything about our lives is different since Daniel arrived, from parking the car to getting the newspaper to waking up in the morning to sleeping at night. Why should sex be immune to change?"

"You don't eat less. Why should we screw less?"

No comment.

Not that Alex is angry. After all, she's had her first orgasm in eight, maybe nine months—a stellar event, however achieved. Almost equally stellar was the $6,800 salary increase she received last week. Considering that she spent two months of 1990 on maternity leave and worked part-time for a month thereafter, she knows the raise is an unequivocal sign of her good standing.

It was granted during a week in which Rob sold absolutely nothing. "It's good I'm used to being less successful than you," he told her, "or I might be jealous."

**TUESDAY, JANUARY 15**
**Manhattan**

ULIET FEELS LIKE AN IDIOT, JUMPING AROUND AND SINGING "THE Itsy-Bitsy Spider" at her first Gymboree class. She thought Lily would like it, but the baby seems shell-shocked. And the other mothers just aren't *copacetic.* She hoped to make friends, but no one talks to her.

Sam was away at a conference all last week. Juliet managed well until Friday, the day he returned. The weather was freezing, a play date canceled, she had no sitter, and Lily was cranky. Sam walked in the door to find a shrieking baby refusing to eat dinner and a wife at the end of her tether. "It's been a complete disaster," Juliet wailed in greeting.

For the next twenty-four hours her manner was brusque, and Sam was hurt. Juliet never told him she was happy to have him back; she picked on him; she ordered him around. By Saturday night, everything she said came across as an attack. He thought she might be punishing him for going away, as she used to do in years past. He tried not to overreact or challenge her and waited for her mood to change. By Sunday, it had.

Today, after the Gymboree fiasco, Juliet and Sam take Lily to a pediatric opthalmologist recommended by their pediatrician, who is concerned that Lily's left eye doesn't tear. The specialist tells them that Lily has either a blocked duct or no duct in that eye; the problem will have to be surgically corrected. Without a tear duct, the doctor explains, bacteria accumulate and eventually cause blindness. He gives them the name of a lachrymal surgeon.

Juliet fears Lily is too young for anesthesia. She cannot imagine the baby undergoing the operation without it. The opthalmologist assures her that the risks of anesthesia for a baby at six months or older are no greater than for an adult.

Sam, however, can't bear the thought of Lily under anesthesia. To wait helplessly while someone he loves is unconscious and under a knife—it's too close to what happened with Juliet.

**TUESDAY, JANUARY 15**
**Queens**

ODAY IS THE DEADLINE FOR IRAQ TO PULL OUT OF KUWAIT. JOE has a knot in his stomach that won't go away. He's had bronchitis, tonsillitis, and a sinus infection for the past five days; everything in his body aches, from his fingernails to his knees. He missed four workdays and is sure that any chance he had to become an acting supervisor has been compromised by excessive sick leave. But none of that matters compared to what may happen to Tony in the next twenty-four hours.

It has been a miserable few weeks. Maria has been sick but won't take time off from work. Luis has an ear infection, Tracy is unable to babysit because she had foot surgery, and Joe's various ailments render him useless around the house. The Reyeses' guardian angel this time is Joe's mother, who has been staying with them since Luis's baptism. She cooks, does laundry, cares for the baby. *God bless her,* Joe thinks.

Maria feels guilty about burdening her mother-in-law and is worried about Joe. She tries to protect him from the TV news, brightly proposing a game of Parcheesi when he reaches for the remote-control device. One night, while Joe sleeps, she turns on the TV and catches a report about how sickness can linger in depressed people. Maria thinks of Joe's incessant cough and the aches in his body that cause him to walk like an old man. He eats nothing but soup and has lost ten pounds in ten days.

Tonight she watches him lie on the bed, staring up at the ceiling, not moving or speaking.

"Are you all right?" she asks.

"I'm scared," he whispers.

### TUESDAY, JANUARY 22
#### Cape Cod

HE DAY AFTER WAR BROKE OUT IN THE GULF, "BOMB SHEETS" were distributed to teachers at Ben's synagogue preschool, with instructions for what to do in the event of an attack. The teachers were so frightened that the extended afternoon program, which Ben attends, was canceled, as was Sarah and Michael's counseling session with the rabbi, which Sarah had finally agreed to.

Sarah couldn't understand the mass panic. "Why would anyone bomb little Cape Cod?" she wondered aloud to another synagogue member.

"You don't get it," the woman said, "because you weren't born

Jewish." Sarah thought this comment so silly she didn't bother reacting.

She is less concerned about enemy invasion than about her and Michael's still unfinished renovation plans. She told Michael to call the architect to check on his progress. He complied and reported that they'll have the plans next week. Sarah hopes so; she wants to get going on it. She feels imprisoned in this small house, this small town.

Today a friend of hers, a woman with three children, confides in Sarah that she has been thinking of committing suicide. She says she's depressed and drinking too much, as people do on the Cape in winter. (Sarah shares the impulse, though with alcoholism in her family, she's too conscious of the danger to indulge to excess.) Personally, Sarah never thinks of killing herself. But she sympathizes with her friend. *Three children, winter, Cape, isolation, drinking, suicide . . . it makes perfect sense.*

**WEDNESDAY,
JANUARY 23
Queens**

J OE PREPARES TO TAKE THE DOG FOR A WALK. HE BENDS TO TIE HIS sneakers, and when he straightens up his eyes are filled with tears and his body is shaking.

"I can't take it," he says to Maria, who is looking at him with alarm. "There's something wrong with me. At work I'm like a robot, I'm making dumb mistakes, my heart is always racing. I feel like I'm having a nervous breakdown. I wonder if I should see someone."

Maria remembers how he *lost it* when his newborn nephew died a year ago. She thinks, *Oh no, not again. Why doesn't he get a grip on himself?* She asks if he wants her to call the parish priest and set up an appointment for counseling.

"Yes," Joe says. He pauses. "If I get out of hand, please let me know."

"Babe, you've really been good," Maria says. "Your mother tells me she can't believe how you've matured, what a homebody you've become. And you're so good with Luis. You always talk about how proud you are, and that makes me feel great."

Joe hugs her. He grabs Nico's leash and leaves the apartment for a twenty-minute walk. When he returns, he tells Maria he wants to go to the Superbowl, on January 27 in Tampa. His beloved Giants are playing. The ticket is expensive, but he'll economize by driving down with a friend from work. They'll leave early Friday morning, spend the night with Theresa in Georgia, arrive in Tampa Saturday afternoon, head back to New York on Monday.

"I feel a little guilty about going while Tony sweats it out in the desert, but it might clear my head," he explains.

Maria responds with a lukewarm *hmmm.*

"I don't want you to think I'm using this as an excuse to get away from you or anything," Joe says quickly. "It's a once-in-a-lifetime opportunity."

Maria's mind races. She figures the minute Joe sees Theresa and her kids he'll lose control, and she won't be there to help him. She fears the Superbowl will turn out to be more painful than invigorating; they'll keep breaking in with war news. Recalling the thriller *Black Sunday,* she thinks about terrorists. And Joe has been so angry at the world lately that she worries he'll get into a fight with someone who happens to look at him the wrong way. But she says only, "If you want to go, go."

"I'm so happy with my son, and with you . . . I don't know what I'd do if you weren't here. I really love you." He reaches out and grabs her hand, squeezing it hard.

**THURSDAY, JANUARY 24**
**Westchester**

 LEX'S TRIP TO ATLANTA THIS WEEK YIELDED LUCRATIVE NEW business, but she was upset about having ruined her best bikini in the overly chlorinated hotel pool. The suit, a beauty in olive and gold, was the only one in her collection high enough to cover her cesarean scar. She returns home tonight to find that Daniel has started crawling. It upsets her to have missed seeing it.

When she walks in, Rob is sitting at the dining table enjoying his mother-in-law's chicken cutlets Milanese. Alex waves hello to him, hugs Daniel, and goes to unpack in her bedroom, where she sees that the baby's humidifier is empty of water. She gave Rob one instruction before leaving for Atlanta: fill the humidifier with water. She leaves the bedroom to ask Rob why he didn't do it.

"I forgot."

"It's not an 'I forgot' issue."

"I have a job, I'm busy. Certain details escape me."

"This detail takes one minute a day, and it has to be done no matter how busy you are," Alex says. "You're not doing it for me, you're doing it for Daniel. Okay?"

"Okay." Rob picks up an envelope lying on the table. "And while you're giving orders, mule, I should tell you that for the first time in eleven years I made more money than you. So there." He waves the tax form indicating his 1990 free-lance income from the consulting job: $28,000. *"That's* why I allowed you to have sex with me the other night," he whispers, so his mother-in-law won't hear.

"Very funny." Alex tries not to smile.

Later, rummaging through the hall closet, Alex finds a package of condoms. She considers taping one to Rob's sink in the second bathroom but decides not to. She has too much pride. *Let him worry about it,* she thinks.

**SATURDAY, JANUARY 26**
**Manhattan**

 AM IS AGAINST WAR, PERIOD. HIS FEELING ABOUT THE GULF SITUA- tion is that there should be a ceasefire and negotiation; if Hussein won't talk, the boycott should continue. Juliet gen- erally shares his pacifism but is ambivalent about this conflict. It's unusual, and troubling, for her not to have a strong opinion about an important issue, or to be unable to engage Sam in debate when he says to her—with, she thinks, annoying self-righteousness—"How can you abandon your principles?"

This morning Sam has a long phone conversation with an old friend from law school who shares Sam's sixties-style leftist thinking: the Gulf war is an elaborate plot to get the country out of the recession, because war pumps up the economy. Sam and his friend agree it was a lot easier to be a pacifist during the Vietnam war. Unlike Ho Chi Minh, Saddam Hussein is clearly a bad guy . . . Juliet overhears this conversation, which meanders endlessly, and finds it moronic.

Later Sam and Juliet go out with Lily. Walking in the park, Juliet makes comments about Sam's self-indulgent, outmoded perspective. He is furious at her portrayal of him as some washed up ex-hippie. Okay, he says, maybe he did drone on with his friend, and yes, he still buys into the whole anti–military-industrial establishment thing, but she ought to mind her own business and not eavesdrop on him.

They have dinner without Lily at a neighborhood restaurant and use the time to deconstruct their argument. Juliet promises to stop monitoring Sam's phone calls and he agrees to stop pretending it's still 1968.

Sam has been in a grim mood, the kind of mood Juliet sees him in no more than once a year. He lost an important civil rights case recently, and he's not used to failure. He is filled with a sense of incompletion and disgrace. He tries distracting himself with Lily, which doesn't help. He once thought that all he would need to do to forget his troubles would be to pick up his baby, but he's learning that's not the case.

His malaise evaporates in time for Lily's dreaded appointment with the eye surgeon. It goes better than he expected; the doctor seems experienced in dealing with parental anxiety. He prescribes a new medicine and says there's a 10 percent chance the problem will clear up on its own. If not, he'll schedule the operation. He explains that the longer they wait, the more damage will accrue to the tear duct, making surgery more complicated.

After the appointment, Juliet and Sam fight, ostensibly about their opposing interpretations of a point the doctor made but really to displace their anxiety about Lily. Sam gets the last word, something they always compete for, because the cab pulls up to his office building just as he finishes speaking.

Juliet goes on to a less than glorious day with Lily. The sitter is on vacation, and Lily screams whenever Juliet tries to get her to take a nap. At four Juliet calls Sam at work. "Get home right now," she says. "I've had it." Sam comes home forty-five minutes later and takes over. He is not annoyed by Juliet's intrusion into his workday. He feels like a hero to walk into the house and rescue her.

**TUESDAY, JANUARY 29**
**Queens**

HERESA SEEMS SO COMPOSED AND STRONG WHEN JOE VISITS HER before the Superbowl that he is envious, and worried anew about his stability. When she says, "I guess it won't really hit me until the ground war breaks out," he wonders, *God, what will happen to me?* He fears Luis can sense his distress, will see him as weak, unable to handle life—though he wonders how much a seven-month-old can understand.

Arriving in Tampa is a welcome relief. The football fans' high spirits are infectious. Soon Joe is in an antic mood, making strangers laugh. He calls so much attention to himself that he gets quoted in the local paper as a die-hard Giants fan from distant New York City.

At the Superbowl, reminders of the war are everywhere. The pregame parade is dominated by Vietnam vets, and all around the stadium people are dispensing yellow ribbons. The performance of the national anthem is punctuated by shots of soldiers against a movie screen, drawing tears from Joe and everyone else. The halftime events feature appearances by the children of people stationed in the Gulf. And the game itself—Joe feels like he's sitting on a razor blade watching the Giants, in whom he feels a personal stake, triumph over the Buffalo Bills at the last second. When he returns home, he changes the outgoing message on his answering machine to *Giants 20, Bills 19 . . . nothing more to say.*

Maria is so happy to see him back safely that she can't stop telling him how much she loves him. Joe wraps his arms around his wife and son, thinking about what his mother said to Maria, how he has changed, matured. His mother is right. He no longer hangs out in clubs or plays basketball every night like he did in his first marriage. The reason, he realizes, is simple. He has Maria and Luis to come home to.

**SUNDAY, FEBRUARY 3**
**Westchester**

 OB AND ALEX TAKE A WEEKEND AWAY FROM DANIEL. THEY GO on a ski trip with one of Alex's clients and his wife, subsidized by Alex's company. When they arrive, Alex hurries into the three-bedroom chalet she rented, tours the place quickly, ahead of her client, and instructs Rob to place their luggage in the modest second bedroom. She wants the client and his wife to have the master, with its king-size bed and Jacuzzi.

"Why did we get this one?" the client asks.

"Because I'm sucking up to you this weekend," she says, making him laugh. She genuinely likes this man, who has already given her

100 percent of his business for 1991. The purpose of the trip is to ensure that he does so for the rest of the decade.

Rob and Alex ski by day and entertain the client and his wife at night with seamless renditions of what they call *The Rob and Alex Show,* feeding each other lines with perfect comedic timing. One night they have dinner at a pretentious French restaurant, where Rob purposely mispronounces the words on the menu ("Excuse me, waitress, I'm not from around here, what is a, um, *poo-let?*"). He orders steak au poivre *(poy-vree),* setting Alex up for the joke to follow. The room is quiet, with people talking in whispers as if in a library. When the waitress places the steak in front of Rob, Alex waits a beat and then says loudly, "Waitress, he'd like some ketchup." The waitress looks at both of them disdainfully—*ketchup on steak au poivre?*—and Alex's guests are charmed.

The weekend, Alex tells Rob, feels like old times; she senses nothing missing. Rob disagrees: Daniel is missing. When they get home, he wants to race out the door to pick up his son, who is with Alex's mother. But Alex insists on unpacking. She knows that once Daniel is in the house, Rob will consider the rest of the evening playtime and leave all the work for her. So Rob puts away the ski equipment and Alex does the rest.

The next day, Alex works at home and notices that the new babysitter, Yvonne, doesn't measure Daniel's formula carefully enough. She also notices that Daniel screams whenever she goes into her office and shuts the door. *From a child's perspective,* she decides, *it must be a lot tougher to have a mother who works than one who doesn't.*

**MONDAY, FEBRUARY 4**
**Southern Maryland**

HE FIRST DAY OF PRACTICING THEIR NEW ROUTINE, TOM AND Erin took Katie to the sitter's together. Erin found the leave-taking so upsetting that Tom did it by himself the second day. Listening to Lorraine's reports on what Katie ate, when she napped, and how she behaved, Erin realized that her daughter had less trouble adjusting to the change than she did.

Erin used the two free days to get organized, stocking up on groceries, doing laundry, trying on her office wardrobe. As she feared, few items still fit. She pulled those out of the closet and went at them with her iron, plotting the diet she will begin any day. She tried to contain her apprehension about the juggling act to come—accomplishing what she needs to in a shortened time frame at work, picking Katie up, feeding her, making dinner for herself and Tom, and somehow fitting in a class or two toward her degree in business administration. She could take one on Friday mornings, leaving Katie with Lorraine, but then she would sacrifice time with her daughter.

Tom and Erin, with Katie in the stroller, spent Sunday touring Annapolis. Katie was on her best behavior; Erin was depressed. She fought tears, fraught with guilt about the next day's separation from the baby. Returning to work, she believes, is the right choice for her but not for Katie. *How do working women ever resolve this conflict?* she wondered.

Katie is asleep when Erin leaves this morning, saving her the agony of saying goodbye. She drives to a downtown hotel to meet Philip, her boss, who invited her to breakfast. Philip's wife, also a lawyer, just gave birth to their second child; he is unremittingly sympathetic as Erin expresses her conflicts about being a working mother.

Erin reaches the office at ten and is shocked at how alien it seems. She was on maternity leave in October when the two firms merged physically; this is the first time she has been in the new building. The computer and phone systems, even the location of the ladies' room, are unfamiliar. During the day she picks up the phone six times to dial Lorraine's number, but each time resists the impulse. She doesn't want to seem interfering or nervous. *If there's a problem,* she tells herself, *Lorraine knows how to reach me.*

Lorraine brings Katie to the door within seconds of Erin's ring. Erin hugs and kisses her daughter with such emotion that she feels embarrassed. She lies Katie down to put the baby's jacket on before taking her outside to the car. To her dismay, Katie starts to cry. *Don't be an idiot,* Erin tells herself. *She's only four months old. It doesn't mean she doesn't love me.*

UDDENLY, OR SO IT SEEMS TO MARIA, EVERYTHING SHE DOES OR says elicits disdain from Joe. The brief exchange they have today while looking at a co-op is typical. The broker tells them the co-op is in public school district twenty-four, among the city's best, but later, when Maria glances at the information sheet the broker gave them, she mentions to Joe that P.S. 24 isn't listed.

"What are you talking about?" he says. "Weren't you paying attention? It's *district* twenty-four, not P.S. 24." His derisive tone offends her. She throws the paper on the floor and walks away.

Joe thinks the tension between them is generated by Maria. He feels she has somehow *isolated* him.

At night, just as Maria is on the verge of sleep, Joe sits up in bed.

"What's the matter?" asks Maria. She can barely keep her eyes open.

"You've been so cold lately—you've been a bitch. Everything's bugging you."

"It's not me, it's you. You act like everything I say is wrong. It's like you've been away for years. First you were sick and out of it, then you went to the Superbowl and we lost track of each other . . ." In the middle of her sentence, Maria falls asleep with her head on Joe's chest. He lies there thinking she may have a point. He's had this cloudy feeling in his head for weeks because of the war. It must be affecting him in ways he can't see.

He decides to avoid the news, which invariably agitates him. He will stop himself from seeing Tony's face whenever he looks at Luis; he will tell himself, *This is your boy here, not some ghost.* He will be careful to watch his tone around Maria, which should prevent her from freezing him out.

Still, the cloudy feeling won't go away.

OB FINALLY BUYS CONDOMS. HE AND ALEX BEGIN HAVING SEX regularly, though less often than before pregnancy. The infrequency reinforces Alex's realization that her life has been forever transformed. She is nostalgic thinking of their childless years, but can't reminisce about them with Rob because he accuses her of regretting their having Daniel.

"That's not it," she protests. "I'm only acknowledging that things have changed completely."

"What was so great about the old days?" Rob says. "What the hell did we do with our time before Daniel? We slept late and we went out. Big fucking deal." He wants another child, he tells her, as soon as possible.

"Forget it. I'm not getting pregnant again for a long time, if ever. You don't understand the toll Daniel takes on my work. I'm always backlogged. Yvonne leaves at five, you don't get home until eight, and those used to be the hours I wrote reports. I can't do them during the day because I'm on the phone. You're insane if you think I'll endure a further assault on my time."

"You're holding up the idea of a second child as a weapon between us."

Alex is too aggravated to continue. She says only, "You *are* insane."

N SUNDAY, JOE AND MARIA OFFERED $75,000 FOR A RENOVATED two-bedroom co-op listed at $80,000; the seller compromised at $77,000. Maria is ecstatic. All the place needs is painting and some minor detail work. There's a dishwasher and a microwave; the bathroom is newly tiled, the bedrooms freshly carpeted; the neighborhood is quiet and safe. Best of all, Joe decided to give the dog away to a friend. Maria would never have suggested it; Nico is Joe's dog and she felt it wasn't her place to say, *Get rid of him.* But Joe realized that Nico would destroy the apartment sooner or later, which is one thing when you only rent, quite another when you own.

Theresa called that afternoon with a message from Tony: he's fine and hopes to be back as soon as May. But people on the base, she added, predict that the ground war will start this week.

Maria focused on the first part of Theresa's news. "That's great, he might be back in May," she said to Joe. He heard only the second part: "Don't you realize, the ground war is starting and Tony is on the front lines."

When Maria gets home from work today, she enters quietly, not wanting to disturb Luis in case he's napping. In the living room she finds Joe slumped into a corner of the couch, Luis in his arms, his head bent over the baby's. For a minute Maria thinks they're both asleep, but as she moves toward them Joe looks up, his face sad. He points wordlessly to a letter lying on the couch. She picks it up and reads it. It's from Tony, dated February 1. "Hey Guys, Hey I'm still here and still kicking . . . I know I'm going in to Iraq very soon, I know I'll have to shoot. I know it's not going to be easy, and I know that I want to come home alive! . . . I don't know what the future will hold, so just in case this is my last letter please remember that I love you all very much."

Maria thinks the letter is selfish—*Tony wants us to feel sorry for him.* She doesn't tell that to Joe. "Honey," she says, "don't worry about it, he doesn't know what will happen." She goes into the kitchen to start dinner and comes out a few minutes later to check on Joe. He is staring into space, clutching Luis, who is still asleep. It looks to Maria like Joe is holding on to the baby for dear life, and then she realizes *he is.* The only way he can counter the terror that Tony might die is by hanging on tight to the flesh and blood he created. She sits down on the couch next to him and rubs his neck. "You have to think positive," she whispers, feeling like a broken record. *Damn Tony,* she thinks.

C ALL IT DELAYED POSTPARTUM DEPRESSION OR JUST A BAD DIP in self-esteem—whatever it is, Erin feels she's failing in every area of her life. Everything overwhelms her. She's crying too much, and eating too much. Tom has been patient with her tears, her short temper, her constant fatigue, but she wonders how long he'll be willing to weather her moods.

At work she thinks about Katie, often feeling jealous of the sitter, but when she's with Katie she worries about work. Erin's job is no less demanding than before, but now she has twenty-five hours instead of forty in which to accomplish the same tasks. She'll have to quit or go back full-time; neither alternative seems acceptable. Her days are drearily repetitive: she gets up, goes to work, battles traffic, picks up the baby, cooks dinner, puts Katie to bed, goes to sleep, gets up . . . the same thing all over again. *This,* Erin realizes, *is what they mean by the rat race.* Today she gets to see Katie roll over for the first time, but the thrill is brief because it reminds her of the other firsts in her daughter's development that she expects only the sitter will witness.

Katie's baptism, held last week, resulted in an estrangement with Erin's one unmarried sister, Judith. Judith was angry with Erin for scheduling the event on a weekend when she had to be away on business. Erin explained that she had to accommodate the grandparents and godparents first, but Judith felt she should have had priority. Erin feels like a horrible person for causing a rift in her family and already worries about what Christmas will be like if she and Judith are still feuding.

Erin, Tom thinks, is on overload. She won't give herself a break; she thinks she has to be everything to everyone all the time. The situation with Judith is the perfect example. She tries so hard to please and is so devastated when she fails that she can't see that Judith is being a bitch. Four members of Erin's family have birthdays in February, including Erin, and they celebrate together each year. At the party yesterday,

Tom saw Erin's tortured expression when she realized that Judith had sent a gift to everyone but her. She left the room; he found her upstairs, crying.

Tom realizes that things were easier on everyone when Erin wasn't working. He had thought the first three postpartum months would be the roughest time and felt pleased they had managed them with relative ease. Now he sees the time went smoothly only because Erin was home, without the conflicts aroused by her return to work. Now he sees *the full picture.*

As for sex . . . It used to be so simple. It didn't need to be planned; it happened and he enjoyed it without having to make an effort to enjoy it. But now he and Erin are so uptight about everything —her work, his work, Katie crying in the next room—that sex is no longer pleasurable. It's just another chore.

The last time they tried, he thought again of Katie's birth and lost his erection. Erin continues to feel that she is no longer attractive to him, especially now that she's gained ten pounds. She won't believe him when he protests, *that's not it.* The less she believes him, the more he feels he must perform in order to convince her; that pressure, of course, makes failure inevitable. After the last attempt, there was another outburst that Tom should find himself a younger, thinner woman. That was almost two weeks ago. Since then they haven't gone near each other.

They'll have a sex life again; he's certain of it. But considering they're both dead tired by 9 P.M. and distracted by other concerns the rest of the time, he doesn't know how, or when, it will happen.

**MONDAY, FEBRUARY 25**
**Manhattan**

AM IS QUOTED PROMINENTLY IN TODAY'S *TIMES*, WHICH NORmally would make his day. But this morning he and Juliet take Lily back to the lachrymal surgeon, who determines that her eye is getting worse and schedules the operation for next Wednesday. Sam questions the doctor repeatedly about the risk of anesthesia. The surgeon insists it's no greater than taking a cab to the hospital, which would be reassuring if Sam hadn't seen the movie *Coma* so many times.

Within hours of being taken to the surgeon, Lily develops a fever. *It's like she's trying to avoid the operation by getting sick,* Juliet thinks. If the baby is still feverish tomorrow, when she's scheduled for preoperative testing, the surgery will be postponed. Juliet wouldn't mind. She continues to hope that the problem will disappear if they wait long enough.

Parents aren't permitted to observe the administration of anesthesia or the procedure itself, nor are they allowed into the recovery room. Thinking of Lily waking up alone in an unfamiliar environment makes Juliet profoundly uneasy. And the night before the surgery sounds like hell. Lily isn't allowed to eat from midnight on; she'll be hungry, eager to nurse, and Juliet will have to deny her. *But Lily is a feisty, resilient kid,* Juliet tells herself. *Nothing really awful could happen to her.*

**WEDNESDAY,
FEBRUARY 27
Queens**

 ARIA AND JOE ARE ON THE WAY HOME FROM A BIRTHDAY party on Sunday, driving separate cars. They stop alongside each other at a red light. Maria looks at Joe and sees an expression of terror on his face. "Something's not right," she says to her sister-in-law, who is sitting in her car. Joe rolls down his window and leans his head out. "The ground war—it started," he says.

Then, almost before it has begun, the war is over. "Thank you, Lord," Joe says, over and over, when he hears the news. He wants to wake Luis, but Maria convinces him to wait until morning. "I'll never be able to sleep tonight," Joe says, but by ten he's out cold.

At 4 A.M. the alarm goes off. Joe jumps out of bed, goes to the crib, lifts up the still sleeping baby. "Hey, you're gonna meet your uncle after all," he says, kissing his son's eyes. Luis opens them. He reaches for his father's mustache with tiny fingers; he drools on the shoulder of Joe's postal uniform; he cries for his bottle. "I guess this is just another day for him," Joe says to Maria, sounding surprised.

**SATURDAY, MARCH 2**
**Cape Cod**

I T IS THE EVENING BEFORE HANNAH'S FIRST BIRTHDAY. SARAH'S SIS-
ter, Allison, six months pregnant, is spending the weekend with the Coens and will attend Hannah's party tomorrow. At dinner tonight at a local restaurant, she wears a high-necked, lace-trimmed maternity dress, the kind of insistently virginal dress Sarah would never have worn.

Allison lacks her sister's fashion sense, but she is no less acerbic. Throughout the meal the sisters talk contemptuously of their hypocritical mother, their chauvinist pig brother, and his skinny, submissive wife. Michael sips his wine and listens. He has heard this sisterly vitriol before, but it always fascinates him. He never gossiped with his brother this way.

Sarah and Allison's dialogue is interrupted when a bejeweled

woman in a fur coat stops at the table. She belongs to the same synagogue as the Coens do, and natters on to Michael about the Purim
party to be held tomorrow morning. Michael tells her that he and Ben
will be there. "Bring Tylenol, you'll need it," she says, waving goodbye. "On second thought," she adds, "bring Valium." She giggles and
drifts back to her own table.

"On third thought," Sarah says, mimicking the woman's chirpy
voice, "bring heroin." Everyone laughs.

The conversation turns to the Coens' plans for renovating their
house. As Sarah describes the hoped-for transformation to Allison,
Michael has a sinking feeling; he pictures Sarah in the kitchen trying to
fit another box of cereal into an already full cabinet or a utensil into a
drawer that won't close, muttering, "I hate these cabinets, I hate these
drawers, I hate this kitchen." *No matter how many cabinets we build or
how big our new kitchen is,* he thinks, *it will never be enough.*

At home the next morning, Michael slices bagels for breakfast while
Allison mixes chocolate batter for a cake that will be served to the
adults at Hannah's birthday party later. The children will eat the cake
that Sarah made, a cat-shaped, orange-frosted creation decorated with
chocolate whiskers, ears, and eyes.

Hannah, now a pudgy, curly-haired, blue-eyed child with a ready
smile, tools around the kitchen in her walker. Ben has gone back to
bed—a reaction, Michael guesses, to all the attention focused on his
sister today. Finally Ben emerges from his room, to find his father
sitting on the bench bouncing Hannah on one knee. Michael pulls
him onto the other one. "That's why people have two knees, one for
each kid, right, Daddy?" says Ben. He and Michael decide to go to the
playground rather than to the Purim party, given the unusually balmy
weather.

Pushing Hannah in her stroller down the long driveway, Sarah
shudders at the Valentine's Day present Michael gave her, now affixed
to her car: a vanity license plate that reads SARAH. More to her liking is
another Valentine's gift, the sapphire and diamond ring glittering on
her left index finger. In exchange, she gave Michael a night of wonderful sex—not such a rare thing anymore. In general she is much

more interested in lovemaking: her tubes are tied, removing her fear of pregnancy, and Hannah is finally sleeping through the night. Sarah has renewed energy for her husband, in bed and out of it.

The first crocus of spring blooms in the Coens' yard; yellow ribbons indicating support for U.S. soldiers in the Gulf still flutter on the mailbox at the end of the driveway. While Hannah sleeps in the stroller, Sarah continues walking to the beach. There she looks at the tranquil sea from the sandy shore of a half-moon–shaped cove and breathes a sigh of relief. The events of the past year—her mother-in-law's death, Hannah's traumatic birth—seem remote. It was a year she tries to forget.

At the playground, Ben romps with his friends while Michael sits at a picnic table, thinking of his mother. The anniversary of her death was in January, but Margery has been very much on his mind as Hannah's birthday approached. *She would have loved to be here today,* Michael thinks. He envisions her arriving at the house with shopping bags full of gifts for her only granddaughter. Inside the bags are rectangular white boxes wrapped in pale pink paper with shiny pink ribbons; inside the boxes are frilly, intricately smocked dresses of velvet and fine Swiss cotton.

Ben never knew Michael's father but often talks about Margery, calling her *Bubbe,* the Yiddish name for grandmother. As Bubbe's presence fades in his young mind, Michael will be able to show him scrapbook pictures of the two of them, grandmother and grandson. Hannah has no pictures, no memories . . . *Never mind.* It hurts to think about Margery, just as it hurts to talk about her, to Sarah or anyone, and Michael tries to block out anything that hurts.

It's almost 2 P.M. Michael has to pick up the hot pink balloons with streamers of emerald-green ribbon Sarah ordered from a party goods store. He plays a quick game of catch with Ben, then hustles him into the car. They collect the balloons and go home, where Sarah has set the birthday table with a hot pink paper cloth and matching cups, plates, and silverware; emerald-green party hats are clustered in the center. Kids of different ages stream into the house and onto the deck.

Hannah, in an expensive pink dress with a matching ribbon tied around her curls, plays with her toys on the kitchen floor, oblivious to the festivities in her honor.

"Everyone will be out of here in an hour," Sarah whispers to Allison as the onslaught begins at three. At 3:50 she places Hannah in her highchair and calls everyone into the kitchen. Michael rolls the video camera as Sarah places one candle—and another to grow on—in the center of the cat-shaped cake. She lights the candles and brings the cake to Hannah. Ben has the preassigned task of blowing out the flames. By 4:15, everyone is gone.

The first year of Hannah's life has ended. Michael is optimistic about the future. He has to be. *Otherwise,* he thinks, *what's the point?*

**MONDAY, MARCH 11**
**Queens**

"I 'M SICK OF THIS DAMN PLACE AND THIS DAMN DOG," MARIA SAYS to Joe when she walks into the apartment after work and sees that Nico spit pieces of pork chop bones all over the floor. "I have no time to relax, I have no time with the baby. I brought work home tonight because I'm so far behind."

"Why don't you take a nap," Joe suggests—not what Maria wants to hear.

"That's easy for you to say. You can sit there watching TV, but I can't. The house is messy enough without you using the highchair as your personal closet. Your corduroy pants are still lying there. What do you think, the maid's coming or something?"

Maria feels she's constantly in motion and getting nowhere. She tries to research interest rates at various banks because Joe has no access to a phone at work, but the loan officers rarely get back to her. When they do, she can't answer their questions because Joe has the information. One night she stayed alone with Luis until Joe came home from the gym at 9:30. The next night she planned to take advantage of a department store sale, but by the time Joe got home from his haircut and *his* errands, it was too late to go. "I had important things to take care of," he explained, which Maria interpreted as saying that *her* things aren't important, *she* isn't important. She was furious.

Joe mops up Nico's mess and walks into the kitchen. He sees the sink full of dirty pots and pans and starts swearing loudly. *If she's going to be nasty,* he thinks, *then I will too.*

"What the hell is your problem?" Maria says.

"Your pots and pans are all over the place!" he yells. She thinks, *The nerve of you! I come home tired every night and one time, just one time, I leave something in the sink and you go nuts and meanwhile you won't even hang up your goddamn pants!* (Maria never asks Joe to do the dishes; it was his chore growing up in his mother's house, and he hates it so much that Maria accepts it as her exclusive duty.) But she says nothing, not even when Joe takes Nico for a walk in the rain and brings him back dripping wet so he can stink up the place all over again. Maria washes the offending pots and pans and allows herself a few minutes to sing a lullaby to Luis before beginning her ironing. Joe goes to bed at 11, but she continues working until 12:30. He wakes when she enters the bedroom. "Babe," he mumbles, "why are you still up?" She ignores him.

The next night she tells Joe, "You've been unfair and selfish." He looks confused.

"I can't believe you're still upset about not being able to go shopping," he says.

"That's only part of it. How dare you lecture me about the pots and pans?"

"Well, what if someone comes to visit? They were all over the place."

"That's too bad. I work all day."

"Okay. You want me to say I'm wrong? I'm wrong."

Not the most heartfelt apology, Maria thinks, but she knows she's at fault, too. She needs to tell Joe what bothers her right away, not hold it in for days. *But,* she thinks, *there's never enough time to get past the anger part.* If she's mad about something at seven, and the baby's up till nine, and Joe goes to sleep while she's still doing chores, how will they ever resolve anything?

OB IS PUZZLED WHEN ALEX COMPLAINS THAT HE NEGLECTS HER in favor of Daniel. He thinks this is another version of how he delayed too long fixing the crack in his windshield, or how she can't get her job done in the time she has, or how he works too many hours for too little money. *It's about expecting life to be perfect.* She cycles in and out of this so regularly that he can predict it almost to the day. (He wonders if it's PMS, though it seems to occur every six weeks.) The first clue is her quiet hostility, a failure to laugh at things she normally finds funny. The hostility builds until it spikes into violent anger and accusation, lasting about twenty-four hours and fading away. Then she returns to her entertaining, wise-cracking self.

*Women,* Rob concludes from a twelve-year study of Alex, *are not like men.* Alex handles a screwdriver as well as he does; she lays tile as precisely as her father laid brick. But she is still as mood-driven as any other woman, Rob thinks, however much she tries to deny it.

O MUCH FOR ERIN'S SHORTENED WORKDAY. WITHIN A MONTH OF her return to the office, she voluntarily lengthened her hours. Now she arrives at eight instead of nine, but she is still unable to complete everything by 4:30, when she has to leave to pick up Katie.

Tonight she casts an anxious look over her desk, stacked with legal briefs and faxes and phone messages. She wears black-and-white-checked stirrup pants with a long black blazer, hoping to conceal her extra weight. At this time a year ago she was three months pregnant and weighed ten pounds less.

Erin has so much on her mind these days, none of it pleasant, that she has insomnia. Last night at nine she took two Tylenols with codeine, but they had no effect. At midnight she popped three Advils and lay sleepless, listening enviously to Tom's rhythmic breathing. She watched the hours go by on the illuminated clock radio. At 4:30 she heard Katie crying and followed the rule the books advise: wait fifteen minutes before going in. By 4:45 Katie was asleep again, but Erin wasn't.

She drives south on the beltway, fiddling with the radio tuner until she catches the Mamas and the Papas singing "Monday, Monday," which aptly mirrors her funk. She thinks of the many things that agitate her.

Their sex life is hopeless. On Friday night they left Katie with Erin's parents, hoping for a romantic evening—dinner out with lovemaking to follow. Erin had her period, so there was no need for birth control (removing one of Tom's excuses for not being able to perform). But she was so worried about another failure, and so tired and crampy, that when they got home from the restaurant she went to sleep.

Her sister Judith, still angry about the scheduling of Katie's baptism, refuses to talk to her. The station is in terrible shape, judging by Tom's recent cryptic comment that he'd rather close it down than declare bankruptcy. She isn't sure if he's considering such a drastic move or just expressing general anxiety, but his statement alarmed her. She had always thought of the station as their security. If it becomes a liability . . . In her head she plays out the nightmarish scenario: Tom loses the station. She goes back to work full-time and her relationship with Katie deteriorates because she's never home. Tom takes a job as a mechanic and is miserable not being his own boss. He quits or gets fired. Erin's income isn't enough to cover their expenses; they lose their house.

Erin is as depressed about her life as she was four years ago, when she and Tom separated. This time she doesn't blame him for her problems, but that doesn't make it any easier to accept what she regards as her disturbing lack of accomplishment. She still has no college degree; her job is only slightly removed from the secretarial pool; she has no consuming interests. She's not a *project person,* like Tom, who just last weekend laid a tile floor in the laundry room. The things Erin does, like making bottles or doing laundry, aren't noticeable. She does have Katie, who gives her pleasure and enriches her life and her marriage, but anyone can have a child. Procreation is not what she means by accomplishment.

And that rat race she runs every day—is it ever going to change? Is it ever going to get better? She fears the answer is no. *This is adult life,* she thinks, *and it's only going to get worse.*

Erin is feeding Katie when Tom walks in, exhausted. He revives himself with a beer and a shower, then goes to pick up dinner at a takeout place nearby. The food sits in its foil wrapping on the table until Katie is asleep. The Wrights eat at 9:15.

"It's funny if you think of how we grew up." Tom laughs. "Our moms had dinner on the table every night at five-thirty."

"When I wasn't working, I cooked every night." Erin is defensive. "The house was clean, the baby was clean, I was clean . . ."

"You were Mrs. Stepford," Tom says gently. "I think you're happier working, and Katie doesn't seem to be suffering."

"That's true." Erin butters her baked potato. "And if I hadn't gone back to work we wouldn't have an extra nickel, and that would put me over the top."

"You're terrible the way you worry about money. You'd like to pay all the bills in advance."

"You'll be late for your funeral, and I'll be early for mine."

"Things have been so marginal this year," Tom says. "I should make more money, but you can't in this business anymore. Last year we made $11,000 or $12,000 a month on gasoline; this year it's down by half. I've seen the good times, and that keeps me going. But if I had $30,000 sitting in the bank right now, I'd feel a helluva lot better."

Erin sighs. She reaches for a box of mint Girl Scout cookies and empties the contents onto a plate.

"What about the schedules?" she asks. (Tom normally drops Katie at the sitter's. He wants to do the pickups instead so he can supervise the station's critical early morning shift.)

"Let's switch for a week, on a trial basis."

"But I can't keep going back and forth on it, it will cause problems at work," Erin says irritably. "It will be impossible for me, I'll lose an hour—and when you get home at six you'll have to do what I do: feed her, throw in some laundry . . ."

"Okay," Tom says. "It's worth it to me, because if I can get to the station at seven, I can fix a lot of problems."

"But now you get up at seven-fifteen. You're talking about getting up by five, five-thirty latest, to get to the station by seven."

"Talk to Philip. See what he says."

"He'll be ecstatic. He hates it when I leave at four-thirty." She pauses. "Okay, let's try it."

Erin leaves the house at 7:16 the next morning, sixteen minutes off schedule. She can't resist lingering; at this hour, Katie is at her most engaging.

Just before eight, Tom drops Katie at Lorraine's and stops at a convenience store for coffee. His mood is buoyant: last night he and Erin finally made love. He's convinced it worked because it was the tail end of Erin's period and he didn't use protection. In the distant past, before Katie, condoms were no problem for him, but in the distant past he didn't have the memory of the birth, nor did he have to contend with the lack of spontaneity that has made sex something to be *put on the schedule*.

Now he can dispense with the terrifying thought that something is wrong with him.

### SATURDAY, MARCH 16
#### Manhattan

ILY'S EYE SURGERY HAS BEEN POSTPONED UNTIL NEXT MONTH, SO the family takes a trip together, the first since last summer's stay on the island. Their destination is Boston, where Sam has to see a client.

For him, the weekend is filled with nostalgia. He and Juliet lived together here in the seventies, and when they drive by their old house he chokes up, thinking of the good times they had there. Juliet teases him for being so sentimental.

They stay with old friends, Mark and Sally, who have a one-year-old son named Eric. Sally is the head of a large division of a major company, which in Juliet's view has made her life an absolute hell. With the exception of her office Christmas party, Sally hasn't been out alone with her husband once since Eric's birth. She works long hours and comes home exhausted, but keeps Eric up late because she feels guilty she's not with him during the day. Juliet watches them closely. Whenever Eric whines, Sally picks him up. "Oh, Eric," she says, "are you tired, am I not paying enough attention to you?" They keep at it while Mark cooks dinner, serves it, clears the plates, and does the dishes. Sally holds Eric on her lap until he falls asleep, around 11 P.M. Juliet looks at Sally and thinks, *My career is nonexistent, but I'd hate to be torn like that.*

**WEDNESDAY, MARCH 20**
**Westchester**

 OB IS NOW THE TOP SALESMAN IN HIS COMPANY, WHICH HE credits to Daniel's presence in his life. He feels restless. He needs a new goal. He's thinking about moving to a bigger corporation—IBM, for instance, which he envisions as Mother Earth, taking good care of its workers. Alex is eager for him to leave his current employer, who offers no benefits beyond Social Security—a ridiculous setup, she thinks, for a man with a family. (Alex has a company-subsidized retirement plan and family medical insurance.) She believes that Rob's insecurity as a provider is partially caused by this situation, which is reason in itself to move on to a company that cushions its employees. Rob's fear of rejection, he knows, has kept him from seeking out the *big ponds,* but now, for Daniel's sake, he's prepared to risk it.

Alex returned from her last trip and was matter-of-fact when Daniel again held back from her open arms. Rob wondered why she wasn't devastated. "There's no point in getting upset," she told him. "It won't change anything. I have to travel in order to do my job."

When she's away, she misses Daniel—but not much. On this last trip she imagined what it would be like if Daniel just disappeared. Because the thought failed to panic her, she wonders if she's really less maternal than other women purport to be. How is it she can cry while watching a Shirley Temple movie but not feel much of anything when she contemplates her son being gone—not kidnapped or hurt or dead, just *gone?* The more Rob makes Daniel the focus of his life (she compares the two of them to Rhett Butler and his daughter, Bonnie, in *Gone With the Wind),* the more Alex finds herself pulling back emotionally from both of them. Already her traveling places her at an uncomfortable remove from her family, and from control of Daniel. On the road she negotiates multimillion-dollar contracts, but she comes home wondering what her son has been eating and when he last had a bowel movement. It seems ridiculous that everyone but her —the babysitter, Rob, her mother, her mother-in-law—knows the answers to such questions.

Rob tells her she ought to get up with Daniel on weekend mornings, when she doesn't have to think about work and can enjoy him fully. Yet he seems possessive about guarding that time, often telling Alex how precious Saturday mornings are because he has Daniel all to himself.

Alex's company has scheduled a five-day conference for sales executives in Florida at the end of this month. Children and spouses are invited, all expenses paid. When Alex learned of the trip, eight weeks ago, she told Rob it was important to her that he lose weight. (She has often observed that people—especially the men she works with, who all seem to be six-foot-two and 165 pounds—tend to write off overweight human beings as sloppy and lazy.) But when they went to the mall last weekend to get resort clothes for him, he had to buy size 38 pants. He wore 30 in college. Alex knows people tend to get heavier as they get older, but *size 38?*

Alex is now the sexually rejecting partner. She thinks Rob knows his weight has something to do with it. He no longer appeals to her physically, but more significant, they are engaged in a power struggle. His smoking, his eating, his excessive focus on Daniel are his way, she thinks, of saying *fuck you* to her. Fine. She can say the same thing.

Rob knows he promised to lose weight before the trip, and he hasn't . . . *but,* he thinks, *so what?* Alex will be busy with her colleagues all day and he'll be with Daniel at the beach, listening to people tell him what a gorgeous son he has. Who needs to be thin for that?

**THURSDAY, MARCH 21**
**Queens**

LL MONTH, JOE HAS WAITED FOR NEWS OF TONY'S HOMECOMING, which was supposed to have occurred first on March 9, then on the 15th. He began to wonder if Tony had already returned, and Theresa had convinced him not to tell anyone for a while so she could have him to herself.

Today after work, Joe runs errands, thinking that his suspicions must be correct; the war's been over nearly four weeks now. Where in hell is his brother?

When he gets back to the apartment, there's a message on the answering machine: "Joe, this is Tony. I'm home. Uh, correction—I'm in New York. I'll be home in about two hours. See you later." *Damn.* If only Joe had known, he could have been there. Tony called between flights from La Guardia Airport, just twenty minutes away.

Joe calls Theresa and proposes that he and Maria and Luis drive down tonight. Theresa says unenthusiastically, "Yeah, he'd like that," and changes the subject. Joe lets her evade him; he'll wait to see what Tony says.

He sits on the couch with a stiff Scotch, throwing pillows at Maria, teasing and tickling her, glancing now and again at the NCAA championship basketball game on TV. By 10 P.M. he has called Tony's house three times, only to get a machine.

At 11:15, Tony calls. "Listen," Joe says, "I really want to see you."

"Then make it happen." Tony's voice is deep, commanding, unemotional, just as Joe remembers it.

"Did you see action, did you get me anything?" Joe had asked Tony to bring back a blood-soaked Iraqi turban as a souvenir.

"There was an Iraqi prisoner," Tony says slowly, "but it was so sad, I didn't have the heart to get it for you." *Sad?* That doesn't sound like Tony.

"Are you okay, brother?" Joe is alarmed.

"We'll talk."

Joe sets the alarm for three o'clock, but he and Maria sleep through it. They wake at seven. "It's too late," Maria says. Joe agrees. Now that Tony is safe, he can be patient. He'll go by himself when Maria and Luis visit her parents in Puerto Rico next month.

He has lost that cloudy feeling that prevented him from thinking straight, but Maria, he thinks, is out of it. Joe can't decide if she's angry with him or just angry at the constant mess in the house. He suggests she organize herself better; her busybeeing, he tells her, makes her too flustered to accomplish much. He thinks she's burning herself out. He teases her and tries to make her laugh. In the old days it was easy, but since becoming a mother she's always tired, always busy, always harassed. She complains he's not helping her but doesn't see that even when he appears to be doing nothing, he's mulling over things that affect both of them—the paperwork for the mortgage, his new responsibilities at work (he was recently made an acting supervisor), decisions about car insurance. He concedes that Maria does more of the housework, but he's in charge of the mental stuff, and gets no credit for it.

Since Maria rarely sits down before midnight and Joe tries to be asleep by eleven, their lovemaking, once an almost daily activity, is frustratingly infrequent. There are evenings when Luis is asleep and Joe sits on the couch stark naked thinking, *Hey, can't you take a hint?* "I just gotta get this done," she'll say, and he gives up and goes to sleep. The next morning she'll tell him she tried to wake him up. "Yeah, right," he'll say.

O ALEX'S EMBARRASSMENT, ROB IS *AN EATING MACHINE* HERE.
Even one of her colleagues comments on it. "You can really put it away," the man says to Rob one night at dinner.
And it isn't just Rob's gluttony that aggravates Alex. She
grits her teeth each time she hears him say, in response to someone's
question about Daniel, "Yes, he's our first," implying there will be a
second.

She asks him several times to take a picture of her alone.

"Why?" he says.

"All the pictures you've taken since Danny's been born are of me
and him. It's like he's my permanent appendage."

"But he's in our life now," Rob says, missing her point.

When Alex was four she asked her mother, "Who do you love
more, me or Daddy?" Expecting her mother to say "you," Alex was
shocked to hear "your father." She knows now that her mother's
attitude served her parents well. Neither of them suffered when their
children grew up and moved away, because neither depended on their
offspring to fulfill their emotional needs; they had each other. *Rob
doesn't get it,* Alex thinks.

At least, she tells herself, the weather here is perfect, and the accom-
modations are more than satisfactory. They have two balconies, one
for sunning and one for breakfast; they can see the sun set over the
Gulf of Mexico every evening. Away from Rob, Alex enjoys herself,
spending as much time with her colleagues on the golf course as in the
conference room. One day she goes on a company-sponsored fishing
expedition; she is the only woman on the boat, and catches the biggest
fish. She and Rob have sex once or twice, but Alex is too annoyed
with him to find it pleasurable.

Rob has a fine time—whenever he's alone with Daniel. Alex is
gone all day, leaving early in the morning; he orders a room-service

breakfast, which he eats on the balcony, feeding Daniel bits of cereal and fruit. He takes the baby down to the pool and they play in the water for a while. He dries him carefully and applies sunblock all over his body, invariably prompting some elderly woman to come over and say, "You handle your baby better than any man I've ever seen." Then Daniel naps in his stroller while Rob reads Saul Bellow's *The Dean's December*. One day he takes the baby to a Red Sox exhibition game in Sarasota. He wheels the stroller around the stadium, earnestly explaining to his nine-month-old the cosmic significance of the Red Sox's trade of Babe Ruth to the Yankees in 1918.

When Alex is around, the atmosphere is strained. Every meal becomes a battleground; Alex criticizes even the amount of ketchup he puts on his hamburger. Her attitude makes it impossible for him to enjoy sex. *It's not easy,* he thinks, *to get excited about someone who spends at least two hours of every single day telling you you're no fucking good.*

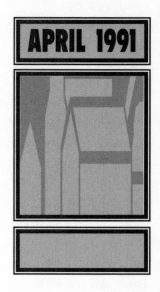

**TUESDAY, APRIL 2**
**Southern Maryland**

ODAY ERIN ATTENDS A TEAM–BUILDING SEMINAR AT WORK WITH nine colleagues. The leader discusses the four major personality types—dominant, steady, compliant, and influential—and singles out Erin as an example of a steady-compliant combination. She tells Erin, "I can see you're very comfortable with who you are." Erin says, "You're right," thinking to herself, *You're a liar.* But later she decides it's possible to be dissatisfied with and accepting of yourself at the same time.

To her surprise, the new schedule is working out. She and Tom alternate the evening pickups, and she does all the morning drop-offs. She now has the flexibility to complete projects or run errands two nights a week, while Tom gets time alone with his daughter and has vastly improved the workflow at the station by arriving at seven instead of nine.

There is only one problem: Erin's feeling of being replaced. It gnaws at her each morning when Katie holds out her arms to the sitter.

J ULIET MADE THE MISTAKE OF READING A. S. BYATT'S INTRICATE novel *Possession* a few days before Lily's operation. One of the stories-within-the-story concerns a Victorian woman who secretly, shamefully, bears a child out of wedlock; what happens to the child is a mystery until the end. There are oblique, poetic references to "squandered Nourishment," to breasts spilling with milk: "We run with milk and blood/What we would give we spill/The hungry mouths are raised/We spill we fail to fill . . ." Juliet thought of her own breasts spilling with milk in the hours preceding Lily's surgery, and of her daughter's hungry mouth, denied nourishment. She felt haunted.

They arrive at the hospital at seven this morning. For two hours, until Lily is given a shot to make her sleep, Sam and Juliet exhaust themselves trying to distract their daughter from Juliet's breasts. The doctor is late; by the time Lily is taken from her parents, the effect of the shot has worn off—she is awake and crying. Juliet is horrified to realize that she will be conscious when they put the mask on her.

The ordeal takes far longer than the forty-five minutes the surgeon predicted. Sam recalls the aftermath of Lily's birth and thinks, *Why don't doctors overestimate the length of procedures so you don't tear your heart out worrying something has gone wrong?* Two hours pass with no information whatsoever, leaving Sam and Juliet to imagine the worst. Finally a nurse tells them she saw Lily being wheeled into the recovery room. Twenty minutes later, the doctor approaches. Lily had a marble-size abscess in her eye, he explains; the operation was more complicated than expected. He had to reconstruct the tear duct and insert a plastic thread to keep the system from closing up again. "They'll bring her up from recovery in a half-hour to an hour," he adds.

Two hours later, Juliet goes downstairs to recovery and demands to see her daughter. Lily is sleeping, she is told; she must leave. But she can hear the baby crying. "Look," Juliet says, "what's going on? She's not sleeping, she's *crying*. Let me have her." She rushes to the gurney where Lily lies, her eye swollen and blood flowing out of her nose. As soon as Juliet picks her up, Lily smiles. For the rest of the day Lily's behavior is normal, though her face looks abused.

Back at home, after the baby goes to sleep, Sam and Juliet take a shower together. Sam starts to cry when the image of Lily's bloodied, swollen face floats into his mind. Juliet is unable to soothe him; she can barely maintain her own composure. She steps out of the shower and grabs a towel.

"I'm sorry, I'm not being very nice," she says. "I'm afraid to talk about it, I'm too upset. I just want to go to bed." And she does.

Sam goes into the living room and sits on the couch, thinking, *She didn't have to apologize. There are times in marriage when one person needs comfort and the other can't give it.* This, he sees clearly, is one of them.

**FRIDAY, APRIL 5**
**Queens**

ARIA AND LUIS LEFT THIS MORNING FOR PUERTO RICO; IN A few hours, Joe will be on his way to see Tony. These last few days, Maria was frenetic—organizing the paperwork for her temporary replacement at the office, washing what seemed to be every stitch of clothing in the house, dashing to the store for last-minute items. Joe was busy himself, running out to Brooklyn to buy the strawberry cheesecakes from Junior's that Tony loves. He couldn't manage to fulfill Maria's one request that he gather clothes that needed laundering.

The Reyeses expected to get their loan commitment this week, but no one from the bank has contacted them. Joe says if they get turned down they could move back to their old neighborhood in Brooklyn. It's not the safest environment, but all his buddies are there. He misses going with them to bars and the fights at Madison Square Garden. Rental apartments in Brooklyn, he reasons, are cheaper; Maria could get pregnant and quit her job.

Joe desperately wants another child, and is hopeful for a second son. He wants to play baseball with his boys while he still has the energy. As it is, when Luis is ten he'll be forty-five—*an old man.*

A LEX DEVOTES THE MORNING TO SCOURING THE APARTMENT IN preparation for a visit from her sister. Rob watches her race from room to room, cleaning utensils in hand, and thinks, *her sister comes over several times a week, for Chrissakes. So what if there are a couple of toys lying around? The toilets are flushed, there's no dirty underwear hanging from chandeliers. Why can't she sit down and have a cup of coffee like a normal person? Why can't she realize the price she's paying? The apartment is spotless, but the spouses are miserable.*

Alex's sister comes and goes. Around 2 P.M., while Daniel naps, a real-estate agent calls to say she has a buyer for their apartment. Alex puts down the phone very slowly. She stares at Rob, who is paging through classified ads for houses. She realizes the absurdity of pretending they will just move along, onward and upward—sell the apartment, buy a house, have another child—as if their arguments aren't serious, as if they're about what color to paint the walls.

Since they returned from Florida a week ago, Alex has wondered if she wants to stay married. She has even considered the custody arrangements they would make about Daniel and how daunting the logistics would be; she imagines Rob picking him up late or not at all, or on a different day than scheduled, because to him such details are trivial.

"I don't think we should sell this place unless some things are resolved between us," she says. Rob puts down the ads and looks at her quizzically.

"If we separate," she continues, "it'll be a lot easier not to have to deal with a huge mortgage."

Rob is silent for a minute and then gets agitated. "What about your son?" he says. *"What about Daniel?"*

"That's exactly my point. You're talking about Daniel's life, I'm talking about mine. He's only part of it."

"So what *is* your life?"

"Stop yelling! Your parents hated raised voices and you'd raise yours and they'd give in to you."

"I'm yelling because I'm frustrated, but okay, I won't yell," Rob says in an exaggerated stage whisper. "Let's list the problems, one at a time—here we go. 'The kid exhausts me and he's not my whole life. My husband is okay but he could have been better, in fact I thought he was going to be better. He has an okay job but he should have a better job and he should have had a better job sooner. The apartment is nice but we should have a house. Other people have pools and back yards, why don't we. My career is okay but I have to travel too much and I resent and hate having so much of the financial burden on my shoulders, and yeah, I have plenty of help with the kid but this is my space and I can't have my privacy.' Have I missed anything? Take it from someone who knows: you need professional help." Before Alex can respond, Daniel wakes up.

They drive to a seaside amusement park and walk along the boardwalk, pushing Daniel in the stroller, talking calmly about everything that is bothering Alex. When she says she suspects that Yvonne is stealing diapers, Rob doesn't laugh (it's hard not to—*only Alex would keep a tally of how many diapers are stacked on the changing table*). She complains she has trouble getting her work done on Mondays and Fridays, when she has no help, and Rob is sympathetic.

"Why don't we have Yvonne come four days instead of three?" he suggests. "It'll be another fifty bucks a week. We won't even notice it."

"You look at it as another fifty bucks a week, I look at it as another $2,500 a year."

"All right." Rob laughs. "And over the next hundred years it'll be a quarter of a million. Come on, Alex."

She tells him he's oblivious to things that need to be done around the house, leaving everything to her. He promises to be more attentive. When they get home, he hangs all the damp laundry (Alex doesn't like the smell of machine-dried clothes). His unbidden action, Alex thinks, must mean she finally got through to him. She begins to feel slightly more hopeful about the marriage.

**SATURDAY, APRIL 13**
**Southern Maryland**

S PRINGTIME IN THIS PART OF THE COUNTRY MEANS AZALEAS, FISH-ing, yard work, and above all, crabs. Soon the Wrights, along with their neighbors, will organize the first hard-shell crab orgy of the season. Each couple puts in fifteen or twenty dollars, someone volunteers to go to the Annapolis seafood market to pick up several pounds of steamed shrimp and a multitude of crabs, and everyone settles down to a communal feast. It's a time of year when families gather outside after work; the parents drink beer and gossip as they watch their kids play. Erin and Tom have stopped talking about moving north, because now it seems that everyone they like lives down here.

Tonight, with Katie asleep, the Wrights sit outside, enjoying the gentle spring breeze. Erin is in a reflective mood. "Our lives are so complicated now," she tells Tom. "Being with each other seems like an easy thing to sacrifice with so much else going on, but it's a mistake. I don't want to turn around one day and think, *Who is this person I married?* We've got to make time to sit down and relax like this more often." To Tom's relief, her tone isn't critical or tearful, which makes him more inclined to pay attention.

Erin asks his advice: she needs to resume her schooling, but can't figure out how to fit even a single class into her life. "I want to set a good example for Katie," she says.

"You'll get your degree well before Katie is old enough to know what 'college' means," Tom says, "but there's no point in pushing it right now while you're already overwhelmed."

*True,* Erin thinks. *Here I am worrying about setting a good example and Katie doesn't even crawl yet. I have five or six years to accomplish this, not five minutes.*

She tells Tom she feels split. Once, he would have nodded sympathetically without really hearing her, but tonight he feels her words deep within his gut. He knows what she means.

"It's the way things are, it's not you," he says. "I tell myself the same thing every day. There's work, there's our relationship, there's Katie; you can only give what you can, and nothing's going to get one hundred percent. You've got to learn to be satisfied with that." He pauses, thinking, *Easier said than done for someone who wants to be the perfect employee, mother, wife.* "You don't have to do the laundry or start making bottles the second you get home," he adds. "Spend that time with Katie. We'll do the other stuff together, after she's asleep."

His suggestions are simple but had never occurred to her. Erin thinks, *He is not just my husband, he is my friend; I'd forgotten.* "I love you," she whispers, so softly that he doesn't hear it.

For a moment, Tom regrets that his own laconic nature requires her to initiate these conversations that end up bringing them closer together. Then he realizes, *At least I had the sense to marry her.*

**WEDNESDAY, APRIL 17**
**Westchester**

LEX IS IN SAVANNAH, OR JACKSONVILLE, OR ATLANTA. *SHE COULD be anywhere,* Rob thinks. As usual, she hasn't left an itinerary.

Rob is staring into her closet, at the neat rows of sensible low-heeled pumps and conservative, knee-covering dresses that compose her business wardrobe (nothing remotely provocative that might offend her southern customers). The pumps are navy and black and beige, the dresses various shades of red . . . He recalls a story Alex loves to tell about herself. Beginning when she was seven, her mother repeatedly took her shopping for a pair of slippers, and all they could find were pink ones. "Try these," her mother would say, and Alex would respond stubbornly, "No, I want blue." (Pink, of course, was too frilly.) Two years went by before she found blue slippers.

Alex thinks the story illustrates one of her virtues: she will not settle for second best. Rob finds it disturbing. He wonders how she ever brought herself to marry. Why she chose him is even more bewildering. He has two theories: her entire family was against their union, which made it more desirable; she thought he was someone other than who he was, or would turn out to be.

Three years ago, Alex was working for another company. The firm employed 25,000 people worldwide, but she was well known to the top executives because she was so successful. During her final two years at that company she was miserable, with a boss who humiliated her. She would negotiate a multi-million-dollar contract and her boss would criticize her because her expenses during the month in which she made the deal were a couple of hundred bucks too high. It was absurd, Rob thought at the time, the way this man harassed her, looking for flyspecks. Now she's doing the same thing to him.

He loves her no less than he did a decade ago; in fact, because of Daniel, he loves her more. The attention he pays to his son, which Alex seems to begrudge, is in direct proportion to his desire to help her. He can't help wondering if she feels trapped in the marriage. Does she resent Daniel because he makes divorce a more complicated and painful undertaking?

Alex is vehemently opposed to a second child. "Our one and only," she comments, even to strangers, when she introduces Daniel. Rob knows that her difficult pregnancy and delivery militate against a second try. He could *fucking strangle* her doctors for letting her throw up for eight months before taking her off the vitamins, for letting her endure fifteen hours of labor and then performing a cesarean anyway.

Rob's strategy from here on is to say, "I've changed my mind; I definitely don't want another kid." The more he tells her he wants another, the more he'll guarantee it won't happen.

TONY WAS AT THE GATE WHEN JOE STEPPED OFF THE PLANE IN Savannah. Joe dropped his carry-on bag on the ramp and rushed to him. Their embrace was strong enough to make their backs ache. Joe expected him to look wasted, but he was as husky as ever.

Tony lost a friend in the war, saw him loaded onto a helicopter in a body bag. At one point, he told Joe, he himself was pinned under the hatch of his vehicle with shells detonating in a circle around him, and yet he emerged unharmed. "I've always had faith," he told his skeptical brother, "but now I'm going to church."

After the first day in Georgia, Joe found himself yearning for Luis. He had been so focused on seeing Tony that he hadn't prepared himself for the separation from his son—the longest ever.

"Never again," Joe says to Maria when the family is reunited several days later. Luis gets the first kiss, but she doesn't mind.

Maria's vacation wasn't exactly her ideal, which would be to stay in a hotel and go to the beach every day. But it accomplished her purpose: her father got to know his grandson. Luis and Maria spent so much time together that the baby has been clinging to her ever since. When she gets home from work now, Luis won't let go of her. Joe feels slighted. "You must have spoiled him down there," he grumbles. "Now he wants to be picked up every second, and only by you."

This morning, they go to breakfast at the House of Pancakes. Maria notices a young woman about her age with three kids in tow and another in her belly. "How does she do it?" she wonders to Joe.

"Maybe they live in a cruddy apartment."

"No way. Look at her leather jacket. Look at how well dressed her kids are." It makes Maria jealous to see large, prosperous families. It seems impossible to have a lot of kids and not work and still have enough money, and equally impossible to have a lot of kids *and* work, because you'd go crazy.

"These dumb young chicks who get pregnant, have three, four kids —they stay home because they go on welfare," Maria says. "It upsets me that they have all those kids and I don't. We could go on welfare too."

"That's cheating. We can't cheat."

"But everybody does it."

"Not us. We'll have three kids, we'll have four. We'll make it happen."

Maria nods. She doesn't ask, *How?*

**WEDNESDAY, APRIL 24**
**Westchester**

 INCE THEIR TALK IN THE AMUSEMENT PARK, ROB HAS BEEN COMING home earlier and offering to take Daniel out of the house so Alex can write her sales reports. He has even tidied the apartment a few times without being hounded. Alex believes in positive reinforcement and tells Rob how much she appreciates his efforts. He is mystified by her praise. He thought it was understood that he's always happy to take Daniel for a few hours; he only reminded her that she should take advantage of those hours to catch up on her work. He believes their rapprochement has nothing to do with him and everything to do with her: *she's out of her anger cycle and into her mellow one.*

Alex has a painful eye infection. She sees a specialist, who thinks it might be caused by a virus, possibly herpes. She tells him she had shingles (a form of herpes) in her eye five years ago; the doctor raises his eyebrows in disbelief. Alex finds his attitude insulting (she regrets having worn jeans, which probably invited his disrespect) and his questions odd: "Have you had any operations, any transfusions?" He doesn't ask if she is promiscuous, but it occurs to her an hour after the appointment that he may have been hinting at AIDS. *It can't be possible,* she thinks, *I've been monogamous for twelve years.* But Daniel is recovering from an infection of some kind, and for the last few nights Rob has been sweating profusely and feeling alternately feverish and chilled, symptoms that disappear during the day. Alex is alarmed but forces herself to be logical. *I should get our life insurance in order,* she thinks.

She wonders if Rob's newly considerate behavior is related to her eye infection. The circumstances are similar to those that brought on her attack of shingles. She and Rob were thirty then, married five years, living in Brooklyn. It was during the period in which Alex hated her former job and had begun feeling (as she does now) that they had stopped moving forward with their lives because they hadn't bought a house. Rob and Alex fought bitterly over this issue, and Alex developed the infection. She was told by her doctor that it was related to stress. Two weeks after she recovered, she and Rob purchased the condo. Rob said it was her eye infection that galvanized him to make the move.

Alex has an appointment with the specialist again tomorrow. She'll ask him point-blank if he suspects AIDS. Instead of jeans she'll wear a severe black suit, which she hopes won't turn out to be chillingly prescient.

### THURSDAY, APRIL 25
#### Southern Maryland

RIN CONTINUES TO FEEL OVERWHELMED. THERE IS UNREMITTING pressure on her at the office, and she again senses resentment directed at her by coworkers. On the days she leaves early to pick up Katie, she gets this "Do you expect us to do your work?" attitude, which her boss, who until now has been her ally and mentor, seems to share. As Erin leaves the office today, she calls to him, "See you Monday."

"Oh yeah," Philip says. "I forgot, you're a lady of leisure. Enjoy your lying around." Erin is stung by his remark.

On the way to a restaurant where she is meeting a friend for dinner, she drives through the neighborhood where she lived during her brief days as a single woman. She recalls the word Tom used to describe her then: "carefree." *Well,* Erin thinks, *no wonder. Life was easy then. Now everything is a struggle.* For the most part she wouldn't go back—

wouldn't trade her marriage, or Katie, for her youthful freedom. *But this business of being a mother and having a career, this juggling act:* it is her life now, and it's anything but easy.

Erin's dinner companion, Liz, has a two-and-a-half-year-old child and is trying to conceive another. She doesn't work; she feels strongly that a mother should devote herself to mothering, and Erin is conscious of Liz's implicit disapproval of her. As far as Erin can tell, Liz has no ambivalence about any aspect of parenthood. Listening to her explain why she doesn't believe in preschool, Erin feels a nagging insecurity. *Everyone but me knows what they're doing,* she thinks. *I'm just winging it.*

**THURSDAY, APRIL 25**
**Westchester**

N HER SEVERE BLACK SUIT, ALEX CONFRONTED THE EYE SPECIALIST. "Were you asking me AIDS-type questions the other day?"

"No," he said. "I have no reason to suspect it. Do you?"

"No, but none of us were virgins before we were married, right? And who knows what our other partners have been doing." He laughed *(the black suit worked!)* and gave her a prescription for eyedrops. Her condition improved, while Rob's deteriorated.

His fever and night sweats continued for five days; then he developed a sharp pain in his lower back and had difficulty swallowing. His father exhibited the same symptoms when he was diagnosed with pancreatic cancer. *I'm going to die,* Rob thought. *I won't see Daniel growing up.*

Alex saw the frightened look in his eyes and reassured him. "You're not going to die," she said, reading his mind. "Let's find out what's wrong."

Today she takes him to the emergency room of the hospital where she gave birth. She observes his agitation each time someone draws blood and finally says, "I was in labor for fifteen hours in this place. How can you complain about getting stuck with a needle?"

"I should be used to it. You've been drawing blood from me for twelve years." He manages a weak laugh. "What's the status of my life insurance?"

"I'd wait to die for a few days if I were you."

Initial tests reveal nothing conclusive, but everything is off just enough to suggest a serious problem. For years Rob has had a heart murmur; because of it, the doctors can't identify his normal heart sounds. They fear endocarditis, an infection around the lining of the heart that could turn fatal within days if untreated, so they put him on intravenous antibiotics. Rob's liver enzymes appear abnormal, which might mean hepatitis or worse; his blood oxygen is low, which might indicate a pulmonary clot. A CAT scan has been scheduled to test for lymphoma—which, the doctor assures them, is extremely unlikely.

"We know how to identify all the terrible things," he says, "and once we rule them out, it becomes 'virus of unknown origin,' which we don't worry about."

When Alex calls to tell Rob's mother that her son is in the hospital, her mother-in-law has to go and take ten milligrams of Valium. Then she accuses Alex of not being "upset enough," whatever that means. Alex wants to say, *If you and your son are both going to be basket cases until this thing is resolved, I'm going to have to be calm.*

She tells her mother-in-law about the testing that has been done so far. "Rob is on antibiotics," she says, "because of his heart murmur."

Her mother-in-law draws a sharp breath. "What heart murmur?" she says. Rob never told her about it, though Alex has known since college. "He cuts me off from his life," she wails. "He doesn't tell me anything."

"You panic," Alex says briskly. "That's why he doesn't tell you." Her mother-in-law doesn't get the message.

"Why aren't they giving us any answers? Are you sure he's getting good medical care?"

*She's acting hysterical,* Alex thinks, *just like Rob did when I was pregnant.* "Don't take this the wrong way," she said firmly, "but bad answers come fast. The longer they take, the more things they've crossed off their list."

Once Rob is checked into a room, Alex forces him to get on a scale. "Two-oh-four," Rob says. "Are you satisfied?"

"Are *you* satisfied? You ate yourself into this."

"If I don't die in the next few days, I'm going to lose weight, and I'm not ever going to smoke again. If I do die, I'm not worried about you. You'll marry that good-looking blond customer of yours. He'll adopt Daniel, and they'll look so much alike that you'll never tell him the guy's not his real father." They laugh.

Alex figures the longer Rob is in the hospital, the better, because he can't smoke there. Even five days should help break his addiction. In the interim she'll remove the cigarette packages, half-smoked butts, and matchbooks from his car.

After four days in the hospital there's still no diagnosis, though the doctors have eliminated the possibility of cancer. Rob is scared, depressed, and bored. He can't concentrate on reading. There's little to do other than stare at the four walls, and little to say to his doctors other than *What do I have?* He misses Daniel terribly, but when Alex brings him to visit, Rob is too feeble to hold him.

In some ways, Rob suspects, Alex is glad he got sick. They both know that only a life-threatening situation would make him quit smoking—for Daniel's sake.

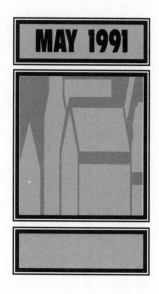

OB IS DISCHARGED FROM THE HOSPITAL KNOWING ONLY THAT whatever he has isn't fatal. The doctor tells him to take aspirin, drink liquids, and avoid sharing food or eating utensils with Daniel.

At home Alex bustles about, taking care of everyone. She makes Rob nourishing, fat-free dinners and spreads pictures of Daniel on the coffee table so he can study them without moving from the couch. When Daniel refuses to go to sleep unless Rob rocks him, she takes the baby for a long drive in the car until he passes out.

Rob asks Alex how things went at home while he was hospitalized, hoping she'll say, "I missed the smell of your aftershave" or "I missed your lusty loins." Instead she says, "There was no water dripping in the bathroom or cabinet doors open in the kitchen. Everything was in its place." The response (so typically unsentimental that Rob is more amused than hurt) makes him think of that old song about the woman who loses her man and tries to shrug it off: "One less bell to answer, one less egg to fry . . ."

Rob has no desire to smoke. He came out of the hospital with a new perspective: *We're all dying, and just because some people can put a name and time frame on it doesn't change the fact that life is limited. All you can do is forestall death as long as possible and enjoy what you have.*

**WEDNESDAY, MAY 1**
**Manhattan**

J ULIET TURNS THIRTY-SEVEN TODAY. SAM GIVES HER A MEMBERSHIP to the Film Forum, a mauve blouse, a linen jacket, and a videotape of an obscure British movie called *Scream of Fear,* which has haunted Juliet since she first saw it at the age of twelve. Every day this week he has brought her flowers—tulips, then lilacs, then roses.

They spent the weekend with Lily on the island, their first visit of the season. Sam rattled happily around the house, fiddling with the plumbing and checking for cracks in the ceiling. Lily crawled around the garden while Sam planted sixty gladiola bulbs. She rolled around on the grass with Juliet and splashed in tidepools with her parents.

The weekend evoked rich and complex associations. The weather was unusually warm, and the island was buffeted by the southern breezes that Sam and Juliet remembered from the day of the miscarriage scare in October 1989. Juliet relived the recent past, from that first bleeding episode through the agony of Lily's birth and the idyll of last summer. It felt to her like an adventure novel filled with danger and love and death and suspense and joy. She was amazed to think that these events all took place within the past eighteen months; it seemed like generations.

They left the car on the island for use during the summer and flew home. When there was turbulence, Juliet cautioned her ashen-faced husband, saying, "Get hold of yourself—you can't transmit your fears to the baby." Sam knows she's right. In the coming months they've planned two family trips involving lengthy plane rides—Wyoming in June, Hawaii in July. He must control his terror.

OB IS DIAGNOSED WITH CYTOMEGALOVIRUS (CMV), A HERPES virus. How he got it is a mystery—"probably from standing next to someone in a store," the doctor says, adding that Alex and Daniel may or may not have been exposed to it. So far, neither show any symptoms.

Rob has lost eight pounds and has not smoked. Still suffering from night sweats and exhaustion, he spends most of his time in bed. He drags himself out for an occasional sales appointment in response to subtle pressure from his office: *Take it easy, and by the way, give this client a call.*

Alex was somewhere in Minnesota when a serious offer was made on their apartment. Rob had to respond to the bid within hours. But he felt miserable, Daniel appeared to be getting sick, and the sitter was late. He decided it was enough of an emergency to do the unspeakable: he tracked Alex down through her secretary, reaching her ten minutes before an important meeting.

The call threw Alex off completely. To control her guilt about being away from Daniel, she struggles to maintain the attitude *This is my job; there's nothing I can do about it.* At the same time, she believes she's the person best equipped to deal with anything that might happen to her son; all he has to do is cry and Rob falls apart. She heard the panic in Rob's voice: "I have to take us both to the doctor, Yvonne's not here, what's her number, what should I do?"

Alex quizzed him about Daniel's symptoms; Rob was afraid he had CMV. "It sounds like he has a cold," Alex said. "Calm down. Yvonne will be there within the hour." She rushed into her meeting, shaken. As soon as she was free, she called Rob back.

"Everything is fine," he reported.

"From now on, I won't even tell you what state I'm in."

"I don't care where you're going, I don't care if you fall off the face of the fucking earth. I just don't understand why you won't give me your number."

"Because you bother me. It's for my self-preservation. You don't really need me, you just want to reach out and touch someone. But I'm not going to tell you where I'm going."

"I know where you're going," Rob teased. "Dinners with men who give you business on the chance you'll sleep with them."

"I ought to," Alex says.

**FRIDAY, MAY 24**
**Queens**

ARIA DOES NOT GET HER WISH TO BE IN THE NEW CO-OP BY her twenty-seventh birthday, which is today. They don't have a closing date or even a copy of the sales contract. They're stuck paying another month's rent, and their letter of commitment from the bank expires on June 10, when they will have to pay $250 to renew it. They gave notice to their landlord some time ago; by July 1, they have to vacate. Joe wants to get out of the co-op deal. He feels the seller's delays have been unethical and unfair.

"Look," Maria tells him, "there's nothing we can do right now; it's Memorial Day weekend. But on Tuesday, I think we should try to sue them for breach of contract."

"First we've got to *look* at the contract, and our own damn lawyer won't send it. We ought to dump the bastard, but we're too far into it with him now." Joe slams his fist into the sofa cushions.

"Babe, you can't let things get to you like this. It won't get us the place any faster." She's trying to be logical. She doesn't see the point in both of them walking around with attitude.

Joe calms down until morning, when he finds that someone tried to steal the station wagon. The lock was jimmied; the thief must have been scared away in mid-act. Joe takes it as a portent. He has to get his family the hell out of here.

He gave Maria her birthday gift: money to buy clothes. As usual, he was resigned to hating whatever she selected, which turns out to be a pair of neon-green wide-legged pants. He thought she would want to dress more conservatively once she became a mother, but if anything she has gone in the opposite direction. He watches her in these pants as she feeds Luis a bottle and thinks, *That looks weird.*

"This garbage you buy," he complains, "it'll be out of fashion in a week. I wish you'd dress like a real woman, not like a teenager."

"No, like a hick." Maria is disdainful.

"Then go ahead, look like Michael Jackson, but you better watch how you dress at the job."

The next day Maria defiantly wears the neon pants to the office. "What parade," Joe calls out to her, "are you marching in today?"

**FRIDAY, MAY 24**
**Westchester**

LEX REGARDS HER LIFE ON THE ROAD AS NOT QUITE A SECRET existence, but definitely a private one, in which she doesn't worry about anyone but herself. Traveling through Atlanta this week, she makes a conscious effort to enjoy every moment; she finds it helps keep her mind off Daniel. She takes time to swim in the hotel pool and soak in the Jacuzzi, and one night she goes out looking for a good meal instead of ordering room service. Driving her rented car, she spots a place with a packed parking lot (a good sign, she thinks, unless it means a bar scene). It turns out there isn't much of a bar, let alone a scene.

Alex orders steamed mussels, a veal chop, salad, and a glass of red wine. She pulls the latest Ludlum paperback from her purse (she prefers male soap operas to the Danielle Steel variety) and reads it throughout her meal, occasionally looking around her, thinking, *No crying baby, no sick husband, no disorder* . . . It occurs to her that life on the road is one thing that hasn't changed, which is why it feels more normal than life at home.

She and Rob haven't made love for so long she can't remember the last time. Now that Daniel routinely sleeps not just in their room but in their bed, sex is impossible. She tells Rob that having Daniel in bed with them is a bad pattern they ought to break sooner rather than later, but Rob says he likes having the baby there. (The possibility that he may be using Daniel as a sexual avoidance technique has crossed her mind more than once.) The last time Rob pleaded with her to have another child, Alex laughed bitterly. "It looks like it'll have to be an immaculate conception," she said.

**MONDAY, MAY 27**
**Southern Maryland**

HINGS HAVE DEFINITELY CHANGED FOR THE WORSE BETWEEN Erin and her boss. The understanding and support that characterized their relationship have evaporated, making Erin feel paranoid and self-critical. And the general atmosphere at the office is so *rinky-dink* since the firms merged that she is constantly aggravated.

At a staff meeting, the office manager lectures everyone for talking too much and standing around in the hall—*third-grade stuff*—and Erin resents it. She surprises herself by storming into the manager's office afterward.

"You attacked all of us for something that applies to very few people," she says. "It was unfair, and it's not good management."

"I have a large staff; I don't have time to single out perpetrators."

"But that's your job. You can't sit there and chew everyone out and make us all feel like shit."

"Oh, Erin, you know I didn't mean you. I wish I had a hundred more like you."

"Well, thanks, but you ought to change your tactics."

Erin gets such satisfaction from initiating this confrontation that she decides to have it out with Tom, too. "You're not around enough," she tells him later that night, "and it's not fair. Everyone thinks that because you work so hard at your job, you should be excused from everything else. I work hard too, but I don't get excused. In the last two months I've gotten eleven different birthday gifts and cards for your family and my family. Where is it written that I have to make time for this and you don't?"

"Okay. I've got to plan better, especially on weekends. Every spare moment I'm doing something, and that's my fault. I'm working so much I can't enjoy what I have."

"The most important thing you have is Katie, and you're not spending enough time with her."

"I know that. You and Katie are the ones who are suffering. And I feel stuck—burned out, ever since she was born. I'm always being pulled in one direction or another. It's like I don't exist."

"I feel the same—like I don't have a *life* anymore. But you can't let your job control everything."

"When it's between taking weekends off or going out of business, I don't feel I really have a choice. But I worry about it all the time. I don't want to get to a point where Katie doesn't know me."

Erin suddenly feels sorry for him. "You won't let that happen," she says.

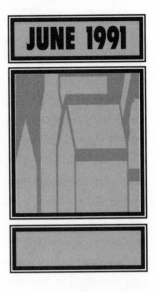

**SATURDAY, JUNE 1**
**Grand Teton National**
**Park, north of Jackson**
**Hole, Wyoming**

HE SLIDING GLASS DOORS OF SAM AND JULIET'S GROUND-FLOOR cabin at Teton Lodge open onto a patio surrounded by meadows where deer and moose roam freely. Beyond the meadows is a spectacular view of a lake framed by the Grand Teton mountain range, a craggy, towering granite formation resembling the Swiss Alps. Watching Juliet and Lily cavort outside in the fresh mountain air, making faces at each other, Sam is struck by the effect the baby has on her mother: she brings out the clown in Juliet, enabling her to let loose with a kind of abandon Sam has never before observed.

Juliet looks at her daughter, thinking that in just ten days she will be a year old. Soon she will be walking, talking, changing from baby to toddler. *Should I risk having another?* Juliet wonders. Before leaving for Wyoming, she asked Sam if he wants a second child. Yes, he said—he believes that Lily's traumatic delivery was a fluke, unlikely to happen again—but he made it clear that the decision is Juliet's.

She is six months late for her six-month postpartum checkup. She has procrastinated about making an appointment with Bernstein because she fears it will be the beginning of an emotionally arduous process—reviewing her medical chart, getting second and third opinions, reliving what she went through a year ago in an attempt to assess the risk of going through it all again. But with Lily about to celebrate her birthday, Juliet feels increasing internal pressure to make a decision. If she is going to give Lily a sibling, she wants them close enough in age to be playmates. She can't stall forever. Now, as she begins a game of pattycake with Lily, Juliet decides to call Bernstein's office as soon as she returns home.

Later, after breastfeeding, the baby dozes off. Juliet lays her down gently and hurries across the room to Sam, who is lying on the other bed absorbed in the newspaper. "She's asleep," Juliet whispers. "Let's do it." As if programmed in discretion, Lily wakes up ten minutes after her parents finish making love. Sam thinks, *Once you have a child, if you delay your chance to have sex even for five minutes, the window of opportunity can shut for a week or more.* He feels fortunate that he and Juliet run on the same sexual clock. If they both weren't eager for that window to open, tension might result—one person would want sex and the other would feel pressured.

In the afternoon, while Sam putters inside the cabin, Juliet sits in a chair on the patio, filming Lily with a video camera. The baby crawls toward the picnic table a few feet away from Juliet's chair, grabs the edge of the table, and pulls herself up. Suddenly she lets go of the table and starts to walk toward her mother. *Lily's first steps!* "Sam," Juliet yells, "come here!"

The next day they return to New York. Their journey is plagued by thunderstorms, not Sam's favorite kind of weather for flying. During takeoff from Denver, where they change planes, he sees lightning strike the runway. He takes Lily on his lap and holds on to her as a fearful child might clutch a stuffed animal. Soon he finds that the baby's soft weight comforts him more than any amount of Valium or beta blockers ever did. He thinks back to nearly two years ago, when he boarded the Los Angeles-to-New York flight the day after he learned that Juliet was pregnant; he remembers how he considered her pregnancy a talisman, psychic armor against terror. And now he has Lily.

Sam still sees death staring at him through the window. But the image, for the first time, is blurred.

**SUNDAY, JUNE 9**
**Valley Stream,**
**Long Island**

HE SITE OF LUIS'S BIRTHDAY BASH IS DISTINGUISHED FROM OTHER Sunday gatherings in this vast wooded park by a cluster of balloons, a long table draped in a "Happy Birthday" paper cloth, and a banner strung between the trees. The guests, some forty adults and half as many children, represent Joe and Maria's extended family of relatives and friends.

Luis stands in a portable playpen, watching the action. Maria, in black biker shorts and a trapeze top, leads the older kids through pin-the-tail-on-the-donkey and *sopa de zapato* ("shoe stew"—everyone throws their shoes in a pile, and the first person to find his own and put them on wins). Frisbees sail through the air; water balloons and squirt guns provide relief from the ninety-degree heat.

Joe is shirtless, grilling chicken legs, hamburgers, and hot dogs on the barbecue. He is upset that his daughter, Cheryl, has a piano recital today and can't be here—but Tony is. Joe rarely takes his eyes off his brother. When Tony comes over to fill his paper plate, Joe embraces him, then slaps him an exuberant high-five. Tony wears a sweatshirt with the sleeves cut off to reveal thick, muscular arms. He spends much of the afternoon holding court at a picnic table; the men cluster around him, listening to tales of combat.

Later there is a raucous game of tug-of-war, accompanied by Latin music blaring from a boom box. When the adults are pleasantly buzzed on quantities of Budweiser (poured discreetly into opaque plastic tumblers, since alcohol consumption is against park rules), Joe gets a conga line together and snakes it through the middle of the picnic area. Today is the annual Puerto Rican Day parade in Manhattan, but he thinks the best parade of all is happening right here in Valley Stream State Park.

Perversely, the lively strains of the lambada sour Maria's frisky mood. She is reminded of Joe's refusal to let her make the rounds of the Latin dance clubs last week with her sister, who came in from Oklahoma for Luis's party. "It's not that I don't trust you," he said. "I don't trust *them*"—the men she might encounter. *I don't care for the morons out there,* Joe thought. *They're Casanovas. I'm jealous, but what Hispanic isn't?* Maria has a passion for Latin dancing—Joe knew this from the beginning. Their relationship began in the clubs, though Joe was never much for dancing; he went there to drink and hang out, and later to be with Maria.

*Why is it,* Maria thinks, *that he can go out with the guys to a bar and drink, but I can't go out with the girls and dance?* Even when she told him that her brother would go along as a chaperone, even when she promised to dance only with her women friends, he was unyielding.

After the Desert Storm parade tomorrow afternoon, Joe and Tony are taking Luis to Lake George. Maria will have two evenings to herself. Tuesday is Latin Night at the Copacabana; she's tempted to go. Joe will find out, of course, but she feels like saying, *The hell with you*—though she's nervous about openly defying him and causing a screaming match or worse in front of the baby.

Joe breaks into her reverie: he has invited some guys back to the apartment after the picnic to watch a basketball game. *Gee,* Maria thinks, *thanks for asking.* Oblivious to her tight expression, he adds, "Babe, let's do the birthday cake."

Joe calls everyone to the table and steadies the video camera on a tripod. Maria holds Luis next to the chocolate and vanilla custard sheet cake with "Happy Birthday, Luis" piped across the top (the bakery misspelled it *Louis,* but Joe carefully corrected the mistake). After the guests finish singing the birthday song, Maria blows the single candle out. Joe offers a special toast to Tony for being here and to God for allowing it. Then he smears Luis's nose and mouth with icing, mugging for the camera.

It takes more than an hour to open all the gifts. When they're done,

Joe says to loud applause, "There are too many clothes here. We've gotta make another baby."

"Yeah, right," says Maria. Her tone is sarcastic, but she is grinning.

OM AND ERIN LEAVE KATIE WITH TOM'S SISTER AND DRIVE TO Middleburg for the wedding of one of Erin's high-school girlfriends. Tom finds instant common ground with the men, who all own boats; Erin commiserates with the wives about the expense of maintaining their husbands' water toys. "Look how much you women spend on clothes," one husband says. The other men nod vehemently, while the women insist that the analogy doesn't hold. Erin and Tom are comforted and amused by the familiarity of this gender-based argument, which goes on almost verbatim in their house at the start of each boating season.

After the reception, they check into an appealing bed-and-breakfast, a refurbished house built in 1832, filled with antiques. They proceed to have what Erin thinks is the best time ever, including their honeymoon. They make twenty-four hours of freedom from responsibility seem like a year. Taking full advantage of their sumptuous four-poster bed, they nap and lounge and make enthusiastic love whenever they please, which is often. They have a candlelit dinner at another historic inn, where they agree they must make this kind of time for themselves on a more regular basis. "We need it," Tom says. "It's amazing what a little weekend can do, it's just *amazing.*"

As for Erin, the weekend amounts to a confirmation of why they chose to be Mr. and Mrs. Tom Wright.

TILL WITHOUT A CLOSING DATE ON THE CO-OP, JOE AND MARIA extend their lease on the apartment until July 31. Then their lawyer calls. The co-op owner, he says, has offered to let them move into the place on Saturday, even though they haven't closed and the apartment is still unfinished. Two days later, Joe learns that a "neutral exchange" has opened up in the postal system; someone in the Orlando station wants to switch places with someone in New York. He notifies his supervisor that he wants the slot. "You've got the seniority," she says. "There shouldn't be a problem." Joe calls Maria to tell her, stunning her into silence.

"Talk to me," Joe says.

"I'm at a loss. I feel numb . . ."

"If I get it, I may have to leave in two weeks."

"What if we're stuck with the co-op? I'll have to move in and try to sell it. You'll go ahead without me and Luis, get a place for us."

"I don't want to leave you two."

"Don't think about that now; let's worry about getting out of the co-op."

Their best hope is that the place won't be ready when the second letter of commitment expires on July 10. But the lawyer calls again to say the work will be completed by morning. If they try to get out of the deal at this point, he warns, they'll lose the $7,700 down payment and possibly incur a lawsuit. Minutes after that sobering conversation, Maria's sister calls to tell them that a four-bedroom apartment in a two-family house on her street, with a two-car garage and back yard, is available for rent for less than $850 a month. *Why does all of this have to come up now?* Maria frets.

She wants to live in Florida and has already plotted the move in her mind. Her fantasy goes like this: somehow they get out of the co-op with the $7,700 intact. They put their things in storage until Joe finds a place down there. Maria and Luis move in with her brother; without having to pay rent, she can use her salary to get rid of their debts. She and Joe will be apart no more than two or three months. In Florida she won't go back to work right away—she won't need to. The cost of living is cheaper down there. She'll take care of Luis, have another baby; maybe Cheryl will join them. Eventually Maria will get a part-time job for the airlines or in a travel agency so the family can fly north at a discount or for free to visit Joe's mother, unless she moves to Florida with them; Joe would love that . . . And then Maria is jolted back to reality, where everything is uncertain and she and Joe are being tortured by possibilities not quite within reach.

"Florida is something we both want," she tells Joe. "You pursue that, and I'll deal with the co-op." Maria thinks she can sell it to a neighbor who expressed interest. "I'll try to unload it for $82, $83,000," she says. "Make $6,000 or something on it. I'll take them to see it when it's finished."

"If we can't sell it, maybe we could rent it. If we could get $1,200 to cover the payments . . ."

"Well, let's pack some more boxes. I was teasing Luis this morning: 'You were born in New York and raised in Florida . . .'"

"I might not get the transfer, you know."

"If you don't, we'll have the co-op, or that place my sister told me about. The point is, we'll be out of here."

"It's crazy," Joe says. "One minute we can't get anything, and the next minute everyone's knocking at our door saying, 'Hey, you want this, you want that?'"

"So what?" says Maria. "At least we're going *somewhere.*"

**THURSDAY, JULY 11**
**Westchester**

HE NIGHT BEFORE LEAVING FOR A WEEK'S VACATION *EN FAMILLE,* Alex smelled cigarette smoke on Rob. She confronted him; he denied it. Not believing him, she went to the garage to search his car and found two packs of Vantages in the glove compartment. She raced upstairs and strode across the living room to Rob, who was sitting at the dining table. Without a word she reached out and yanked his hair, the most severe punishment she could think of for a man terrified of going bald. "If you want to do this to your lungs," she yelled, shoving the cigarette packs into his face, "then your hair is fair game!"

Rob sheepishly accepted what he thought of as a disciplinary action. He swore he would never smoke again. Alex didn't believe him, and he couldn't blame her. Even he knows he's lying.

The next day they left for Kiawah Island, a resort near Charleston, South Carolina. On the way, Rob got a speeding ticket and Alex got her period. To her it meant they wouldn't have to use birth control when—*if*—they had sex.

"Don't you get the feeling Daniel's watching us?" Rob said to Alex after lovemaking on the second day of vacation.

"You really do come from a bumper crop of Jewish nuts, don't you?" Alex snorted. Rob laughed so hard he nearly cried. That became their line of the week, *a bumper crop of Jewish nuts.*

They rode bikes several times a day along verdant trails, played with Daniel in the wading pool, and never bothered with babysitters. At night they barbecued on the terrace of their one-bedroom condominium, three floors above the sandy beach and the Atlantic beyond. By the end of the trip they were relaxed, tanned, in high spirits—even in love. For once Alex was charmed to hear Rob gush over Daniel's resemblance to Mike Love of the Beach Boys.

They returned to Westchester on Sunday and made love that night. Rob seemed distracted and in a hurry. Alex could sense his awareness of Daniel, asleep in his crib across the room—could hear him thinking, *Is the baby about to wake up?* Alex likes kissing, foreplay, exploration. This felt like *cut to the chase, do not linger.*

On Monday she left for a three-day trip with misgivings about being away for most of Daniel's first birthday on the tenth. While on the road, she reflected on this time last year—buying Levolor blinds the day she went into labor; crouching at the door to the emergency room, unable to stand because of her contractions; staring at the grout between two tiles on the floor of the room when she was given an enema; refusing to open her eyes in the recovery room because she wanted to float in a world without pain. She understood for the first time why her mother gets upset when her children fail to visit her on their birthdays. *It's really* her *day,* Alex thought, *not ours.*

Rob was home alone Tuesday night watching the All-Star game with Daniel on his lap. He mused about the beauty of baseball, which reminds him of a Van Gogh painting—lovely from a distance, the mastery of it visible only up close, where you can see every brushstroke, every play. Watching baseball always takes Rob back to his childhood. He can feel the dirt under his feet, the slide into base, the impact of a fly ball caught in his glove. He wants Daniel to share the game with him as his own father never did. Rob stared at the golden surfer boy snuggled against him and marveled at his inexplicable luck in this one part of his life. A line from *The Great Gatsby* came to mind: "If personality is an unbroken series of successful gestures, then there was something gorgeous about him." Rob thought, *My life is just a series of years, months, hours, much of it pivoted around things that didn't turn my way—until Daniel.*

Alex got home the next night, her son's birthday. Rob and Daniel picked her up at the airport at eight. They went directly home and proceeded with a raucous celebration that had been Alex's idea: they put Daniel on top of the dining table and allowed him to destroy a chocolate-and-vanilla ice cream cake. The baby seemed shocked at first by the coldness but soon was happily smearing himself and his parents, who were busy smearing each other, with gobs of ice cream, while a video camera set up on a tripod recorded their antics.

This morning Alex notices the speeding ticket Rob got on vacation, still taped to the refrigerator door with a note from her saying, "Please pay this and mail by the tenth." She is annoyed that he couldn't accomplish this simple task. When she sees that her keys, and the hundred-dollar silver ring from Tiffany's to which they were attached, are missing from their usual place on top of the stereo speaker, she is apoplectic. She doesn't travel with them because she is afraid of losing them.

"Are you sure you didn't take them with you?" Rob says, prompting Alex to call her mother, who was in the house on Monday. Her mother says she saw the keys on top of the speaker Monday night. Yvonne, the babysitter, said she didn't use them at all during Alex's absence.

Alex wastes a workday looking for the keys, retracing her steps on the road, calling car rental companies and hotels and clients. (It particularly galls her to call her customers; the last thing she wants is to appear airheaded and disorganized.) Her search is futile. Alex decides that Rob must have grabbed the keys Tuesday morning by mistake and suggested that she took them to shift blame from himself.

By the time Rob comes home, eager to play with Daniel, Alex is in a rage. *She* has had no time for Daniel after a day spent hunting for the keys, taking Yvonne to the train station, making dinner, and doing two loads of laundry.

"I couldn't write a single report," she says to Rob.

"Big fucking deal. Are you going to lose your job over it?"

She is in no mood for sarcasm. "You fail to realize I *have* my job because I write reports. There's a direct correlation between my paperwork and my sales."

"You got a million-dollar order on this trip. Why would anyone care if you get your report out tomorrow instead of today?" Rob doesn't understand why a little thing like missing keys can so upset her. "Something else must be bothering you. What is it?"

"There's nothing else. That was a Tiffany key ring. I want it back."

"So buy another one. It's only a hundred bucks."

"In other words, throw money after the problem—your typical solution."

Rob stares at her in frustration. Alex decides to drop it; nothing will be resolved by arguing. (Her willingness to fight is related to the amount she travels. Lately she's been traveling a lot, so they argue less. *What's the point?* she thinks. *I'll be gone in a few days.*) She takes Daniel into the bedroom and lies down with him, grateful to escape from Rob. As Daniel sucks on his bottle, she thinks about her husband. *I chose him because he was incredibly funny, incredibly smart, and a wonderful lover, and at twenty-two you don't think it can get better than that,* she muses. *But in marriage, what matters over time is how well your day-to-day styles mesh.* From that perspective, she's not sure if she and Rob are so well matched.

*Only when you're older,* Alex concludes, *do you realize that the physicist who is so brilliant he can figure out how many holes are in the universe has no fucking idea where his laundry is.*

**SATURDAY, JULY 13**
**Southern Maryland**

OM HAS REGAINED HIS SEXUAL CONFIDENCE: THAT USELESS, scary feeling of wanting to have sex in the worst way and not being able to has left him. He used to be so concerned about whether he could sustain an erection that the slightest distraction would ensure failure, but now Katie can cry or the dog can bark and it doesn't affect him. His complaint now, which pre-dates parenthood, is that he wants sex more often than Erin does. She'll beg off, claiming exhaustion (her weight gain is part of it—she looks in the mirror and thinks, *How can he possibly find me desirable?),* and sometimes he'll respond with a sarcastic "Why don't you just call me when you're ready?" But this problem, at least, is more hers than his. He can handle it. Now that his impotence is a thing of the past, he doesn't think having a child has affected their sex life either way.

But Katie has had a definite impact on Tom's approach to work. In the past, if he planned to leave at 6 P.M. and a customer came in at 5:45 with a problem, he would stay and fix it. Now his attitude is *If I can't get it done when they want it and they don't understand, tough.*

His eagerness to please, he now comprehends, was never worth the sacrifice of his time and energy. *Thanks to Katie,* he feels, *I'm less desperate about accommodating everyone.*

**SUNDAY, JULY 21**
**Westchester**

HE ELUSIVE TIFFANY KEY RING SURFACED LAST WEEK—IN ROB'S bathrobe pocket. He allowed Alex countless *I told you so's* and was vastly amused when, two days later, it disappeared again. Alex couldn't blame him this time because he was away overnight on business. She thinks Daniel threw it in the trash.

The apartment has been sold. The deal will close around September 1; they'll move in with Alex's mother until they find a house. Uncertainty about the future rattles Alex in general, and not knowing where they'll end up living, or how long they'll be at her mother's, makes her especially tense. She's concerned about how Rob and her mother will get along in close quarters. If Rob thinks Alex is a stickler for neatness, he has no idea what he's in for with her mother, who makes Alex seem like a slob by comparison.

Tonight Alex and Rob get down on the living room floor to play with Daniel. Rob coaxes peals of laughter from the baby and looks up at Alex in rapture. "I think he really *likes* us!" he says.

"Who the fuck cares if he likes us? One day he'll get down on his knees and thank God we're his parents, but along the way he's supposed to hate us and wish we were dead so he'll be able to strike out on his own. You're too focused on his approval. That's not the message you should transmit."

*Touché,* Rob thinks. Alex commands both respect and affection from others; he is always ready to forgo the former because he's afraid it will obliterate his chance at the latter. *If I were more secure,* he muses, *I wouldn't look to Daniel to validate my existence.*

"It would be nice for Daniel to have a sibling," he says, thinking that another child might blunt his own tendency to center everything on his son.

"Yes," Alex says, "it would be nice. But you don't realize how impossible the logistics would be."

Later Alex convinces Rob to take the daring step of moving Daniel's crib to the study so they can make love in the bedroom without Rob's being distracted. As he wheels the crib, with Daniel sleeping inside it, across the living room, she checks the expiration date on the condom packet. *No way,* she thinks, *will I allow another accident.*

**THURSDAY, AUGUST 8**
**Southern Maryland**

RIN WALKS INTO THE HOUSE AT 7 P.M., DISGRUNTLED. "TGIF, I'LL tell you," she says to Tom, who guides spoonfuls of vegetable-beef soup into Katie's mouth.

"For you, anyway." Tom sighs. Tomorrow is Erin's day off.

"Almost for you," Erin says. "I feel like we haven't seen each other in weeks. I have to work on Sunday—ugh." Wearily she scans the mail. "I started my diet yesterday, and today I'm a beast. Cranky and starving."

At ten, with Katie in bed, the Wrights sit down to dinner.

"Every day at work," Erin tells Tom, "something comes back that I've screwed up. I'm just not *there* anymore. Yesterday I sent a prospectus out to eleven different clients, and today I found I'd forgotten the cover letter explaining why they would want to buy the damn bonds in the first place. My work used to be beyond reproach. Now it's like I had a stroke that erased my brain."

"Hey, you didn't get dumb all of a sudden, and you didn't get dizzy all of a sudden." Tom is amused at the idea of Erin without a brain. "You're second-guessing yourself. The more conscious you are of making mistakes, the more you make them—sorta like sex. Once you think you're not going to be able to perform, then for sure you can't."

Erin considers the analogy. "That's true, I guess, but I don't know what to do about it. I could lose my job. A lot of people who have to do my work on Fridays are pissed off that I'm not there."

"You have to commit. Once you consider leaving a job, it's always on your mind, and it'll keep you from giving everything you've got."

"I don't have any more to give. There's only so much of me. I still question myself every morning when I see Katie crawl happily to Lorraine and not give two hoots whether I'm there. And when I get home and look at all there is to do . . ."

"Think how much worse it was this time last year," Tom reminds her. "I had the porch to finish, you were pregnant, business was awful, there were all these unknowns. Now it's just your work."

"And all the stupid stuff I've been doing there."

"When I have a customer counting on me to do something, I get to a point where if it's gross negligence on my part I beat myself up, but if it's a judgment call, I'm not going to worry about it."

"On judgment calls, yeah. I've gotten reamed out by clients more times than I can remember because I didn't do something the way they wanted it done. I apologize and hang up the phone saying, *Up yours*. But these things going on with me now are completely within my control."

"I don't think the solution is for you to stay home all day with Katie, even if we could afford it. I think it would drive you absolutely nuts."

"If I had two kids, I'd have to stay home."

"Well, I'd say that's ninety-nine percent a given. But I'd like to feel a little more confident about the station before that happens."

Erin kicks off her shoes and rests her feet on the empty chair next to her. She exhales deeply. "I'm going to sit down this weekend and really psych myself into getting through the next month at work. It helps if I think of it that way, in month-long blocks—get through one and go on to the next."

"Tomorrow you might find out you're twenty million dollars richer, you know," Tom teases her. "Don't forget we have ten bucks riding on the lottery."

"And guess what? I'd quit my job, first thing."

"Before the Mercedes and the diamonds, or after?"

"Very funny." Erin smiles. "Before. And I suppose you'd just keep plugging away at the pumps, right?"

"Uh . . . right," Tom says, abashed.

**FRIDAY, AUGUST 9**
**Queens**

OE DIDN'T GET THE TRANSFER TO FLORIDA, AND THE CO-OP SALE closed yesterday. He dragged the proceedings out as long as possible, reading every piece of paper three times, staring out the window, cursing under his breath. *They dicked around with us for so long,* he fumed, *and now we're stuck with the place.*

Today they move in. Joe feels better when he sees Luis merrily exploring his sunlit room—*his own room,* no more crib and changing paraphernalia cluttering up the marital bedroom—and hears Maria exclaiming over the pristine kitchen appliances. Several of their new neighbors stop by to introduce themselves and bring homemade cookies. This old-fashioned friendliness, Joe and Maria agree, was never in style in their old neighborhood.

It is close to dinnertime; men are lighting barbecue grills and kids are scampering on the grass. Joe remembers seeing a Little League field a few blocks away. He thinks, *I can't wait until Luis is old enough to play on it.* From their front steps, he and Maria observe the peaceful environment: the modestly scaled series of two-story, two-family brick buildings with neat white trim, facing each other across wide green lawns with well-tended plantings, divided by a quiet street dominated by bicycles, not cars.

"It's still not a house," Maria says to Joe apologetically, wondering why he's so quiet. "Is that what you're thinking?"

"No," Joe says. He points to Luis, engaged in dismantling a daisy beside them. "I'm thinking, this is ours now."

He puts his arm around her shoulder and pulls her close. "It's going to be okay," he says.

**THURSDAY, AUGUST 15**
**Westchester**

LEX USUALLY MENSTRUATES WITH PRECISION ON THE TWENTY-eighth day of her cycle. When she went in for her yearly Pap smear, her period was one day late.

"Am I pregnant?" she asked Carl anxiously as she lay on the examining table, feet in stirrups.

"I'm good," Carl said with a laugh, "but not that good."

"Rob and I had unprotected sex once this month, on Day Two of my period, and I was bleeding actively . . . it seems impossible."

"That's how I got my second child. My wife had her period, we had sex without contraception, and then she went on a lengthy business trip. There was no way I was even in the same state with her when she was ovulating, but sperm can theoretically live inside you for seven days."

For a moment Alex was speechless. "That's not exactly what I want to hear," she said. "I'm going to pretend I didn't. Let's talk about birth control. I want an IUD." Driving home, she thought, *This can't be.*

On the thirty-fifth day of her cycle, she took a home pregnancy test. It was positive. Rob said, "Let's call him Kiawah," after the vacation spot where Alex conceived.

"Baby Jesus seems more appropriate. Getting pregnant during your period . . ."

Now that she's over the shock, she isn't conscious of any emotion, one way or the other. *Okay*, she thinks, *I'm pregnant, I'll throw up for another eight months, have the kid, go back to work . . . Those are the facts; nothing else matters.* Her concerns are practical ones, such as how to find a house large enough to accommodate live-in help and how to tell her boss, who just promoted her to product manager, that she'll have to take another maternity leave.

"You'll be getting a vasectomy before I leave the hospital with this baby," she tells Rob.

"No way."

"You are such a fucking pussy."

"Will another baby short-change Daniel?" Rob worries.

"If anyone gets short-changed, it will be the second child, not the first."

As Alex focuses on logistics, Rob grapples with conflicting feelings. His instantaneous reaction—*Omigod, this isn't what I wanted at this moment*—was followed by joy, then fear. He hopes for a girl, so he won't have to compare two boys in a competition destined to be loaded against the younger one. *How could anyone measure up to Daniel?* he thinks, angry at himself for already playing favorites.

Unlike the way he felt during the first pregnancy, Rob has little medical anxiety. Today, as Alex is about to leave for her first prenatal appointment with Carl, his only comment is "We're not going through labor again. We'll have a scheduled cesarean. Whatever the doctor thinks is irrelevant." Alex agrees and relays this to Carl. He suggests they wait to make such a decision until the thirtieth week, when he'll have a sense of the baby's size.

"Okay," Alex says, "but I'm humoring you. I've decided on a section no matter what. Also, my husband refuses to have a vasectomy, so I want my tubes tied as soon as I give birth."

"That's an extreme attitude." Carl is amused, but adds that he strongly recommends against an immediate ligation. "The most critical time of an infant's life is within the first four to six weeks," he explains. "You ought to be sure everything's okay before you eliminate the possibility of conceiving again."

Alex is off by only two days on her calculated due date. Carl confirms it will be April 7, 1992.

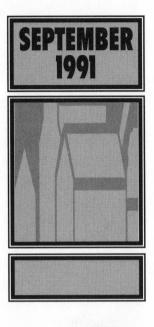

**SEPTEMBER 1991**

**WEDNESDAY,
SEPTEMBER 18
Southern Maryland**

 RIN TOOK TOM'S ADVICE AND MADE A MENTAL COMMITMENT TO stay at her job at least until February. Now she can concentrate; she has found her mind. She and Tom have adjusted schedules so she can be available as the workload demands— at night, on Fridays, sometimes on weekends—and no longer feels the tacit resentment from colleagues that she had found so debilitating.

Post–Labor Day business at the station has been unusually strong; Tom tells Erin he has turned the corner. Slowly, he's paying off debts and building up reserves.

If things continue to go this well for both of them, Erin wants to devote the Caribbean cruise they plan to take early next year, in celebration of her thirtieth birthday and their tenth wedding anniversary, to making another baby.

HE HOUSE, A 2,800-SQUARE-FOOT, FIVE-BEDROOM COLONIAL ON the grounds of a golf course, came on the market at $439,000 just after Labor Day. Rob and Alex have shopped around enough to know this one is a steal. The kitchen hasn't been renovated in thirty years, but the large, level yard, the solid prewar construction, the imposing Mediterranean facade, the stunning original woodwork, the spacious master bedroom, the maid's room and bath off the kitchen, which will allow Alex to hire a live-in house-keeper—the place is, Alex thinks, *a bride's wet dream.* They offered the asking price and found themselves in a bidding war with another buyer. Each party was requested to submit a sealed bid. Rob guessed the competition would offer $450,000, so he and Alex topped it by $500. They won. The paperwork toward a January closing began.

It will be none too soon. Alex is weary of stumbling out of her mother's bathroom, weak from nausea, only to hear her mother say that having a second child is crazy, since Alex doesn't spend enough time with the first.

Once again, Rob is certain he will lose his job, though he is still his firm's top salesman. He remembers going through this when Alex was pregnant the first time. *There's something about expecting a child,* he thinks, *that provokes my worst insecurities. God cannot possibly allow me this much good luck: a beautiful son, a child on the way, a perfect house.* Alex goes over the numbers with him, trying to demonstrate that they can afford the place and deserve to live in it. "We're homebodies," she tells him. "We should have a home worth being in."

The purchase and the subsequent anxiety spur Rob to make his move with IBM. He met an IBM executive at a sales conference in Atlantic City a few months ago; the man seemed impressed with his credentials. "Call me if you want to explore the possibilities," he said, handing Rob his business card. Rob finally called him last week to set up a meeting. He prepared for it by enlisting Alex as his coach.

"What are your goals?" Alex asked, playing the role of the inter-
viewer.

"To work for your company."

"No, no, no," said Alex as Alex. "To find out if you *want* to work
for the company. Don't sell yourself short. Let the guy know you have
a lot to offer *him*. Make it clear that you are interviewing him as much
as he is interviewing you."

But this afternoon's meeting with the executive leads nowhere. The
man tells Rob that IBM isn't hiring but downsizing, encouraging early
retirement. Rob says quickly that he's not looking for a job, only for
direction. The executive gives him some names to contact and ushers
him out.

Rob went into this meeting already feeling dejected. Today is the
one-year anniversary, on the Hebrew calendar, of his father's death.
He spent the morning in the cemetery with his mother and brother,
and as he stared down at the grave, his old fear of repeating his father's
life—having everything and then losing everything, his business and
his self-respect—reasserted itself.

Yet if not for his father, Rob thinks, there would be no Daniel, who
was conceived accidentally as Rob's father lay dying. Instead of being
out on a sales call or at a baseball game, Rob had to stay within reach
of his family. *It was the fact of his dying,* Rob thinks in wonder, *that
placed Alex and me in bed together having sex at that particular time.* For
that, he blesses his father.

**FRIDAY, OCTOBER 4**
**Southern Maryland**

AST SATURDAY, TOM WAS BUSY INSTALLING THE CEILING ON THE new porch after spending both days of the previous weekend engaged in a bluefishing tournament.

"Let's just rest tomorrow," Erin said. "Be together as a family for a change." Tom agreed. But in the evening his neighbor and fishing partner, Larry, called to invite him on a flounder-fishing expedition beginning at 5 A.M. sharp the next day. The offer was irresistible. Flounder is elusive in the Chesapeake Bay. Catching it is more of a challenge, and more pure sport, than catching the ubiquitous bluefish.

As Tom and Erin prepared for bed, he mentioned Larry's proposal. "It will only take up half the day," he said.

"You mean you're going?" Erin asked, wondering how he could even consider it after spending all last weekend away.

"Oh, I don't know," Tom said, though his mind was made up. Erin would be upset, he knew, but he reasoned that by the end of the month, fishing season will be over. *She's gotta realize,* he thought, surreptitiously setting the alarm for 4:30, *it's not that I don't want to be with her, but I can be with her all year. I just need a little bit of time to myself.*

The next morning Tom shut the alarm off within seconds, hoping not to wake Erin. But she heard the shower running. When he emerged from the bathroom, she was livid.

"It's not fair," she said. "I don't hear you saying, 'Why don't we all do something together?' All I hear is 'I'm going fishing.' I've talked to other fathers, people I work with, and they say, 'Once you have kids, there's a lot you have to give up.' I've given up a lot, but I don't see how what you do with your free time has changed one iota. You're a part-time dad. I think it stinks."

"This is the last weekend I'm going to fish this year."

"You say that now, but there will be plenty of other opportunities, this month and you won't pass them by."

"I'll be around all wintertime."

"That's just because you can't fish, it's not because you want to. And thanks for giving me the weekends when it's three degrees out-side."

"Okay. I won't go."

"You're missing the point," Erin said, teeth clenched. "You made your choice, so go, get out of my house."

He went, but he felt so guilty that the outing wasn't worth it. He was pissed off, and pissed off about being pissed off, and he couldn't shake it. The weather didn't help; the water was so rough they had to turn back an hour ahead of schedule without catching a single fish.

Erin spent the morning stewing over Tom's selfishness. People are always telling her how lucky she is to have a husband who routinely alters his schedule to suit hers, who willingly takes care of the baby two nights a week. But Erin thinks parenthood *should* be a fifty-fifty part-nership. Her own father worked two jobs for years and still managed to spend more time with his family than Tom does. So how is she *lucky?*

Tom got home at 2 P.M. The grim expression on Erin's face told him she was still angry, but he saw no point in pursuing the subject. The week went by with few words spoken between them.

Today Erin takes Katie, with her parents, to the mountains. They'll stay over at a lodge and return home tomorrow for Tom's day off. When Erin calls to say they arrived safely, Tom announces his plan to drive up in the morning.

"Don't bother," Erin says. "It's a two-and-a-half-hour trip. It's not worth it."

"No," he insists. "I want to spend the day with you."

"You will. We'll be home tomorrow afternoon." They leave it at that.

Katie and Erin are at breakfast the next morning when Tom strides into the lodge. Erin guesses he's trying to make up for last weekend. He denies this, but she appreciates his effort, getting up before six instead of taking advantage of the rare opportunity to sleep in. By the end of a blissful day in the crisp mountain air, capped by Tom's welcome proposal that they stay an extra night, Erin's anger has evaporated.

**TUESDAY, OCTOBER 8**
**Westchester**

LAST THURSDAY, IN HER MOTHER'S YARD WITH DANIEL, ALEX tripped on a brick. She twisted her body to avoid falling on Baby Jesus and landed on her side, badly wrenching her shoulder. She tried to ignore the pain, allowing herself a Tylenol only when she felt close to screaming, but by Sunday she succumbed to Rob's pleas to get medical help. The doctor in the emergency room put her arm in a sling. The next day, still in agony, she flew to Toronto.

At her first appointment, with a female client, the woman took in the sling and Alex's pained face. "You look terrible," she said. "I'll take you home and make you some lunch." Alex was touched by the offer. The woman drove Alex to her house and told her to lie down on the couch, then served her cider and a sandwich and asked if she wanted a painkiller. Alex declined, explaining that she is pregnant. After that, they talked as if they'd been friends for years.

Alex didn't mention business, which seemed inappropriate considering the setting. Instead they dissected the Clarence Thomas–Anita Hill case, which had dominated the news all week. Alex explained her view of sexual harassment: It's a fact of life for any woman who isn't ugly, particularly when you're between twenty-two and twenty-eight and ambitious but still junior—a fresh piece of meat to middle managers in their thirties and forties. That Hill stayed in touch with Thomas over the years, despite his alleged conduct, seemed to Alex the politically expedient and therefore correct approach. Her new friend agreed.

Alex went on to recount how her former boss had pressured her, intent as much on flexing his power as on sleeping with her. She had to fend him off after every meeting and every business dinner. The man was clearly a *pig,* but Alex never viewed herself as a victim. Her three older brothers had prepared her for the ways of a man's world by warning that everyone has an agenda. "Anyone who sends you flowers just wants to get laid," they would say, words that echo to this day.

Back home, Alex feels awful. Her shoulder still hurts, and she is constantly nauseated. This morning, Daniel, who is in an aggressive stage, bites her hard on her leg, bruising it. She slaps him across the face and won't let her mother comfort him when he starts to cry. She hurls every bit of bad psychology she can think of: "Bad boys bite, Mommy doesn't love bad boys." She regrets her harshness later—he's only fifteen months old, after all—but she feels so sick, so tired, so overwhelmed by the idea of being sick and tired for several more months, that somehow she lost control. That feeling, foreign to her, is most upsetting of all.

Later she tells her boss about the pregnancy with trepidation, but he takes the news in stride.

"Are you happy being pregnant again?" he asks.

Alex pauses. "Well," she says finally, thinking about the next seven months before the baby is born, "I guess I'm resigned to it."

Hanging up the phone, she realizes she has never allowed herself to consider how she feels about it. The fact is, she hates being pregnant, but having another child is something else entirely. *In the long term,* she thinks, *it will be good for all of us.*

"S O HOW ARE YOU?" TOM SAYS CHEERILY TO ERIN, WHO HAS JUST arrived home with several bags of groceries. She utters a perfunctory "Fine." She knows she is, in fact, premenstrual and therefore irrational, which means that for the next thirty-six hours she will be annoyed by everything Tom does or says.

Erin ignores him as she stocks the pantry and cleans a cut-up chicken for tomorrow's dinner with the neighbors (a regular Wednesday ritual, the responsibility rotating among three families). On the counter beside her is a long list of tasks to be accomplished for Katie's first birthday party on Sunday. Erin selected the theme—*101 Dalmatians,* one of her favorite movies—while browsing in the Disney Store in Annapolis. The full roster of weekend houseguests, who descend on Friday night, numbers eight adults and three kids. Erin has yet to buy the food for the party, not to mention the subsequent preparation of crudités, dip, baked beans, and enough hamburger patties for forty-five people.

Tom interrupts Erin's list-studying with a few questions, and doesn't seem to notice her curt responses. Yes, she picked up the battery for her electric garage-door opener at Radio Shack today; no, the dog didn't eat; no, she's too tired to put Katie to bed, he should do it.

At 7:30 Tom takes Katie upstairs, reads her a story, and leaves her in her crib. When he returns to the kitchen, Erin is sitting at the table, paging through *Newsweek.*

"I made your haircut appointment with a different person," she tells Tom, "so maybe this time it won't look butchered." Her tone is so hostile that Tom reacts to it.

"What'd I do this time?" he asks.

"It's just me about to get my period and being irritable and needing someone to take it out on," Erin explains in a softer tone, pleased that he finally picked up on her mood.

"Oh," Tom says, puzzled. "I had no reason to think you were mad. Unless it was last night, when I came home with that bad headache."

"You sat in that chair all night long chilling out while I did the laundry, cleaned the kitchen, took care of the dog, took care of Katie . . . and I was dreading having to talk to Lorraine about readjusting Katie's eating schedule. I was going to do it this morning, but I couldn't get up the nerve. I don't want her to think I'm criticizing her, but I don't want her giving Katie a bottle at six, because she won't eat dinner."

"Lorraine is your employee," Tom says. "She can't do the job right unless you let her know how you want things done."

"True. Is it a problem to flip-flop our nights next week? I have a closing Monday and I have to work late."

"We'll work it out," Tom says. "Fishing season being almost over, I will put in equal—"

"Equal *what?* This I have to hear."

"Equal time."

"Oh." Erin's voice exudes sarcasm. "You think so?"

"You just wait and see."

"You know, it would have only taken you ten minutes, but you never got around to finding the timer for the water-treatment system," Erin points out. "I called the plumber myself yesterday. It was supposed to be your assignment."

"There's just so much I can do."

"I have more to do than you," she retorts. "My lists are longer than yours." From her purse she retrieves one example, inspired by the bombshell her boss dropped during a long, private lunch last week. Philip is planning to leave at the beginning of the year to start his own practice and wants Erin to come with him. Once she would have jumped at the opportunity. But next year at this time she hopes to be pregnant, working no more than three days a week. If she goes with Philip, she'll face more pressure, longer hours, and greater risk. The three-page list in front of her, which she prepared for him voluntarily, details everything she can think of that would be required in a startup, from furniture to fax machines to personnel.

Philip, Tom believes, is offering Erin a once-in-a-lifetime chance. If she doesn't try it, she'll regret it. His sister left a large firm when her boss started up his own company. The company struggled for a while, and Tom's sister was often given stock in lieu of salary. Then it became successful and was bought out by a conglomerate at double the stock value, leaving his sister with a great deal of money. There's no way to know whether Erin will be blessed with similar good fortune, but Tom ardently hopes she will give the idea a shot. He sees it as giving her the kind of autonomy and leverage over her destiny she can't get elsewhere without a college degree. It has limitless possibilities, Tom thinks, for someone as highly motivated and organized as Erin.

"Which list am I on?" Tom says, shuffling the papers he pulls from her purse.

"The one for the party."

"What are my assignments?"

"Pick up the rug for the family room and clean the house on Sunday."

"That's it?"

Erin senses what he's getting at. "I think so. You may have to watch Katie for a couple of hours on Saturday while I get the food for the party, but you'll probably be able to fish in the morning."

Tom grins. "We'll have to check the list and check it twice. And if I'm naughty I'm not goin' fishin', but if I'm nice I am."

Erin tries to look stern, but laughs instead. "Really," she says, knocking herself on the side of her head, "this ought to be my 1992 resolution: *Lighten up, Erin Wright.*"

### SATURDAY, OCTOBER 12
#### Cape Cod

HE TEMPERATURE IS AN INVIGORATING SIXTY DEGREES, THE leaves are red and gold and orange, the sky is bright blue, the sea breeze is fresh and strong. The bride-to-be, who spends the early afternoon receiving a French manicure as a wedding gift, cannot help but consider the glorious weather a good omen. It is Sarah and Michael's wedding day.

Instead of going to Paris, as they once planned, they will commemorate their tenth anniversary by marrying each other again, this time in a traditional Jewish ceremony. Years ago, when Sarah converted, Michael said it "might be fun" to be married again by a rabbi, an idea that was forgotten by both of them until this year, when Michael's mother died. Sarah thought about how Margery had accepted her from the beginning as her own daughter and wished she had expressed her gratitude more fully when she had the chance. A Jewish wedding would be one way to thank her. "Let's do it," she said to Michael in midsummer.

"Michael is such a wreck," Sarah confides to Betsy, her friend and manicurist. "He has spent the entire day on the toilet."

Betsy laughs. "Why? I thought he only gets that way when he's facing some big change."

"He hates being the center of attention," Sarah says, admiring her elegant nails. "I love it."

"Well," Betsy asks with a mock grimace, "are you going to consummate your marriage tonight, after the wedding?"

"I bet we won't. We'll probably be too drunk. Maybe in the morning . . ."

Later, in the car, Sarah unsuccessfully scans the radio stations for live coverage of the Thomas-Hill hearings. With the Kennedy family compound nearby and Chappaquiddick a couple of ferry rides away, Sarah isn't the only Cape resident snickering over Ted Kennedy's presence on the Senate Judiciary Committee. *He shouldn't be up there,* she thinks, reflecting the local consensus. *Who is he to judge someone else?* Her sympathies are with Anita Hill, though she can't comprehend why the woman waited so long to step forward.

Sarah once worked for a man who was notorious for seducing female employees in exchange for Jaguars and promotions. When he started in on Sarah, inviting her out for drinks and dinner, she told him *no way.* "Come on," he said, "I'm the president of the company, everyone wants to go out with me." "Don't flatter yourself," Sarah said. He never spoke to her again. When a position for which Sarah was eminently qualified opened up, the president gave it to his latest girlfriend, who was woefully inexperienced. Sarah was neither surprised nor upset. *No promotion,* she thinks, *would have been worth sleeping with that scumbag.*

After a visit to her hair stylist for a trim and blow-dry, she drives home, worrying that the rabbi will be long-winded during the ceremony. It's supposed to last just half an hour. If he blathers on, she'll say, within earshot of the assembled guests, "Okay, time to wrap this up." And if he dares to correct her pronunciation of the Hebrew prayers . . . Not willing to admit to nervousness on that score, Sarah adopts a defiant attitude.

At four she arrives at her house, now doubled in size; the renovation is nearly complete. The interior displays her urbane modern taste and color sense. The showpiece is the new family room, with a soaring sixteen-foot ceiling, skylights operated by remote control, and a massive stone fireplace against one wall. The walls are the palest pink with a subtle hint of purple. The existing woodwork and floors, once deeply stained, have been stripped and bleached. French doors lead to a new outdoor deck.

A winding pickled oak staircase leads from the living room to the loft, which has walls of the same purplish pink tone and a new pullout sofa to accommodate guests. It is also intended to be Michael's office. A door separates it from the master bedroom so he can work on his computer or watch TV without disturbing Sarah.

Michael has faith in Sarah's aesthetic judgment and no complaints about the feminization of his living quarters. But he did make one suggestion: with all the new pinkness, she might consider repainting the fuschia bathroom. Sarah had already reached the same conclusion. The bathroom, she decided, looked like a whore's lair, so she had the walls painted in a stone color. The neutral hue provides a backdrop for her collection of hand-painted tiles, commissioned from a Vermont artist, which depict exaggeratedly voluptuous figures of nude women.

The old living room is now a formal dining room, with pale mint walls stippled with hints of pink. The kitchen has been gutted and rebuilt. There Sarah prepares a plate of cheese and crackers for houseguests, expected within the hour. She checks the bar and fills the ice chest. On a wall calendar under today's date, she has written *Married/ 7:30.*

Michael comes in after dropping the kids at Kim's, the sitter. Sarah kisses him warmly. He wants to respond, but holds back. When she offers to fix him a snack, he looks at her quizzically. He has endured a week of conjugal strife, heightened by money worries (the renovation went considerably over budget), disciplinary problems with Ben, another respiratory illness of Hannah's, and the backlash from Sarah's maniacal organizing (for the party, the houseguests, the five-day second honeymoon trip to Disney World with Ben, and arrangements for Hannah to stay at Kim's). It culminated Tuesday morning in one of Sarah's "I'm sorry I ever had kids" outbursts. Even Michael admits that having two children is exponentially more complicated than having one, but her comment hurt him more than ever before. *Here I'm spending all this money setting up the house the way she wants it,* he thought, *and she acts like she doesn't want to be here.* "The door's open, you can leave anytime you want," he told her. Then he shut down, refusing to speak.

Sarah regretted her anger and its effect on him. That afternoon she met with the rabbi to discuss the ceremony. "I'm not sure Michael wants to marry me again," she said in a jocular tone that didn't fool him. After she left, the rabbi called Michael at work. "Can I see you today?" he asked. Michael trusts and respects the rabbi but declined the invitation, feeling too hopeless to talk. On Wednesday, sitting in his office, he reconsidered. He dialed the rabbi's number.

"You haven't been yourself," the rabbi began when Michael arrived at the synagogue an hour later. "What's wrong?"

"It's been a rough week," Michael said. He summarized his trials. The rabbi listened and consoled but offered no solutions. Michael left the synagogue feeling frustrated. *My marriage is a rocky road,* he thought, *and there are no answers.*

His mind flickered back two years to the beginning of Sarah's second pregnancy and the end of the seventh year of marriage. *Things are better between us now than they were then,* he concluded. He and Sarah still don't resolve their disputes, but somehow the conflicts dissipate more quickly. *I used to retreat into a corner and Sarah would follow, punching me all the way, and now she backs off before I reach a dead end . . . or maybe I'm more effective at protecting myself against her punches . . . or maybe I'm just getting older and more resigned.*

By Thursday, Sarah had shifted into her sweet act. *That's our little marriage game,* Michael reflected. *If we're expecting company, she makes up to me.* Still wounded by Tuesday's fight, he tried to resist her attempts at peacemaking—to punish her as she punished him—but felt himself softening. Today, he knows he will surrender.

Outside, he hears cars pulling into the driveway, the doorbell ringing, Sarah's joyful voice greeting their guests: Deborah, Sarah's friend from childhood; Peggy, a colleague from her New York retailing days; Lauren; and their husbands. *Let the fun begin,* Michael thinks sardonically. But he feels a rush of affection for his wife. He joins her at the door, where he hugs the women, shakes hands with the men, and beams at the oh's and ah's as people take in the transformation of his home. In the kitchen, Sarah offers drinks; Michael declines. "Remember what happened last time," he says. Everyone laughs—they were there for the first wedding, when Michael nervously downed three shots of Scotch before the ceremony and was so inebriated that "wedded wife" came out as "wedded woof."

The guests reminisce about the nuptial events ten years ago. There was Sarah's bachelorette party, which her friends promised would involve nude male dancers, but after driving an hour to the seedy bar they learned that the act had ended weeks ago. (Sarah made the women pretend otherwise to Michael, so everyone devised a different risqué story with which to tease him.) There was Sarah's prewedding glee when Michael told her that it is a custom in many Jewish families to slip envelopes containing large checks to the groom, and her subsequent disappointment. Michael's mother told her friends that Protestants expect serving trays as gifts, so instead of the thousands of dollars Sarah envisioned, she wound up with thousands of serving trays.

The guests drift off to their rooms. Sarah, in a tea-length cream chiffon dress, departs for the synagogue an hour early, arm-in-arm with Michael. There they meet their children, supervised by Kim. Hannah toddles around in a beautifully detailed white dress that Michael's mother would have loved, a white flower in her Shirley Temple curls. Ben wears a navy blazer and a serious expression only slightly less tense than his father's. Michael is apprehensive about flubbing his Hebrew in front of eighty people, but Sarah is serene. She twines white satin ribbon attached to long-stemmed white roses around the poles of the simple *chuppa* as if she's been doing it all her life. (She is, in fact, improvising; she has no idea what this Jewish nuptial structure is supposed to look like.) Then she gives final instructions to the caterer and peeks approvingly at the three-tiered white wedding cake decorated with pink roses and baby's breath.

Michael watches Sarah admiringly. *Why isn't* she *nervous about the Hebrew?*, he thinks, and then realizes sadly that no one besides the rabbi is likely to notice a mistake in pronunciation. *How ironic,* he muses, *to finally have a Jewish wedding with no Jews to witness it.* His mother is dead; his brother has a prior engagement; Michael has no other immediate family. (He never questioned his brother's decision to attend the twenty-fifth wedding anniversary of friends of his wife's, plans made a month before he and Sarah announced their party, though Sarah was outraged and told his brother so.) Sarah's mother won't be here—she said she can't afford the plane fare—but her sister, brother, father, and their families will.

At precisely 7:30, Michael and Sarah walk toward the chuppa from different sides of the room. They meet in the middle, grasp hands, and mount the steps to the altar, where the rabbi and cantor await them. Michael's palms are damp with sweat; Sarah's are dry. "Mommy!" Hannah cries from the first row. She tries to squirm off Kim's lap to run to Sarah, but Kim restrains her. Sarah blows her daughter a kiss.

After a series of prayers and the sharing of the first cup of wine, the rabbi begins his sermon by paying tribute to Michael and Sarah, his friends and contemporaries as well as congregants. "Together you are so very, very much," he says. "I can't imagine that either of you would be nearly so much as you both are together. You not only are parents together, you are supporters of each other in ways that are too complex to quite fathom and understand. This is obvious to those of us who can stand back . . . I pray that this moment will give both of you the chance to do just that, to stand back and take a look from a distance . . . and notice how far you have come . . ."

He tells a seafaring parable from the Talmud: "The rabbi is asked how it is that there are always great celebrations at the beginning of the voyage . . . no one knows how well that voyage is going to go, it's only a hope, a dream, an expectation . . ." Michael's mind wanders. He thinks of Sarah's underclothes—a provocative one-piece lace teddy instead of bra and panties. *That's the advantage of remarrying your own wife, you get to watch her dress for the wedding . . .* He snaps to attention when the rabbi nears the end of the parable.

"At fifty years perhaps we have a celebration to say how well that voyage went . . . yet the point of the voyage is not just to arrive safely in port, but to have fun along the way. It's the ability to say gee, this is a little work, and sometimes not altogether comfortable; sometimes the rolling and pitching of the deck brings feelings that we wish weren't there . . ." Michael knows the rabbi's last sentence directly refers to the talk they had this week.

". . . The real reason people go on journeys is not so much to get to the other side, but to be where they are—the joy of the journey itself . . ." Michael's eyes fill with tears. *We keep forgetting that part,* he thinks. *The joy of the journey itself.* Sarah, resisting the tug of deeper emotion, has an urge to giggle. *This has to be the end,* she thinks.

The rabbi concludes his sermon and leads Sarah and Michael through the repetition of vows, first in Hebrew, then in English. When Michael gets to the word "wife," he purposely stalls; only the jab of Sarah's elbow in his side keeps him from saying "woof." He smashes the traditional glass with one stomp of his foot and turns to kiss the bride. The kiss is prolonged; the audience applauds. Before they release each other, Sarah whispers to Michael, "Thanks for not saying 'woof.' " "You don't know how hard it was not to," he whispers back. Holding hands, laughing, they leave the altar.

In the synagogue's party room, music is supplied by a singing piano player and a saxophonist. Bartenders pour champagne and wine; waitresses pass skewered Thai chicken and tiny potatoes crowned with caviar. Sarah talks vivaciously to her guests, holding Hannah in her arms. Ben stays close to his father, occasionally joining his cousins in boisterous play outside in the hall. After a cold buffet, the two-man band strikes up "It Had to Be You." Michael leads Sarah onto the dance floor and guides her expertly. As cameras flash, they kiss, and kiss again.

By midnight the synagogue is dark and silent, but the party continues at home. The houseguests, now in jeans and sweats, cluster around a vigorous fire, drinking more champagne and dissecting the evening with Sarah. Michael is in the kitchen, wrapping platters of leftover food in cellophane to be served at tomorrow's brunch. "Michael," Sarah calls merrily from the family room, "come here, we have to open presents."

It is close to three before the party breaks up. Michael and Sarah do not make love that night, and the next morning they sleep through the alarm. At 9:15, Sarah careens out of bed. "We've got fifteen people coming here in an hour," she says to her husband. *"Get up."* Michael throws on a pair of jeans and makes a run to Dunkin' Donuts for Thermoses of coffee, necessary for champagne hangovers. Hannah and Ben, who slept at Kim's last night, make a brief appearance at the brunch. Ben, bored with the adults, tells Sarah he wants to go back to Kim's to play with her kids. "Take Hannah with you," Sarah says to Kim. By 2:30 the guests are gone, the dishes are done, and Sarah and Michael have two and a half hours to themselves before they have to fetch the children. They go upstairs to consummate their marriage.

It is the quintessence of what Sarah considers mad, passionate love-making, enhanced by the sensuous rays of the sun streaming in through open French windows above the bed. When they finish, they lie naked and entwined, feeling the warm breeze on their bodies, gossiping about the party, dozing off now and again—a postcoital luxury they haven't indulged in at home since before Ben's birth. They toast each other with Diet Pepsi, poured into Sarah's best crystal. Together they take a languorous shower.

And then, at five, with the sun fading fast, they hurry to the car with a tray of leftovers for Kim's family. They are jarred by the abrupt return to reality. *Pick up the kids, load their overnight stuff . . . don't leave Hannah's stuffed bear and Ben's Ninja Turtles at Kim's . . . Race home, make supper, draw baths, read stories, do the laundry, finish packing for the honeymoon à trois . . .*

"Ben will be absolutely starving," Sarah says grimly.

"Happy Meal," says Michael, turning on the ignition. "McDonald's!"

# Epilogue

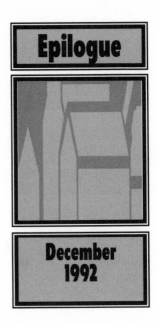

## December
## 1992

*Cape Cod:* The ceremonial reaffirmation of their love did not, of course, magically put an end to Sarah and Michael's problems. Over his initial resistance, they entered marriage therapy in February. They have just concluded the course of treatment.

Both report progress. In one session, Michael revealed his deepest fear: that Sarah will leave him. Genuinely shocked that Michael read the threat of abandonment into her angry outbursts (especially the oft-repeated "if it weren't for you I wouldn't have had kids"), Sarah insisted she has never contemplated leaving him and never will. These days, she tries both to control her urge to lash out and to reassure him of her love. Her moods still fluctuate, especially depending on how much sleep she's getting—which isn't much because of Hannah's frequent asthma-induced night wakings. But she is more patient, Michael is more forthcoming, and the discordant atmosphere that once gripped the household has eased perceptibly.

It is no coincidence that Sarah's relationship with Ben, who is now six and in first grade, has also improved. Though their willful personalities still clash, Sarah responds less aggressively. (She can't remember the last time she spanked him.) Ben, in turn, is beginning to show her the affection and respect she realizes she has yearned for. Her hostility toward her son, Sarah now understands, was a cover for feeling rejected by him. She has never had to struggle in the same way for Hannah's love; at two and a half, she is by nature sunnier and less complex than Ben—and clearly adores her mother. As her children grow older and more independent (Hannah is already in preschool five days a week), Sarah feels increasing freedom to pursue her entrepreneurial interests. With three female partners, she is finalizing a business plan for an interior-design company and has several projects underway.

One recent Saturday, Sarah received a letter from the college student who served as the kids' live-in au pair during the summer, and read it aloud to Michael. " 'I was talking about the two of you in my women's issues class the other day. I said that you have a great marriage . . .' "

Great? Not quite, but getting there. At the beginning of treatment, when the therapist asked them to rate the quality of their marriage on a scale of 1 (lowest) to 10 (highest), Sarah gave it an 8, Michael a 5. Now, both give it a 9.

*Westchester:* Alex and Rob moved into their dream house in January, and in April their second child, a daughter, Jessica, was delivered by scheduled cesarean. Alex hired a live-in housekeeper-babysitter and returned to work in June; a few months later she received a major promotion. Though her traveling schedule is grueling, she enjoys her job more than ever. But for the first time she feels torn, missing her kids intensely while she's away, guilty that she may be sacrificing them for her career. This conflict is a measure of the increasing pleasure she takes in motherhood.

Daniel has grown more attached to her and she to him. Jessie is a delight, one of those rare babies who sleeps well, cries infrequently, and causes no trouble. Rob continues to be the model father, but Alex is now as devoted to their children as he is. On weekends the four of them get down on the floor in the den to play, a portrait of the perfect nuclear family.

The marriage, however, is suffering. Rob and Alex have not had sex since Jessie was born; Alex refuses. She finds Rob physically unappealing—he now weighs close to 215—but beyond that, she seems to be punishing him for all the things he won't do: go on a diet, quit smoking, organize his time.

She views the problem as Rob's: he is self-destructive and ignores her concerns. He views it as hers: nothing he does makes her happy. Their pleasure comes from their children, not from each other. Parenthood has only exacerbated the differences between them. They are in deadlock, waiting for the other to change. Alex recognizes they need help but is too proud and too stubborn to suggest it.

When she told Rob that she felt they'd reached the lowest point of their marriage, he seemed startled. He maintains that what is wrong is that nothing is wrong. His income has increased dramatically this year. He has a beautiful home, two beautiful kids, a beautiful wife . . . He loves her, he says, even though she won't sleep with him. He claims to be almost entirely happy. The extent to which he is not is minuscule. He compares it to having a small pebble in your shoe: most of the time, you don't feel it.

For Alex, the pebble is a sharp rock; the tension between them rarely abates. She has been angry, but her anger is slowly and perilously turning to disinterest. When she imagines going on like this forever, she feels panic.

Within the solid walls of the dream house, their marriage is in danger of collapse.

*Queens:* After Luis's second birthday in June, Joe and Maria decided to have another baby. The pregnancy was confirmed in September. Joe began looking for a second, part-time evening job to pay off their debts. Maria, happy to be pregnant but daunted by the financial and logistical complications of a second child, debated her options: putting both kids in day care with Tracy, who is still Luis's sitter, and returning to her job in Manhattan; staying home during the day and working nights at a local hospital; hiring live-in help, preferably a family member . . .

Then she started spotting. In her ninth week of pregnancy, a sonogram revealed she had miscarried. The following days were sad, but Maria and Joe soon rallied by turning their attention to the future. Maria began to investigate courses in business and health administration. If she takes classes while retaining her full-time job, she is entitled to tuition reimbursement and will eventually make more money in a position of greater responsibility. Joe has reached the postal service's maximum base-salary level and also plans to go back to school, earn a degree in medical technology, and switch careers.

Their marriage, sound before Luis's birth, remains so. They are comfortable in the two-bedroom co-op they bought with so many misgivings over a year ago. Luis, a vigorous and engaging little boy, goes everywhere with them; neither Joe nor Maria feel the need to get away alone. They are a *family*, tightly knit, secure in each other's love. All they wish for is greater financial security and another child, maybe two.

Maria is only twenty-eight; there is still time. In February or March, they will try again.

*Manhattan:* By fall, Sam determined that he was sure he wanted a second child, as long as giving birth to that child would not endanger Juliet. Juliet remained ambivalent, her desire for Lily to have a sibling weighing against her fear of another traumatic delivery and her hesitancy about incorporating a second child into the family. Although Lily has enriched the marriage and life in general, Sam and Juliet have little time to concentrate on each other, and a new baby would mean even less.

To resolve the more concrete medical question, they waited six months until a specialist in high-risk pregnancy, Victoria Muller, could review Juliet's case and offer a second opinion. (Dr. Bernstein had already said that Juliet's risk of hemorrhage would be no greater than any other woman's, especially if the delivery was by scheduled cesarean under controlled circumstances.) Because Muller's office changed the appointment at the last minute, Sam couldn't be there to hear the doctor tell Juliet that she has a 50 percent chance of hemor-rhaging during a second delivery. When Juliet asked if a hysterectomy would be the worst-case outcome, the doctor replied, "I'm not going to lie to you; there is a very small chance that you would die." None-theless, Muller said she should go ahead and get pregnant if she wanted to.

Juliet told Sam she had made a decision based upon her meeting with Dr. Muller: she will not risk bearing another child. She suggested they consider adoption.

Sam, while not against adoption, wondered if Juliet may have misin-terpreted what the doctor said. If a second delivery would be so dan-gerous that death was a possibility, however slight, why would Muller tell Juliet to get pregnant anyway? Seeking clarification, Sam called Muller himself. The "50 percent chance of hemorrhage," he learned during this conversation, referred to *any* excessive bleeding, not neces-sarily requiring transfusion, anesthesia and possible hysterectomy. The risk of death would be only marginally greater than the odds of any woman dying in childbirth, which are slim indeed. As Sam suspected, the situation was far less dire than Juliet had made it out to be.

Now in agreement that the medical issue is no longer the absolute determining factor it once was, Sam and Juliet are back in the same foggy middle ground: do they—more specifically, does Juliet—want a second child or not? For the moment, with neither of them feeling particularly urgent about making a decision, they've tabled the discus-sion.

Whether or not they have another child, Juliet and Sam are explor-ing the possibility of "co-housing." They've heard about a group of people developing such a project in lower Manhattan, in which each family would have separate living space but share certain common areas. Such an environment, they think, would alleviate their feeling of social isolation—given Sam's laziness and Juliet's timidity when it comes to initiating new friendships—and would be good for Lily, who likes being around other children.

Juliet's days are quite free (Lily attends nursery school in the morn-ing and has a sitter in the afternoon), but though she's been writing steadily she has made little headway selling her work. Sam still travels frequently and his fear of flying has been blunted only slightly by a new prescription for Xanax. The marriage, once fairly seamless, frays more easily now. They fight more often and recover less quickly because so much of their free time and energy is centered on Lily. But because they place a premium on resolving their differences, they avoid the build-up of resentment that can lead to emotional estrangement. And the passion that has always grounded their relationship remains intact.

*Southern Maryland:* Erin joined her boss, Philip, in his newly formed law firm, as Tom hoped she would. The risk has paid off. Instead of being "just a secretary," Erin's title is firm administrator. She directs her own staff of three secretaries and a receptionist. She received a $45,000 bonus this year, equal to her full annual salary. Her self-esteem has surged. The downside is her guilt about being an absentee mother; she works full-time and then some. But under her skillful administration, the law office is now running so smoothly that in February she plans to work a four-day week, devoting Fridays to Katie. By summer, she hopes to get pregnant. Her schooling is still on hold, but she knows she will, somehow, someday, get her college degree.

To accommodate Erin's demanding schedule, Tom has taken on more responsibility for their daughter, picking her up at the sitter's every night, feeding and bathing her before Erin gets home. Yet his business is doing so well that he has just finalized the purchase of a second station at a bargain price. It had been in dire financial shape, but with proper management, Tom is convinced, it can become profitable.

Eighteen months ago, Tom was close to despair, unable to take home a salary, contemplating bankruptcy. He credits his turnaround to a more mature attitude wrought by fatherhood. He no longer views his business as his life; his life begins when he leaves at five to pick up Katie.

Both he and Erin complain of too little time together, an inevitable corollary of combining dual careers with parenthood. Their days are long and harried but, on balance, far more rewarding now than in years past. They have not forgotten what caused their separation in the spring and summer of 1987. There was no baby then, no juggling of schedules, an abundance of personal freedom—but there was also no apparent common ground, no attention paid. Their daughter is a source of mutual joy and eternal connection, but they know that being parents together cannot in itself guarantee their relationship will flourish over time. They understand that to counteract the process of attrition otherwise known as daily life, they must make an effort to sustain an ongoing dialogue; have the patience and flexibility to adjust continually to each other's shifting needs; maintain the conviction that bad times eventually get better; be willing to see, if only for a nanosecond, through each other's eyes.

Independently, and with equal assurance, both Tom and Erin offer this assessment of their marriage after parenthood: it gets better every year.

# Acknowl-
# edgments

Essential background sources (in addition to those mentioned in the Preface) included: Arlie Hochschild's *The Second Shift*; Deborah Tannen's *You Just Don't Understand*; Betty Friedan's *The Feminine Mystique*; George E. Vaillant's *Adaptation to Life*; Donald Katz's *Home Fires*; Tracy Hotchner's *Childbirth and Marriage*; Myra Leifer's *Psychological Effects of Motherhood*; Sara Ruddick's *Maternal Thinking*; *Father and Child* (edited by Stanley H. Cath, Alan R. Gurwitt, and John Munder Ross); *Balancing Acts: On Being a Mother* (edited by Katherine Gieve); and long-term studies on the transition to parenthood conducted by Jay Belsky and colleagues at Pennsylvania State University.

For their assistance in my search for couples, I thank Nancy and Mark Kaufman, Lansing and Iliana Moore, Alan Skvirsky, Gwenn Snider, Wendy and Larry Steinhardt, and the following obstetricians: Jay Lupin of White Plains Hospital in White Plains, New York; Sara

Imershein of Columbia Hospital for Women in Washington, D.C.; Frank Silverman and his assistant, Laura Jiannaris, of New York University Medical Center; and most particularly, Jon Snyder of NYU Medical Center, who not only provided me with useful leads but was unfailingly generous with his time and insights into the practice of obstetrics. Additional medical wisdom was provided by Laura Popper, a pediatrician affiliated with Mount Sinai Medical Center, and Kent Sepkowitz, a specialist in infectious diseases at Memorial Sloan-Kettering Cancer Center, both in New York City.

I thank Nancy Evans and Paul Bresnick for their editorial guidance and encouragement in the early stages. I am indebted to Steve Rubin for his unflagging support from beginning to end.

I am blessed with three steadfast friends who also happen to be gifted writers and readers. They soldiered their way through myriad drafts, challenging my assumptions and offering invaluable suggestions: Marilyn Johnson, Elizabeth Kaye, and my very own intellectual scourge, Daphne Merkin.

For their sharp-eyed comments on portions of the manuscript, I thank Betsy Carter, Jan Cherubin, Lisa Grunwald, Deborah Pines, Nessa Rapoport, and Carolyn White.

The unflappable Casey Fuetsch, my editor, was unerring in her literary instincts, infinitely patient with my obsessive tinkering, and always responsive to my needs.

For her shrewdness, candor, enthusiasm, and killer negotiating skills, I thank my agent, Kathy Robbins.

The Writers Room and its director, Renata Miller, provided me with an affordable and wonderfully collegial haven in which to work.

I had more than a little help from my friends, who listened to, cajoled, calmed, fed, and in one way or another, sheltered me: David Blum, Will Blythe, Maggie Brenner, Michael Brod, Judith Dan, Marti Devore, Roger Director, Carole Dvorkin, Gary Guenther, Peter and Ann Herbst, Joanie Kubisch, Leslie Larson, Jerry Madison, Sèamus McCotter, Terri Minsky, Stephen Randall, Alan Richman, Barry Siegel, Betsy Steyer, Annette Sue, Sally Dixon Wiener, and Ellen Ziskind. I am especially grateful to Tony Schwartz for his astute counsel and vigorous cheerleading on my behalf.

My family, as always, sustained me. Elienne Squire lent her own writerly eye to the manuscript; David Squire, Pat Squire, Jon Squire, and Rebecca Guenther were willing sounding boards. Max Hirshey came through with weekly contributions of sushi and moral support. Helen and Aaron Spiegel freely provided emergency babysitting. Esther Weltman is and always will be a source of inspiration in ways I could never adequately express.

My husband and in-house cliché detector, David Hirshey, had the forebearance and good humor to live with me and my anxieties, most of which he shared. My delicious daughter Emily kept me focused on my work: the more I produced each day, the sooner I could return home to her. I owe them both, big time.

Finally, I thank the five brave couples who permitted me to invade their lives for three tumultuous years. This book would not exist without them.